THE CALLING OF THE NATIONS:
EXEGESIS, ETHNOGRAPHY, AND EMPIRE
IN A BIBLICAL-HISTORIC PRESENT

Green College Thematic Lecture Series

The Green College Thematic Lecture Series provides leading-edge theory and research in new fields of interdisciplinary scholarship. Based on a lecture program and conferences held at Green College, University of British Columbia, each book brings together scholars from several disciplines to achieve a new synthesis in knowledge around an important theme. The series provides a unique opportunity for collaboration between outstanding Canadian scholars and their counterparts internationally, as they grapple with the most important issues facing the world today.

PREVIOUSLY PUBLISHED TITLES

Governing Modern Societies, edited by Richard V. Ericson and Nico Stehr (2000)

Risk and Morality, edited by Richard V. Ericson and Aaron Doyle (2003)

The Shifting Foundations of Modern Nation States: Realignments of Belonging, edited by Sima Godfrey and Frank Unger (2004)

Love, Hate, and Fear in Canada's Cold War, edited by Richard Cavell (2004)

Multiple Lenses, Multiple Images: Perspectives on the Child across Time, Space, and Disciplines, edited by Hillel Goelman, Sheila K. Marshall, and Sally Ross (2004)

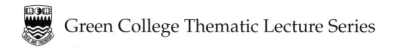

Green College Thematic Lecture Series

The Calling of the Nations

Exegesis, Ethnography, and Empire in a Biblical-Historic Present

Edited by
Mark Vessey, Sharon V. Betcher, Robert A. Daum,
and Harry O. Maier

UNIVERSITY OF TORONTO PRESS
Toronto Buffalo London

© University of Toronto Press Incorporated 2011
Toronto Buffalo London
www.utppublishing.com
Printed in Canada

ISBN 978-0-8020-9241-0 (cloth)

Printed on acid-free, 100% post-consumer recycled paper
with vegetable-based inks.

Library and Archives Canada Cataloguing in Publication

The calling of the nations : exegesis, ethnography, and empire in a
biblical-historic present/edited by Mark Vessey ... [et al.].

(Green College thematic lecture series)
Includes bibliographical references and index.
ISBN 978-0-8020-9241-0

1. Nationalism – Biblical teaching. 2. Nationalism – Religious aspects.
3. Religion and state. I. Vessey, Mark II. Series: Green College thematic
lecture series.

BS680.E85C35 2010   220.8'32054   C2010-905023-1

University of Toronto Press acknowledges the financial assistance
to its publishing program of the Canada Council for the Arts and
the Ontario Arts Council.

 Canada Council Conseil des Arts   ONTARIO ARTS COUNCIL
for the Arts   du Canada   CONSEIL DES ARTS DE L'ONTARIO

University of Toronto Press acknowledges the financial support of the
Government of Canada through the Canada Book Fund for its
publishing activities.

Contents

Illustrations

Preface

A leading European literary critic and theorist spoke recently of the present age as a '"global" time of migration and of ... questioning of both the nation-state and the unmarked dominance of Christianity.'[1] This volume shares that time and those questions. It originated in a series of lectures at Green College, University of British Columbia (UBC), on issues of land-title, territory, and national identity arising from narratives that connect peoples and cultures of an ancient and 'biblical' Near East to those of a modern, putatively 'post-biblical' West and Far West. The lecture series was complemented by an exploratory workshop ('Promised Lands'), held at the Peter Wall Institute for Advanced Studies, UBC, on Christian missions and colonial histories in the millennium between the fall of the Roman Empire in the West and the onset of European colonization of the Americas; two of the following chapters are based on papers given at the workshop.

As was to be expected, the appointed topics of workshop and lecture series elicited widely and at times passionately discordant responses, both from our invited speakers and from those who came to hear them. We have tried to recapture some of the dynamics of the original discussion in the chapters of 'commentary' that conclude each of the three main parts below (and to which contributors were at liberty to respond in writing). The introduction is based on opening remarks made at the original workshop, while the epilogue – which takes up the discussion anew, and proposes additional terms for it – was written expressly for this volume. It is our hope that the collection will help to disengage the main lines of a shared discourse on the ways in which *biblical* understandings have shaped 'Western,' especially European and North American assumptions of and about communal identity, nationhood, territorial entitlement, and collective destiny over the first two thousand years of the 'Common Era.'

The keywords of our subtitle signal three areas of central concern:

– *exegesis*, the means and methods of biblical understanding;

– *ethnography*, the use – in this context – of particular biblical understandings, in order to speak about or in the name of a given or postulated 'people' (howsoever otherwise imagined); and

– *empire*, a power relationship that may at times be articulated or contested on the basis of a biblically derived view of actual and desired relations between peoples.

On either side of this triad, the framing elements of the title encapsulate the primary claim of this book – if a book written from so many different personal and affiliative standpoints and with so sharp an awareness of the risks of book-staked claims may in good conscience profess such a thing. The claim is this: that the 'global' time of the present is still far more deeply contoured by biblical-historical, especially *Christian* biblical-historical, intuitions of nationhood than the secular creeds of most Western liberal commentators (and perhaps especially liberal academics) customarily allow.

It is beyond the ambition of this book to explore all the implications of that fact, for which other arguments continue to accumulate, some of them far more powerfully persuasive than academic prose. Ours was not the only project planned at the beginning of the millennium to have been overshadowed by the events of September 11, 2001, and their sequels. As the essays below collectively suggest, however, the dread of being overtaken by events may prove in the long run somewhat less lethal than the desire to anticipate the future with perfect assurance. Our aim, in any case, has not been to draw political conclusions but to provide elements for a richer and more nuanced consideration of these questions than is typically possible in the heat of public debate on national and global emergencies or in the pressurized atmosphere of government policy-making. The maintenance of such a space of leisurely and serious consideration is, we believe, still the proper function of scholarly critics and historians, if they are to answer their own calling.

As the Compiler or Ecclesiast could almost have said, 'Of the making (and unmaking) of nations by the book there is no end,' not even for those who read from Genesis towards apocalypse. The phrase 'calling of the nations' is not quite literally biblical either, but it will serve here as shorthand for the class of biblical references that are, in the same act, namings, citings, or summonings-to-appear of a social and often geo-political entity that in ordinary speech, as in standard translations of Jewish and Christian scriptures, is called a 'people' or a 'nation.' The processes of such *doubly* biblical citation are in practice highly various, ranging from a bare identification of terms ('Ulster is Israel') to the most elaborate recastings, recallings, and re-citations of history and prophecy. Common to all of them, however, is a free defiance of the alien logic that distinguishes as we did in our first paragraph above between 'biblical' and 'post-biblical' times, and an equal insistence, beyond any debate over canonicity or closure of the canon, on the *biblical* coordinates of a history that not only comes down to the present, but that has also in some sense already encompassed the future.[2] Taken together, with all their differences, this volume's essays may be seen as offering an informal taxonomy of such *biblical-historical* figures of thought and expression, together with reflections on their often momentous practical consequences.

The introduction takes its cue from a newspaper story in a Western Canadian province where public interest in the ancestral tales of regional 'First Nations' runs parallel with anxiety about native land claims, and finds there a model of ethnographic expropriation with visible attachments to a particular tradition of 'Western' Christian hermeneutics. It then sketches a historical understanding of that model, here dubbed 'the archeophone' (after a customized version in the National Library of Canada) for its capacity to call new nations into the place of older ones, in spite of ordinary distinctions in space and time. As it engages the work of such noted twentieth-century critics and theorists of culture and nation as Michel de Certeau, Benedict Anderson, and Erich Auerbach, the inquiry leads backwards and eastwards – to early modern and medieval Europe, and to the ancient Mediterranean and Near Eastern worlds in which the Jewish and Christian bibles were redacted.

After this reverse excursion across the 'Common Era,' chronological sequence is resumed in Parts One and Two, though without any expectation of a fulfilment over time.

Part One ('Biblical Possessions') presents a series of comparative studies of strategies for translating or converting biblical texts into new realities within and beyond the target language. Summarizing arguments that he has developed at length elsewhere, Donald Harman Akenson reviews the exclusionist ethnographies, topographies, and polities devised respectively by ancient Christianity and Rabbinic Judaism, taking modern Irish nationalism as a corroborative instance

('Perhaps God Is Irish: Sacred Texts as Virtual Reality Machine'). In Nabil Matar's essay ('Protestant Restorationism and the Ortelian Mapping of Palestine') it is Islam and the qur'anic understanding of the Abramic land promise that supply the extra term of comparison, at the close of a study focused on the cartographic premises of the 'heretical' strain of Protestant biblical literalism known as Restorationism, here dated and located to seventeenth-century England. The restoration would be of the Jewish people to the land of promise, in fulfilment of a *Christian* eschatology. As observers of the contemporary religious scene – especially in the United States of America – are only too well aware, this 'heresy' and the larger 'orthodoxy' that lies behind it are far from extinct. In a subsequent piece that makes a poignantly disjoint doublet with Matar's, Laura Levitt ponders the dilemmas still posed for American Jews by a biblical legacy that until recently seemed assured only by the good offices of their Christian co-nationals and co-sharers in the liberal dream of seamless social integration ('Beyond a Shared Inheritance: American Jews Reclaim the Hebrew Bible').

If the essays and commentaries of Parts One and Three do their work, there should be no danger that Part Two ('Confounding Narratives') will be read as a serial account of anything so tractable, and hence conceivably so *re*-tractable, as a single, unified Western discourse of biblical exegesis, ethnography, and empire. It is true that certain ways of biblical understanding have proved remarkably long-lived, despite the 'secularization' of modern Western societies, and also probably because of the diversion created by the modern, Western myth of a 'secular' society. Yet from a critical-historical point of view, the most serious mistake one could make would be to impute the millennial logics of a biblical 'calling of the nations' to *The Bible*, as if there were indeed but one, divinely designed device, technology, 'great code,' or 'archeophone,' the ownership and use of which would have passed from one people or power to another, often by more-than-hermeneutical violence, until finally it came to rest ... wherever it may now be for the time being, like a certain piece of military equipment at the end of the film *Raiders of the Lost Ark*. If this Hollywood-inspired scenario seems plausible (and sales figures for books like *The Da Vinci Code* and *The American Prophecies* suggest that it is irresistibly appealing to a great many people), that may be because 'the Bible,' as an idea curiously severed from any actual compilation of texts, has proved amenable over the centuries to many different improvisations of power, both by those in positions of dominance and by the dominated.

The essays in Part Two recall a number of critical instances of this sort of improvisation, beginning in the time of the first influentially 'Christian' Roman emperor (Constantine) and a few decades before the declaration of the first ever 'Christian' empire (by Theodosius I). Harry Maier (in 'Dominion from Sea to Sea: Eusebius of Caesarea, Constantine the Great, and the Exegesis of Empire') and Karla Pollmann (in 'Unending Sway: The Ideology of Empire in Early Christian Latin Thought') show how elements of a traditionally Roman imperial ideology were variously adopted and transmuted in Christian propaganda and preaching between the Constantinian and Theodosian eras. Then, in Ian Wood's contribution ('"The Ends of the Earth": The Bible, Bibles, and the Other in Early Medieval Europe'), we watch as Christian missionaries working beyond the limits of a formerly Roman world, from the eighth century onwards, adapted their biblically coordinated histories and ethnographies to the new realities encountered and imagined by them in the mission field.

Part Three ('Colonial and Postcolonial Readings, Premodern Ironies') opens with another scene of contact between European Christian colonists and the indigenous inhabitants of remote regions, this time in North America. In an essay devoted to one of the most successful Christian missionary orders of all time ('The Amerindian in Divine History: The Limits of Biblical Authority in the Jesuit Mission to New France, 1632–1649'), Peter Goddard traces an attempted reconciliation between biblical and ostensibly extra-biblical presents, fixing a temporal horizon within which, for a while at least, the long-standing hermeneutics of the 'archeophone' would seem to have been suspended, even if not necessarily to the advantage of native peoples. The next two chapters address some of the ambiguities latent or indeed patent in verbs such as 'inherit' and 'reclaim' when used by Levitt and others with respect to a bible and its presumptive people(s). What opportunities may biblical self-identification or 'auto-ethnography' still hold out for those whose collective identity does not conform absolutely or indeed at all easily to the social, geo-political unity of the (modern) 'nation'? Granted the history of its use in support of missionary and colonial-imperial dispossessions, what potential does the (Jewish, Christian, or Jewish-Christian) bible have as a *counter-hegemonic* text? How can it be kept from reassimilation into the dominant cultural narrative? In addressing those questions – which will also be central to the epilogue – the essays by Laura Donaldson ('Joshua in America: On Cowboys, Canaanites, and Indians') and Jace Weaver ('Premodern

Ironies: First Nations and Chosen Peoples') subject long-standing and catastrophic colonial-American exegeses of Old Testament promises to counter-readings that, ironically or not, may finally owe more to poetry than they do either to 'history' or to 'theory' as such.

The editors wish to express their gratitude to Green College and the Peter Wall Institute for Advanced Studies at the University of British Columbia, and to the Vancouver School of Theology, for their funding and hosting of the lecture series and workshop from which the present volume derives. For invaluable assistance in its preparation for the press we are likewise greatly indebted to Dr Dania Sheldon and to our indexer, Natalie Boon.

M.V., S.V.B., R.A.D., H.O.M.
Vancouver, August 2010

NOTES

1 Mieke Bal, 'Religious Canon and Literary Identity,' in Erik Borgman, Bart Philipsen, and Lea Verstricht, eds, *Literary Canons and Religious Identity* (Aldershot, 2004) 9–31, at 25.
2 Cf. Harry Harootunian, 'Remembering the Historical Present,' *Critical Inquiry* 33 (2007): 43–66, opposing to this kind of imagination of times an alternative model in which 'experience turns back to a historical present, which now remains open to a history made in the present founded on the fashioning of expectations based on an unforeseen future' (57).

THE CALLING OF THE NATIONS:
EXEGESIS, ETHNOGRAPHY, AND EMPIRE
IN A BIBLICAL-HISTORIC PRESENT

1

Introduction
The Bible in the West:
A Peoples' History?

MARK VESSEY

7 Remember the days of old, consider the years of many generations: ask
thy father, and he will shew thee; thy elders, and they will tell thee.
8 When the Most High divided to the nations their inheritance, when he
separated the sons of Adam, he set the bounds of the people according
to the number of the children of Israel.
9 For the Lord's portion is his people; Jacob is the lot of his inheritance.

Deuteronomy 32 [The Bible, 'King James Version']

68 What stories they have have been brought in a book

_____

_____

Stories are fed to them

_____

69 from a place without caribou, moose, wolf, lynx.

_____

_____

from a book.

_____

70 _____

Without whiskeyjack, black spruce, beaver or bear.

They are taught to call it the Holy Book.

---

71 **They are taught to call it the Holy Land.**

Robert Bringhurst, *New World Suite*, no. 3: 'Four Movements for
Three Voices' ('I: All the Desanctified Places')

Nation and Recitation: The 'Archeophone'

A few years ago the *Vancouver Sun* reported a wonder. 'The Songcatchers'
ran the headline on the front page of the review section of that Saturday's
paper: 'Paul McKay explores a Canadian musical miracle, resurrecting
long-forgotten recordings that preserve Nisga'a tradition' (Vancouver
Sun 2002). The accompanying black-and-white photograph showed an
elder of the Nisga'a, one of British Columbia's 'First Nations,' singing a
lullaby to his grandchild in 1927. The singer's name was Tralahaet in
his own language, Frank Bolton in Christian English. The article tells
how in August 1927, at the prompting of Québécois Rhodes Scholar
and anthropologist Marius Barbeau, this Nisga'a man, with others from
his Nass River community in northern BC, laid down recordings of
dozens of their traditional songs, singing them 'into the elegantly fluted
horn of an Edison wax cylinder recording machine.' They sang of
family histories, of hunting and fishing grounds, of love and loss, of
victory and defeat in fights with neighbouring tribes. McKay describes
the mechanical process: 'Each melody and age-old lyric, often accompanied by drum beats or a raven-shaped rattle, reverberated inside a
narrowing sound channel, then pulsed a rubber diaphragm attached to
a crude needle. The needle then dug one continuous groove, circling

the outer surface of a hollow cylinder of hardened wax about 300 times to make each two-minute recording.' What happened in the Nass Valley, he writes, 'may be the most astonishing miracle in Canada's musical history.'

What was the miracle?

If Tralahaet and the other Nisga'a singers in those far-off August days marvelled at the workings of the Edison recording device, we hear nothing of it. Did they? Unchecked, a long tradition of vulgar ethnology could dispose at least some of us to think that they must have done. The figure of the awestruck 'native' was a piece of the late-imperial British stagecraft with which I was brought up. Although I no longer recall the name of the B-movie, black-and-white and presumably of the 1940s, I do remember the scene from it in which tropical islanders gather round a washed-up wireless set, which then suddenly crackles into life, startling them with its human voice. 'Voicey-box' they called the contraption, in the pidgin English expected in such cases by audiences such as the one in which I then sat, some winter Saturday evening in the late 1960s, in one of the nicer Christian boarding schools of southern England, a time of the year and week when, if we were not watching worn-out prints of U-certificate films, we would be listening to a lecture (with slides, if we were lucky) by some recently returned traveller to foreign lands, a missionary or perhaps a retired military man, brought in to widen our horizons and fire our minds with a desire to know more about places that had until lately been coloured pink in our atlases. Our vulgar ethnological wonder was easily excited in those days, but amazement at a technology capable of conveying human speech across vast distances was reserved for others. Had there been natives on the moon when Neil Armstrong stepped off the ladder, it would have been their role to marvel at our technical ingenuity, while we studied their appearance and behaviour.

At first glance there would seem to be no wonder at all about the reputed 'miracle' on the Nass. While clearly a remarkable man, Marius Barbeau only did what other ethnologists of his time were doing across North America and elsewhere, transcribing the traditional 'myths,' beliefs, and practices of peoples whose ways of life were being rapidly transformed by contact with 'modern civilization.' For their part, Tralahaet and his fellow Nisga'a performers were only doing what by then came no less naturally to them, cooperating with white men who had an interest in them, whether as missionaries, cannery owners, or folklorists. There was nothing miraculous about their behaviour either, at least not at the time. Whatever may have taken place in 1927, the marvel reported in the *Vancouver Sun* was evidently of more recent date. At the end of the article one read an invitation: 'To hear a 1927 recording of Tralahaet singing a Nisga'a song, go to www.enchantedear .com.' There at length was the wonder: that it was possible, here and now, to hear songs sung by the Nisga'a in another time, as if in another world. (The URL has since been taken over by a company marketing hearing aids.)

The structure of vulgar ethnology remains intact. As with the 1960s English schoolboy's wonder at films or slide-shows of tropical island-ers, so with the *Vancouver Sun* reader's on-line enchantment by 'an-cient' Nisga'a song: the miracle for 'us' lies not in the technology of representation but in the effect of distance created by the encounter – for the visitor to that website, the distance imagined in time between the ear now hearing and the singer of so long ago, strangely heard again. It is the gap, not the mediation, that awes 'us.'

Even now, with our carefully policed multicultural awareness, we are probably still readier to attribute techno-wonder to others than to ourselves. On a trip to the Nass Valley, the *Sun* reporter discovered a Nisga'a man busy smoking salmon in the old way. His commentary continues in the best tradition of vulgar ethnography:

> On a serenely sunny August afternoon, encircled by the regal, rugged mountains that surround his ... village of Aiyansh, it may be that no mo-ment is as unassumingly sacred for George Gosnell as this. Except this. Seconds after he is surprised with a CD copy of two of Marius Barbeau's 1927 wax cylinder songs ... Gosnell's legs surge with electric currents, he hums out loud, nods to the polyrhythms, and an amazed grin creases his handsome face.

A moment later he was dancing. A photograph showed Gosnell with a personal CD player, earphones on, salmon hanging in rows in the back-ground. Who could say what that 'amazed grin' expressed or con-cealed? We have only the newspaper's account: the latest audio technology meets a 'timeless' way of life; belated instant of cultural en-counter; on the part of the native performer, delight, amazement, an overwhelming experience of the sacred; an immediate, hard-wired re-sponse, current surging from hi-tech instrument to natural man; the new, improved voicey-box. In this version of the story, the native people of British Columbia were still cooperating with 'outsiders' at the begin-ning of the twenty-first century.

Like all such native peoples in Canada in the 1920s, the Nisga'a of that time were under tremendous pressure to assimilate to settler culture. Native forms of cultural expression, such as the potlatch and ceremonial dress, had been banned, and the use of indigenous languages was in steep decline. Then there were the missionaries. The *Sun* reporter interviewed Tralahaet's eighty-two-year-old granddaughter, who remembered how he used to take her and other children to his fishing and hunting grounds along the Nass. 'I heard him singing to himself,' she recalled, 'in Nisga'a, in the woods ... I wanted to know that song, the words, how to sing it. But he told me now he was a Christian; the priests had told him not to pass our songs on to the children and grandchildren.' And so a breach was made in memory. This woman had lived all her life as a Christian: 'A permanently opened Bible waits by her favourite window-side chair, and her heart still lifts, she says, when she hears the gospel songs of Elvis Presley.'

The mention of that open bible caught my eye when I read the piece in the *Sun*, reminding me of the headstones I had seen a few months earlier, in a salt-stung graveyard outside the village of Masset (Ghadaghaaxhiwaas) on the northern edge of Haida Gwaii, 'The Islands of the People,' otherwise Queen Charlotte Islands (but only since 1787). The memorial stones, many of them cut by masons as far away as Nanaimo on Vancouver Island, are for Haida men and women who died in the later decades of the nineteenth century. In the carved figures on one series of monuments, animals sacred to the Haida (raven, eagle, killer whale, etc.) appear alongside the open book of the Christian gospel. Haida ways of life underwent the same assault as did Nisga'a. On those islands too, grandparents were discouraged from passing on tales and songs to their grandchildren. That outsiders now have any ear for what was once told and sung in Haida Gwaii is due in large part to the transcriptions made around 1900 by the American linguist John Reed Swanton. Again no miracle: only, at this distance and for us, the thrill of another belated encounter, the shock of 'a story as sharp as a knife' – the phrase used by poet Robert Bringhurst to introduce his acclaimed translation of 'classical' Haida texts (Bringhurst 1999).[1]

Some of the finest of those Haida oral narratives were performed for Swanton by a man who, on being baptized as a Christian for the third (!) time, had taken the name of John Sky. Possibly, suggests Bringhurst, 'he had ... been told that John was the poet among the evangelists and that Saint John's totem animal, the eagle, corresponded to his own' (Bringhurst 1999, 75; Skaay 2001). Of all the canonical Gospels, John's plays most explicitly on the relations of voice and letter, spoken word and written book, beginning as it does 'In the beginning was the word ...' (1:1) and ending 'And there are also many other things which Jesus did, the which, if they should be written every one, I suppose that even the world itself could not contain the books that should be written' (21:25 [KJV]). Although Jesus' injunction to his disciples to evangelize all nations occurs at the end of Matthew's Gospel, it is there at the close of John's that we find the original, as it were 'missionary' warrant for the permanently open book on the Haida headstone or Nisga'a woman's table, a book that tells a story without end this side of the eschaton and yet that is already mysteriously complete between two covers – a story that implicitly encompasses all stories without omission or remainder. For woe betide anyone who would add to or take away from the words of this book (Rev 22:18–19; cf. Deut 4:2)!

In fact, the Nisga'a woman's story in the *Vancouver Sun* does not end with the mention of her open bible and the gospel songs of Elvis. She could not forgive the silencing of her grandfather: '"That was a terrible thing," she says with uncharacteristic vehemence. "I hate that the preachers here then did that to him ... What kind of a Christian is that – to say his songs were a sin?"' But then, we are told, 'her serene smile returns.' Why? Because what was lost had been recovered. 'Now she knows the wax cylinders recorded ... in 1927 have been found, and can be copied on to countless CDs for her and her grandchildren to hear ... "I have waited a long time," [she] sighs, "... Now I think my prayer has been answered."' Her grandfather's voice had returned. The silence was over. 'In the beginning was the word ...' and so on (presumably) until the end foreseen by every faithful rendition of the gospel, by Elvis or any other singer.

And not only, we are to believe, for this woman and her descendants. Barbeau's recordings of Nisga'a songs are only a small part of the total sound archive that he left behind. Other cylinders, with recordings of other indigenous peoples of Canada, including neighbours of the Nisga'a, the Gitxsan, remained to be transcribed. The problem in the past had been that every playing of them would degrade the original recording. 'But now,' we learned,

those petrified sounds can be miraculously brought back to life. The National Library [of Canada, in Ottawa] has recently purchased a custom-made $25,000 'Archeophone' that can instantly convert wax cylinder and pre-war vinyl records into digital data. Perfect copies can then be stored on computers, duplicated as countless CDs, sent to other museums, and posted on the Internet for public access. Better still, sophisticated computer software can eliminate much of the crackling and hiss found on most old recordings.

All that was needed now was more money to pay for these 'instant conversions.' Then miracles would multiply, dead formats come to back to life, whole cultures be miraculously regenerated. Here was the 'resurrection' to which the headline referred. Thanks to the customized 'Archeophone,' the tales and songs of several of Canada's First Nations might soon sound again almost as they did before, and go on resounding perfectly for as long as there was world and time and a serviceable electronic platform for them.

Erase the details that identify this story of a wonder-working machine in its present version as North American, Canadian, British Columbian and putatively Nisga'a, remove the particulars of early-twentieth-century colonizing process and early-twenty-first-century postcolonial aspiration, delete the proprietary language of Edison and his successors, and we are left with a single plot motif or the motor of a simple plot: the artificial 'playback' of a people's memory, nation as recitation, the working of the archeophone (lower-case 'a' to distinguish the generic device from the latest model in Ottawa or any other late imperial capital).

The *archeophone*: a machine that no one has ever seen; a technology, the wonder of which is to go unnoticed most of the time; the subject of the essays in this book.

What *is* surprising, if not strictly miraculous, about the functioning of the customized, capital-A Archeophone in Canada's capital city, is that it reportedly rendered the voices and musical accompaniment of those Nisga'a performers of the 1920s without distortion. To be surprised at this, we have only to compare an earlier, more characteristic instance of the operation of the generic or archetypal 'archeophone.' *The Indian Speaks* is a 1941 illustrated anthology of native stories, jointly produced by Marius Barbeau, 'an ethnologist of the National Museum of Canada,' and Grace Melvin, head of the Department of Design at the (then) Vancouver School of Art (Barbeau and Melvin 1943). The shock one now feels on opening such a book is of a technology that makes itself remarked. The following quotations are from the preface:

> The Indian is here shown from within, under his own terms, as he used to express himself through his myths, songs, and stories. In this light he

belongs to humanity at its best; he can speak to us and we can understand him, for he is a person of high intelligence, of culture, and deep feelings. When he tells us how the world was created, how it collapsed at the time of the Flood, how the Earth Mother holds up our island – America, how the Great Raven conjured the first people out of a clam shell into the world … we might smile with incredulity if we did not remember our own Biblical symbolism … Here as we pass, we ponder on the differences, and sometimes the similarities, in traditions handed down from the dim past on distinct continents; we cannot help but feel that the ancient American somehow is our distant kinsman … (7)

…

Stripped of his hunting grounds and his primeval heritage, the red man may appear before us today with pick and shovel or, perhaps too often, in rags and tatters. For this he owes us no gratitude; in spite of the activities of our missionaries, we never really undertook to be his guardian or his redeemer. As a result he is well on his way to complete disappearance … (8)

This Indian has never been more comfortably 'our' kinsman than at the moment of his imminent disappearance, clasped in the stories that he has told and the songs that he has sung 'before lapsing into silence forever.'

The book, we are told, was assembled largely from 'unpublished records previously made for the National Museum of Canada among the native survivors of a past age,' including the same Edison wax cylinders of which there has been more recent report. These had been supplemented from other sources, among which were 'stories of the Mackenzie River Athapascans … adapted from Father Petitot's [1838–1917] published recollections in French which date back to about 1870.' In fact, the first ten stories in *The Indian Speaks* represent 'an old Huron legend' from the 'new Indian village' of Lorette, near Quebec City. All of them reflect the long history of Christian missions in that region. In the first, an old Huron 'saint' breaks into song one Christmas Eve. The song he sings is 'a Christmas carol … which Father Jean de Brébeuf, the Jesuit missionary [1593–1649], had composed for the converts among his people.' A snatch of it is recorded and translated: 'Jesus was born in the manger.' This opening sequence of Huron songs is concluded when the geographic focus of the collection shifts to the far west of Canada, for a story taken 'from songs and records of the Nass River,' that is, of the Nisga'a or Gitxsan. The title of that story is 'The Last Pagan.' His name was Geetiks, he had three wives already, and he dared to hold a potlatch for his wedding to a fourth. Others in the village were impressed. 'Whether they were all true Christians or not,' the story ends, 'an ancient train of thought among them was now awakened, which the missionaries have not yet succeeded in stamping out' (48).

The last item in *The Indian Speaks* is quite devoid of Christian colouring. It is the Haida tale of how the raven stole the moon. The same story would be chosen by Haida artist Bill Reid and by poet Robert Bringhurst as the title piece for their popular volume of illustrated versions of Haida myth in English, *The Raven Steals the Light*.[2] Unlike Barbeau and Melvin, Reid and Bringhurst had no interest in the imminent disappearance of the American Indian. Nor would they have been half so easy as their predecessors with the assimilation of native tradition to ancient biblical myth. Indeed, when occasion demanded, Reid was ready to turn the idiom of the 'King James Bible' against the would-be inheritors of the Queen Charlotte Islands. Writing in support of the preservation of Haida Gwaii from logging and other forms of commercial exploitation, in the same year (1984) in which he and Bringhurst published *The Raven Steals the Light*, he took his text from the Book of Genesis: 'A few thousand years ago, a mere tick of the cosmic clock, but quite a respectable time when measured by the rapid pace of a people intent on overtaking their own destiny as soon as possible, the god of a then obscure tribe came up with a rather questionable dictate: "Be fruitful and multiply, and replenish the earth and subdue it"' (Reid 2000, 206). In this ironic cranking of the archeophone, the operation of the machine itself becomes audible.

For Barbeau, whatever remained for missionaries to do in places like the Nass Valley, 'the last pagan' had already had his day. If the 'Canadian' Indian still spoke, he did so from beyond the grave, in the accents of the white men and women who had settled the country from Québec to British Columbia and beyond. The Indian was history – and the history, like the land, was 'ours.' That much would have seemed perfectly obvious to most Canadians in the 1930s, when Barbeau and Melvin were putting together the materials for their anthology. In British Columbia, writes Paul Tennant,

> government Indian agents ... were [then] at the height of their influence and control over local Indian communities. The great majority of Indian children were ... in the religious schools ... [O]ver the next half century, Whites growing up in the province or emigrating into it remained immersed in their own society's comforting myths and learned virtually

nothing of Indian issues or past white policies towards Indians ... and with aboriginal land claims suppressed, Indian political activity appeared at an end. (Tennant 1990, 114–15)

As present-day residents of the province of British Columbia know well enough, the issue of native entitlement to land has a special connection with the Nisga'a. Late in 1927, within weeks of Barbeau's packing up his Edison recording device in the Nass Valley, a committee of the federal government in Ottawa threw out a case for the restitution of land to native people that had been actively pursued for more than a decade by the Allied Tribes of British Columbia, the Nisga'a foremost among them. That judgment stood until 1973, when the Supreme Court of Canada ruled in favour of a claim by the Nisga'a to have held title to their lands before the assertion of British sovereignty over mainland British Columbia in 1858. The 1973 case (known as *Calder*) led to changes in the Canadian constitution that cleared the way for legal pleadings by native peoples in British Columbia and for the new treaty-making process set up in the province in the early 1990s, of which the Nisga'a Agreement, ratified in 2000, is to date the most important result.[3]

It is time to end this excursion into local history and widen our gaze to the horizons of this collection as a whole. The image of the 'archeophone' provides a convenient device for doing so. The archeophone, in the generic sense that I have been invoking, is itself a device of transition, translation, and cultural transfer. As the customized, proprietary 'Archeophone' in Ottawa is supposed to enable both native and non-native peoples of Canada to revise their senses of 'national' identity through auditory encounter with lyrical performances from a past made miraculously present by state-of-the-art technology, so too, I suggest, has the generic archeophone known in Western cultures as 'The Bible' or 'The Holy Scripture(s)' traditionally facilitated the transfer of *idioms of nationhood* between a past recognized as remote ('Remember the days of old,' the Deuteronomist says) and a contemporary reality understood as being at once modern and providentially continuous with the historical reality of the Bible. Other commentators have found other metaphors for representing one or another aspect of this 'communication of idioms,' a process truly as mysterious in its way as the mingling of divine and human attributes in the person of Christ for which Christian theologians use that phrase.

Canadian historian Donald Harman Akenson, after Northrop Frye and the poet William Blake, has spoken in this connection of the

Jewish-Christian Bible as a 'great code' (Akenson 1991, 9).[4] Another inviting line of approach, and one that may more fully license the emphasis here placed on *the artificial temporality of a biblical-historic present*, lies through Michel de Certeau's reflections on the 'scriptural operation' and Benedict Anderson's theorizing of 'imagined communities.' Anderson relied for a crucial piece of his reasoning on a sense of epoch that he derived from Erich Auerbach's great study *Mimesis: The Representation of Reality in Western Literature* (1946). It is this sense of epoch that, in his analysis, separates the modern consciousness of nationhood from earlier – including Christian, biblically based – convictions of transhistorical community. With Auerbach's sanction, Anderson would deny the continuity-into-modernity of the technology of the biblical-historic present. As we shall see, however, Anderson misrepresented Auerbach. Far from supporting a thesis of the radical supersession of biblical by modern computations of time and nationhood, the argument of *Mimesis* – now as then – attests to the powerful currency of biblical thought-ways and the fragility of what has been taken for secular modernity.

Ethnography, or the Operation of Scripture

In an often-cited essay in *The Writing of History*, Michel de Certeau used testimony from Jean de Léry's *Histoire d'un voyage faict en la terre du Brésil* (1578) to mark the appearance of a new 'law of writing,' presented by him as constitutive of modern history and modern ethnology alike, and of Western modernity as a whole. This 'modern practice of writing' was an instance of what Certeau elsewhere called 'heterology.' It was a way of organizing the world of human experience, knowledge, and power relations through an 'utterance (*parole*) instituted *in the place of the other* and designed to be understood *otherwise* than it speaks' (210), 'a problematic that founds its mastery of expression on what the other keeps silent' (3).[5] The stakes of such a discursive regime are summed up in Certeau's commentary on an engraving that showed Amerigo Vespucci encountering 'America' in the person of a naked aboriginal woman:

> An inaugural scene. After a moment of stupor on this threshold marked by an avenue of trees, the conqueror is going to *write* the body of the other and therein trace his own history ... [The image] represents the beginning of a new function for writing in the West ... [W]hat is really initiated here

is a colonization of the body by the discourse of power. This is *writing that conquers*. It will use the New World like a blank (desert) page on which to write the western will. It transforms the space of the other into a field of expansion for a system of production. On the basis of a division between a subject and an object of the operation, between a *will to write* and a *written body* (or a body to be written), it constructs western history. (xxv)

Although the science of ethnology as such would be only one of the modes of the new 'writing,' it could be considered to have a uniquely reflexive relationship with the modern Western practice of history, inasmuch as 'ethnology is especially interested in what *is not written*' (210). With this line from Claude Lévi-Strauss, Certeau opened the single chapter in *The Writing of History* to deal directly with 'New World' discourse, entitled 'Ethno-graphy: Orality, or the Space of the Other – Léry.' Léry's text provided a 'figure of modernity' by presenting 'the equivalent of a [Freudian] "primal scene" in the construction of ethnological discourse.' As read by Certeau, the *Histoire d'un voyage* laid bare a 'scriptural operation [*opération scripturaire*] which produces, preserves, and cultivates imperishable "truths" … on the strength of a rumour of words that vanish as soon as they are uttered and are therefore lost forever' (212). This chapter on 'Ethno-graphy' echoed and overwrote another in Lévi-Strauss's *Tristes tropiques* ('A Writing Lesson') that had been ferociously critiqued by Jacques Derrida in *Of Grammatology* ('The Violence of the Letter: From Lévi-Strauss to Rousseau').[6] If only for its repetition in scholarly literature, the scene from Léry and its homologues would now count as primal for a certain ethnography.[7]

A Huguenot refugee who, after a sojourn in Geneva, spent time among the Tupinamba of Brazil and later published an account of his experience, Léry (in Certeau's account) employs the figure of the 'savage' as a discursive means of making himself at home again in Christian Europe. The successful closing of the outward-homeward circuit depends on an experience of radical alterity located towards the psychological mid-point of the narrated journey: 'The story effects his return to himself through the mediation of the other. Yet something still remains over there, which escapes the words of the text; namely, the speech of the Tupis. It is that part of the other that cannot be retrieved – it is a fleeting act that writing cannot capture' (213). The experience of irreducible orality is registered in Léry's text by his account of a ballad sung by Tupinamba women, the instantaneous effect of which upon him he describes as a kind of ecstasy or 'ravishment,' even though he could not understand what was being sung. The memory of the ecstatic moment is so sharp, he says, it can still reproduce the effect long afterwards, as if the song were yet in his ears. 'The hole in time,' suggested Certeau, 'is identical with the absence of meaning' (ibid.). When the song was explained to him by a translator, Léry learned that the singers had been lamenting their valiant forbears, consoling themselves with the thought of seeing them again beyond the High Mountains, declaiming threats against their enemies, and recalling a time when floodwaters rose so high that everyone on earth had drowned except their ancestors, who survived by climbing the highest trees in the country. Impressed at the time by what he took for a poetically embellished reminiscence of the biblical Great Flood, Léry now reflected that, lacking any kind of writings ('privés de toute sorte d'écritures'), the Tupinamba were naturally unable to preserve an accurate memory of events in the distant past. In Certeau's reading, it is the opportune recovery of a reference point in biblical history that, by restoring meaning, also restores the narrator to himself and makes possible his homeward journey. The return to Christian Europe was thus a return to and by means of written narrative (*récit*), in scripture and in the *Histoire d'un voyage*. As Certeau explained it, 'productive time is restored [and] the generation of history resumes' after the heart- and time-stopping moment when, ravished by the voice of the other in a suspended present, 'the observer forgot himself' (214).

To support his exegesis of this scene, Certeau referred to an earlier chapter of the *Histoire* in which Léry considered the religion of the Tupinamba. Entitled 'Nulle écriture et nulle connaissance du vrai Dieu' ('No writing [*or* scripture] and no knowledge of the true God'), the chapter contains a claim for the God-given advantage of writing ('l'art d'écriture') that would be echoed in other narratives of 'New World' encounters.[8] Certeau pursued his own generalization. Writing accumulates over time and extends itself in space; it is archival and expansionist; it capitalizes and colonizes. The power of writing

> is caught in the play of a double *reproduction*: as history and orthodoxy, it preserves the past; as mission, it conquers space by multiplying the same signs. This [i.e., Léry's] is the period in which the critical work of the return to origins, by exhuming written 'sources,' goes forward on the basis of the creation of the new empire made possible by the indefinite repetition, through the printing-press, of identical products. (216)

At this point, Certeau's repetition of Léry's primal ethnographic scene restates the main argument of *The Writing of History* about the origins and sources of Western modernity, which is in fact an argument about the processes by which 'origins' and 'sources' come to be subject to a new regime of writing.

As elsewhere in Certeau's work, the development of the thesis proceeds via a tacit equivocation on the sense of *écriture*.[9] Introducing Léry's chapter on Tupinamba religion ('Nulle écriture ...'), Certeau paraphrased its subject-matter as 'the relation between the Christianity of Scripture [*le christianisme de l'Écriture*] and the oral traditions of the uncivilized world' (214). After a long quotation, he heads his next section 'La reproduction scripturaire.' The adjective 'scripturaire' here equivocates between 'Scripture' (*l'Écriture*) and 'writing' (*écriture*) in a way that English cannot convey. The historical drift in Certeau's texts is from the former sense towards the latter. A similar slippage already appears in Léry's, which began:

> Quant à l'écriture, soit sainte ou profane, non seulement aussi ils ne savent que c'est, mais qui plus est, n'ayant nuls caractères pour signifier quelque chose ... (de Léry 1580, part 4, ch. 1)
> [As for writing, be it sacred or profane, not only do they likewise not know what it is, but moreover lack any characters by which to signify things ...]

As with the later comment that the Tupinamba are 'privés de toute sorte d'écritures' ('deprived of any kind of writings'), the initial reference to 'sacred or profane writing' must be to writing(s) as documents, books, or historical narratives rather than to a semiotic system as such. Having just spoken of the natives' ignorance of God, Léry now spoke of their similar ('aussi') ignorance of any kind of authoritative *text*. It was only the additional and even greater wonder ('qui plus est') of their apparent ignorance of all written signs that inspired his studied digression on writing as 'art' and 'invention.'

'Scripture' in the sacred sense nonetheless remains a major axis of understanding in the *Histoire*, fully justifying the emphasis laid by Certeau on the importance of specifically *biblical* coordinates for the narrator's self-recovery after the momentary, as it were atemporal, ravishment of native song. A few pages after that episode we find Léry astounding his Tupinamba audience with the biblical story of Creation. When an old man breaks in with a story of other foreigners who had come long ago with similar tales, which the people had chosen not to believe, the narrator surmises that St Matthew must once have made a landfall in Brazil! Then, as the old man relates how these earlier missionaries had punished the natives by teaching them the use of weapons, he makes a connection with Revelation 6:4 ('And there went out another horse that was red: and power was given to him that sat thereon to take peace from the earth, and that they should kill one another: and there was given unto him a great sword'). While the strangeness of the Tupinamba may be radical and irreducible, it is at the same time largely containable by a biblically derived hermeneutics.

In fact, according to Certeau, the *Histoire d'un voyage* amounts to nothing less than a 'hermeneutics of the other':

> It transfers to the New World [*transporte sur le nouveau monde*] the Christian exegetical apparatus which, born of a necessary relation with Jewish otherness, has been applied successively to biblical tradition, to Greek or Latin antiquity, and to many other foreign totalities besides. Once again, it extracts effects of meaning from the relation to the other. *Ethnology will become a form of exegesis which has not ceased to provide the modern West with a means of articulating its identity through a relation with the past or the future, with foreigners or with nature.* (221, italics mine)

Despite the millennial continuity suggested by the first two sentences of this statement ('Once again …'), Certeau clearly meant to signal a break between ancient/medieval and modern; hence the future tense in the last sentence ('Ethnology will become …'). The transfer of Christian exegetical apparatus to the 'New World' somehow also *transforms* that apparatus. In the next sentence we read of 'this *new* [i.e., post-biblical] "hermeneutics of the other,"' otherwise 'ethnology.' Similarly, Certeau granted Léry's status as a *religious* writer only to take it away again: 'Through all this Jean de Léry appears to be a good Calvinist … But he is already displacing the theology that inspires him. He is *laicizing* it' (217, italics mine). The more obviously Christian religious elements of Léry's discourse, Certeau suggested, fall on the uncivilized, unlaborious, timeless, ecstatic-prophetic side of the division marked by his narrative – on the opposite side, that is, from the historical and productive (capitalizing, conquering, colonizing, scientific) work of *modern writing*. Even the reminiscence of the biblical Flood in the natives' song was worth nothing until rendered by an interpreter and inserted by the narrator into the extra-biblical plot of the *Histoire*.

The 'scriptural operation,' as Certeau understood it, must therefore be distinguished from the workings of any traditionally biblical hermeneutic. The 'new law of writing' is something other and more than a re-application of the scriptures. Yet the relationship between the Bible and the modern 'law of writing' is still assumed to be close, indeed critical for Western modernity. Certeau's clearest statement on this subject appears in another essay:

> One could hardly overestimate the importance of the fundamental relationship between Western culture and what was for centuries considered writing par excellence, the Bible. If we simplify history ... one can say that before the 'modern' period, that is, until the sixteenth or seventeenth century, this writing (Holy Scripture) speaks. The sacred text is a voice ... For reasons analyzed elsewhere, the modern age is formed by discovering little by little that this Spoken Word is no longer heard, that it has been altered by textual corruptions and the avatars of history ... 'Truth' no longer depends on the attention of a receiver who assimilates himself to the great identifying message. It is the result of work – historical, critical, economic work ... Another writing is imposed little by little in scientific, erudite or political forms: it is no longer something that speaks, but something made. Still linked to what is disappearing, indebted to what is moving away into the distance like a past but remains an origin, this new writing must be a practice, the endless production of an identity that is supported only by an activity, a moving on that always depends on something else to provide an available space for its advance, to the degree that the voice proper to Christian culture becomes its other and the presence given in the signifier (the very definition of voice) is transformed into a past. The capitalist scriptural conquest is articulated on that loss and on the gigantic effort of 'modern' societies to redefine themselves without that voice.[10]

As history, we may agree, this probably *is* too simple.[11] Like everything Certeau wrote, it is also open to questions about the writer's own desire to hear silenced voices speak again.[12] This much is clear, however: Certeau's thesis about *post-biblical* writing as the dominant 'mythical practice' of the modern West is inextricable from his contention that modernity constitutes itself primarily *by defining the past as its own other*. That is the claim with which *The Writing of History* originally began, before the addition of the preface to the second edition with its exegesis of the engraving of Vespucci and 'America.' In making the claim, Certeau discloses the psychoanalytical bias structuring the narrative of separation and loss in the passage quoted above. 'Modern western history,' he asserts, 'effectively begins with the difference between the *present* and the *past*. By this means, it also distinguishes itself from (religious) *tradition*, from which it never succeeds in separating itself entirely, maintaining with this archaeology a relation of indebtedness and rejection' (2). A vestigially Foucaultian notion of 'archaeology' here takes a Freudian turn reminiscent of the opening of *Civilization and Its Discontents*. Christian 'religious tradition' becomes the premodern 'other' of modern Western historical consciousness, a realm of orality simultaneously buried and mourned by modernity, foundational for its discourses, and forever liable to resurface within them. 'Archaeology,' Certeau states, 'was for me the mode in which I sought to specify the return of a "repressed," a system of Scriptures [*Écritures*] which modernity has *made* into something absent, but without being able to eliminate it' (14). As 'archaeology' for Certeau names both the mode of inquiry and the form in which its object manifests itself, so 'heterology' names each and all of the modes taken over time by *the return of the Scriptures*, transformed, as 'writing.'

Among those modes, as we have seen, the discourse of ethnology occupies a place of privilege. Certeau's musings on Defoe's figure of Robinson Crusoe – ethnographer, colonist, capitalist – in essays of his such as 'The Scriptural Economy' develop the idea more fully. But the essential point is already made, albeit with extreme compression, at the beginning of the essay on Jean de Léry: 'The modern practice of writing becomes the instrument of a double labour which concerns, on the one hand, the relation to the "*uncivilized*" human being [*l'homme "sauvage"*] and, on the other, the relation to *religious* tradition.' The dawning awareness of a 'New World' comes hard upon the 'twilight of medieval Christianity' (211). Ethnology (p)recapitulates Renaissance and Reformations, if not already Enlightenment. The relation to religious tradition that ethnographic narrative inscribes is implicitly supersessionist. For a Frenchman and a Jesuit like Certeau, the encompassing term for such seismic shifts in the strata of European culture or its collective unconscious was 'laïcisation.' The nearest anglophone equivalent would be 'secularization.' Turning an ethnologist's eye on his own society, as he liked to do, he found it to be, above all, one of stories (*récits*):

Captured by the radio (the voice is the law) as soon as he awakens, the listener walks all day long through the forest of narrativities from journalism, advertising, and television, narrativities that still find time, as he is getting ready for bed, to slip a few final messages under the portals of sleep. Even more than the God told about [*raconté*] by the theologians of earlier days, these stories have a providential and predestining function: they organize in advance our work, our celebrations, and even our dreams … Our society has become a recited society in three senses: it is defined by stories [*récits*] …, by *citations* of stories, and by the interminable *recitation* of stories. (de Certeau 1980, 186)[13]

Echoing Certeau's analysis without acknowledging it, the opening section of this chapter was titled 'Nation and Recitation.' The final section will attempt to justify the borrowing, by showing how readily Certeau's understanding of the 'scriptural operation' lends itself to a discussion of the modern (Western) discourse of nationhood, including components of it that would seem to have little to do with modernity as customarily defined.

Imagined Continuities: The Biblical-Historic Present

In his 1983 book *Imagined Communities*, Benedict Anderson argues that the rise of 'vernacular print-capitalism' in Europe in the sixteenth and seventeenth centuries made possible the emergence of modern forms of nationalism (Anderson 1991). Belief in the nation provided people with a sense of social cohesion and intergenerational continuity that transcended the bleak facts of their own mortality, imparting a meaning to their lives that would otherwise have been lacking. It was a substitute for the religious assurance that had been lost with the break-up of the former community of (Latin) Christendom.

Anderson's reflections on the twilight of traditional Christianity are in the same key as Certeau's, with the onset of 'secularism' duly substituted for that of 'laïcité':

In Western Europe the eighteenth century marks not only the dawn of the age of nationalism but the dusk of religious modes of thought. The century of the Enlightenment, of rationalist secularism, brought with it its own modern darkness. With the ebbing of religious belief, the suffering which belief in part composed [i.e., consoled] did not disappear … What was then required was a secular transformation of fatality into continuity, contingency into meaning. (Anderson 1991, 11)

The answer to this urgent requirement was the nation. In order to fulfil its collective-psychological function, however, the fiction of the modern nation had to conceal the facts of its own emergence. Hence, while the idea of the nation-state would be of something new and newly *histori-cal*, the nationhood to which it gave expression was always seen to 'loom out of an immemorial past.'

These formulations of Anderson's have their exact counterpart in Certeau's conjuring of the ghost of Jules Michelet, author of a *Histoire de France* (1869), as a reminder to us that modern, nation-centred his-toriography begins at the tombside, 'the border at which, from Virgil to Dante, *fictions* were constructed that were not yet *history*' (de Certeau 1988, 2). The discourse of nationalism was central to the practice of 'modern writing' theorized by Certeau.[14] Yet despite these pregnant references to Virgil and Dante, poets par excellence of the Roman Empire and Catholic Christendom, he has little to say about the pro-cess of transition from 'fictions' that did not yet count as 'history' to those that would. Anderson is more forthcoming. He explains the waning of the imagined community of Western Christianity from the late Middle Ages onwards partly as an effect of increasing knowledge of the non-European world and partly as a corollary of the collapse of a pan-European religious discourse based on Latin Scripture. On both points he remains close to Certeau, though without evincing any knowledge of the latter's work. But in Anderson's account neither the encounter with the exotic 'other' nor the silencing of the scriptural Word appears as truly decisive. Instead, the decisive factor is a new apprehension of *time*. Whereas Certeau, following a tradition as old as Renaissance humanism itself, located the onset of modernity in a rad-ical separation of past from present, Anderson finds it in an imagina-tion of translocal *synchronicity* made possible by new media.[15] For him the primary index of modernity is not the 'writing' of heterology but a print-borne intuition of sameness or homogeneity in time.[16]

To establish a context for this change in collective sensibility, Anderson quotes a key section from Erich Auerbach's *Mimesis: The Representation of Reality in Western Literature*. Auerbach is one of three inspirational guides named in the acknowledgments to *Imagined Communities*, along with Walter Benjamin and anthropologist Victor Turner (Anderson 1991, ix). The merging of a scheme from *Mimesis* with an aphorism from Benjamin enables Anderson to state a hypoth-esis about 'modern time' on which he then bases his main argument for the role of print-capitalism in the formation of national identities. Without underestimating the appeal of Benjamin's visionary prose, one can fairly say that Auerbach's contribution is historiographically the more substantial. Though evidently taken 'as read' by the majority of those who have since made Anderson's work their own point of departure, *Mimesis* is the linchpin of his ambitious chronology.

Such a re-application of Auerbach's work in a book otherwise so heavily influenced by anthropology would be merely singular, were it exceptional. But it is not. If we turn from political to literary science, the treatment of Auerbach as an honorary ethnographer begins to seem like a norm of contemporary 'cultural studies.' Stephen Greenblatt not long ago traced his own and others' practice of 'new historicism' or 'cultural poetics' to the impact in the mid-1970s of Clifford Geertz's *The Interpretation of Cultures* on a generation of literary scholars still under the spell of *Mimesis* (Greenblatt 2000, 31ff.).[17] Edward Said made Auerbach one of the exemplary representatives of a tradition of 'secular anthropology' that would begin with Vico and include what Said himself liked to call 'secular criticism' – which has been taken for a species of postcolonial critique.[18] These are just two of the most pertinent 'Auerbachian' revivals for our present theme; the list could easily be extended.[19] How is one to account for the influence on the current critical study of Western discourses of culture, nation, and colonization of a Prussian, Jewish philologist of Romance literatures, who wrote his best-known book in Istanbul in 1942–5 and died in the United States in 1957? Anderson does not say why he feels able to treat *Mimesis* as an authoritative text. Nor, unlike Said and Greenblatt, does he stop to consider how Auerbach's personal sense of the fatality and contingencies of modern existence may have shaped his work. He merely cites him for his authoritative description of a 'form of [temporal] consciousness' held to be characteristic of Christian men and women of the Middle Ages and 'wholly alien to our own' (Anderson 1991, 24). This citation will bear a more studied reading. A great deal potentially depends upon it.

The quoted passage, which occurs near the end of the third chapter of *Mimesis*, is only intelligible in relation to the larger design of Auerbach's book. In the famous essay of chapter 1 ('Odysseus' Scar') Auerbach has juxtaposed a scene from the hero's homecoming in the *Odyssey* with the story of the near-sacrifice of Isaac in Genesis 22, in order to illustrate what he takes to be a radical difference between Homeric-Greek and Judaeo-Christian biblical styles of representing the world of human experience. In the epic there is only one temporal horizon; even events narrated in flashback, like the goring of young Odysseus by a boar, appear in 'a uniformly illuminated, uniformly objective present,' beguiling our senses and rendering superfluous any activity of exegesis: 'The Homeric poems conceal nothing, they contain no teaching and no secret second meaning' (Auerbach 1953, 7, 13).[20] In contrast to this serenely hospitable Homeric representation of reality, a biblical episode such as Isaac's sacrifice, according to Auerbach, is so 'fraught with background' and 'mystery,' so layered 'with depths of time, fate and consciousness' (12), that it compels the reader to refer its every detail to an encompassing narrative-doctrinal unity; only by dint of such externally validated interpretation can he or she hope to grasp the story's essential but concealed meaning.

This hermeneutical imperative is presented by Auerbach as the corollary of the Bible's absolute claim to historical truth:

> The Bible's claim to truth is not only far more urgent than Homer's, it is tyrannical – it excludes all other claims. The world of the Scripture stories is not satisfied with claiming to be a historically true reality – it insists that it is the only real world, is destined for autocracy. All other scenes, issues, and ordinances have no right to appear independently of it, and it is promised that all of them, the history of all mankind, will be given their due place within its frame, will be subordinated to it. The Scripture stories do not, like Homer's, court our favor, they do not flatter us that they may please us and enchant us – they seek to subject us, and if we refuse to be subjected we are rebels.
>
> Let no one object that this goes too far ... (14)

The possible objection that it is religious doctrine, rather than the stories themselves, that stakes the claim for absolute authority is ruled out with an assertion that 'doctrine and promise are *incarnate* in them [i.e., the stories] and inseparable from them' (15, italics mine).

If this language of 'incarnation' sounds a prophetic note, then that is no accident either, since Auerbach's attempt to explain the eventual emergence in the West of a kind of literary realism supposedly unknown to Homer and other authors of classical antiquity is grounded on a reading not of the Hebrew but of the Judaeo-*Christian* Bible. As he begins to argue in chapter 2, in a few almost blindingly dense pages on the Gospel scene of Peter's denial of Christ, it is the 'Jewish-Christian literature' of the New Testament, 'the story of Christ, with its ruthless mixture of everyday reality and the highest and most sublime tragedy' (555), that, in contravention of the norms of classical rhetoric, furnished the model for a style of realism that would one day be capable of treating seriously the experiences and fates of ordinary people – of presenting all its characters, irrespective of their social station, as equally caught up in 'the unfolding of historical forces' (44). The fulfilment of this Hegelian possibility is reserved by Auerbach for the French novel in the age of historicism: 'Michelet and Balzac are borne on the same stream' (473). By then we are in chapter 18. Before this 'modern realism' can be revealed in its fullness, there is a long story to be told of successive realizations and progressive revisions of the 'incarnational' logic of the Christian Gospels, beginning with St Paul. For whatever importance he may accord to Peter as a biblical character, it is Paul, on Auerbach's telling, who is the first 'author' of the Western Bible as a work of literature.

Although there is no Pauline text among those excerpted in *Mimesis*, Paul's agency is signalled early on, as Auerbach enlarges upon his description of the Bible as an all-inclusive and hence highly exclusive 'history of all mankind':

> The Old Testament [unlike the Homeric poems, which allow for boundaries in time and space] presents universal history: it begins with the beginning of time, with the creation of the world, and will end with the Last Days, the fulfilling of the Covenant, with which the world will come to an end. Everything else that happens in the world can only be conceived as an element in this sequence; into it everything that is known about the world, or at least everything that touches upon the history of the Jews, must be fitted as an ingredient of the divine plan. (16)

By a centuries-long process of (re-)interpretation, the 'original frame' of this 'Jewish-Israelitish realm of reality' was made to accommodate such 'new and strange world[s]' as those of Assyrian, Babylonian, Persian, Greek, and Roman history, with inevitable effects on the shape of the frame itself. Without using the term, Auerbach evokes the expansion of a scriptural 'canon' as well as the multiplication of exegetical procedures. He continues:

> The most striking piece of interpretation of this sort occurred in the first century of the Christian era, in consequence of Paul's mission to the Gentiles: Paul and the Church Fathers reinterpreted the entire Jewish

tradition as a succession of figures prognosticating the appearance of Christ, and assigned the Roman Empire its proper place in the divine plan of salvation. Thus while, on the one hand, the reality of the Old Testament presents itself as complete truth with a claim to sole authority, on the other hand that very claim forces it to a constant interpretative change in its own content; for millennia it undergoes an incessant and active development with the life of man in Europe. (16)

As at other places in *Mimesis*, one must allow here for the telescopic effect of Auerbach's expository method. Speaking of 'the first century of the Christian era,' he summons not only Paul but 'the Church Fathers,' and refers to a hermeneutic synthesis which, in order to have 'assigned the Roman Empire its proper [i.e., definitive] place in the divine plan of salvation,' cannot be dated long before the time of Augustine's *City of God*, begun soon after the sack of Rome in 410.[21]

Sure enough, apart from another fleeting mention of Paul's mission to the gentiles and of his 'method of revisional interpretation' tacked on at the end of chapter 2, discussion of this definitive and definitively Christian hermeneutic synthesis is reserved by Auerbach for a sequel to the reading of a passage from Augustine's *Confessions* that forms the climax of chapter 3. Here too the connection to what has come before in the book is somewhat inorganic. Like the analysis of the scene of Peter's denial, the analysis of the *Confessions* focuses on the anti-classical treatment of 'everyday reality,' once again held up as a distant precursor of modern literary mimesis. And yet, Auerbach is obliged to grant, such effects of realism are still rare in the Latin Church Fathers: 'They are no poets or novelists and, on the whole, no historians of their present' (73). Far more often than they represent current reality, they *interpret* it, and they typically do so for the purpose of 'bringing [it] into harmony with the Judaeo-Christian view of history.'

It is at this point, with Augustine's *City of God* as his chief exhibit, that Auerbach explains in detail, for the first time in *Mimesis*, the 'figural' method of revisional-historic interpretation developed by the Church Fathers on hints from St Paul.[22] This is the source of the passage quoted by Anderson in the section of *Imagined Communities* entitled 'Apprehensions of Time.' I repeat the quotation, restoring (italicized) a number of clauses that he omits:

This type of interpretation [says Auerbach] *obviously introduces an entirely new and alien element into the antique conception of history.* For example, if an

occurrence like the sacrifice of Isaac is interpreted as prefiguring the sacrifice of Christ, so that in the former the latter is as it were announced and
promised, and the latter 'fulfills' ... the former, then a connection is established between two events which are linked neither temporally nor causally – a connection which it is impossible to establish by reason in the
horizontal dimension *(if I may be permitted to use this term for a temporal extension)*. It can be established only if both occurrences are vertically linked
to Divine Providence, which alone is able to devise such a plan of history
and supply the key to its understanding. *The horizontal, that is the temporal
and causal, connection of occurrences is dissolved;* the here and now is no
longer a mere link in an earthly chain of events, it is simultaneously something which has always been, and which will be fulfilled in the future; and
strictly, in the eyes of God, it is something eternal, something omni-tem-
poral, something already consummated in the realm of fragmentary
earthly event. *This conception of history is magnificent in its homogeneity, but
it was completely alien to the mentality of classical antiquity.* (Auerbach 1953,
73–4, cited by Anderson 1991, 24)

Anderson italicizes the word 'simultaneously' in the last sentence of
the passage as he quotes it, then continues in his own voice:

[Auerbach] rightly stresses that such an idea of *simultaneity* is wholly
alien [*sic*] to our own. It views time as something close to what Benjamin
calls Messianic time, a simultaneity of past and future in an instantaneous present. In such a view of things, the word 'meanwhile' cannot be of
real significance. Our own conception of simultaneity has been a long
time in the making, and its emergence is certainly connected, in ways that
have yet to be well studied, with the development of the secular sciences.
But it is a conception of such fundamental importance that, without taking it fully into account, we will find it difficult to probe the obscure genesis of nationalism. What has come to take the place of the mediaeval
conception of simultaneity-along-time is, to borrow again from Benjamin,
an idea of 'homogeneous, empty time,' in which simultaneity is, as it
were, transverse, cross-time, marked not by prefiguring and fulfilment,
but by temporal coincidence, and measured by clock and calendar.
(Anderson 1991, 24)[23]

Having delivered these generalizations, Anderson goes on to show how
two new media of the eighteenth century, the novel and the newspaper,
played on the emergent sense of 'simultaneity in homogeneous, empty

time' to represent 'the *kind* of imagined community that is the nation' (25). Calendrical coincidence, whether assumed in the plotting of incidents involving different characters in a novel or asserted by the date on a newssheet reporting events from different places, and underlined in both cases by the shared textual experience of separated readers, helped establish the 'imagined linkages' out of which a modern consciousness of nationhood could grow. Such a creation was only possible, however, because more ancient solidarities – *including, crucially, that founded on the pre-consummated unity of biblical history* – had already broken down.

The synchronicities of Anderson's narrative of the making of nations are so striking, his own linkages so insightful, it will perhaps seem ungrateful to stick at a single quotation. I do not quibble with the minor finesses of this one. It is easy to see why Anderson omits Auerbach's repeated statement that 'horizontal' denotes an axis of 'temporal and causal connection' (i.e., 'along time' rather than 'across time') when his own use of the phrase 'horizontal-secular, transverse-time' (37) will rotate that axis by ninety degrees. Likewise, the deeply felt tribute in *Mimesis* to the 'magnificent homogeneity' of the providentialist world view, left in place, could only have got in the way of an assimilation of its opposite to Benjaminian 'homogeneous time.' These sleights of hand undoubtedly conceal difficulties in Anderson's adaptation of Auerbach. More immediately revealing, however, is his silent conversion of Auerbach's claim for the radical novelty of the Jewish-Christian conception of history with respect to *classical* norms into a claim for its utter strangeness ('wholly alien') to *modern* ways of thinking – and hence to the idea of the nation in the modern, capitalist, and colonial era.

There would be nothing untoward about such a claim, considered on its own terms, in a book published in 1983. It would be just another statement of the modernization-as-secularization thesis that has been taken for granted, until quite recently, by most humanistic research on the history of European or Western culture(s) since the rise of scientific historicism in the nineteenth century.[24] That *Imagined Communities* was squarely grounded on such a thesis is made plain again in the final section ('The Biography of Nations') of the second of two supplementary chapters appended in the second edition (1991). After several pages devoted to Michelet as the first historian to 'write *on behalf* of the dead' (197), Anderson adduces the modern genres of biography and autobiography as further instances of narratives that are 'set in homogeneous, empty time' and therefore constrained to establish links to larger social and cultural unities. It is this necessity, he suggests, that explains why the biographer is at pains to record the calendrical, A.D. dates of two biographical events which his or her subject can never remember: birth-day and death-day. Nothing affords a sharper reminder of this narrative's modernity than the opening of the Gospel according to St. Matthew. For the Evangelist gives an austere list of thirty males successively begetting one another, from the Patriarch Abraham down to Jesus Christ … No dates are given for any of Jesus's forebears, let alone sociological, cultural, physiological or political information about them. This narrative style … was entirely reasonable to the sainted genealogist because he did not con-ceive of Christ as an historical 'personality,' but only as the true Son of God. (205)

'As with modern persons,' Anderson continues, 'so it is with nations,' except that for nations there are no given dates of beginning and end. Because they are not begotten but made, and do not die naturally, their biographies 'can not be written evangelically.' The history of the mod-ern nation, like that of a modern person, is fashioned in a time and for a temporality that are alike strictly post-biblical and 'secular.' Michelet communes with the dead in order to create an artificial memory, be-cause there is no preordained national genealogy. Other times, other scribes. To write an 'evangelical' or biblical-genealogical history of a nation would be as odd today, Anderson affirms, as 'to end a life of Hitler by observing that on 30 April 1945 he proceeded straight to Hell.'

That is almost the end of *Imagined Communities*. Although Anderson does not cite *Mimesis* in these closing pages, the memory of a book writ-ten by a Jewish refugee from German National Socialism (and dated from Istanbul, 'May 1942 – April 1945') is not altogether submerged.[25] The contrast between 'evangelical' and 'secular' modes of writing only makes sense, to the extent that it does, as a reprise of Auerbach's dis-tinction between *Christian-figural* and *secular-historicist* modes of real-ism. For it is, let it be said, a highly idiosyncratic version of the secularization thesis that Anderson, along with other recent revivers of Auerbach, takes over from *Mimesis*, a version in which, as late as the final chapter of that book, a scene of the narrator's father in Proust's *À la recherche du temps perdu* 'standing like Abraham in the engraving after Benozzo Gozzoli … telling Hagar that she must tear herself away from Isaac' can be cited in illustration of 'the symbolic omnitemporality of an event fixed in a remembering consciousness' and, on the same page, Joyce's *Ulysses* can be described as 'a symbolic synthesis of the theme "Everyman"' in which 'all the great motifs of the cultural history of

Europe are contained,' even though the novel's 'point of departure is very specific individuals and a clearly established present (Dublin, June 16, 1904).' No one who has read the intervening chapters since 'Odysseus' Scar' will fail to infer that, in Auerbach's eyes, the greatest of modern or modernist European fiction had somehow saved the 'magnificent homogeneity' of the Jewish-Christian apprehension of time and history, albeit now without any vertical link to Divine Providence. Alien as such a 'figural' vision of reality may have been to the Homeric or 'classical' mind, there is no sense in treating Auerbach as an authority for its radical strangeness to the 'modern' – so long as modernity begins with print-capitalism, the Reformations of Christianity, and the European colonization of the Americas. Indeed, it is more plausible to see his own philological work as a sustained attempt to interpret the history of European literature in the light of 'symbolic omnitemporality,'[26] or to make another Scripture out of Literature.[27]

Auerbach had a clear notion of a process that could be called 'secularization' and unhesitatingly located its literary-historical beginning in Dante's *Commedia*. In Dante, on his view, the distinctively Christian, incarnational-eschatological sense of the significance of individual human personality in history became so artistically powerful that it began to eclipse theology. For Auerbach, however, *the beginning of the end of a theological world view did not entail the winding-down of biblical-figural time.* On the contrary, the continuity of European literature – and, by extension, of European or Western culture – depended for him on a conviction of the seriousness of 'everyday' human experience that would always be exactly datable from the coming of God as a human being, as first represented and interpreted in the Gospels. *Pace* Anderson, then, it was precisely because the evangelists did *not* conceive of Christ 'only as the true Son of God' but also 'as an historical "personality"' that later writers and readers were able to conceive of a human present more fraught with past and future, for the individual and the collectivity, than had been imaginable in classical times. Hence, far from being an unequivocal sign of secular modernity, as Anderson claims, the fact that every biographer is now 'at pains to record the calendrical, AD dates' of his or her subject's birth and death would, on an Auerbachian view, be a literal reminder of the lingering pervasiveness of the Christian-figural scheme of reality: even if there were no longer a Hell for Hitler, calendrical time (AD or CE) could never be *empty*.

To speak in this way of the pervasiveness of such a scheme in the West is of course not to assume its persuasiveness, now or at any time, for all persons or peoples. Auerbach's commitment to Christian figuralism in literature did not make him a Christian, nor could he be at all confident that the 'reality' he discerned in his texts would last beyond the middle of the twentieth century. Certainly he had no illusions of his own powers of prophecy. Contrast the certainty of the opening of his book, in its sure-footed reference to well-known passages from Homer and the Old Testament, with the lonely and faltering tone of its conclusion:

> It is still a long way to a common life of mankind on earth, but the goal begins to be visible. And it is most concretely visible now in the unprejudiced, precise, interior and exterior representation of the random moment in the lives of different people. So the complicated process of dissolution [in modernist fiction] which led to fragmentation of the exterior action, to reflection of consciousness, and to stratification of time seems to be tending towards a very simple solution. Perhaps it will be too simple to please those who, despite all its dangers and catastrophes, admire and love our epoch for the sake of its abundance of life and the incomparable historical vantage point which it affords. But they are few in number, and probably they will not live to see much more than the first forewarnings of the approaching unification and simplification. (553)

As a terminal episode, this is less like Odysseus's homecoming than Abra(ha)m's setting-forth. Yet little if anything remains of the spirit of that 'man of faith' who answered the Lord's call to 'get thee out of thy country ... unto a land that I will shew thee' and who received the promise of future nationhood and a legacy of land in return for his obedience.[28] Auerbach in 1945 could see no further than the approaching end of his own scattered generation, which for all he knew could mark the close of an epoch in 'western history.'[29] 'In 1880 or 1930,' he had represented Stendhal as thinking in 1830, 'I shall find readers who understand me!' (462). He could hardly have imagined the reissue of his own book in a 'Fiftieth-Anniversary Edition,' complete with an introduction to proclaim its continuing timeliness.[30] There is no figure in Mimesis of which that event would be the fulfilment.

Said spoke of Mimesis as one of 'only a small number of books [that] seem perennially present and, by comparison with the vast majority of their counterparts, to have an amazing staying power' (Said 2003, ix). That Auerbach's critical-historical work could be hailed at this late date in language otherwise normally reserved for 'the classics' or 'the Bible' was to be put down to its extraordinary success in accounting for the wonder of just such 'perennially present' works of writing. That achievement, Said argued, was due as much to the author's ability to establish a vantage-point (or virtual 'Istanbul') at the edge of the spiritual continent of Western literature-and-scripture as it was to his rare capacity to pass for a resident alien of each of its nations or provinces in turn. Such deeply engaged detachment Said considered to be no less vitally necessary at the beginning of the twenty-first century than it had been fifty years earlier.

In seconding those claims for Auerbach's work on behalf of the present collection of essays, I would also wish to pursue the notion of its timeliness a little further. Easy as it is to admire *Mimesis* as a brilliant evocation of the origin, rise, waning, and eventual disappearance of a biblical-historic sense of the present in Western consciousness, the parabola of such a reading is at once too perfect for the book itself and too peremptory with respect to the history of our own times – that is, *since* 1945. We have seen that Anderson's citation of Auerbach in *Imagined Communities* imposes an epoch that is not borne out by closer reading. The effect of such a realization is to reinforce Certeau's hypothesis concerning the 'operation of scripture' as both 'history' and 'ethnography' in modern societies, while blurring even more than Certeau does the boundary between the *récit(s)* of Christian religious tradition and those of a conjecturally 'post-Christian,' 'secular' culture. Those inferences made, the present timeliness of *Mimesis* will have less to do with its deployment of excerpts or anecdotes in the service of some kind of literary anthropology of the West, than with the original (and lingering) shortness of its final horizon.

In its apparently effortless joining of times and cultures from the ancient Near East to the modern West, *Mimesis* mimics the operation of what I have been calling the 'archeophone.' Were it not, however, for Auerbach's acute awareness of the unbridgeable gap opening before him *at the time of writing*, his prevision of 'a common life of mankind on earth' would be no more promising than any other brand of universal prophecy-as-policy, of whatever date CE or BCE. The sequels of such mono(archeo)phonic performances are well enough known to us from history and the newspapers. The polyphony of Robert Bringhurst's *New World Suite*, excerpted for an epigraph above, is part of a west-coast Canadian poet's reckoning with them. His too are the lines on which we may most fittingly end, modelling as they do an inspired shortsightedness that matches Auerbach's at the last and a weariness, born like his of an exhaustion of narrative recitation, that may yet be one of our better hopes for a future life in common here on earth.

The speaker, known as Moses, recalls how the people used to come at his bidding:

> Once I used to sing them
> a song about an eagle and a stone, and each time
> I sang it, somehow the song seemed changed,
> and the words drifted into the sunlight. I do not
> remember the song now, but I remember
> that I sang it, and the song was the law, and the law
> was the song. The law is a song, I am certain …
> And I climbed to the head of this canyon. They said
> I could look down at the new land
> if I sat here, and I think it is so, but my eyes
> are no longer strong, and I am tired now of looking.[31]

NOTES

1 Volume 1 in the three-volume set of *Masterworks of the Classical Haida Mythtellers.*
2 Reid and Bringhurst 1984, with a preface by Claude Lévi-Strauss.
3 Tennant 1990, ch. 16: 'Aboriginal Title in the Courts.' See also McKee 2000 and Harris 2002, esp. ch. 10: 'Towards a Postcolonial Land Policy.'
4 'Transformed from a literary metaphor to a historical one, the concept of the scriptures as a code is perfect. They are a code not in the sense of something to be deciphered, to be broken, but in the sense that one speaks of organisms as having a genetic code. For certain societies, in certain eras of development, the scriptures have acted culturally and socially in the same way the human genetic code operates physiologically. That is, the great code has, in some degree, directly determined what people would believe and what they would think and what they would do. Equally important, the code has provided the fundamental workings of these societies' cosmologies. In this second aspect, the great code determined the ground rules under which new information entered the particular culture, how this information was evaluated, and what were the alternative courses of behaviour in any particular situation. Societies that took the Hebrew scriptures as their basic cultural code were formatted just as firmly as a

present-day computer disk.' For an alternative image of scriptures as a 'virtual reality machine,' see Akenson's essay in the present volume.

5 de Certeau 1988. Parenthetical references are to pages of Conley's English translation; in many cases, however, I have preferred to make a more literal translation.

6 Lévi-Strauss 1973, ch. 28; Derrida 1976, part 2, ch. 1. In *Tristes tropiques*, writes Derrida, 'the "Writing Lesson" marks an episode of what may be called the anthropological war [*la guerre ethnologique*], the essential confrontation that opens communication between peoples and cultures, even when that communication is not practiced under the banner of colonial or missionary oppression' (107). I would underline Derrida's remarks (113) on what he calls the 'empirical violence' of the genre of the ethnographic anecdote, and his diagnosis of the concealed teleology and eschatology at the heart of the classic ethnographic narrative from Rousseau onwards, 'the dream of a full and immediate presence closing history, the transparence and indivision of a parousia, the suppression of contradiction and difference' (115).

7 The scene is reprised by Greenblatt (1991, 14–19), with acknowledgment of Certeau. For Greenblatt's own treatment of the operation of 'writing' (but not 'scripture') in situations of 'New World' encounter, see the Commentary on part 2, below.

8 Jean de Léry, *Histoire d'un voyage*, part 4, ch. 1. For a modern translation, see de Léry 1990. Compare this statement of Léry's with that made by the English compiler of travellers' accounts, Samuel Purchas, discussed in my commentary on the essays in Part 2 below, 219.

9 Cf. the Translator's Introduction to *The Writing of History*, xx: 'The homologies of literature, Scripture, and history are implicit in the French, locating – in the formulation of Certeau's title – the doubly identical mission [*sic*] of literature as both *écriture* and chronicle.'

10 De Certeau 1984, 'The Scriptural Economy,' 136.

11 For the beginning of a critique, orientated on the history of the Latin Bible, see my introductory remarks in Pabel and Vessey 2002, 3f.

12 Certeau raises the questions himself: 'Concerning ethnological discourse, I would like to explain what it articulates in exiling orality outside of the areas which pertain to Western work, in transforming speech into an exotic object. But even so, I do not escape the culture that produced this discourse. I only reduplicate its effect. What ex-voto is my writing dedicating to that absent speech? For what dream, or what lure, is my writing a metaphor? There can be no answer. Self-analysis has been

disenfranchised, and I would not know how to replace with a text what only a voice that is other could reveal about the place in which I am writing' (de Certeau 1988, 211). This confession must be at least partly a response to Derrida's criticisms of Lévi-Strauss: above, n6.

13 From a chapter called 'Believing and Making People Believe.'

14 See esp. de Certeau 1988, 26, anticipating Anderson at several points: 'When the religious unanimity of Christendom was broken down into the diversity of European states, a knowledge was needed to take up the slack of belief and allow each group or each country to receive a distinctive definition. With the effects of the printing press, of a growing literacy and education, knowledge became a tool of unification and differentiation.'

15 Cf. *Imagined Communities* (Anderson 1991) 68, where Anderson cites Auerbach on the Renaissance humanists' 'discovery' of historical perspective; but this is a minor emphasis. Anderson's privileging of print culture, his claims for the discourse of nationhood as a distinctively *modern* formation, and his neglect of religious factors (especially the Christian Bible) in the continuing processes of nation-building have been fairly criticized by Hastings 1997, in terms largely consistent with those of the present volume.

16 As we shall see, however, the difference is less profound in its implications than could appear from this phrasing. For both Anderson and Certeau the protomodern discourse of 'secular' ethnicity, community, or nationhood is forged in the aftermath of a more-than-millennial tradition of (Christian) religious solidarity. Whereas one focuses on the displacement of an old technology, namely, 'Scripture' in the most Catholic and universalizing sense of the word, the other focuses on the coming of a new one, namely, print.

17 For a trenchant view of Greenblatt's use of Geertz, see van Oort 2004, who detects in it a latter-day aestheticizing variant of an older anthropological quest for 'elementary forms' of culture, whereby 'classic texts are [now] reread for signs of the experience of sacrality, and the historical archive is opened to the search for strangeness, for the alterity that will show us *in fictional form* something of the original mystery of a world still enchanted by the sacred' (624). Greenblatt himself acknowledges having wanted 'the touch of the real in the way that in an earlier period people wanted the touch of the transcendent' (Greenblatt 2000, 31) at precisely the point in his essay at which he turns from Geertz to Auerbach.

18 Said 1983, 5–8; Said 1993, 43–7; Said 2003; Mufti 1998.

19 See also, in particular, Lambropoulous 1993, whose preliminary analysis situates *Mimesis* as a 'colossal tautology [and] a monument of ethnocentrism'

(6), and Dawson 2002, a conscientious attempt to revise Auerbach's method-
ology in the cause of contemporary Jewish-Christian dialogue.

20 These and other generalizations about classical literature have not always
been ratified by specialists. Nor, apparently, did Auerbach himself see any
need to defend them too strenuously; see Auerbach 1954.

21 For Augustine's biblical-providentialist understanding of Roman history,
which differed significantly from the triumphalist perspective enshrined
in such works as the *Chronicle* of Eusebius of Caesarea (adapted for the
West by Jerome) and the *History against the Pagans* of his own protégé
Orosius, see Markus 1988. Complementary perspectives can be found in
Vessey, Pollmann, and Fitzgerald 1999.

22 He had treated the topic at length in his article 'Figura,' first published (in
German) in 1944; English translation in Auerbach 1984, 11–76. Auerbach's
theses on 'figuralism' in Christian exegesis and European literature have
attracted extensive commentary: see esp. White 1999, ch. 5, and Dawson
2002, ch. 4 and passim.

23 The quotations of Walter Benjamin are from the 'Theses on the Philosophy
of History,' completed in 1940, first published in German in 1950, as
translated by Harry Zohn in Benjamin 1968. The context is a distinction
between historicism and historical (dialectical) materialism: 'Historicism
rightly culminates in universal history. Materialistic historiography differs
from it as to method more clearly than from any other kind. Universal
history has no theoretical armature. Its method is additive; it musters a
mass of data to fill the *homogeneous empty time*. Materialistic historiography, on the other hand, is based on a constructive principle ...
Historicism contents itself with establishing a causal connection between
various moments in history. But no fact that is a cause is for that very
reason historical. It became historical posthumously, as it were, through
events that may be separated from it by thousands of years. A historian
who takes this as his point of departure [i.e., a historical materialist] stops
telling the sequence of events like the beads of a rosary. Instead, he grasps
the constellation which his own era has formed with a definite earlier one.
Thus he establishes a conception of the present as the "time of the now"
which is shot through with chips of *Messianic time* ... The present, ... as a
model of *Messianic time*, comprises the entire history of mankind in an
enormous abridgement' (262–3, italics mine).

24 See the important collection of essays edited by Peter L. Berger (1999),
especially Berger's introductory essay, as well as Howard 2000.

25 The dates of composition for *Mimesis* are given in a note on the copyright
page of the original German edition (Bern, 1946). On the last page of the

'Epilogue' Auerbach records that 'the book was written during the war and at Istanbul, where the libraries are not well equipped for European studies' (557).

26 Elsewhere Auerbach is perfectly plain on this point; see the introduction to his *Literary Language and Its Public in Late Latin Antiquity and in the Middle Ages* (1965).

27 Cf. Lambropolous 1993, 13: 'Rephrased and completed according to its messianic perspective and eschatological yearning, the subtitle [of *Mimesis*] should now read: "The Biblical Interpretation of the Prefigurement of the Fulfillment of the Covenant in the Tradition of the Secular Scripture."' The idea of 'literature' as a 'secular scripture' was popularized by Northrop Frye in *The Secular Scripture: A Study in the Structure of Romance* (1976).

28 As observed by Kugel 1998, 296n1, God's summons to Abra[ha]m to depart for Canaan at Genesis 12:2 is closely echoed by the command at 22:1 to sacrifice his son on a mountain 'which I will tell thee of.' He also notes that 'of all the Hebrew Bible's narratives that were read *typologically* [or, as Auerbach would say, *figurally*] – that is, as prefiguring the events of the New Testament – perhaps none was so evocative as the story of Abraham's offering up of Isaac, which was understood by Christians from early times as a foreshadowing of the crucifixion' (Kugel 1998, 306, with subsequent reference to Augustine, *City of God* 16.32 for a definitively figural – but spiritual, *not* territorial – reading of the Abrahamic covenant). Although the link is never made explicit, Auerbach's choice of Abraham's trial as the primary *petite histoire* of *Mimesis* cannot have been uninfluenced by the Christian *grand récit* in which it was customarily interpreted. As the movement in chapter 1 is away from Odysseus's homecoming to Abraham's sacrificial outward journey, so in chapter 20 a matching rendezvous with Joyce's *Ulysses* gives way in its turn to a last reading of Woolf's novel as a locus of readerly self-surrender (Auerbach 1953, 551–2).

29 Cf. Auerbach 1953, 557, the final paragraph of the Epilogue: 'With this I have said all that I thought the reader would wish me to explain. Nothing now remains but to find him – to find the reader, that is. I hope that my study will reach its readers – both my friends of former years, if they are still alive, as well as the others for whom it was intended. And may it contribute to bringing together again those whose love *for our western history* has serenely persevered' (italics mine).

30 Said 2003. Said's introduction has been reprinted in *Boundary 2* 31.2 (2004): 11–34 ('Erich Auerbach, Critic of the Earthly World') as part of a special issue devoted to his intellectual legacy. In a prefatory piece, Aamir R.

Mufti argues that Said's advocacy of 'secular criticism' requires us to understand the term 'secular' in a catachrestic sense, opposed not to religion as such but to nationalism. 'In this sense,' he writes, 'the secularism implied in secular criticism is a *critical secularism*, as I am calling it here, a constant unsettling and an ongoing and never-ending effort at critique, rather than a once-and-for-all declaration of the overcoming of the religious, theological, or transcendental impulse' (Mufti 2004, 3).

31 'Deuteronomy,' cited, like the second epigraph, from Bringhurst 1995, 46 and 196–7, with the author's permission. Bringhurst writes in the Foreword: 'Writing, if it lives, is rooted in speaking, and speaking, if it lives, is rooted in listening for the speech, the calling, of being. There, I think, is where the real work of poetry occurs' (12). For a rendition of the poem of the first epigraph that makes more audible its quality of song than the King James Bible, see the New Jewish Publication Society translation of *The Tanakh* (1985): 'Then Moses recited the words of this poem to the very end, in the hearing of the whole congregation of Israel ...'

REFERENCES

Akenson, Donald Harman. 1991. *God's Peoples: Covenant and Land in South Africa, Israel, and Ulster*. Montreal and Kingston: McGill-Queen's University Press.

Anderson, Benedict. 1991. *Imagined Communities: Reflections on the Origin and Spread of Nationalism*. Rev. ed. London: Verso.

Auerbach, Erich. 1953. *Mimesis: The Representation of Reality in Western Literature*. Trans. Willard R. Trask. Princeton: Princeton University Press.

– 1954. 'Epilegomena zu Mimesis.' *Romanische Forschungen* 65: 1–18.

– 1965. *Literary Language and Its Public in Late Latin Antiquity and in the Middle Ages*. Trans. Ralph Mannheim. Princeton: Princeton University Press.

– 1984. 'Figura.' English translation in *Scenes from the Drama of European Literature*, ed. Wlad Godzich and Jochen Schulten-Sasse, 11–76. Minneapolis: University of Minnesota Press.

Barbeau, Marius, and Grace Melvin. 1943. *The Indian Speaks*. Toronto: Macmillan.

Benjamin, Walter. 1968. 'Theses on the Philosophy of History.' Trans. Harry Zohn. In Walter Benjamin, *Illuminations*, ed. Hannah Arendt, 253–64. New York: Schocken Books.

Berger, Peter L. 1999. *The Desecularization of the World: Resurgent Religion and World Politics*. Washington: Ethics and Public Policy Center.

Bringhurst, Robert. 1995. *The Calling: Selected Poems 1970–1995*. Toronto: McClelland and Stewart.

– 1999. *A Story as Sharp as a Knife: The Classical Haida Mythtellers and Their World*. Vol. 1 of *Masterworks of the Classical Haida Mythtellers*. Vancouver: Douglas and McIntyre.

Dawson, John David. 2002. *Christian Figural Reading and the Fashioning of Identity*. Berkeley and Los Angeles: University of California Press.

de Certeau, Michel. 1980. *The Practice of Everyday Life*. Trans. Steven Rendall. Berkeley and Los Angeles: University of California Press, 1984.

– 1984. *L'Écriture de l'histoire* (1975). 2nd ed. Paris: Gallimard.

– 1988. *The Writing of History*. Trans. Tom Conley. New York: Columbia University Press.

de Léry, Jean. 1580. *Histoire d'un voyage fait en la terre du Brésil, autrement dit Amérique*. 2nd ed. Geneva: Antoine Chuppin.

– 1990. *History of a Voyage to the Land of Brazil, Otherwise Called America*. Trans. Janet Whatley. Berkeley and Los Angeles: University of California Press.

Derrida, Jacques. 1976. *Of Grammatology*. Trans. Gayatri Chakravorty Spivak. Baltimore: Johns Hopkins University Press.

Frye, Northrop. 1976. *The Secular Scripture: A Study in the Structure of Romance*. Cambridge, MA: Harvard University Press.

Greenblatt, Stephen. 1991. *Marvelous Possessions: The Wonder of the New World*. Chicago: University of Chicago Press.

– 2000. 'The Touch of the Real.' In Catherine Gallagher and Stephen Greenblatt, eds, *Practicing New Historicism*, 20–48. Chicago: University of Chicago Press.

Harris, Cole. 2002. *Making Native Space: Colonialism, Resistance, and Reserves in British Columbia*. Vancouver: UBC Press.

Hastings, Adrian. 1997. *The Construction of Nationhood: Ethnicity, Religion, and Nationalism*. Cambridge and New York: Cambridge University Press.

Howard, Thomas A. 2000. *Religion and the Rise of Historicism: W.M.L. de Wette, Jacob Burckhardt, and the Theological Origins of Nineteenth-Century Historical Consciousness*. Cambridge: Cambridge University Press.

Kugel, James L. 1998. *Traditions of the Bible: A Guide to the Bible as It Was at the Start of the Common Era*. Cambridge, MA: Harvard University Press.

Lambropoulous, Vassilis. 1993. *The Rise of Eurocentrism: Anatomy of Interpretation*. Princeton: Princeton University Press.

Lévi-Strauss, Claude. 1973. *Tristes tropiques*. Trans. John and Doreen Weightman. New York: Athenaeum.

Markus, R.A. 1988. *Saeculum: History and Society in the Theology of Saint Augustine*. 2nd ed. Cambridge: Cambridge University Press.

McKee, Christopher. 2000. *Treaty Talks in British Columbia: Negotiating a Mutually Beneficial Future*. 2nd ed. Vancouver: UBC Press.

Mufti, Aamir R. 1998. 'Auerbach in Istanbul: Edward Said, Secular Criticism, and the Question of Minority Culture.' *Critical Inquiry* 25: 95–125.

– 2004. 'Critical Secularism: A Reintroduction for Perilous Times.' *Boundary 2* 31.2: 1–9.

Pabel, Hilmar M., and Mark Vessey, eds. 2002. *Holy Scripture Speaks: The Production and Reception of Erasmus' Paraphrases on the New Testament*. Toronto: University of Toronto Press.

Reid, Bill. 2000. *Solitary Raven: The Selected Writings of Bill Reid*. Ed., with intro., Robert Bringhurst. Vancouver: Douglas and McIntyre.

Reid, Bill, and Robert Bringhurst. 1984. *The Raven Steals the Light*. With a preface by Claude Lévi-Strauss. Vancouver: Douglas and McIntyre.

Said, Edward W. 1983. *The World, the Text, and the Critic*. Cambridge, MA: Harvard University Press.

– 1993. *Culture and Imperialism*. New York: Knopf.

– 2003. 'Introduction.' Fiftieth-anniversary edition of the English version of Eric Auerbach, *Mimesis*, ix–xxxii. Princeton: Princeton University Press.

– 2004. 'Erich Auerbach, Critic of the Earthly World.' *Boundary 2* 31.2: 11–34.

Skaay. 2001. *Being in Being: The Collected Works of a Master Haida Mythteller, Skaay of the Qquuna Qiighawaay*. Trans. Robert Bringhurst. Vol. 3 of *Masterworks of the Classical Haida Mythtellers*. Vancouver: Douglas and McIntyre.

The Tanakh: The New Jewish Publication Society Translation ccording to the Hebrew Text. 1985. Philadelphia: Jewish Publication Society.

Tennant, Paul. 1990. *Aboriginal Peoples and Politics: The Indian Land Question in British Columbia, 1849–1989*. Vancouver: UBC Press.

Vancouver Sun. 2002. 'The Songcatchers.' Saturday August 31: E1, 6–7.

van Oort, Richard. 2004. 'The Critic as Ethnographer.' *New Literary History* 35: 621–61.

Vessey, Mark, Karla Pollmannn and Allan D. Fitzgerald, eds. 1999. *History, Apocalypse, and the Secular Imagination: New Essays on Augustine's 'City of God.'* Special issue of *Augustinian Studies* 30.2.

White, Hayden. 1999. *Figural Realism: Studies in the Mimesis Effect*. Baltimore: Johns Hopkins University Press.

Part One

Biblical Possessions

2

Perhaps God Is Irish: Sacred Texts as Virtual Reality Machine

DONALD HARMAN AKENSON

This is a 'religious' series of essays, in the sense that everyone in it understands that there are such things as sacred texts. In the homiletic tradition, I should like to introduce a text (a non-sacred one, to be sure) that will exemplify the thought pattern I am trying to impose on our discussion. It is one that you almost certainly know: David Lodge's mock-Arthurian masterpiece *Small World* (1984). It featured, you will recall, Persse McGarrigle, a young innocent farmer's son from Mayo, who was educated at University College, Galway, and received his MA from University College, Dublin, for a thesis on the influence of Shakespeare on T.S. Eliot. A mundane topic at best, but by virtue of a clerical error he breaks through into the postmodern moment, just at the time it is most fashionable: some publisher thinks the book is about the influence of Eliot upon Shakespeare and the lad's life careens off in ways he never expected.

There's a lot more in Lodge's rich volume, but that's the sequence-of-narrative point I want us to embrace. What David Lodge has presented as parody and as downright silly is actually the truth.

It permits me to tell you the unspoken truth about my own profession, history – a truth so basic that we never tell our graduate students about it. This is that time's arrow runs only one way and, in the history business, that way is backwards. That is, we always start any journey of historical research with our own selves, ego in the original sense of the term, and we move through time from 'now' back to something that we define as 'then.'

The next step is that, as historians, we impose a very rigid literary structure upon all the material that we collect. We arrange it in a form in which we claim that time's arrow runs forward. In this regard, we are very much like conventional scientists. If one picks up any scientific journal one will find that a rigid rhetorical form is employed, one that presents data acquisition and explanation according to the scientific method. Each article implies a narrative sequence of events and a causal explanation of them. But talk to any top-level scientist and you'll be told that this rhetoric and the reality of scientific behaviour are laughably unrelated. As I say, in the historical profession, we do something similar, so I am not casting stones.

On this occasion, however, I should like to start where history begins – in a temporarily frozen now (in reality, 'now' just keeps moving, so this is a conceit that you have to buy, just as you suspend disbelief when at the theatre). The 'now' we will deal with is Irish nationalism in its pure, or classic, form. Then we will move backwards.

I

Ireland, even more than most countries, believes in its own exceptionalism. Therefore, our overall purpose of arriving at some cross-cultural generalizations is antithetical to the nationalist mindset and will not be met with approval by its devotees. It will be called in what is today a right-wing slur word, 'revisionism.' So be it.

How does Irish nationalism work? Notice the word 'work.' Belief systems are machines and this one does a lot of heavy lifting. It's a good one.

The fundamental piece of work that Irish nationalism has achieved, the basis for all of its later constructions, was a piece of successful linguistic imperialism. Namely: the capture for itself of the magic term on which everything else depends, the name of the polity. It has frequently been pointed out that if one used the term 'Irish nation' in, say, 1790, it meant Protestants – that is, the politically active class. Yet, a century later, it meant Catholics and by quiet consensus, albeit not explicit ideology, excluded Protestants. How this occurred is a complex matter, but three compact periods of history are crucial. The first is the 1820s, when Daniel O'Connell's brilliant campaign for Catholic Emancipation (meaning the right of Catholics to sit in parliament) mobilized the Irish Catholic population in a cause in which they asserted their right to be the Irish nation. Second, as Brian Walker has demonstrated, the general elections of 1885 and 1886 provided a topographical recognition that Protestants and Catholics were different. Put simply, what is now southern Ireland voted nationalist-liberal; the north, save for three seats, voted anti-nationalist (Walker 1996, 15–63). And thus it has remained.

And third, after the end of the Anglo-Irish war of 1919–22, the Protestants of southern Ireland, called at that time the Irish Free State, saw the future and about one-third of them left. They correctly predicted that they would face cultural, political, and economic discrimination in the new Free State. (As it turned out, the discrimination was quite subtle and relatively mild.) Thus, although there were 327,000 Protestants in the Free State in 1911, the number was only 221,000 by 1926. This represents the biggest single movement of population in twentieth-century Irish history and is usually erased from the official memory (Akenson 1988, 4; see also Delaney 2000). This made easier the theocratization of southern Irish society, with Eamon de Valera's 1937 constitution reading as if it were a set of footnotes to Catholic canon law.

Of course the matter of cultural identity is extremely complex, and most people have multiple identities which are exhibited according to the demands of their immediate context. However, there is no denying that at a level of demotic understanding, Irish and Catholic became synonymous to the degree that the Catholics owned the brand name and Protestant assertions of Irishness were muted at best, save for a few eccentric individuals. The easiest illustration of that is found on this side of the ocean. Until the middle years of the Clinton presidency, every St Patrick's Day celebration at the White House had Catholic politicians flown in from the Old Country, and nary a Protestant in sight. Which is to suggest that worldwide – not just in the homeland – the linguistic imperialism was successful.

One should not underestimate the willpower required to obtain control of the magic word 'Irish.' To stay with the US case for a moment, there was no accurate information on the religious make-up of the American-Irish ethnic group until the 1970s and 1980s. Then, a large-base study by the National Opinion Research Center of the University of Chicago, a smaller study by the Gallup organization, and a third, very large-base work by the Graduate Center of the City University of New York independently came up with the same results: that between 54 and 59 per cent of those persons who identified their ethnicity as primarily Irish were Protestants (Akenson 1993, 219–20). Now, the United States is a special case, but it illustrates the crucial point that grabbing control of a magical label has nothing to do with reflecting reality. It is, however, the first step in creating a sacred text. No Holy Name, no sacred text.

A second act of Irish nationalism was predictable: *association of the Holy Name with a specific piece of land*. This was quite easy in Ireland, because it is a small enough island to be thought of as one piece of property, at least in modern times. Before the canal age and then the railway age, most Irish residents probably thought of themselves as inhabitants of Connacht or Munster or smaller units: baronies and parishes. Still, there is something slightly bemusing about the Irish nationalist embrace of the hydraulic theory of nationhood: as the 1960s pop ballad said, 'Thank God we're surrounded by water.'

Manifestly, a grabbing of the Holy Name by one group and the application of that name to a specific piece of land implies an *ethnography, an exclusionist one.* The people with the Irish name should own the island of Ireland.

It is at this point that it becomes necessary to *develop a set of texts* that justify the exclusionist ethnography and the appropriation of the Holy Name. These texts must, among other things, include a genealogy. Genealogy is justification. And, as Harold Bloom has remarked (in relation to tractate Aboth in the rabbinic literature), 'The prestige of origins is a universal phenomenon' (Bloom 1975, 46). The Irish nationalist texts that provide genealogies are numerous, but one of the most revered is the High Victorian volume usually called *Speeches from the Dock*. It was in its twenty-third edition in 1882 and has never been out of print since. Two other basic texts, almost sacred to Irish nationalism, are John Mitchel's *The Last Conquest of Ireland (Perhaps)* (1860) and the Irish Declaration of Independence of Easter Week 1916. If one takes these three texts as bedrock items of a much larger textual edifice, it is clear that they evince two other characteristics in addition to a strong sense of pedigree. They are Manichean in defining themselves as virtuous and everyone else as virtueless. And they place a great emphasis on MOPE-dom. This is a specifically Irish phrase, but it is portable. The MOPE aspect presents the Irish as the Most Oppressed People Ever. It is a rhetorical reflex that allows the presentation of all Irish migrants to new worlds as being *exiles* and those remaining within the country (until full freedom is obtained) as being *internal exiles. The trek out of bondage,* either past or proleptic, is fundamental to the texts of classic Irish nationalism.

So, what a modern case, that of Irish nationalism, suggests is that a politico-cultural movement can do well if it embraces the following tricks: engage in linguistic imperialism, demand a specific geographic site or block of land, define an exclusionist ethnography, and develop a set of sacred texts that justify the preceding activities. These texts will include a genealogy, a sharp sense of our rightness and of the wrongness of others, a detailed catalogue of our own sufferings, and an exile myth.

II

At least it worked for the Irish. Let us look at a really big parallel case, all the time agreeing that, of course, nothing is ever fully parallel and that each culture is unique. That said, the most important previous effort with which I am conversant was the invention of what we now call Judaism. That is, rabbinic Judaism, which comes into being in the years 70 CE to, roughly, 600 CE.

The rabbis (I will call them that, although other scholars prefer proto-rabbis or, simply, leaders of the Pharisees) had an immense problem. The Roman-Jewish War of 66–73 CE destroyed the physical setting upon which the ancient Yahweh-faith had depended, and it scattered once again the religious savants: some to outback villages in Eretz Israel and later, increasingly, to foreign lands. If you wish to pick a date for the beginning of the invention of modern Judaism it is the beginning of July (the 'ninth of Ab' in traditional laments), in the year 70 CE. On that date the Temple was almost completely destroyed.

This is the single most underrated event in the religious history of the period, although, granted, it is recalled more often by Jews than by Christians. This event was nothing less than a nuclear blast that ended forever the world in which Jesus and Hillel and Paul and Gamaliel had existed. The religious life of Eretz Israel of the pre-70 period had possessed both prescription of practice and precise definition of a holy site where God's house was located and where the covenant with Yahweh was daily re-enacted, through blood sacrifice. And, although less consequential, it is not irrelevant that Herod's Temple was probably the largest, most ornate, and impressively decorated religious building in the world.

All that: gone.

The problem for the survivors of the Yahweh-faith was: how to create a new religion – new circumstances, new religion – while maintaining with a straight face that they were merely continuing the old. Their solution, worked out over five hundred years, was to replace a visible temple with an invisible one, a blood-letting priesthood with a law-splitting Rabbinate, and to use text and oral tradition to create a new definition of holy places, making each home an altar to the Almighty.

The primary sources on which I am here relying are truly amazing documents, and I mention them briefly with a feeling of immense inadequacy, for, collectively, they are among the most intricate and fascinating of religious documents ever composed. Specifically, I am referring to the Mishnah, the Tosefta, the Sifra on Leviticus, the Jerusalem Talmud, and the Babylonian Talmud. Together they comprise roughly ten million words. I know of no one who has truly mastered the lot, for that is literally beyond human capability. However, we owe an immense debt of gratitude to Professor Jacob Neusner for the monumental achievement of translating this material into candid, usable American English. Full translations exist in no other modern European language.

Of these volumes, the foundation – upon which the rest are mostly commentary – is the Mishnah. This is a most curious document in several ways. It gives no clear indication of when it was converted from an oral to a written text; it is silent about its own genealogy; and it asserts authority with a self-confidence that is teeth-rattling. It is such a tough entity – both in the sense of being difficult and in being brass-necked – that most of the rest of the rabbinic corpus is given over to gentling the Mishnah's tone and explaining its most difficult sections: for it is almost entirely Haggadah – that is, case law. The Mishnah appears in written form about 200 CE, the traditional date, but, I suspect, began to be written in portions after the Bar Kochba debacle of 135.

Now, to take this rabbinic corpus as a whole, what do we find? First, that it is not a continuation of the wildly pluralistic religious world that had swirled around the Jerusalem Temple. There, easily three dozen 'denominations' or 'factions' or 'parties' coexisted uneasily (of which, incidentally, Yeshua of Nazareth's version of Yahwehism was one). But only one is represented in the rabbinic corpus; only one becomes the basis of modern Judaism, and this is Pharisaism – at least, if the traditions of the rabbis are accurate and the judgments of most modern scholars are correct. So, we have one sect, among dozens, that comes to own the Jewish franchise.

How is this done? You know the answer – they acted Irish.

That is, they articulated an exclusionary polity. The fascinating thing about the Mishnah is that it scarcely pays any attention to anyone but itself. 'We are the only form of the Faith,' it implicitly says. Not that it is naive: its inventors clearly know of rival forms of Yahwehism still existing – most notably the religion that becomes known as Christianity – but they don't deign to utter a word of recognition. Only in later commentaries (in the proto-Talmuds and the Talmuds) are heretics discussed and damned, and even that is done as a sidelight to more demanding discussions. The rabbinic corpus is exclusionary in the most compelling way possible, for it implies that if you are not deeply immersed in our system of thought, you exist, if at all, as dung on the heels of the heathen.

Basic to this particularly successful attempt at seizing the remains of the Yahweh-faith (I say particularly successful because it has one, and only one, skilled rival, the Yeshua-followers) is an act of double linguistic imperialism. The term Jew, to use the English word, had a currency in the Ancient Near East that made its ownership valuable. Its origin of course was in reference to the tribe of Judah and later to the area in the south of Eretz Israel, which had its focal point at Jerusalem. Since Judah had long been the regnant tribe of Eretz Israel and 'Judaism,' or 'Jewish,' one of the brand names of its religion, to seize the right to determine who was or who was not Jewish was crucial. The rabbis did this in a distinctive fashion: not by defining an orthodoxy to which all Jews must ascribe, but rather an orthopraxy – that is, a code of behaviour that all Jews must honour. And the rabbis declared themselves to be the only legitimate interpreters of that code. Thus, the extremely detailed arguing on law cases which often seems to modern eyes to be mere pettifogging is not, for by assuming control of the code of social and religious practice, the rabbis controlled who could properly be called a Jew. What had once been a priestly power now was assumed by legal scholars.

There was more to their imperialism. They also took control of the name Israel, which is the most important collective name for the Chosen People. Now, in fact, Israel had not existed since the Assyrians destroyed the northern kingdom (leaving only Judah as a power base) in 722 CE, and there was no palpable contact, save in the name itself, with the ancient kingdom: indeed, the best case for actual genealogical descent from Israel was that of the Samaritans, whom the rabbis despised. Still, the word Israel was magic. The rabbis made it their own property.

Obviously, the rabbis had a problem. Their Temple no longer existed and, after the mid-second century, most of the better scholars were in diasporal lands. (Thus, the most impressive of the rabbinic texts is the Babylonian Talmud.) So the texts that they created, if they were to be successful, had to be a *virtual reality* machine.

And successful they *are*. The rabbinic corpus, especially the Mishnah, preserves in loving and precise detail the lines of the old physical Temple. But now it is a Temple of the mind. And it is declared that learning the details of the now-vanished Temple worship is the equivalent of actually serving in the Temple. And the rabbis, with their immense learning and parsing of legal matters, are declared to be the equivalent of the ancient priests. Declared by themselves, of course, but that is how a successful power grab works. By talking and talking and talking about their virtual world, the rabbis came to control the everyday world of the scattered peoples of the earlier multiple denominations of Judaism.

Their texts became reality.

The texts talk about exile from specific pieces of land, they lament great moments of pain within the culture – just like the Irish texts. But what is most fascinating to me is the extreme, but curiously sloppy, way that a genealogy is asserted for these new texts. The Mishnah, in its basilisk-like way, gives no hint of the pedigree of the legal arguments it presents, beyond associating certain arguments with certain sages. But at most, the sages mentioned in the Mishnah go back to the mid–first century before the Common Era. The Mishnah, if one can personify it, just does not care about origins: it is so strong in its self-belief that it simply says, 'here are the rules; now get on with them.' That, though, does not satisfy an audience that places heavy emphasis upon contact with origins and that distrusts anything avowedly new.

So, in the rabbinic corpus one finds two attempts at pedigree. The first is the tractate Aboth (meaning 'the Fathers') that was written at least a generation, and probably two, after the Mishnah was completed, and is simply stapled on to the Mishnah. Stapled? It refers to people living at least half a century after the Mishnah was compiled and it is entirely Aggadah, whereas the Mishnah is virtually all Halakha. In every way it is in a stylistically inconsonant register as far as the Mishnah is concerned. Yet, it does one thing that makes it beloved and believed: Aboth traces a spiritual genealogy from Rabban Gamaliel II, son of Judah the Patriarch, redactor of the Mishnah, all the way to Moses. The only problem is that once the inventors of this genealogy get into the blank spaces before the Maccabeans, they lose verisimilitude. They haver between various styles of genealogy and introduce figures unknown in either biblical or rabbinic tradition, and then they just make huge jumps to assemblies of elders that are as indeterminate as the inside of a fog bank. (A further expansion, 'Aboth de Rabbi Nathan,' was still being worked on in the eighth century and is not here germane.) Now, as far as pedigrees go, this is not very convincing, but Aboth is useful if the audience is already pre-sold; that is, if it wants, desperately, to be assured that rabbinical knowledge goes back to Sinai and to Yahweh and is not a new religion.

More compelling is the second set of pedigrees that the rabbis provide for themselves, for they are conceptual entities and therefore do not trip on the details of human descent. The point underlying Aboth, however, is powerful: namely, that there was a valid tradition, independent of written scripture, that came from the same mountain as did the written material. This idea is not pressed in a flashy way, but in the Bavli one finds three references to the oral Torah, which is to be taken, like the written Torah, as coming from Yahweh.

This is the plinth on which the later (medieval) doctrine of the dual Torah stands. It holds that the rabbinical tradition, as first written down in the Mishnah and as later articulated in various Talmuds and commentaries, is equal in authority to the books of Moses and subsequent documents that are labelled sacred.

The final stage comes in the high Middle Ages and is a matter of practice rather than pedigree: the students in most Yeshivot spend a great deal more time studying oral Torah – that is, the writing of the rabbis – than they do in studying the scriptures. Yet, all this is done while it is being strenuously asserted that nothing new is being invented, and that only clarification and reinterpretation are taking place.

A brilliant success: the rabbis define a new religion, articulate a set of texts whose virtual reality surpasses the remembered physical actualities of Jerusalem and its priests and its limited scriptures. The new text is the power and power over the text is power over the people. Amen.

III

In respecting the way that history runs backward, from the present to earliest times, the next logical case is Christianity. But let us not call it that, because the term is a misleading anachronism. The term was not at all widely used until the second century and applying it to people who never heard it – Yeshua of Nazareth, for example – implies our acceptance of a line of false continuity between earlier and later generations. In fact, what we wish to appreciate is the immense creativity required for that line of false continuity to overcome the radical disjunctures in the story, and calling the first and second generations 'Christians' makes the extraordinary seem banal. So, let us refer to the Yeshua-faith, at least for the duration of the first century.

Now, although it seems counter-intuitive, the religion and the pattern of textual creation of virtual reality that distinguishes the

Yeshua-faith antedates the creation of similar patterns by the founders of rabbinic Judaism. To put it simply, Yeshua's followers were quicker off the starting line than were the rabbis and, therefore, they somewhat limited what the rabbis could do, for any imitation of the opposition was disdained by the rabbis.

I said 'starting line.' By that I mean to imply that the Great Destruction of 70 CE had the same effect upon the Yeshua followers as it did on the surviving sages. Here you may baulk. You may well have accepted that the rabbis began their replacement of physical reality with textual reality on the 9th of Ab, for the date plays a big part in present-day liturgies. But few, if any, present-day Christians shred their shirts when remembering the Destruction of the Temple. Nevertheless, I am asking you to consider the possibility that the most important date in the transformation of the Yeshua-faith from an obscure Jewish sect into an independent religion was the same 9th of Ab, in the year 70 in the present system of dating. To even consider this you must swallow hard, for I am saying that the birth, actual words, and eventual execution of Yeshua of Nazareth were secondary in importance.

How can I say that? Well, to answer a question with another question, would you please show me one of Jesus' letters – say, to his mother or to one of his disciples? Or will you please show me any contemporary report – say, by a Roman equivalent of a police constable – detailing the words and actions of this particular person? Or even a boat rental slip on the sea of Kinnereth. No?

The point is obvious. No text, no Jesus.

And, I would assert, there is no credible text, save the letters of St Paul, that can be dated prior to 70 CE. Whenever it may have begun, the transformation of Yeshua-of-Nazareth, whomever he might have been, into Jesus-the-Christ was crystallized by simple necessity. When the Temple was destroyed, the Yeshua-followers had the same problem all the other Jewish sects had – namely, how to have a Temple religion without a Temple. The texts that tumble into existence – the Gospels and the various non-Pauline epistles – are drop-dead brilliant, not least in the way that they are aggregated, arranged, and censored to produce a harmonious whole, the New Testament. Jesus becomes both the Temple and the sacrificial lamb within the Temple. Belief in him has the same cleansing effect that animal sacrifice to Yahweh once had; and more, for it yields not just purification, but salvation. A fever of textual production follows the Destruction and the scattering of the central figures of the Yeshua-faith. To put it simply, I would argue that the

Yeshua-faith began to turn into Christianity at exactly the same time that Pharisaism began to turn into rabbinic Judaism. Only these two, of all the Jewish denominations, prosper, *and it is because they substitute textual reality for physical reality* and do so with immense skill.

Most of you probably are aware that in New Testament studies either the matter of 70 CE is ignored or an immense amount of effort is expended in trying to force pips out of the post-70 texts. Some of these efforts are sensible, most are not. I have discussed them in *Saint Saul: A Skeleton Key to the Historical Jesus* (2000), and do not wish to go through those issues now. However, since Paul's seven authentic letters (as they are usually termed) are the only direct internal source we have on the nature of the Yeshua-faith prior to the year 70, it is worth noting the things they tell us about the faith communities and then surmising what the Great Destruction might have done to those faith collectivities. First and foremost, Paul makes it painfully clear – and it clearly gives him pain to have to do so – that the Yeshua-faith after the death of Yeshua was controlled from Jerusalem. It was directed, to Paul's distaste, by members of Yeshua's family, individuals who had not followed the Master when he was alive. Paul has some regard for Yacov, the ascetic brother of Yeshua, but he has little time for the other brothers and sisters, who travel about on church funds, while he, Paul, has to pay his own way. And, most irritating, Paul has to pay the equivalent of a franchise fee to the Jerusalem church if he is to be permitted to carry on his ministry to the Gentiles. To the very end of his days, Paul is schlepping his begging-bag around Asia Minor and worrying that the Jerusalem authorities will not accept his collection as adequate. Although the Yeshua-faith under Yacov is not quite a caliphate, it is very close.

Post–70 CE texts do not wish to remember all this, especially the hegemony of Jerusalem. Nor should we expect them to do so: the Yeshua-followers were rapidly dispersed after the levelling of Jerusalem and soon Rome became the central headquarters. And, increasingly, the Yeshua-followers expanded among non-Jews. So writing threnodies on the fall of Jerusalem would hardly have been good salesmanship. Nevertheless, we have a phenomenon of some moment: before the Great Destruction there are no texts for the Yeshua-faith – only Paul's letters, some crabbit, some brilliant – and then, by the year 100, there are scores of texts. These texts, taken together, form a virtual reality, but their coming into existence – the Big Bang in what is now Christian history – was immediately after a real-world event: the 9th of Ab. In any other discipline than biblical history, the conjunction of massive social dislocation with the creation of palliative texts related to that dislocation would be viewed, perhaps, as causally relevant, especially given that there is solid documentation of the occurrence and dating of these events, and of very little else in the early story of the 'Christian' faith.

(Here, a historiographical aside. That these new texts, rich and inventive as they are, do not memorialize the fact that they result from the destruction of the Jewish metropole is hardly surprising, given the constraints I have just mentioned. What remains a disappointment to me is the refusal in biblical studies to both recognize and celebrate the immense creativity and intellectual achievement of the last thirty years of the first century when Christianity is a-borning – that is, when texts are turning Yeshua of Nazareth into the detailed and mythic Jesus-the-Christ. Instead, we have trainloads of studies trying to find the historical Jesus. Despite the surface statement of recent studies which almost universally affirm that Yeshua was a Jew, there is an unwillingness to see the early Yeshua-faith as what it was: one of dozens of fairly weird Judaisms in the Second Temple Era. And there is a refusal to apply the standards of the historical profession as to what can be known about that Yeshua-faith in its early days – very, very little. Most disappointingly, despite the surface bowing towards Judaism, there remains an extreme reluctance to accept the real Jewishness of the Yeshua-faith, as a Temple-based, Jerusalem-controlled congeries of sects. And therefore the survival of the faith and its magnificent blossoming after the Destruction of 70 CE is virtually occluded. I wish to say this very gently here, but I think the desperate attempts of generations of scholars to get behind the texts of 70–100 CE are in part normal intellectual curiosity, in part spiritual thirst to find a historical Jesus; but they also have been, and still are, a product of the unconscious and unintentional affirmation of the anti-Semitism that lies at the heart of the virtual reality which is formed by the Christian scriptures.)

Those comments aside, the intellectual fecundity and the instinctive shrewdness of the texts of the last thirty years of the first century are amazing. Jesus-the-Christ replaces the Temple and the Temple sacrifice, as I have mentioned earlier.

Particularly shrewd is the way the new texts simultaneously create an exclusionary ethnography and imperialize the sacred name. Significantly, the writers of the biblical texts are effective because they are not greedy. They do not attempt to grab both the magic names: Israel and Judah. Instead (following Paul's example, which is pre-70), they declare the Yeshua-faith to be the true Israel. The genealogy of this Israel is that it has been in God's eye since before Abraham – Paul's seeming view in Romans (e.g., 9:6–7) – or even before time began (John's view, I think). This is to claim that they, Yeshua's followers, are the true Chosen People.

Notice, though, that they do not claim to be Judah. This, in part, is just practicality: to go around saying that 'we are the true Jews' would be an uphill struggle, since even in the Diaspora, Jews numbered more than a million and were formally recognized as a licit religion by the Roman Empire. More importantly, by not seizing the mantle of Judah, only of Israel, the writers of the basic texts were able to create a perfect them-versus-us situation. The Jews become the evil Other that opposes the True Israel. This theme develops slowly, starting in Paul and working into charges of deicide in the later Gospels. In any exclusionist ethnography, it is always helpful to have someone to hate.

And note here a very subtle temporal displacement of hatred. The 'Jews' that the scriptures use as hate figures are pre-70. (They have to be, because that's the era in which Yeshua's life was lived.) But the Jews with whom emerging Christianity is having to fight are the only other significant surviving sect from the dozens of multiple Judaisms of the late Second Temple Era: the Pharisees, who evolve into the rabbis. So this Christian ethnography is immensely shrewd in the way it displaces its aggression. It attacks its main rival in the post-Destruction era by vilifying the precursors of that rival as they existed in the *pre*-Destruction period. That's hate literature at its most skilful. (And here, do not take me as being excessively hard on the Christian scriptures: our two previous cases, Irish nationalism and rabbinic Judaism, are themselves inclusive of very effective forms of hate propaganda. It is not possible to have an exclusionary ethnography that is 'nice.')

The creation and character of the early Christian texts and of the central corpus of rabbinic Judaism differ in two signal ways. First, the speed with which the Yeshua-followers worked is amazing. By comparison, the rabbis were virtually leisurely. And second, the Christians used primarily narrative; the rabbis used it not at all in the Mishnah and only sparingly elsewhere. Even in the Bavli, the most developed of the rabbinic texts, Aggadah (story) is at most one-third of the context and then it is never extended story. The texts that we call Christian involve long stories and, crucially, the narratives are almost entirely historical in form. (Whether or not they are historically accurate is another question and not here relevant.) That the rabbis did not use narrative

one might guess is in large part because their rivals, the Yeshua-
followers, got there first and rewrote the ancient Hebrew scriptures
with such skill that anything the rabbis did in that genre would have
looked merely imitative.

So gloriously well tuned are the Christian scriptures that one could
spend years parsing the details. Here I shall only mention that all the
motifs that we saw in the Irish template – genealogy, bondage, exile,
oppression, exodus out of bondage – are incorporated. All save one. The
New Israel that Christianity declares itself to be is not immediately tied
to any specific piece of land. God's land and the good land are not one.

Not for a while. The Book of Revelation ties the ultimate triumph of
Christianity to a sanguinary conquest of Eretz Israel, but that is a prophecy so distant in fulfilment that it is not prescriptive in the present.

Seemingly, Christians (as they recognizably are by the early second
century) can live in the land of the spirit, in the virtual reality defined
by their text, and do not have to acquire real estate to fulfil their divine
mission. Text replaces topography. Except … except that the actual history of Christianity from the fourth century onward is one of territorial
warfare and genocidal bloodbaths.

To put it another way, the one place where the Christian attempt at
virtual reality falls short of the rabbinic and the Irish examples is that,
unlike the other two, it renounces topography. And it breaks apart in
practice at the very instant it hits the ground. Humanity cannot live by
faith alone, apparently, but requires a purchase on this earth, even if
humanity's faith is in the heavens.

IV

If we take one final step, following time's arrow as it flies from the
present back to the infinite past, we might well look at the earliest full
example we possess of a belief system that follows the Irish pattern:
that of the ancient Yahweh faith. Constraints of time prevent my repris-
ing material that I have presented in *God's Peoples: Covenant and Land in
South Africa, Israel, and Ulster* (1991) and in *Surpassing Wonder: The
Invention of the Bible and the Talmuds* (1998), except in the most compressed fashion. The points I will make here, however, are quite simple
in outline, if complex in unspoken detail. The first is that the primary
text of the religion of Yahweh – Genesis through Kings in the order as
given in the Hebrew Bible – was brought together at a moment when,
like the invention of the early rabbinic and Christian texts, an analgesic

was needed: in this case, during the Babylonian Captivity of the sixth century BCE and the destruction of Solomon's Temple. Exactly like the previous two examples, a text is set in place to fill the void left by the destruction of God's house and by the necessity of leaving the precincts that surround the now-ruined edifice. And, like the Jewish and Christian examples, this extraordinarily powerful text implied an exclusivist ethnography (including some dandy pogroms), a special deal with the Almighty, a catalogue of oppressions, an exile myth, and a deliverance from bondage. Unlike the Christian scriptures, the ethnography and the covenant with Yahweh involve grabbing a specific piece of land, Eretz Israel. And, although the Chosen People are later said to be displaced from this land, it is to be theirs under a law of return that has no expiration date. The entire exercise is leveraged by a lovely piece of linguistic imperialism. Although the Chosen People are by the time of the Exile only the southern kingdom, these Judaean-based peoples subsume into their own cosmology the heritage of the long-destroyed northern kingdom and even prefer to call themselves 'Israel.' That is the one thing they certainly are not, but the name is magic and in this form of thinking, taking the sacred name is as important as imperializing holy ground.

At this point let us stop and consolidate our questioning.

We have a pattern of belief systems that are remarkably similar, although not completely congruent. Irish nationalism obviously is presented here as a metonym for several other modern nationalisms. It is an appropriate one not only because of the wonderful articulateness of much of its literature, but because Ireland was the first nation to carry out a reasonably successful war of independence against the Second British Empire.

In the context of the present volume, my intention in using it as the metre stick against which to gauge other, major belief systems was to raise the question, Is there necessarily much difference between colonial belief systems and those that oppose them? Would the vulnerable cultures of the land of Canaan have been any happier dealing with the anticolonial Irish than with the conquering Chosen People?

Maybe. But I would maintain that most successful resistance to imperialism requires using many of the conceptual methods of the conqueror. And if one acts like an imperialist, it is not long until one thinks like one; soon, who can tell the difference? Witness the post-independence history of southern Ireland with its radical declension of who belonged and who did not.

At heart, I think this collection of works is asking of the Judaeo-Christian tradition and of its relative, Islam, 'Can religion be cured?' That is, can belief systems be shifted out of their self-protecting exclusivities and also moved away from identity with sacred land, however defined?

The immediate answer is 'of course,' in the sense that humanity is capable of almost anything. But is it likely? If so, how will it be accomplished? And lurking behind those issues is the single biggest question of all: will our civilization have the ability to survive monotheism?

It comforts me only slightly that, indeed, God *is* Irish.

REFERENCES

Akenson, Donald Harman. 1988. *Small Differences: Irish Catholics and Irish Protestants, 1815–1922: An International Perspective*. Kingston, ON: McGill-Queen's University Press.
– 1993. *The Irish Diaspora: A Primer*. Toronto: P.D. Meany.
Bloom, Harold. 1975. *A Map of Misreading*. New York: Oxford University Press.
Delaney, Enda. 2000. *Demography, State and Society: Irish Migration to Britain, 1921–1971*. Montreal and Kingston: McGill-Queen's University Press.
Sullivan, T.D., A.M. Sullivan, and D.B. Sullivan, eds. 1868. *Speeches from the Dock*. Dublin: Gill and MacMillan.
Walker, Brian. 1996. *Dancing to History's Tune: History, Myth and Politics in Ireland*. Belfast: Institute of Irish Studies.

3

Protestant Restorationism and the Ortelian Mapping of Palestine (with an Afterword on Islam)

NABIL I. MATAR

This essay examines the cartographic representation of Palestine in the first European Atlas, Abraham Ortelius's *Theatrum* (1570). Although Ortelius relied on previous authorities for his map, the success of his atlas ensured the longevity of his biblical rather than empirical view of Palestine. Focusing more on the Israelites' exodus route and the division of the land among the twelve tribes than on current or recent political and geographical information, Ortelius gave rise to the heresy of Restorationism: the idea that Jews should 'restore' their kingdom by conquering Palestine, then convert to Christianity and so hasten the return of the Messiah. The essay concludes with a brief discussion of the qur'anic view of the exodus, and its geographic non-specificity – along with the reaction that Ottoman cartographers would have shown to Ortelius's purportedly 'new' cartography.

I

On 20 May 1570, the *Theatrum Orbis Terrarum* was published in the prosperous city of Antwerp, and proved so successful that four more editions were printed in that same year (Binding 2003, 201). Consisting of fifty-four maps, all of them drawn by mapmakers whom Abraham Ortelius scrupulously credited, the *Theatrum* was an elegant tome chiefly about the European *orbis*, since forty-six maps were of Europe, leaving the rest for the non-European world. The atlas opened with maps of the continents, followed by maps of European countries, employing the most recent and up-to-date information in geography: 'nova' and 'recentior' and 'novissima' were repeatedly used adjectives in the titles to assure readers of accuracy, contemporaneity, and order.

As John Gillies states, the atlas was 'the single most famous manifestation of the new geography in the sixteenth century' (Gillies 1994, 79).

In plate 50 (figure 3.1), Ortelius introduced a map of the Ottoman Empire, 'Turcicum imperium,' from the Austrian borders through Anatolia and the Levant to North Africa. In the 1570s, this was the world of the fearsome Muslim enemy, the 'scourge of Christendom.' Typically of Ortelius, however, there is no sensationalizing of the subject: the region is accurately conveyed, showing seaports, rivers, natural formations, and social groupings. Included in one corner of the Ottoman Levant is 'Iudae,' confusedly shown as a kind of existing administrative division in the Ottoman Empire; it lies below 'Soria' and next to a vignette of two ships in battle. Because 'Iudae' would be of interest to the devout Christian reader, Ortelius continued his 'narrative form of cartography' (to use James Akerman's phrase)[1] with a map showing 'Palestinae sive totius terrae promissionis nova descriptio,' the 'new delineation of Palestine or of the whole Land of Promise' by the German mapmaker Tileman(nus) Stella (1525–89). As with the rest of the maps in the *Theatrum*, Ortelius re-drew and coloured Stella's map, adding to it his own cartouches.

Stella's original copperplate engraving of 1557 (republished in 1559) is cluttered with flower and leaf decorations, cartouches in both German and Latin, vignettes of ships and a coat of arms, all of which occupy nearly one-third of the map. The coastline extends from Byblos in Syrophoenicia to the Nile Delta, and from the Mediterranean coast eastward as far as 'Syriae Pars' and 'Moab.' Stella's purpose in preparing the map could not have been either navigational or topographical: his was neither a portolan map nor a map that could serve, as other maps did, in travel or contemporary commercial enterprise. Rather, his map was theological, showing the many miraculous and divine locations and signs on the Israelite exodus: 'Itinera Israelitarum ex Aegypto loca et insignia miracula diversorum locorum et patefactionum divinarum descripta.'[2] With pious precision, Stella traced the Israelite departure from Mansio to Suchot to Etham, to the crossing of the Red Sea (showing, in small, the drowning and destruction of the Egyptians); the trail then picked up at Marah and Elim, continuing serpentinely all the way to Almon, Diblathaim, and finally to Abarim, northeast of a banana-like Dead Sea.

In preparing his map, Stella drew on two earlier mapmakers, Jacob Ziegler (1470–1549), who had produced a *Tabula Universalis Palaestinae* in 1532, and Gerard/Gerhard Mercator (1512–94), who had produced

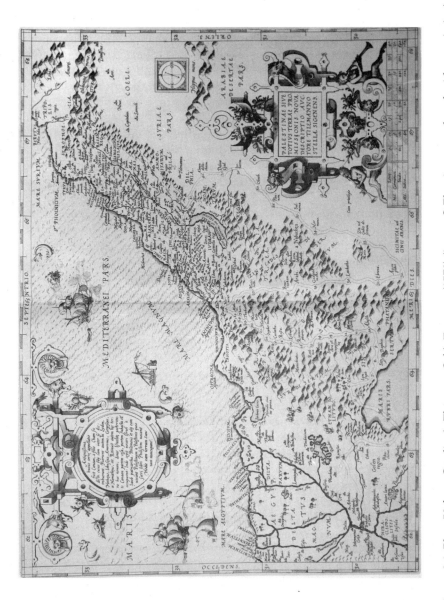

Figure 3.1. Plate 50 from Ortelius's *Theatrum Orbis Terrarum* (1570) (image © Elsevier; reproduced with permission)

in 1537 a map of *Terra Sancta* showing the territories of the twelve Israelite tribes and the route of the exodus. The latter map, along with Stella's, was the first in the history of European cartography to chart the course of the exodus; no maps before the sixteenth century had attempted such supposed historical accuracy. The reason for this innovation was the new Reformation theology with its emphasis on the literal interpretation of the Old Testament. Martin Luther had discarded the multilayered levels of Catholic interpretation and had insisted that the scriptures be read within their historical, linguistic, and geographical context. The Lutheran edition of the Bible that appeared in 1526 included a map of the holy land, as did Miles Coverdale's English Bible of 1535.[3] Stella, having studied at Luther's university, Wittenberg, and having been a student of Philipp Melanchthon, the heir of Luther in Germany, adopted the historical method of interpretation and produced his map.[4]

Ortelius positioned Stella's map immediately after the map of 'Turcicum imperium,' since Palestine fell within the contemporary Euro-Christian conflict with the Islamic Empire.[5] In the map of 'Turcicum imperium,' one of the two ships in battle near the coast of Palestine has the Ottoman crescent firmly on its sail. With such danger in mind, the reader of the atlas might well have expected the map of Palestine to show Ottoman military bases, settlements, and cities along with the exposed ports that could be used for naval and military intervention. Instead, Ortelius violated chronology by moving backward to a classical/biblical map of the land, thereby obliterating Palestine's present geography and confirming, as his cartouche states, the Judaeo-Christian past:

> Antiquissima huius terrae appellatio fuit Canaan, à filio Cham sic dicto: cuius filii eam inter se distribuerunt. Fuerunt autem hi Sydon, Hethaeus, Iebusaes, Amorreus, Gergesaus et Hamathaeus, etc. Retinuit autem hac terra hoc nomen, donec Israelitae posteritate Canaan partim caesa, partim subacta eam occuparent: Inde caepit uocari Israel à Iacob patriarcha. Ptolomeus et alii eam uocant Palestinam à Palestinis quos sacri libri Philistim uocant[.] Hodie eam terram Sanctam nuncupant.[6]

There was nothing about Palestine 'at this day' except the information from Ptolemy. Palestine, for Ortelius, was a predicate of Toranic Judaism and not of modern geography or Ottoman jurisdiction: it was a palimpsest of what the Canaanites and the Mosaic scriptures had inscribed. Although some cities on the coast showed the classical as well as the contemporary names (Azotuus/Asdod), many others, both on the coast and inland, carried names that did not exist in the East Mediterranean geography of the sixteenth century (Rhinocorvra; Catachrysea; Salem). The map of Palestine followed in the narrative which had started in 'Turcicum imperium,' but it was different from any other map in the atlas: it was a piece of invention, a map that was supposed to be 'nova' but that did not reflect the contemporary political history or even geography of the region. The map showed 'Iudae' and 'Samaria,' regions that did not exist in the Ottoman Empire of the sixteenth century, mixed with Roman names,[7] the twelve divisions of the land among the sons of Jacob, and, most prominently, the exodus route of the Israelites with its forty-one landmarks. Buyers of the *Theatrum*, some of whom had ventured to the ends of the earth in search of markets and merchandise, were expected, as they stared at Ortelius's map of Palestine, to suspend their disbelief and remove themselves from geography to biblical history, and from the 'hodie' to eschatology.

While Ortelius, being the royal geographer of the Spanish king, would not have presented to his discriminating buyers maps other than those that would help them in their global commerce, he had no qualms about presenting Palestine as a meta-Palestine, a holy land without contemporary accuracy. Indeed, even the introduction to the map mentions nothing about the present-day conditions: rather there is information about King Solomon, Herod Tetrach, and Josephus. By placing a biblical map among fifty-three other maps of the contemporary world, Ortelius delegitimized sixteenth-century Palestine and re-inscribed in the minds of his European readers a land of scriptural faith, dominated, as it was, by the prominent route of the exodus. Joshua 18:4–5, 9 had told how after the conquest of the East Bank of the Jordan River, the Israelite leader ordered 'three men of each tribe ... to walk through the land [of Canaan] and describe it ... and divide it into seven parts.' For Ortelius and his audience, Palestine had been 'mapped' as far back as biblical times and therefore its cartographic borders had been finalized by divine authority. Jesus later added to that cartographic finality his incarnation on Roman soil. In his map of 'new' Palestine, therefore, Ortelius presented the old-testamental-cum-Roman geography as changeless: no amount of history, conquest, religious transformation, or empirical evidence could alter the eternal design of God in 'Palestina vel terra sancta.' The map of Palestine was inerrant because the word of God in the books of Exodus and Joshua was inerrant.

Ortelius was not ignorant of the changes in the sixteenth-century sanjak of Ottoman Syria, part of which was Palestine. Many maps before his had shown an Ottoman-dominated Palestine: the 1484 map that was included in Braun and Hogenberg's atlas, the *Civitates Orbis Terrarum* (which began serialization in 1572), had clearly shown who was in control of Jerusalem and the rest of the land. At the forefront of the map stand a few Turks donning their well-recognized turbans in an act of assertive presence. Furthermore, when Ortelius wrote about Persia in the foreword to his map of that region, he did not describe the Persia that had been mentioned in the scriptures, but the Persia of his own day: 'Persarum Imperium vti olim, sic etiamnum hodie maxime clarum est, amplissimasque Regiones comprehendit' (49).[8] And as he spoke about the Persians, he again referred to real not imaginary people: 'Gens natura liberalis est, & ciuilitatis amans; litteras & artes colunt; nobilitatem agnoscunt,' who were different from the Turks in their religion and character.[9] Similarly, in the case of the Ottoman Empire, the reader was referred to books which described its greatness, 'qua hodie nobis minari videtur,' 'that today is seen to threaten us' – the emphasis being on the 'today' not of Ptolemy but of the year 1566 (50). When he wrote about North Africa, 'Barbary,' he referred to people with specific complexions, talents, and abilities: 'Ab hominibus subfusci coloris inhabitatur. Qui Ciuitates incolunt, sunt in architectura, atque inuentione Mathematica mire dexteri' (53).[10] Again, when he described the Italian peninsula, he listed the old place names ('Antiqua') and next to them the new names ('Recentia'): he showed how 'Latium' had become 'Campagna di Roma,' and 'Magna Graecia' 'Calabria Superiore' (32). On the map, Ortelius included only the new names, confirming a real Italy with a contemporary geography. In Italy as elsewhere in the world, there was a past to be differentiated from the present, and archeological sites that had changed into contemporary names. Indeed, as he mapped America, which had only recently been colonized by Europeans, Ortelius did not show the map of native Americans but of Europeans: change in America was part of history, even if history had started less than eighty years before the *Theatrum*. There were not even illustrations of Indians, only of the European seafaring ships that had carried the makers of the new geography.

Ortelius was not concerned that he had situated his Palestine map of scriptural and classical invention next to maps of commercial, cartographic, and contemporary knowledge – knowledge that he often gathered from travelling correspondents. For what was important in the mapping of Palestine, and unlike any other map in his atlas, was not the land 'hodie' but the invention of a land, an invention that coincided with the larger project of invention in early modern Europe. The sixteenth century is often viewed as the age that invented America, as José Rabasa has shown in particular reference to the cartographic contributions of Ortelius and Mercator.[11] What Rabasa meant by 'inventing' was the transformation of a region of the world into a palimpsest where the colonizer obliterated the past through the present, coined names that eradicated whole regions and cities, and created vacuum and 'terra incognita' in spaces that were supposed to exist but about which he knew nothing. Depending on personal, national, religious, or commercial ambitions, the conquistador and the trader, the missionary and the searcher for Eldorado defined, imagined, populated, and depopulated the vast *terrae incognitae* of America and the rest of the undiscovered world. As Walter Mignolo commented, the map of the American *mundus novus* 'was far from being geographically neutral and politically unmarked' (Mignolo 1995, 262). For it was to provide the invaders with religious legitimization for inventing borders and geographies. Less than two decades after the discovery of America, in 1507–8, Johannes Ruysch (like Ortelius, an Antwerp man) referred in his *Universalior Cogniti Orbis tabula ex recentibus confecta observationibus* to the new world as 'Terra sancte crucis sive Mundus novus' ('Land of the Holy Cross, or the New World') (Mignolo 1995, 265). It is as if immediately after the 'discovery' of America came the invention of America's holiness – a Christian holiness that endowed legitimacy on the Christian conquerors.

If 'naming is a powerful weapon of the cartographic propagandist,' as Mark Monmonier observed (Monmonier 1996, 110), then in renaming the regions of America, as Colin Calloway added, Europeans instituted a process of dispossessing indigenous populations and effectively excluding 'Indians from the New World they created on parchment and paper.'[12] Similarly, Ortelius (and his predecessors) renamed the cities and regions in Palestine in order to legitimate the same process of dispossession and obliteration: there is not a single printed map of Palestine before 1500 that does not show the biblical divisions of the land among the twelve tribes[13] – divisions that were not in existence in the sixteenth century. In the way that names in America had been Europeanized, indicating which lands were seized by the European conquistadors, so was Palestine de-Arabized and its names biblicized, in the expectation of Christian/European possession. In the preface to the map in the 1606 English translation of the *Theatrum*, the following explanation was given: 'That which the ancients called Palestine and Phoenicia, all the Europeans generally now call the HOLY LAND, under which name they comprehend that whole country which God gaue unto the Israelites by the name of the Land of Promise, to them and their seed' (Ortelius 1606, 111). The land did not have a name, only an 'ancient' and presumably unused one in these modern sixteenth-century times: the name 'HOLY LAND' belonged to the Europeans who 'now' gave it to the land. As lands which the Europeans did not possess in the New World became nameless '*terrae incognitae*,' signifying the link between knowledge and domination, so did the land of Palestine became a '*terra sancta*,' signifying the link between European sacralization and European domination.

The most prominent feature of Ortelius's invention of Palestine was the inclusion of the exodus route. The route was part of Stella's literalism of Protestant exegesis, but the exodus itself was an important *figura* in the allegorical tradition of biblical interpretation. The exodus was not only a historical event but also a prophetic one that pointed to, and anticipated, the exodus of the soul from the condition of sin to salvation, its pilgrimage from this life to the promised land of the hereafter. Ortelius could not have been unfamiliar with this figural interpretation of the exodus in biblical exegesis, but he was also interested in its political/eschatological fulfilment. By placing the map of Palestine/the Promised Land immediately after the map of the Ottoman scourge of Christianity, Ortelius confirmed the other message of the exodus as the re-inscribing of God's narrative of salvation onto the Euro-Christian encounter with Islam.[14] Ortelius knew that his patron, Philip II, to whom he dedicated the *Theatrum*, was earnest about that encounter: in 1570, Philip's fervour towards Jerusalem was intense (although it abated in the following decades) (Housley 2000, 243). Ortelius viewed the Israelite exodus not only as the figural fulfilment of the journey of the human soul to salvation, but also of the *reconquista* and re-Christianization of the holy land. The Israelite exodus to the land and its subsequent seizure from the ungodly anticipated the salvation of the land by Philip from the hands of the infidels, while the map made visible the route that had allegedly been taken by the Israelites, and pointed to the route that should be taken by the Catholic monarch, leader of the new Israel. 'The maps of the atlas are like mirrors, and play the part of images,' wrote Ortelius, images that are affixed to the mind, and taken out 'for use when we desire' (quoted in Binding 2003, 242).

This exodus-modelled *reconquista* recalled the conquest of America (which Philip II was still overseeing) since, as Steven Salaita has noted, 'the conquest of America began with [the conquest of] Canaan' (Salaita 2002, 142). By celebrating the Mosaic conquest of Canaan to the Spanish king, Ortelius's map foreshadowed Spain's conquest of the holy land. Only this conquest motif explains why Ortelius chose to focus on the Christian holiness of Palestine at a time when Catholic mapmakers had shifted the 'privileged scenes of ecclesiastical history ... from the Holy Land to Italy, from the places of the Bible and Christ to the seat of his representative in Rome' (Fiorani 1996, 138). After all, Ortelius printed his atlas within a Catholic environment at a time when all book and print contents were checked 'as regards the religious and political views expressed in them' (Voet 1998, 19): he knew that buyers of the *Theatrum* would carefully scrutinize boundaries, especially the representation of the Spanish-occupied Netherlands. Furthermore, he lived in a period of European history that coincided with the creation of the modern state: cartography created the states because it provided visual documents about authority, jurisdiction, and spheres of influence that were definitive, codified, and exclusive. The map of Palestine was therefore to serve as a blueprint of the future extension of the Habsburg Empire and of the re-inscription 'hodie' of the classical and biblical names. As readers and monarch looked at the Palestine map, after looking at contemporary France and Spain and the Ottoman Empire, they saw both a geographical location as well as a prophetic destination. The *Theatrum* transformed Palestine from a reality into a potentiality whose figural fulfilment lay in the eschatological conquest by Philip II.

Unlike his friend and rival, Mercator, whose map of Palestine was Ptolemaic rather than biblical (and who at least conceded in his *Historia Mundi* the presence of 'barbarous Inhabitants' in the land [Mercator 1635, 842]), Ortelius invented a scriptural Palestine which he framed in a modern atlas – with scale bar, compass rose, graticule, and graduated margin. By imposing the biblical on the Turko-Arab, Ortelius produced a para-colonial ideology that would inform all subsequent cartographic representations of Palestine. Kenneth Nebenzahl has stated that Ortelius's maps of Palestine became the models for early modern cartography, and 'continued to figure prominently in atlases to come' (Nebenzahl 1986, 87); Jerry Brotton confirms that the way in which Ortelius created and presented geographical information has continued 'to influence the field of geography even today' (Brotton 1997, 152).

Indeed, between 1570 and 1624, the *Theatrum* appeared in Latin, Spanish, English, French, Dutch, Italian, and German, and in about forty-seven editions. The editions which Ortelius himself produced, from 1570 to 1595 (he died in 1598) saw an increase in the number of maps from 54 to 147, but at no point was there a single map of contemporary Palestine.[15] Rather, the Ortelian Palestines were inventions showing the peregrinations of Abram, the life of the Virgin, the lands of Judah and Israel, and the wanderings of Paul – all confirming a Christian view rather than a depiction of Palestine as a land to which traders, ambassadors, and pilgrims went – and over which current Islamo-Ottoman jurisdiction prevailed. With their Latinized names and Judaeo-biblical emphases, the maps completely dissociated sixteenth-century Palestine from its Arab and Turkish inhabitants. Theology defeated modern borders, peoples, and historical evolution.

If an early modern Ottoman subject of the 'Turcicum imperium' had seen Ortelius's map of Palestine, or any of the other 'theological' maps in the later editions of the *Theatrum*, he would have found such 'new' maps confusing for relying on scriptural interpretation, and dismally failing to take into account contemporary names and descriptions.[16] The Ottoman would have concluded that the Euro-Christian had an antiquated and archaic knowledge of the Middle East. For a sixteenth-century Ottoman map of the Eastern Levant shows a conception of the Levant that is quite different from the Euro-Christian: there are no cartographic inventions to justify hoped-for conquest, no theological contortions to legitimate prophecy.[17] Both Arabic and Turkish writers of the early modern period often mention in their travels and histories the 'land of Palestine' (*ard filasteen*) or the land of Jerusalem (*ard al-Quds*), as did the first Ottoman mapmaker, who included the name of 'Filasteen'/ Palestine in 1729.[18] But no writer or mapmaker ever alluded to a Mosaic burden of prophetic conquest.[19]

II

Like medieval maps, early modern maps were burdened with 'theological discourse' (Scafi 1999, 50). And no discourse burdened Ortelius's map of Palestine more than the discourse of Exodus. Presenting a map of the Ottoman Empire followed by a map of the exodus to the land which lay in the geography of that Empire figurally anticipated the power of God to inspire a future exodus/conquest of the land. This conflation of

journey and *figura*, faith and cartography, led to the emergence of one of
the strange heresies of the sixteenth century: that the Israelite exodus
was a prophetic anticipation of the 'Restoration' of the Jews to the
Promised Land in preparation for the Second Coming of the Messiah.

As I shall employ the term, 'Restoration' is a proper noun peculiar to
a distinctly English Protestant idea of Jewish conquest of Palestine in
the light of the Abramic covenant and its fulfilment in the Mosaic exodus.[20] The term 'Restoration' does not appear in the King James version,
but the promise to 'restore' the kingdom appears in Jeremiah's post-
exilic prophecy: 'Then will I bring them up, and restore them to this
place' (27:22) – although by the time of Jesus, the restoration was more
of a question than an article of faith: 'Lord, wilt thou at this time restore
again the kingdom to Israel?' (Acts 1:6). In this respect, it is safe to state
that Restorationism began in the Ortelian cartography of the *Theatrum*,
but then developed as a largely English theological interpretation.
Specifically, it dominated Puritan thought from the 1590s on, and fully
matured in the middle of the seventeenth century.[21] Among historians,
the question as to why and how that heresy emerged has been answered
from various perspectives. While some have appealed to Protestant/
Puritan biblicism, others have invoked philo-Semitism as the driving
force behind the emergence of the idea of Restoration.[22] But the idea of
restoration had no theological support in the writings of either Luther
or Calvin, nor in any of the other reformation movements.[23] Furthermore,
there was nothing in the political or military status of Renaissance Jews
to invoke such a Restoration. Rather, until the nineteenth century,
European Jews did not become involved in the Anglo-Christian discussion of their fate because they were not trying to 'restore' to a distant
land, but, more eagerly, to preserve their communities in countries that
were hostile to them on the ground as well as on the stage and in the
pulpit. As the idea of Restoration was debated, praised, or rejected by
theologians and politicians, it was not Jews but British Protestants who,
through sermons and pamphlets, argued its pros and cons and deliber-
ated over the destiny of a community that viewed the Restoration as a
theological means for yet another expulsion from Europe and another
attempt at forcible conversion to Christianity.[24]

The crucial factor that led to the emergence of the idea of Restoration
was the revolution in cartography and the publication of the *Theatrum*.
Ortelius had shown the Turkish Empire – invincible, unshaken, dangerous
– and then the exodus, a figural model of conquest and re-Christianization

of Palestine. As the Ortelian narrative had moved from the map of the Ottoman Empire to the exodus, so too did the theological narrative in English thought move from the exodus of the ancient Israelites to their current Restoration and confrontation with the Turks. Starting in the late sixteenth century, English theologians examined the fulfilment of the Abramic promise, along with the prophetic books of Daniel and Revelation, discovering the figural fulfilment of the Israelite exodus in the Restoration of contemporary Jews to Palestine, their conversion to Christianity, the establishment of the messianic kingdom, and the destruction of the Turks. In 1590, Andrew Willet, one of the most respected and prolific theologians in Elizabethan England, became the first writer to propose the Restoration and establishment of a Jewish kingdom in Palestine[25] – for which heretical view he was jailed and his book burned by the public hangman. But his idea attracted followers, and in 1608, a few years after the appearance of the English versions of the *Theatrum* (which included not only the exodus map, but two other maps of biblical Palestine), Thomas Draxe published *The Generall Calling of the Jewes*. Draxe clarified in his subtitle to this treatise that the Lord would give the Jews grace to 'returne and seeke Iehovah their God, and David their King, in these latter dayes': the Jews would return/be restored to the promised land, but in being restored, he emphasized, they would convert to Christianity. Again, such a view was seen to be dangerous, which is why the authorized version of the King James Bible in 1611 emphatically interpreted the Abramic promise of the land in Genesis as a promise not of a territorial possession of Palestine by the post-exilic Jews, but of the coming of Jesus ('Promise to Abram of Christ'). A few years later, in 1615, George Sandys published an account of his visit to the 'Promised Land' and declared the land truly empty. The map he produced in his account, *Relation of a Journey begun An. Dom. 1610*, showed a completely de-Arabized and de-Turkified land. Although Sandys had travelled through Palestine and at no point had encountered provinces called 'Samaria' or 'Iudea,' his map prominently showed these two names. Later in his description of the land, he stated that it was 'wast and ouergrowne with bushes, receptacles of wild beasts, of theeues, and murderers' (Sandys 1615, 'To the Prince'). Palestine was an empty land awaiting the restoration of the Jews who, upon their conversion, would reclaim it for Christ.

As Ortelius had associated the church's exodus with the war against the Turks, English theologians linked the literal Restoration of the Jews to Palestine with the destruction of the Muslims there. The first full-length treatise to link the Restoration of the Jews with the defeat of the

Turks was *The Calling of the Jewes* by Henry Finch. Writing in 1621, under the strong influence of Thomas Brightman, Finch treated the prospect of the Jews' Restoration in light of contemporary fears in England. For him, the fulfilment of the Abramic promise of the land, and the fulfilment of the exodus *figura* in the Restoration of contemporary Jews would bring about victory over the Turks – and safety for England. Finch described how God had 'layd the red Sea dry, when he brought the Israelites out of Egypt: so once againe will do the like vnto the riuer [in Isaiah 15:16] when the people lending their eare to the Call of Christ, shall make head and repaire towards their former seates' (Finch 1621, 21). The fulfilment of the Abramic promise lay in the exodus, and the fulfilment of the exodus lay in the Jews' Restoration to Palestine, conversion to Christianity, and victory over the 'Turks' – a term used interchangeably with 'Muslims':

> They [the Jews] shall repaire towards their owne country. Esay 11.15, 16 &
>   51.10, 11. Jer. 3.18; Hosh. 1.11
> In the way, Euphrates shall be laid dry for them to passe, as once the Red
>   Sea was. Rev. 16.12. See Esay 11.15 & 51.10, 11.
> The tidings of this shall shake and affright the Turkish power. Dan. 11.14.
> A merueilous conflict shall they haue with Gog and Magog, that is to say,
>   the Turke. Ezeck. 38 & 39. Rev. 20.8.
> And shall be in fore distresse. Dan 12.1.
> This conflict shall be in theire owne country, the land of Iudea. Rev. 20.8, 9.
>   Esay 25.10. Ioel 3.2. Ezech. 39.2, 4 Zach 142.4, 3, 4, 5. Dan 11.44, 45.
> A notable victorie they shall obtaine. (Finch 1621, 3)

Finch confirmed the Restoration as the figural fulfilment of the exodus: 'Gods miraculous hand and power in their deliuerie, and leading them to their country; who as he layd the red Sea dry, when he brought the Israelites out of Egypt: *so once againe will do the like*' (emphasis added). The Jews would become 'Kings and chiefe Monarches of the earth, sway and gouerne all,' whereupon all the kings of the earth would 'bring presents' to them, and all the nations would come 'vnder their dominion' (Finch 1621, 7, 15). Although Finch was careful to state that the Jews would convert to Christianity, that upon their Restoration they would 'not set up the legall ceremonies' (ibid., 102), his allusions to their worldly monarchy resulted in his immediate imprisonment by an angry James I and a denunciation of his Restorationist heresy by

Archbishop Laud. 'It was an old error of the Jews,' preached Laud a month later, 'which denied Christ come, that when their Messias did come, they should have a most glorious temporal kingdom' (Laud 1867, 1:17). Laud realized that the 'restoration' of the Jews would lead them to rebuild the temple and offer sacrifices, which would conclusively prove that Jesus was a false messiah.

In the same year that Finch was writing, 'P.H.' published *Microcosmvs, or a Little Description of the Great World* (1621). Influenced by Ortelius, whom he mentions frequently, P.H. describes a biblical Christian Palestine while mentioning the Crusader 'Christian kings of Palestine' (p. 307). Palestine still belonged to Euro-Christians – even centuries after the defeat of the Crusades. Similarly, Jodocus Hondius's map of Palestine, also influenced by Ortelius, appeared in the 1625 collection of travels by Samuel Purchas, thereby legitimating geographically the inclusion of maps of Canaan and the exodus among the very modern accounts of the world.[26] By 1629 it was perfectly acceptable to print a map showing Palestine from the east, as it might have been viewed by the invading Israelites: Moses stands holding the tablets of the Law with Aaron at his side, as the armies of Pharaoh drown in the Red Sea.[27] By showing a de-Turkified Palestine, the mapmaker offered direct evidence of scriptural revelation, and assisted the audience in realizing their own exodus into the land of covenant, completely oblivious to the present reality of the land. This map consolidated the view that Palestine was a land empty of contemporary history or people, and awaiting transformation. Writing in 1639, the theologian John Goodwin recalled Finch as he urged the following view: 'The Turke is to be overthrown, to make way for the Jews, the kings of the east, under the sixth vial, and to be destroyed by the seventh' (Goodwin 1861, 3:62).

Despite theological and governmental opposition, the idea of Restoration continued to find support among seventeenth-century English theologians, scientists, philosophers, and insane prophets, especially during the tumultuous years of the civil wars. Englishmen – and women – prayed for the destruction of the Muslims at the hands of Jews restoring to Palestine. As part of their contribution to the Restoration project, some 'mechanick' preachers even started planning for the new exodus: they declared themselves anointed leaders of the Jews whose conversion and Restoration would hasten the defeat of the 'Mahometans.' The Jews' Restoration to Palestine was now the Englishmen's burden, providing English men and women with fantasies for redefining themselves and for seeing themselves not only in the spiritual geography of

Christian faith, but in the real Levant of seventeenth-century conflict between Christendom and Islamdom. In 1650, one John Tanny declared himself a leader of the Restoration of the Jews, but was drowned in a little boat as he prepared to sail for Jerusalem (Theuavjohn 1650). George Foster changed his name to Jacob Israel Foster, after he decided to 'bring the Jews into Judea': 'I will now restore them to my power ... bring them into their own Land again, which tidings of their returne they shall have from England first ... and before the fifty years that is now present and coming, he shall be destroyed even the Pope of Rome shall lose his life in 1654 ... and the great Turk shal lose his life in the year 1656' (Foster 1650, 56, 63, 65). By 1652, a map such as Nikolaus Visscher's *Nova Totius Terrarum Orbis* [*sic*] was quite acceptable, with its Crusader flag for the 'Pays de Jerusalem.' Palestine was already reconquered and Christianized.

III

No better example can highlight the imperial paradigm of Restorationism than a comparison with the Ibrahimic promise in the Qur'an. Such a comparison would have served as an ideal conclusion for Robert L. Wilken's *The Land Called Holy: Palestine in Christian History and Thought*. Wilken disingenuously showed the similarity between Jewish and Christian devotion to the holy land – disingenuously because, as Kenneth Cragg has incisively shown, where holiness in Christianity is a predicate of divine drama, holiness in Judaism is a predicate of divine donation (of land) and of exclusion, and as such is completely repudiated in the *kerygma* of the New Testament (Cragg 1997). A comparison with the Qur'an would have shown an alternative to the land covenant that Wilken claims for Christianity. For in one respect, the Qur'an was a critique of the kind of Judaic land covenant that circumscribed God to a geographical place, thereby contradicting His universalism. Specifically, the qur'anic repudiation of the land covenant was a repudiation of the henotheism that marked some Israelite, Moabite, and Graeco-Roman localizations of deities to specific lands and regions.[28]

Ibrahim plays a major role in the qur'anic covenant of monotheism, but the Qur'an does not predicate the covenant on the possession of a land. Nor does the Qur'an designate a specific land for Ibrahim and his descendants, as the Book of Genesis announces for Abram, 'from the Wadi of Egypt to the Great River' (Gen. 15:18). Rather, the Qur'an mentions a blessed (not holy) land to which Ibrahim escapes, after his harassment by the unbelievers: a land 'which we [God] have blessed for (all) peoples' (Q 21:71).[29] But no covenant is established through the land nor does the land have a name, a location, a border, or any distinguishing feature. Where the biblical promise of the land is exclusionary of all who are not descendents of Abram and henotheistic worshippers of Yahweh, the promise in the Qur'an, with its assertive monotheism, is to all peoples.

The Torah inextricably links covenant to land, based on what Akenson calls the conditionality of the covenant: 'if-then' (Akenson 1992, 26). The Qur'an does not replicate this link and makes no geographically specific allusions: indeed, the word land/*ard* occurs only five times in the Qur'an, in contrast with the scores of references in the Hebrew scriptures. Even Mecca and Medina, the cities where Islam evolved, are only briefly mentioned in the text, while other regions are merely exempla/ *ibar* of divine intervention. Even in the allusion to the Prophet's night journey/*mi'raj* to the 'Far Distant Place of Worship' (Q 17:1), there is no specific mention of Jerusalem. Furthermore, the city of Mecca is blessed/ *mubaraka* (not holy/*muqadassa*), not because God blessed and designated it for the people who had submitted to Islam, but because it housed His Ibrahimic house, the Ka'ba. In the whole corpus of the *hadith*, there is no reference to land as part of the Muslim covenant with God.

The de-geographization of the 'blessed' land appears again in the qur'anic account of the exodus. After Pharaoh and his armies are destroyed by the deity, the escaping Israelites are told to settle a land. God 'said unto the Children of Israel after him [Moses]: Dwell in the land; but when the promise of the Hereafter comes to pass we shall bring you as a crowd gathered out of various nations' (Q 17:104). The land, again nameless,[30] is just a dwelling place, without covenantal significance or divine legitimization for conquest. The Qur'an makes no link between the 'blessed' land to which Ibrahim had hoped to go and the land to which Moses and his Israelites were going. The land could be anywhere, to the east of Egypt (a country which the Qur'an does mention) or to the west: the Qur'an makes no mention of the orientation of the land. Neither 'Palestine' nor 'Canaan' nor 'promised land' is mentioned in the Qur'an, either – only 'the holy land' (*al-Ard al-Muqadasa*) (Q 5:21), a phrase that appears once, but without any explanation as to location. And the land is holy because God leads the Israelites into it: as 5:21 shows, God tells the Israelites to 'go into the holy land which Allah hath ordained/*katab* for you' – *katab* meaning commanded, not necessarily covenanted. The land is holy because God has so ordained it – *before* it is conquered by the Israelites. But the Israelites refuse to enter the land for fear of the native inhabitants (Q 5:22). In anger at their defiance (Q 5:24), God punishes them by forbidding them the land: it becomes *muharrama* Q:5:26; God then sends them into the desert for forty years. The wander ends, however, not in Moses' conquest of the land, but in his arrival at the land of Moab, where he dies, having been forbidden the land because of the sins of his people. What is important in the qur'anic narrative is not the possession of the land, as in the Torah, but the Israelites' relationship with the God who is leading them to a land. Because the Israelites disobey God, the Qur'an does not mention anything about the actual conquest of the land (as the Torah so elaborately does) nor that the land is to become the Israelites' forever, as in the Abramic promise. The exodus motif in the Qur'an is shorn of any prophetic mimesis because the land becomes *muharrama* to the Israelites.

From the Renaissance on, nearly all bibles included maps; no Qur'an ever does. Where the Bible focuses on historical geography, the Qur'an focuses on the religious and moral lessons of that geography; where Yahweh has specific residence on earth, Allah does not. The qur'anic God, unlike the Genesis and Exodus deity, does not call for the conquest of a land because it is holy to the believers and unholy to its native (unbelieving) inhabitants. Nowhere does the Qur'an invoke conquest on the basis of geographical and ethnic particularization, and at no point does the qur'anic God revert to the henotheism of associating deity with land.

Despite the advances in cartography and the science of geography, English and other European Restorationists continued to envision a paradigm for Palestine that ignored contemporary reality and geography, and continued to conceive the map of Palestine as a *figura* preparing for the conquest of the land by the twelve tribes. Inspired by the exodus in the latest cartography of Renaissance Europe, Restorationists imposed a biblical past on contemporary geography, thereby delegitimizing both historically and prophetically the reality of Arabo-Ottoman Palestine. This introduction of Restorationism into biblical discourse coincided with the beginning of the European age of empire, and with the Ortelian atlas (and subsequent atlases) that were seen to be instruments of that empire.

The cartographic imagination worked differently in Islam. As Walter Mignolo states in *The Darker Side of the Renaissance*:

Had Islam, instead of Christianity, 'discovered' unknown land and people, not only might America not have been America, but it would not have been the fourth part of the world because, from the perspective of Islamic geography and cartography, the earth was not divided in three parts. Economic expansion, technology, and power, rather than truth, characterized European cartography early on. (Mignolo 1995, 311)

As recent research has shown, the study of cartography has been transformed into a critique of ideology, cultural archaeology, and imperialism. What are the rules that 'allow the construction of a map?' asked Michel Foucault; and much has been done since that question was raised to examine the 'cultural production of maps.'[31] It should by now be clear that the map of Palestine in Ortelius's *Theatrum* with its exodus motif was not a 'value-free image' or a natural act of graphic scientific measurement (Harley 1988, 278), but an act loaded with theological, eschatological, and, ultimately, para-colonial Restorationism.

NOTES

I wish to thank Professor Muhammad Asfour of the University of Jordan for his comments on an early draft of this essay.

1 Akerman 1995. Akerman is referring here to an argument by Denis Wood (1987). See also Binding 2003, 202: by naming his atlas a *Theatrum*, Ortelius emphasized that his work was in line with the stories of 'the solemn plays of the ancients which took human destiny as their subject.'

2 'The route of the Israelites out of Egypt located, and the miraculous signs of various places and of divine revelations described.'

3 See chapter 9 on 'Terrae Sanctae' in Crane 2002.

4 As Catherine Delano-Smith and Elizabeth Morley Ingram (1991) indicate, it was Melanchthon who first thought of including a map of the exodus in a bible (xxii).

5 Ortelius 1570, 3. For binaries in maps, see Friedman 1994, 64–96.

6 'The moste auncient name of this lande was called Canaan of the sonne of Cham, whose sonnes diuided it amont them selues. Theyre names were Sydon, Hethaeus, Jabusaeus, Amorraeus, Gergesaeus, Hammathaeus, & this lande held this name, vntill the Israelites possess it. But Canaans posteritie, being partelie killed, partelie subdued, it began afterward to be called the landde of Israel, of Iacob the patriarch. Ptolomi, and others, call it Palestine, of the Palestines, whom holie scriptures too call the Phillistines, at this day, it is called the holie land' (from the 1606 English translation of the *Theatrum*).

7 Ortelius was the first cartographer to use classical sources for his map of Palestine (Koeman 1964, 25).

8 'The Empire of the Persians as it hath always in former ages been most famous, so at this day still it is very renowned' (1606 English translation).

9 'It is by nature a Gentleman-like and honourable Nation, very ciuill and courteous, loving learning liberall sciences' (1606 English translation).

10 'The people generally of this whole country are of a brownish or tawny complexion. They which dwell in cities, are very ingenious in Architecture and such like Mathematical inuentions' (1606 English translation).

11 See Rabasa 1993, ch. 5.

12 See Calloway 1997, ch. 1.

13 For those maps, see Campbell 1987.

14 Like all maps, Ortelius's had a message that was framed in the context of his patron/audience. For a discussion of the 'message' in maps, see Harley 1989.

15 In the third of his additions to the *Theatrum* in 1584, Ortelius replaced Stella's map with another map of Palestine, derived from the 1570 wall map of Peter Laicksteen [fl. ca 1556–70] and Christian Sgrothen [ca 1532–1608]. The inaccuracy of this latter map is even greater than that by Stella. See reproductions of all the maps in van den Broecke 1996, plates 170–3 and 180. See also see Tooley 1978, 28–31.

16 See, for instance, a description of the coast of Palestine in the sixteenth century (in Heyd 1956).

17 For Ottoman cartography, see Ösdemir 1992, Hamdani 1981; for the Walters Art Gallery maps, see Goodrich 1986, Hess 1974, and Soucek 1996.

18 See a reproduction of this map in my *Turks, Moors and Englishmen in the Age of Discovery*, 133.

19 For a critique of 'Exodus' from an anticolonial perspective, see Said 1988.

20 For a discussion of this term, see my 'The Idea of the Restoration of the Jews in English Protestant Thought: From the Reformation until 1660' and 'The Idea of the Restoration of the Jews in English Protestant Thought: From 1661–1701.'

21 It was European because no similar exegesis regarding 'Restoration' appeared in Christian, Arabic, or Eastern Orthodox exegesis. An Arabic commentary on the book of Apocalypse in 1671 makes clear that the land of promise, *ard al-mee'ad*, had been taken away from those who had possessed it and given to the rest of the nations, *umam*; the true *ard al-mee'ad*, continues the Arabic writer, to which the evangelist refers is that which cannot be taken away and is forever. 'This [promised land] is what God promised to all his saints' (British Library, OR 1329, 57v).

22 See Roth 1964, 149, and Katz 1982; see also the studies by Edelstein, 1982, and Tuchman, 1983.

23 See for instance, Martin Luther: 'For there is no prophet, nor promise, which foretells its [Jerusalem] restoration, as happened in Babylon and Egypt,' in *Against the Sabbatarians: Letter to a Good Friend* (Luther 1955, 47:84). For general discussions of this theme, see Healey 1977 and Toon 1970, 24ff.

24 See my 'The Controversy over the Restoration of the Jews in English Protestant Thought: 1701–1753' and 'The Controversy over the Restoration of the Jews in English Protestant Thought: 1754–1809.'

25 Willet 1590, esp. 32v–3v. Around 1611, Willet had a Venetian Jew living in his house near Cambridge. He did not try to 'restore' but rather to convert the tenant; he failed.

26 Indeed, in the earlier account of the world, *Pvrchas his Pilgrimage*, Purchas had alluded to Willet's work in his description of the Jews' conversion (1613, 242). The map in *Pvrchas his Pilgrimes* depicted 'Canaan' at the time of Jesus (Purchas 1625, 7:465).

27 The map was drawn by Jodocus Hondius the Younger in 1629 and used by the Blaeu publishing firm of atlases for over thirty years.

28 The god Chemosh, for instance, also gave to his people, the Moabites, the land of Moab: Judges 11:24; the goddess Aphrodite gave her name to the island of Cyprus; and the Olympian gods had their residence on Mt Olympus.

29 Translations of the Qur'an (Q) from Pickthall.

30 Later Muslim exegetes, such as Jalal al-Din Muhammad bin Ahmad al-Mahalli and Jalal al-Din Abd al-Rahman bin Abi Bakr al-Sayyut (al-Jalalayn), however, would specify the land as Palestine.

31 See the 'Questions on Geography,' in Foucault 1980, 74–5.

REFERENCES

Akenson, Donald Harman. 1992. *God's People: Covenant and Land in South Africa, Israel, and Ulster*. Ithaca: Cornell University Press.

Akerman, James. 1995. 'From Books with Maps to Books as Maps: The Editor in the Creation of the Atlas Idea.' In Joan Winearls, ed., *Editing Early Historical Atlases*. Toronto: University of Toronto Press.

Binding, Paul. 2003. *Imagined Corners: Exploring the World's First Atlas*. London: Headline Book Publishing.

Brotton, Jerry. 1997. *Trading Territories: Mapping the Early Modern World*. Ithaca, NY: Cornell University Press.

Calloway, Colin G. 1997. *New Worlds for All: Indians, Europeans, and the Remaking of Early America*. Baltimore and London: Johns Hopkins University Press.

Campbell, Tony. 1987. *The Earliest Printed Maps, 1472–1500*. Berkeley: University of California Press.

Cragg, Kenneth. 1997. *Palestine: The Prize and Price of Zion*. London: Cassell.

Crane, Nicholas. 2002. *Mercator: The Man Who Mapped the Planet*. New York: Henry Holt.

Delano-Smith, Catherine, and Elizabeth Morley Ingram. 1991. *Maps in Bibles, 1500–1600*. Geneva: Librarie Droz.

Edelstein, Alan. 1982. *An Unacknowledged Harmony*. Westport, CT: Greenwood Press.

Finch, Henry. 1621. *The Calling of the Ievves. A Present to Ivdah and the Children of Israel*. London: Edward Griffin.

Fiorani, Francesca. 1996. 'Post Tridentine "Geographia Sacra." The Galleria delle Carte Geografiche in the Vatican Palace.' *Imago Mundi* 48: 124–48.

Foster, George. 1650. *The Pouring Forth of the Seventh and Last Viall*. London.

Foucault, Michel. 1980. *Power/Knowledge: Selected Interviews and Other Writings, 1972–1977*. Ed. and trans. Colin Gordon et al. New York: Pantheon.

Friedman, John B. 1994. 'Cultural Conflicts in Medieval World Maps.' In Stuart B. Schwartz, ed., *Implicit Understandings*, 64–96. Cambridge: Cambridge University Press.

Gillies, John. 1994. *Shakespeare and the Geography of Difference*. Cambridge: Cambridge University Press.

Goodrich, Th.D. 1986. 'The Earliest Ottoman Maritime Atlas: The Walters Deniz Atlasi.' *Archivium Ottomanicum* 11: 25–44.

Goodwin, Thomas. 1861. *An Exposition of the Revelation*. In *The Works of Thomas Goodwin*. Edinburgh: James Nichol.

Hamdani, Abbas. 1981. 'Ottoman Response to the Discovery of America and the New Route to India.' *Journal of the American Oriental Society* 101: 323–30.

Harley, J.B. 1988. 'Maps, Knowledge, and Power.' In Denis Cosgrove and Stephen Daniels, eds, *The Iconography of Landscape*. Cambridge: Cambridge University Press.

– 1989. 'Deconstructing the Map.' *Cartographica* 26: 1–20.

Healey, Robert M. 1977. 'The Jew in 17th-Century Protestant Thought.' *Church History* 46: 63–79.

Hess, Andrew C. 1974. 'Piri Reis and the Ottoman Response to the Voyages of Discovery.' *Terrae Incognitae* 6: 19–37.

Heyd, U. 1956. 'A Turkish Description of the Coast of Palestine in the Early Sixteenth Century.' *Israel Exploration Journal* 6: 201–16.

Housley, Norman. 2000. 'Holy Land or Holy Lands? Palestine and the Catholic West in the Late Middle Ages and the Renaissance.' In R.N. Swanson, ed., *The Holy Land, Holy Lands, and Christian History*. Woodbridge, Suffolk, UK: Boydell Press.

Katz, David. 1982. *Philo-Semitism and the Readmission of the Jews to England, 1603–1655*. Oxford: Clarendon Press.

Koeman, C. 1964. *The History of Abraham Ortelius and his* Theatrum Orbis Terrarum. New York: American Elsevier Publishing Co.

Laud, William. 1867. *The Works of William Laud*. Ed. William Scott. Vol. 1. Oxford: Oxford University Press.

Luther, Martin. 1955–86. *Luther's Works*. Ed. Jaroslav Pelikan and Helmuth Lehmann. St Louis: Concordia Publishing House.

Matar, Nabil. 1985a. 'The Idea of the Restoration of the Jews in English Protestant Thought: From the Reformation until 1660.' *Durham University Journal*: 23–36.

– 1985b. 'The Idea of the Restoration of the Jews in English Protestant Thought: From 1661–1701.' *Harvard Theological Review* 78: 115–48.

– 1988. 'The Controversy over the Restoration of the Jews in English Protestant Thought: 1701–1753.' *Durham University Journal* 80: 241–56.

– 1990. 'The Controversy over the Restoration of the Jews in English Protestant Thought: 1754–1809.' *Durham University Journal* 87: 29–44.

– 1999. *Turks, Moors and Englishmen in the Age of Discovery*. New York: Columbia University Press.

Mercator, Gerhard. 1635. *Historia Mundi or, Mercator's Atlas. Lately Enlarged by I. Hondy. Englished by W.S.* London: T. Cotes for M. Sparkie and S. Cartwright.

Mignolo, Walter D. 1995. *The Darker Side of the Renaissance*. Ann Arbor: University of Michigan Press.

Monmonier, Mark. 1996. *How to Lie with Maps*. Chicago and London: University of Chicago Press.

Nebenzahl, Kenneth. 1986. *Maps of the Holy Land*. New York: Abbenville Press.

Ortelius, Abraham. 1570. *Theatrum orbis terrarum Abrahami Ortelii Antuerp. geographi regii*. Reprinted 1964, Lausanne: Sequoia.

– 1606. *Theatrum orbis terrarum Abrahami Ortelii Antuerp. geographi regii. = The theatre of the vvhole world: set forth by that excellent geographer Abraham Ortelius*. Trans. W.B. London: John Norton.

Ősdemir, Kemal. 1992. *Ottoman Nautical Charts and the Atlas of Ali Macar Reis*. Trans. P. Mary Işin. Istanbul: Creative Yayıncılık.

Pickthall, Mohammed Marmaduke. n.d. *The Meaning of the Glorious Koran. An Explanatory Translation*. 15th printing. New York: Mentor.

Purchas, Samuel. 1613. *Pvrchas His Pilgrimage*. London: William Stansby for Henrie Fetherstone.

– 1625. *Hakluytus Posthumus or Purchas His Pilgrimes*. 20 vols. Reprinted 1965, New York: AMS Press.

Rabasa, José. 1993. *Inventing America*. Norman and London: University of Oklahoma Press.

Roth, Cecil. 1964. *A History of the Jews in England*. 3rd ed. Oxford: Clarendon Press.

Said, Edward. 1988, 2001. 'Michael Walzer's Exodus and Revolution: A Canaanite Reading.' In Edward W. Said and Christopher Hitchens, eds, *Blaming the Victims: Spurious Scholarship and the Palestinian Question*, 161–78. London: Verso.

Salaita, Steven. 2002. 'Demystifying the Quest for Canaan: Observations on Mimesis in the New World and Holy Land.' *Critique: Critical Middle Eastern Studies* 11.2: 129–50.

Sandys, George. 1615. *A Relation of a Iourney begun An: Dom: 1610. Fovre bookes. containing a description of the Turkish Empire, of Aegypt of the Holy Land, of the remote parts of Italy, and ilands adioyning*. 2nd ed. London: W. Barrett.

Scafi, Allessandro. 1999. 'Mapping Eden: Cartographies of the Early Paradise.' In Denis Cosgrove, ed., *Mappings*. London: Reaktion Books.

Soucek, Svat. 1996. *Piri Reis & Turkish Mapmaking after Columbus*. London: Nour Foundation and Oxford University Press.

Theuavjohn, Thomas (Thomas Tany). 1650. *I proclaime from the Lord of Hosts the Returne of the Jewes from their Captivity, and the Building of the Temple in Glory, in their owne Land*. London: Charles Sumptner.

Tooley, R.V. 1978. 'Maps of Palestine in the Atlas of Ortelius.' *The Map Collector* 3: 28–32.

Toon, Peter, ed. 1970. *Puritans, the Millennium and the Future of Israel*. Cambridge: James Clarke.

Tuchman, Barbara. 1983. *Bible and Sword*. 3rd ed. New York: Funk & Wagnalls.

van den Broecke, Marcel P.R. 1996. *Ortelius Atlas Maps*. 't Goy, Netherlands: HES Publishers.

Voet, Leon. 1998. 'Abraham Ortelius and His World.' In Marcel van den Broecke, Peter Van Der Krogt, and Peter Meurer, eds, *Abraham Ortelius and the First Atlas*. Utrecht: HES Publishers.

Wilken, Robert L. 1992. *The Land Called Holy: Palestine in Christian History and Thought*. New Haven: Yale University Press.

Willet, Andrew. 1590. *De Vniversali et novissima Ivdeaorum Vocatione.* Cambridge: Cambridge University Press.

Winearls, Joan, ed. 1995. *Editing Early Historical Atlases.* Toronto: University of Toronto Press.

4

Beyond a Shared Inheritance: American Jews Reclaim the Hebrew Bible

LAURA S. LEVITT

In 1985, all three parts of the Bible translation, with revisions, were brought together in one volume entitled *Tanakh* – from the Hebrew acronym for *Torah* (Pentateuch), *Nevi'im* (Prophets), and *Ketuvim* (Writings). The title of the new volume, carefully chosen, underscored yet again the Jewishness of the new translation as a whole: the Jews, even as they share the Hebrew Bible in common with their Christian neighbors, understand much of it differently, and even call it by a different name.

Jonathan Sarna, *JPS: The Americanization of Jewish Culture 1888–1988*

As I wrote these words, Christian citizens of Alabama were holding a vigil at the State's judicial building in order to protest the imminent removal of a two-and-a-half-ton granite monument engraved with the Ten Commandments.[1] It is hard to underestimate the importance of the Bible in American culture and to our definitions of ourselves as a culture, even as we in the United States continue to argue for the separation of church and state, a notion whose very phrasing belies its Christian assumptions. After all, who besides Christians really have 'churches'? Americans see themselves as heirs to a biblical inheritance, as the new Israel, the chosen people who live on a land promised to them by the biblical G-d, a place where we will live out and fulfil his promise and become a light and leader among all the nations of the world. The granite monument is itself an affirmation of this biblical status. It says that the people of Alabama as citizens of the United States of America are part of the new Israel, that justice in America is biblical, that it stands on the foundation of the Ten Commandments, that the foregoing are fundamentally linked.

This essay is also about language and naming. It investigates the slip-
pages and tensions between the various names used in English in the
United States to talk about the Hebrew Bible, the Old Testament, or the
Tanakh, the sacred text at the base of our American national identity, as
a way of looking at the place of Jews in American culture. In placing
such issues in the context of the larger 'biblical' culture of the United
States, I want to ask what it has meant for Jews to claim a space in that
culture, and begin to explore the complex relations among specifically
Jewish notions of scripture, *our* (Jewish) sacred texts, and the various
ways in which the Hebrew Bible connects *us*, as American Jews, to the
dominant Protestant culture of the United States – but also distinguishes us from it. The essay will consider the position of Jews in
American culture by focusing on the seemingly common ground of the
Hebrew Bible. By contextualizing the Jewish Publication Society's decision to call its 1985 translation of the Hebrew Bible the *Tanakh*, I hope to
make clear the contradictions that continue to mark the status of
American Jews. Instead of arguing that there has been a linear progres-
sion from the sense of a shared biblical culture to a fuller appreciation
of a uniquely Jewish approach to scripture, I will place that 1985 decision in a more ambivalent history. My contention will be that the JPS
translation does not – as could be thought – mark a new high point in
the general acceptance of Jews, Jewish culture, and Jewish tradition in
the United States, but that it should instead be viewed as a revealing
instance of a more tense and complicated relationship.

The Silence of the Archives

Just how mindful were the editors of the JPS translation about the decision to name their translation the *Tanakh*? In an attempt to answer this
question I went to the Philadelphia Jewish Archives where the Jewish
Publication Society's papers are housed. I assumed that there would be
abundant information about the decision-making process. To my surprise, however, I found scarcely any documentation on this point. A
search of books and periodicals in biblical studies likewise turned up
little commentary on this decision or its implications. It is true that
there was plenty of discussion about technicalities – word choices, er-
rors of translation, minor points in dispute. But on the most basic issue,
the naming of the text – nothing. What I have come to realize, in my
surprise and disappointment, is that this lack of comment is itself significant. Despite the boldness of the initiative, those responsible for it

apparently chose not to call too much attention either to the decision or to the process that produced it.

I did not draw a total blank. Invoices from printers and distributors yielded small clues.[2] From these and a brief note in the minutes of a meeting of the JPS board of trustees on 6 May 1985, I learned that the decision had been made very late in the day. The note reads, 'The title has been selected: It will be called "TANAKH: A New Translation of the Holy Scriptures According to the Traditional Hebrew Text"' (JPS Papers). Even so, this was not much. Frustrated by how little I had found, I decided to make a direct approach to those in a position to tell me more. Jonathan Sarna, author of a definitive history of the Jewish Publication Society, was able to relay an account given by his father, the biblical scholar Nahum Sarna, who had been on the editorial board: 'He tells me that the suggestion was made by Chaim Potok, who felt that the name TANAKH would underscore the Jewish character of the translation (unlike names like Bible, Holy Bible, or Old Testament, the latter, of course, being a term that would not have been considered). He said the idea immediately captured everyone's imagination' (Jonathan Sarna, personal communication, 3 Feb. 2003). Next I contacted Ellen Frankel, CEO and editor-in-chief of the Jewish Publication Society, who told me that she had learned from the novelist Chaim Potok, who was also one of the editors, that 'it was a decision of the Bible Translation Committee and the Board ... to use TANAKH instead of "Holy Scripture" (the 1917 translation title) so as to educate the public that we Jews have our own name for our Bible just as Muslims have the "Koran" as theirs' (Ellen Frankel, personal communication, 30 July 2002). This matched what Jonathan Sarna had told me and what I had seen in the archives.

It would seem, in short, that the committee had a strong sense of the importance of their decision, but chose not to call attention to it either in their publicity for the translation or, as they might have done, in other scholarly publications subsequently. To me this ambivalence is compelling, and I would like to consider what it may have to tell us about the (changing?) status of Jews in American culture. To do this, I will have to suspend each of the key terms of my title, beginning with American Jews' desire for social acceptance on the supposedly 'common ground' of a 'shared biblical inheritance.' To put it more plainly, I will have to call into question the classic liberal assumptions that have informed popular notions of Jewish 'inclusion' in American society ever since the emancipatory promises of the American and French revolutions in the late eighteenth century brought Jews within the dominant cultures of the West. I use the occasion of the 1985 translation and its remaking of the Hebrew Bible into a more specifically Jewish text as an opportunity for uncovering some of the contradictions and tensions that are necessarily glossed over by the liberal idea of a 'shared inheritance.'

My reinterpretation of the notions of a shared inheritance and of Jewish social acceptance builds broadly on the work of postcolonial theorist Homi Bhabha. I use Bhabha's concept of 'the almost but not quite white' status of colonial subjects to begin to unravel some of the similar constraints built into the liberal social contract that brought Jews into the mainstream culture of the United States and Western Europe. I maintain that the liberal contract is the other side of the colonial project. On the basis of this critique, I take apart the assumptions built into my title and challenge the wider claim of social progress that has always been such a crucial component of the promise of liberal inclusion. In this case, specifically, I challenge the belief that the Hebrew Bible or *Tanakh* has ever been in any simple way a 'shared inheritance' or that American Jews have fully 'reclaimed' the Hebrew Bible as their own. Because we as American Jews are still invested in liberalism as a metadiscourse, it continues to act as a framework for our understanding of ourselves as rational and ethical people. Hence, 'prophetical ethical monotheism'[3] becomes the rational liberal religious faith par excellence, the ultimate enlightened religious position that supports and enhances the social contract that brought Jews social acceptance in the first place. Given this ongoing belief, I argue, American Jews remain vulnerable, unable fully to recognize the ambivalence of such legacies. By focusing on the role of the Hebrew Bible in determining the place of Jews in American culture, I hope to indicate both the practical limitations of the liberal doctrine of inclusion and the contradictions at the heart of this ideal of social and spiritual integration.

Stories in Translation

It is important to see how the 1985 JPS translation both continues and disrupts a much longer legacy of biblical translation, both Jewish and non-Jewish, in the United States as well as elsewhere. Translation is always a contested site in the work of meaning-making, and language and naming are at the core of the Jewish Publication Society's project. On the one hand, the 1985 JPS translation is an acknowledgment that the vast majority of American Jews do not have direct access to their sacred text in its original language. It is a statement about the role of English in the American Jewish community; in America, English is the most prevalent Jewish language. On the other hand, this Jewish translation of the Hebrew Bible is also a text for the larger American public. It is a scholarly Jewish translation of a text that is also read by non-Jews who lay claim to this text from other religious traditions, especially the various Christian denominations that make up the majority culture of the United States.

As the translators and editors of the 1985 JPS translation were well aware, in both these respects their translation stands in a long and rich tradition. Our concern here is with what (Western) biblical scholars call the fourth great moment in the history of biblical translation, the rendering of the Hebrew Bible and the Christian Scriptures into English, and how this affects Jewish understanding of and engagement with the Hebrew Bible. Who reads these texts and what do the translations tell us about such readers, given that they are designed in the first instance for assimilated Jews? How do Jews read these texts as their own? How do they understand the relationship between Jewish and other translations? For example: what might it mean for Jews that one of the Jewish scholars who worked on the JPS translation had also earlier helped translate the (Christian) New Revised Standard Version (NRSV)? What does it mean that in 1985, a moment rather late in the epic of biblical translation, the American Jewish version was named by its Hebrew acronym, comprising the first letters of each of its three constituent parts, *Torah* (the Pentateuch), *Nevi'im* (Prophets) and *Ketuvim* (Writings), an ordering which profoundly differentiates traditional Jewish approaches to the Hebrew Bible from Christian readings?[4] Finally, what is the significance of the fact that all of this happened almost twenty years after the beginning of the celebration of Jewish ethnicity and Jewish cultural difference in America? What do this late rereading and reclaiming of the text at the very heart of the liberal promise of cultural sameness – the Hebrew Bible, and the Prophetic tradition – mean for contemporary Jews and their fellow Americans?

To be in a position to answer these questions, we need to retrace some of the longer history of biblical translation.

Translation of the Hebrew Bible began around 2200 years ago in Alexandria (Egypt) with the Septuagint, as Greek became the vernacular language of Jews in this region, replacing Hebrew and Aramaic. The Hebrew Bible was also translated into Aramaic (the 'Targums') between the last centuries BCE and the first few centuries CE. All subsequent Christian translations followed these Jewish translations, the Septuagint and the Targums, as well as building on the work of the Jewish exegete Philo (ca 20 BCE – ca 50 CE). The Christian Latin translation attributed to Jerome (340–420) became authoritative in the West and was duly named the 'Vulgate' by the Counter-Reformation Council of Trent. Another important Jewish translation, into Judeo-Arabic, was made by Saadia Gaon (882–942), in a style more poetic than literal. During the Reformation, Luther and Tyndale may have used Latin translations of classical Jewish commentaries (Rashi, Ibn Ezra, and Kimhi), which were themselves based on the Aramaic translations of the Targums, to produce their reformed translations in German and English. Tyndale's efforts were crucial for what became the King James (or 'Authorized') Version, completed in 1611.[5]

The first Jewish translation into English in the United States was done by Rabbi Isaac Lesser in 1853, following the lead of Moses Mendelssohn, the Enlightenment German Jewish philosopher who translated the Torah text into German (1780–3).[6] Like other American translations, the Lesser and later Jewish translations attempted to establish a distinctively American way of approaching the biblical text. The translations by various Christian communities in the United States were also a way of establishing the independence and the prestige of American culture as an heir to these ancient sacred writings. Of particular significance in this light were the Revised Standard translation of 1881–5 and the American Standard translation of 1901. Although these American translations were built on the legacy of the King James Version, the translators clearly wanted to place their country on the map by virtue of its scholarship and critical engagement with scripture. In the twentieth century, the effort to make the text speak in an American vernacular would become increasingly important as a way of distinguishing modern American readers of the Bible from devotees of the more formal and antiquated cadences of the King James Version.

At the same time as American Protestants and Catholics were striving to update their translations of the Bible in an American vernacular and support their translations with the latest critical scholarship, so were American Jews. They wanted an English translation for themselves, one that they could be proud of as English-speaking Jews. That was the desire behind the 1917 JPS translation, perhaps the most significant American Jewish translation before the current one. By then, Lesser's translation had come to seem too expansive, too literal, and inconsistent with the best scholarship of the day. There was clearly a need for a new Jewish translation. The team of translators under Max Margolis did not start from scratch. Instead, they used the Revised Standard Version as their starting point and did their best to remove all un-Jewish and anti-Jewish expressions. They also added Jewish commentaries and critical sources. In the end, the 1917 JPS translation became more than just the Jewish version of the RSV. It was a source of Jewish pride. Unlike the more literal Lesser translation, this one was redacted in prose of a quality to set it on a level with the kindred works of Catholics and Protestants. According to the biographer of one of its editors, it was 'a peace offering by Jews to the non-Jewish world. To the Jews it presented a Bible that combined the spirit of Jewish tradition with the results of biblical scholarship, ancient, medieval and modern. To non-Jews it opened the gateway of Jewish tradition in the interpretation of the Word of God' (Neuman in Sarna and Sarna 1988, 101). It could even surpass Christian translations by bringing traditional Jewish scholarship to English-speaking readers. The language around the translation was triumphalist and pluralistic. It offered both Christians and Jews a Jewish account of this shared sacred text even as it focused on American Jewish readers. It also seemed to say that the Jewish version was the definitive version. Solomon Schecter spoke of the text as both 'for Jews and by Jews' (Sarna and Sarna 1988, 102). By the same token, it marked America as a centre of Jewish life and creativity. Like the Standard edition, it followed the King James in diction. As Jonathan Sarna has suggested, this fact can be explained in part by the presence of non-native English speakers on the editorial board. They were committed to replicating what they thought of as the highest form of the English language, that of the King James (Sarna 1989, 110).

The new JPS translation, like its 1917 predecessor, was not an authoritative religious text for any single Jewish religious community, although Reform, Conservative, and Orthodox rabbis were on the editorial board with the scholars who actually did the translation. The impetus for a new translation came after the Second World War. As the United States took its position as a world leader and began to retool industries and educational institutions in accordance with this role, American cultural production also entered a fresh phase. In the forefront of this development was a series of biblical translation projects. A new Catholic translation in 1941 was followed by updatings of the Revised Standard translation (New Testament in 1946, Old Testament in 1952). With these examples before them, Jewish scholars were not slow to see the need for a truly contemporary Jewish translation of the Hebrew Bible. Leading the charge was Harry Orlinsky, a Canadian Jewish biblical scholar who had worked on the New Revised Standard translation. In his 1953 address to the annual meeting of the Jewish Publication Society, Orlinsky made the case for a new initiative. His talk was entitled: 'Wanted: A New English Translation of the Bible.' The 1917 translation, he argued, was no longer serviceable. What was needed was a vernacular translation that was neither too literal nor archaic in its language, that made fuller use of traditional Jewish commentaries and highlighted the value of these sources for modern readers, and that was informed by the latest archaeological and biblical scholarship. His listeners were convinced. In 1955 the new JPS translation project began. It was a huge undertaking. Several years passed before the first section of the translation was completed; the Torah translation appeared in 1962, followed by the Prophets (*Nevi'im*) in 1978 and the Writings (*Ketuvim*) in 1982. The culmination of these long labours was the 1985 publication of the single volume *TANAKH: A New Translation of the Holy Scriptures According to the Traditional Hebrew Text*.

The new translation offered readers a vernacular version that was scientifically up to date and that no longer sounded antiquated. Unlike other translations, it was based primarily on the Masoretic Hebrew manuscript traditions. It built on the insights of new research, especially in archaeology. And it reasserted the importance of Jewish interpretive and translation traditions, making these available to ordinary readers and scholars alike. In effect, the text reclaimed the tradition of biblical translation itself as a Jewish practice. It affirmed that Jews were the first translators of the Hebrew Bible and that all subsequent translations followed their lead. Already these were powerful ways of asserting the Jewishness of the American sacred text. But there was more to it than that.

The Empowerment of Hebrew and the Return to the Land

Part of what distinguished the 1985 translation was that it offered a bold reassertion of Hebrew as a modern language, the language of a vibrant contemporary Jewish nationalism as expressed by Zionism and the post-war creation of the State of Israel. The text was a product not only of the increasingly biblical focus of Israeli culture,[7] its commitment to archaeology, and its role in rebuilding the Jewish nation as it was 'of old,' but also of the new biblical scholarship being done in the new

Jewish state.[8] Israeli scholars were involved in the translation project, increasingly as it proceeded. Unlike the JPS translation of 1917, the work was done this time by North American and Israeli scholars, not by scholars trained in Europe. This shift in the locus of biblical scholarship reflected the growing role of biblical culture in defining twentieth-century Jewish life.

Zionism (i.e., modern Jewish nationalism) gave the ancient language of Hebrew a new lease on life. One could say that the language was returned to the land, through the overlapping logics of Jewish nationalism and the various religious traditions of Jewish chosenness and peoplehood. For modern Jewish nationalists, Hebrew and Palestine both echoed familiar tropes within normative, post-biblical Rabbinic Judaism – notions of a once-thriving people driven into exile and now finally returning home. Jewish nationalists worked to *realize* these mythic dreams. In doing so, they also worked against normative Rabbinic Judaism, which had focused not on the Hebrew Bible but on the oral tradition of the rabbis, placing the Talmud at its centre and taking Diaspora for granted. By contrast, in the twentieth-century vision of Jewish renewal the mythic and the national merge as the reclaiming of a biblical inheritance. Under this logic, an emasculated and diminished Rabbinic Judaism would give way to a heroic alternative, as a beleaguered people returned to its ancient homeland and ancient language. In effect, the same mythic schemes that had inspired many Protestant communities to see themselves as Israel returning to rebuild Jerusalem in the New World were now being deployed by Jews in the guise of Jewish nationalism.[9]

The twin novel features of these narratives – the empowerment of G-d's people through a renewed interest in the Hebrew Bible, and a sense of peoplehood increasingly understood in nationalist, albeit *biblical*-national, terms – would naturally tend to emphasize the fault lines between Christian- and Jewish-American communities. After all, each claimed to be the true Israel, and the very idea of the Jewish people returning to the land conflicted with ordinary Christian supersessionism. How could the Old Testament ever have needed to be completed and the people of the old covenant replaced by the new, if the old promise was being fulfilled by the return of the Jewish people to the land? The metaphors of the biblical text as Christians understood them were being challenged by what one scholar has described as the 'rematerialization' of these tropes or figures (Ezrahi 2000).

Given these factors, the 1985 JPS translation was a potentially risky reassertion of Jewish agency or Jewish power. The *TANAKH* insisted that the Bible was a Jewish text. It said that the Jewish people were the rightful heirs to this sacred inheritance: it is *our* text and as such it can rightfully go by its ancient name, its first and Jewish name. It need not be referred to in the ways that others, even dominant others, have known it. This reassertion of a more ancient Jewish understanding of the text, of how it is ordered and what it should be called, constituted an implicit challenge to Christian readers.

The Zionist piece of this tale is telling in another way. As always when they attempt to embrace Enlightenment principles, Jews must abandon some shame before they are able to claim a more modern Jewish self – in this case a Jewish *national* self. The national self looks back to a pre-Rabbinic past in order to affirm itself as modern. Like the Reformers (those most fervently anti-Zionist of American Jews before the Second World War), these nationalist Jews see themselves more fully in the vision of a *biblical* past. In both classical Reform theology and in Zionism it is the Bible that defines the essence of a modern Jewishness, as either a form of biblical nationalism or a biblically inflected liberalism. Like the Zionists, the Reformers proclaimed themselves the heirs to a biblical inheritance – in their case, the prophetic tradition. In each case, the most ancient became the most modern and an old exilic Judaism was overcome. As Jonathan and Nahum Sarna explain,

> Although Zionists tended to stress different chapters from the Bible than did Reform Jews, they too turned to the Bible for inspiration and ideological justification. The Bible legitimated the Jewish claim to a homeland. Biblical archaeology linked the past and the Jewish present. Spoken Hebrew, revived by the Zionist movement, was modeled on biblical Hebrew, not rabbinic. Secular Zionists may have disdained works of Jewish law and scorned theology, but they respected the Bible. They also respected biblical scholars. (Sarna and Sarna 1988, 104)

Prophetic Ethical Monotheism: A Shared Inheritance?

I am not arguing that it was not until 1985 that Jews claimed the Hebrew Bible in America, but rather that prior to this they had claimed it on other terms. They had indeed understood the Hebrew Bible as a 'shared inheritance,' as that which Christians and Jews had in common with each other. In the United States this sharing has always been conceived in liberal terms. What has been shared by Jews and Christians, especially Protestant Christians, is the 'Old Testament' and, more specifically, the prophetic tradition of ethical monotheism. The shared understanding of that tradition bolstered liberal notions of social responsibility and inclusion, the very political theory that enabled Jews to become citizens of liberal nation-states such as the United States.

What strikes me about this understanding of the Hebrew Bible is that it so obviously overlooks, especially in the first five books, the *biblical* notion of 'inheritance.' Although we are nowadays inclined to think of inheritance chiefly in biological terms, as that which is genetically transmitted from one generation to the next, this is not how it was configured in biblical narrative. In the biblical text, as more generally in traditional societies, an 'inheritance' is a legacy bequeathed by a relative. It is property. It carries legal status and rights. It means gaining something as one's right or portion, becoming heir to it. What is received is something valuable from the past that takes one into the future. In the patriarchal narratives, what is passed on is the promise G-d made to Abraham to become a great nation, a promise of both land and progeny. In the biblical text an inheritance may indeed be shared.[10] But the inheritance is not necessarily shared equally. Typically, when inheritances are divided in the Bible, some heirs are privileged and others marginalized. The question of which child gets the largest share of the inheritance – the question, in other words, of which one is the real inheritor – is at the heart of some of the best-known biblical narratives. Isaac and Ishmael, Jacob and Esau do share an inheritance, but not in an equal or unproblematic manner.[11]

Contestation is another kind of intergenerational legacy; what is passed down is often figured in terms of intimate conflict. In the Hebrew Bible, conflict is transmitted from one generation to the next in the family of the patriarchs. Shared are lingering bad feelings, anger, and jealousy within families and clans. The valuable possessions at issue are neither enjoyed, used, nor experienced jointly. In the Bible there is no sharing of a birthright, a blessing, or a promise. No siblings are depicted as equal partners. Inheritance is an all or nothing affair, usually the rightful possession of the firstborn but often not. The inequity between siblings that emerges in the patriarchal narratives of Genesis, although tempered by later prophetic visions of justice, endures. It persists in the ongoing relationship between Judaism and the various forms of Christianity. All the readings of biblical sibling rivalry by both the rabbis and early Christian commentators point to very powerful arguments for the fact that only one people can be the true Israel.

These long-standing contests among and between Christians and Jews created tensions that were only exacerbated as Protestant communities reformed their Christian identities by appealing to Old Testament models. Such moves brought Protestants seemingly closer to actual Jews, but they also made more vivid the differences in biblical interpretation between Jews and Protestants. Jews living in the United States were of course different from Protestants, even those who attempted to live closer to the edicts of the Old Testament. Liberal Jews in the nineteenth and early twentieth century were still reading the biblical text through the lens of post-biblical Jewish tradition; as much as they privileged the biblical text in their modern self-understanding, they were still very much the heirs of Rabbinic Judaism. Not even Reform Jews could be simply considered the people of the Old Testament.

The idea that certain Protestant groups were actually closer to Jews and could therefore form alliances based on a shared commitment to the Hebrew Bible came under severe strain as these groups got to know actual Jews who did not, as it turned out, live the kind of lives that Protestants imagined Jews to live. Thus, what began as philo-semitism often turned into something altogether different and less tolerant. The notion of commonality could only go so far, leaving Jews to remain on guard; these alliances often became a pretext for proselytizing Jews.[12] And yet, despite such hazards, the theory of a community between Christians and Jews grounded in the Hebrew Bible continued to shape the imaginations of American Jews. By appealing to this shared inheritance, especially to a liberal reading of the prophetic tradition, Jews entered into American culture as full citizens of the United States. They became accepted as familiar others, strangers who shared a prophetic tradition.

Jews and Christians in the West turned to the prophetic tradition in the late eighteenth and early nineteenth centuries to support their progressive visions. Liberalism used the prophets to help justify its universal conception of 'the equality of all men,' or at least all men of property. Liberals relied on the language of the biblical prophets not only for the content of their vision, but also as a common religious source for their claims that 'all men were created equal and endowed by their creator with certain inalienable rights.' In this way, it could be argued that liberalism itself was rooted in the biblical prophetic tradition. And, in turn, it was this kind of argument that made it easier for Jews and Protestants to see what they had in common and why they might be able to live together in peace as citizens of liberal nation-states such as the United States of America. This was also the background to the ecumenical impulse, revived in the 1950s, to see Protestants, Catholics, and

Jews as sharing a 'Judeo-Christian tradition.' The term 'Judeo-Christian' became a way of signalling the shared inheritance of Jews and Christians in the Hebrew Bible and its prophetic tradition (Silk 1984).

The idea of such a biblical inheritance was bound to be especially powerful in the United States. Because the earliest Protestant settlers saw themselves as an Old Testament people, there was already a sense that the New World was infused with the legacy of the older texts of the Christian scriptures. Many of these Protestant settlers had been persecuted in the old world for their allegedly dissident beliefs and practices. Their efforts to see themselves as heirs to the Hebrew Bible prefigured the liberal vision of a more equal relationship, not only between different groups of Christians, but also between Christians and Jews. According to a similar logic, Jews took seriously the texts of the Hebrew Bible in shaping their way of life on this new continent. And yet, as I have already indicated, this theory of community naturally gave birth to contentions. The question would arise: Who was the *true* Israel, the lineal heir to this biblical tradition?

The Limits of Assimilation: Liberalism and Colonialism

The idea of biblical community reflects a desire to make connections across the divide between Jews and Christians while also maintaining a set of inherent tensions – tensions that bespeak a difference that can never be fully resolved. Jews and Christians may read the same sacred texts, but in emphasizing this truth we (and/or they) obscure the practices of reading and living that have shaped our respective, distinct historical relationships to those texts and their interpretation. For American Jews, especially in the nineteenth century, the desire for social acceptance dictated a serious attempt to minimize such disparities. For members of the dominant Protestant culture, however, they continued to signify. The latter did not fully accept Jews as their equals because, despite Jewish efforts to assimilate, Jewish difference still mattered.

'Almost but not quite the same.' This is a dynamic that I have written about elsewhere in terms of the liberal/colonial project (Levitt 1997). My aim was to draw attention to the close relationship between liberalism and its other side, colonialism. The ability of Western nation states to become more open and inclusive depended upon their continuing exploitation of those 'others' or colonial subjects whose land, labour, and resources provided much of their wealth. Building on the work of Homi Bhabha on colonialism, I have argued that even in the liberal West, 'others' such as Jews or women can only ever try to fit in; the harder they try, the more they will remain 'other.' However much such a 'liberal' subject tries to be accepted, he or she is always almost but not quite acceptable. Assimilation remains necessarily partial. As Bhabha explains for the case of the colonial subject, 'By "partial" I mean both "incomplete" and "virtual." It is as if the very emergence of the colonial is dependent for its representation upon some strategic limitation or prohibition *within* the authoritative discourse' (Bhabha 1994, 125). What particularly interests me about the case of American Jews as putatively 'liberal' subjects is the excessive effort of this particular 'other' to be at once the same and distinct: as I see it, both desires are operative from the beginning. The same pattern can be discerned in the attempt by American Jews both to share the Hebrew Bible and to claim it as their own.

In fact, I would argue, it is the *excess* of their efforts to fit in that finally marks American Jews as different. Liberalism and colonialism, as I note above, are two sides of the same coin; each offers the promise of acceptance and, at the same time, its annulment. Emancipation, assimilation, and acceptance are never fully realized in this system. Instead, at the heart of the emancipatory vision is a deferral. The promise is always only partial; it can never be fully realized. And in the gap between the promise and its elusive fulfilment lies the problem. To imagine full acceptance as Jews or women or colonial subjects is always illusory. Liberalism and its version of universalism based on a certain commonality always produce excess as a symptom of the condition of 'almost but not quite.' Jewish investment in glossing over such tensions nonetheless remains great. The desire for a more truly universal polity ensures that Jews will continue to promote liberalism as a means to this end, as if someday it will be possible to achieve it. Giving up on that promise would be too frightening in a world where there are no obvious alternatives. For on what other terms might *we* share? American Jews have yet to make anything of a possibility which feminist and queer theorists have lately been exploring, namely, that of constructing alliances without consensus or sameness as a basic assumption (Jakobsen 1998; Butler 1999).

Because liberalism remains central to how Jews understand their place in US culture, the kinds of internal contradictions that Bhabha describes continue to animate American Jewish life. In the final section below, I offer some further examples of this ambivalence as it marks both the production and the reception of the 1985 JPS translation of the Hebrew Bible.

Tanakh and the Situation of American Jews

Let us return to the question of how the decision to name the single-volume translation 'The TANAKH' was made. Jonathan Sarna explains:

> [Harry] Orlinsky generally referred to the new translation as the 'New Jewish Version' (NJV), emphasizing its 'newness,' as distinguished from the Protestant 'Revised *Standard* Version.' But others involved in the translation objected to the word 'version,' because it implied that the Jewish translation bore official sanction, which, unlike the Protestant and Catholic versions, it did not presume to have. The official title of the Bible published in 1985 strikes a middle ground: *TANAKH: A New Translation of the Holy Scriptures According to the Traditional Hebrew Text* (revised in the third printing to *TANAKH: The Holy Scriptures: The New JPS Translation According to the Traditional Hebrew Text*). (Sarna, JPS Papers, 242)

Another reason that Orlinsky's title was ultimately rejected by the editorial board may have been that a 'version' can also be understood as 'a description or account from one point of view ... a particular form or variation of an earlier or original type' (American Heritage Dictionary). The editors of the new JPS translation did not want their work to be seen as just another 'version' alongside Christian translations.

Orlinsky himself, despite his use of 'New Jewish Version' to refer to the translation in process, evidently took a great deal of pride in calling himself a scholar of *Tanakh*. Although an ecumenist, he used the term *Tanakh* regularly when describing the work he did.[13] In fact, in many ways Orlinsky embodies the tensions that I have been describing. One can only begin to imagine what it must have meant to him and his fellow Canadian and American Jews that this Jewish biblical scholar had been invited to participate in the translation of the New Revised Standard Version (NRSV) of the Bible. He was the first and only Jew to work on such a project in modern times.[14] In doing so, he helped to create the definitive translation of the biblical text for a broad North American readership, but especially for liberal Protestants (Thuesen 1999). For the NRSV was both a 'standard' and quite specifically a Protestant text, the product of a particular Protestant tradition. The inclusion of Orlinsky on the editorial board was thus a statement about ecumenical inclusion, but it also contained a rub. This would never be a 'universal' text in a sense that could include Jews. It remained a (Protestant) Christian text, and nowhere was that more apparent than in the ordering of the Old Testament books. After participating in this project, Orlinsky made his famous speech to the Jewish Publication Society, calling for a new Jewish translation. On the one hand, Orlinsky's inclusion was an honour and an affirmation of Jewish acceptance, but on the other hand it made clear, at least to him, the limits of this same act of inclusion. The text that he had helped create was never going to speak to him *as a Jew*.

In answer to my question about the decision to name the 1985 JPS translation *TANAKH*, Ellen Frankel wrote, 'I am not sure that it was the wisest move since we [JPS] don't get "shelved" in Bible sections of bookstores and many people still don't know what it is, but it was a valiant decision and may pay off in the end' (Ellen Frankel, personal communication, 30 July 2002). In fact, over twenty years and numerous reprintings, the Jewish Publication Society is still struggling to make the Hebrew Bible known as a *Jewish* text. It still gets lost on bookstore shelves and, as a result, is not as widely available to non-Jewish readers as other versions of the Hebrew Bible. It is not picked up by general readers unfamiliar with the acronym behind the title *Tanakh*. In this as in other respects, the most recent Jewish translation of the Hebrew Bible into English remains a contestable property. My hope is that this essay will have helped to explain this situation and at the same time make plain the power of the liberal legacy to keep such ambivalences alive and well in contemporary America.

NOTES

1 I want to thank Matthew Mitchell for his research assistance as I began work on this essay. I express my appreciation to Phil Miller, Ellen Frankel, and Jonathan Sarna for talking to me about these issues. I thank David Watt for his editorial suggestions and helpful comments on earlier drafts of this essay, and I am especially grateful to Catherine Staples for her keen eye and expert editorial assistance with various drafts of this essay. I also want to thank the editors of this volume, especially Robert Daum, for helping me make this a stronger essay.

2 For example, a memo to a distributor in Kingsport, TN, dated 8 July 1985, reads: 'Our Bible: entitled Tanakh,' which may suggest that there had been some confusion on the point (JPS Papers).

3 This term comes from the theology of Liberal Judaism and Christianity, and is exemplified in classical Reform Judaism and the theology of

Hermann Cohen in the early twentieth century. For more on Cohen, see Jospe 1971. On the ongoing legacy of this kind of theological position, especially among Reform Jews, as well as other positions, see Borowitz 1995 and 1978.

4   Unlike either Protestant or Catholic translations, the JPS translation, as its name implies, orders the text in a distinctly Jewish way. The *Tanakh* begins like other translations but starts to diverge after the first five books. There are minor variations in the order of the prophetic texts, but the most profound difference is that the *Tanakh* ends with Writings – specifically with 1 and 2 Chronicles – and not prophetic texts as the Old Testament does for Christian readers. Moreover, the name *Tanakh* is itself an oddity in English. It is a phonetic translation of the Hebrew acronym, which in English becomes a proper noun as the name of the JPS text. The 1985 translation was the culmination of a long series of translations that also followed from the Jewish ordering of the biblical text. The one-volume edition brings together three formerly separate JPS translations: the 1962 translation of the Torah text, the 1978 translation of *Nevi'im*, and finally the 1982 translation of *Ketuvim*. This is a point made by the writer Jack Miles. In his biography of God, Miles makes a point of following the Jewish order of the text. See Miles 1995.

5   There is a whole legacy of modern English translations in the British context, including the influential British Standard revisions and the British Jewish Soncino and Herz translations and commentaries. I thank Richard Menkis for reminding me of this other important tradition of Jewish translation into English, during the question-and-answer period following my original presentation of this material. On the place of the Hebrew Bible and its translations in a Western European context, see Cohen 2002.

6   On this history, see Sarna and Sarna 1988, esp. 87.

7   On these issues see Abu El-Haj 2001 and Benvenisti 2000.

8   As Sarna and Sarna explain, these translations were increasingly done by both American and Israeli biblical scholars, with the editors even meeting in Israel (110–11).

9   Here I have in mind especially the Puritans, who worked to distinguish themselves as a counter-reformation movement by reclaiming the legacy of the Old Testament, as they imagined themselves fulfilling G-d's promise in what would become the United States. See Zaikai 1992.

10   An example of this can be found in Genesis 48 and 49, in which Jacob divides his estate among his sons and two grandsons.

11   For a more charged reading of this question, see Schwartz 1997.

12   See, for example, Ariel 1991.

13 In 1975, on Shimon Weber's Yiddish radio show on WEVD in New York, he corrected Weber when he introduced him as a world-famous Bible scholar and instead used the term *Tanakh*. I thank Phil Miller, head librarian at HUC-JIR in New York, for this story. Telephone conversation, February 2003.

14 Orlinsky took pride in his 'minority' status in this undertaking, not only as a Jew but also as a Canadian citizen. See Orlinsky and Bratcher 1991, 'Appendix: The Canadian Connection,' 311–14.

REFERENCES

Abu El-Haj, Nadia. 2001. *Facts on the Ground: Archaeological Practice and Territorial Self-Fashioning in Israeli Society*. Chicago: University of Chicago Press.

Ariel, Yaakov. 1991. *On Behalf of Israel: American Fundamentalist Attitudes towards Jews, Judaism, and Zionism*. Brooklyn, NY: Carlson Publishing.

Benvenisti, Meron. 2000. *Sacred Landscape: The Buried History of the Holy Land since 1948*. Berkeley: University of California Press.

Bhabha, Homi. 1994. 'Of Mimicry and Man: The Ambivalence of Colonial Discourse.' *October* 28.1 (1994), 125–33.

Borowitz, Eugene. 1978. *Reform Judaism Today: Book One, Reform in the Process of Change*. New York: Behrman House.

– 1995. *Choices in Modern Jewish Thought: A Partisan Guide*. 2nd ed. West Orange, NJ: Behrman House.

Butler, Judith. 1999. *Gender Trouble*. New York: Routledge.

Cohen, Richard. 2002. 'Urban Visibility and Biblical Visions: Jewish Culture in Western and Central Europe in the Modern Age.' In David Biale, ed., *Cultures of the Jews: A New History*, 731–96. New York: Schocken Books.

Ezrahi, Sidra. 2000. *Booking Passage: Exile and Homecoming in Modern Jewish Imagination*. Berkeley: University of California Press.

Jakobsen, Janet. 1998. *Working Alliances*. Bloomington: Indiana University Press.

Jewish Publication Society Papers. Philadelphia Jewish Archives Center, Philadelphia.

Jospe, Eva, trans. 1971. *Reason and Hope: Selections from the Jewish Writings of Hermann Cohen*. New York: Norton.

Levitt, Laura. 1997. *Jews and Feminism: The Ambivalent Search for Home*. New York: Routledge.

Miles, Jack. 1995. *God, A Biography*. New York: Knopf.

Orlinsky, Harry, and Robert Bratcher. 1991. *A History of Bible Translation and the North American Contribution*. Atlanta, GA: Society of Biblical Literature.

Sarna, Jonathan. 1989. *JPS: The Americanization of Jewish Culture 1888–1988*. Philadelphia: Jewish Publication Society.

Sarna, Jonathan, and Nahum Sarna. 1988. 'Jewish Bible Scholarship and Translation in the United States.' In Ernst Frerichs, ed., *The Bible and Bibles in America*. Atlanta, GA: Scholars Press.

Schwartz, Regina. 1997. *The Curse of Cain: The Violent Legacy of Monotheism*. Chicago: University of Chicago Press.

Silk, Mark. 1984. 'Notes on the Judeo-Christian Tradition in America.' *American Quarterly* 36.1 (Spring 1984), 65–85.

Thuesen, Peter. 1999. *In Discordance with the Scriptures: American Protestant Battles over Translating the Bible*. New York: Oxford University Press.

Zaikai, Avihu. 1992. *Exile and Kingdom: History and Apocalypse in the Puritan Migration to America*. Cambridge: Cambridge University Press.

5

Recalling the Nation's Terrain: Narrative, Territory, and Canon (Commentary on Part One)

ROBERT A. DAUM

The forms of colonialist power differ radically across cultural locations, and its intersections with other orders of oppression are always complex and multivalent. But, wherever a globalised theory of the colonial might lead us, we need to remember that resistances to colonialist power always find material presence at the local, and so the research and training we carry out in the field of post-colonialism, whatever else it does, must always find ways to address the local, if only on the order of material applications.

Steven Slemon, 'The Scramble for Post-Colonialism'[1]

Postcolonial readings of nationalist narratives abstracted from textual representations can never be interrogated, unsettled, and complicated sufficiently. Nationalist narratives distort competing narratives, whose presence and social significance may be beyond our ken. The authors, transmitters, and readers of such texts in the past are likely to have had multiple and conflicted identities. Any text represents a compressed cultural moment in a lost conversation amidst myriad other lost conversations. Postcolonial analyses of cultural phenomena, including my own, are not immune to charges of reductivism:

> For all its talk of difference, plurality, heterogeneity, postmodern theory often operates with quite rigid binary opposition, with difference, plurality and allied terms lined up bravely on one side of the theoretical fence as unequivocally positive, and whatever their antithesis might be (unity, identity, totality, universality) lined up on the other. (Eagleton 1996, 34)[2]

With a deep appreciation for the enormous challenges facing, and the significant achievements of, each contributor in Part One, I shall raise some questions with the aim of engaging my three colleagues and others in a constructive conversation about postcolonial theory, interpreting sacred literatures, sacral nationalism, and comparative religious study.

Sacral Nationalism

Donald Akenson's ambitious and very readable chapter can be located within the broad genre of nationalism studies; 'sacral nationalism' is its subgenre. He outlines a straightforward ideological framework or, to use Foucauldian terminology, the rules of formation of several different 'national' discourses.[3] Drawing on an impressive breadth of reading and an array of different cases from antiquity to modernity, Akenson boils down the complexities of foundational myths, sacred texts, heresiologies, and leadership factions in order to identify the 'tricks' of authority construction and nationalist ideology. By 'tricks' he means categories of tropological elements or discursive rules (presuming control of a name, title to a territory, and so on) constituting the authoritative national ideology of each of his several cases.[4]

Akenson draws on a rich scholarly tradition, to which his work makes a provocative contribution.[5] Moving beyond a model of 'ideological diffusion,'[6] Akenson's attention to the agency of elites in his various cases synthesizes ideological and sociological diffusion models of nationalism. Identifying necessary elements of sacral nationalism in very different societies is an ambitious objective.[7] The critical comments that follow are posed in the interest of sharpening and pursuing the lines of analysis that Akenson presents in his chapter.

Akenson is right to underscore the cultural importance of the date of the ninth of Av (47). This comes to serve as a symbolic date onto which other major calamities of Jewish history are collapsed retroactively, from antiquity to modernity. Certainly the destruction is likely to have had a massive impact, and facilitated the eventual eclipse of the Temple-based priesthood. The latter's collapse also provided support for a range of theological and political polemics. Akenson's references to the site's architectural fame are well supported. The site's place in the symbol system of the Temple cult, its meaning in competing value systems, historic associations with it, its role as the foundation of the

Temple-city's hierarchy and economy, and its influence as liturgical and pilgrimage site were unsurpassed for Judeans. In light of the fact, however, that readings of the impact of the Temple's destruction are based disproportionately on a series of *ex post facto* textual representations of the meaning of that event within rabbinic and other motivated sources, a scrupulously diachronic and nuanced analysis is essential.[8]

Catherine Hezser has demonstrated that the Talmud Yerushalmi is nearly silent about Jerusalem (Hezser 2000, 11–49). Isaiah Gafni highlights ambivalent Babylonian amoraic traditions about the Land of Israel, suggesting that some Diaspora Jews felt at home in Mesopotamia (Gafni 1997). Now, one might respond that this is evidence of the ultimate success of the five-hundred-year rabbinic project of replacing the metropole, but I wonder whether that would not be begging the question. There likely were Judeans, Galileans, and, of course, Samaritans who were not devastated by the Temple's destruction.[9] In antiquity right up through the Second Temple era there were competing cultic sites, some of which Judean kings and Hasmonean monarchs sacked. Akenson does not discuss the anti-Temple and anti-priestly discourse (clearly not always the same thing, and some of which is better classified as critical than as anti-Temple rhetoric) of the Second Temple era, which is common to New Testament, Qumran sectarian and rabbinic traditions. Undoubtedly the Temple's destruction changed a fundamental component of the political and cultural landscape; but a variety of cultural and social forces brought about the changes that followed its destruction.[10] Akenson insightfully identifies some important tropes *comprising* rabbinic ideology, but one may be left with the inadvertent impression that these ideological 'tricks' *constituted* rabbinic culture and authority. These tropes may have been necessary causes, but were they sufficient causes of rabbinism?[11]

Daniel Boyarin suggests that 'Judaism was well underway to redefining its locativity and "transferring of shrine imagery to the new community," even before the Temple was destroyed, so we need something else to account for the crisis that produces "religion."' For Boyarin, Justin Martyr (whom he credits with the 'promulgation,' if probably not the invention, of the trope *Verus Israel*) and the Mishnah 'are engaged in the construction of the borders of orthodoxy via the production of the others who are outside. These are heretics, the *minim*, the *gnostikoi*.'[12] Boyarin cites Shaye Cohen's helpful observation that 'the air of crisis which pervades the apocalypses of Baruch and Ezra is conspicuously absent from tannaitic [second- and third-century

rabbinic] literature, even those dicta ascribed to Yavnean figures ...
And even the apocalypses of Baruch and Ezra [are not] concerned with
the cessation of the sacrificial cult *per se*' (Cohen 1984, 28). For Boyarin,
'the defense of orthodoxy through the propagation of the succession list
was a mutual invention of both Christians and Jews at about the same
time, without any clear possibility of assigning priorities and imita-
tions' (Boyarin 2003, 315).[13]

Binary oppositions are not only employed by heresiologists. Akenson
sketches a neat, binary opposition between a 'blood-letting priesthood'
and a 'law-splitting Rabbinate' (47). Complicating this picture is that
the priests also were splitting laws;[14] therefore, they too were legal
scholars, and the rabbis ventured into ritual slaughtering in both texts
and butcher shops. The implication in Sifre Deuteronomy (and elsewhere) is that priests acted as judges in non-ritual cases as well as in
ritual cases. Recognizing that priests were juridical rivals, not merely
cultic functionaries, strengthens Akenson's model. Akenson rightly
points to rabbinic discourse that regards the rabbis as the 'equivalent of
the ancient priests' (49–50). Some rabbis seem to have sought to take the
place of the priests in receiving tithes, some sought mourning rites not
applicable to priests, and rabbinic texts debated whether sanctity akin
to that of the Temple city inhered in, accrued to, or hovered over rabbinic sites outside of Jerusalem. As a sign of rabbinic compromise with
the traditional hereditary priesthood, priests retained special privileges
in synagogue rites and communal life for centuries after 70 CE. The
descendants of priests and Levites still hold some of these privileges. In
some texts the classical rabbis claimed to be the successors of the ancient magistrates, *not* the priests.[15] Moreover, the priests, who also
should not be seen as an undifferentiated social class, were not un-
rivalled rulers either.

Akenson writes that only one faction from pre-70 – the Pharisaic faction – 'is represented in the rabbinic corpus' (48). One problem is that
we possess no Pharisaic texts, only rabbinic texts, so reconstructing precisely who the Pharisees were on the basis of references in the New
Testament, Josephus, and a few rabbinic sources is difficult. All these
sources are motivated to portray Pharisaism in particular ways that
complicate our efforts to reconstruct the historical situation.[16] Second,
rabbinic literature preserves anti-Pharisaic polemics, including a 'hypo-
critical Pharisee' trope found in the New Testament; the relationship
between Pharisees and the rabbis is not entirely clear.[17] Third, priestly
ideology also can be found in the rabbinic corpus, which is not

surprising, inasmuch as there were priests among the ranks of rabbis. Fourth, it is conceivable that some of what Josephus classifies as Essene notions made their way into the rabbinic corpus, and in any event, priests were not the only groups for whom purity was a very important issue.[18] Fifth, if the so-called Damascus Covenant found its way into the Cairo Geniza, one has to consider the possibility that, just as all the priests, priestly traditions, and loyalty to a cultic system centred in Jerusalem did not disappear in 70 CE (an increasingly held position in the field, due to evidence from excavations of Byzantine-era synagogues), other pre-70 'factions' also may have left an imprint on rabbinic teachings. Diachronic reconstruction of the complex social spectrum within which, eventually, rabbinic and Christian orthodoxies emerged is frustrated by the sources reflecting a retroactive, synchronic flattening of traces of disparate traditions and the suppression of moderate or hybridized positions and identities.[19]

Similar problems complicate the task of reconstructing the history of rabbinic–Samaritan relations. Akenson hypothesizes that, in order to claim the name Israel, the rabbis had to displace the Samaritans, 'whom the rabbis despised' (49), because the Samaritans were genealogically more proximate Israelites than the rabbis. The stark simplicity of this formulation may distract a reader from appreciating Akenson's shrewd insights regarding the discursive power of claiming the name 'Israel.' Rabbinic views regarding the Samaritans are conflicted. Akenson is on solid ground to claim that the Samaritans (*Kuthim*) served as a theoretical other for the rabbis, but it is not correct to say simply that the rabbis despised the Samaritans; these attitudes should be read diachronically and examined in the context of regional political, social, and economic tensions. Likewise, New Testament references to the Samaritans are complex. Regional tensions between 'Samaritans' and Jerusalem-oriented Judeans in antiquity are well attested.[20] In the context of a consideration of identity on the basis of tithing practices, Judah the Patriarch ('Rabbi') and his father are cited as authorities holding radically divergent positions: '"A Samaritan is like a Gentile" – in the words of Rabbi. Rabban Simeon b. Gamaliel says: "A Samaritan is like an Israelite."'[21] Akenson's characterization of the rabbis' antipathy towards the Samaritans should be reckoned with the extracanonical tractate *Kuthim*, which includes statements acknowledging the greater stringency in Samaritan observance of some legal traditions. In the context of the tractate, this greater stringency is not necessarily always a point of criticism. To be sure, there is a good deal more negative than positive material about Samaritans in the rabbinic corpus, *Kuthim* poses many historical problems, and hostile attitudes prevail in time; still, the statement needs to be modified.[22]

Akenson's statement that 'most of the better scholars were in diasporal lands (thus the most impressive of the rabbinic texts is the Babylonian Talmud)' (49) calls for comment. Certainly, the Babylonian Talmud is a more highly edited anthology. It bears noting, however, that the bulk of the Babylonian Talmud was edited at least 150 years later than the Palestinian Talmud, and editorial work may have continued for generations. Moreover, current scholarship is coming to recognize the degree to which the Palestinian Talmud has been unfavourably judged, largely because it is unlike the Babylonian Talmud, as well as owing to manuscript problems, rather than because it is inferior on its own terms.[23] Furthermore, his statement privileging the Babylonian rabbis does not account for the fact that much of the classic midrashic literature is attributed to Palestinian sources, that the Babylonian Talmud also contains Palestinian rabbis' teachings (albeit some likely modified and others possibly invented), and that some very important scholarly work was done in Palestine right up to the First Crusade, including the textual productions of the Masoretic scribes, as well as the liturgical poetry known as *piyyutim*.[24] Here again, subsequent literary developments complicate the reconstruction of earlier historical developments.

Akenson states that the 'Mishnah ... does not care about origins' (50), but as he notes subsequently, this is the purpose served by *m. Abot* 1:1, parallels in *m. Eduyyot*, and other iterations of what is known as the 'chain of tradition.' Perhaps one should say that the Mishnah and (purportedly amoraic collections of presumably) tannaitic traditions generally are both radically discontinuous *and* explicitly continuous. Akenson writes (47) that the challenge for the rabbis was 'how to create a new religion – new circumstances, new religion – while maintaining with a straight face that they were merely continuing the old.' He only seems to recognize the 'Yeshua-faith' (in the first century CE, thereafter 'Christians') as serious competitors in the consciousness of the rabbis.[25] I wonder whether Akenson's model implicitly relies too heavily on the rabbis' retroactive reconstructions of their own importance (seeing them as already ensconced at Yavneh or even in the Galilee after Bar Kokhba).[26] In addition, the relative coherence of rabbinic theology, authority, and law (as described, for example, in the writings of Rav Sherira or Maimonides) should be seen as a retroactive representation of rabbinic origins.

Akenson is right to note the significance of sources emphasizing rabbinic origins as fundamentally continuous with ancient (pre-rabbinic) legal institutions (*m. Avot* 1 is perhaps the most famous case), but intriguingly, other sources take a different approach.[27] For example, the mishnaic tractate *'Eduyot* represents a process of considerable innovation, and a body of legislation attributed to the legendary figure Rabban Yohanan b. Zakkai is presented as, in some ways, assertively discontinuous with Second Temple era traditions. Still, the scandal of *innovatio* in the Roman legal context, the disapprobation of traditions lacking an authoritative lineage (*isnad*) in the Islamic legal context, in combination with a complex dialectical formation of rabbinic/Talmudic orthodoxy, contributed to the shaping of an explicitly conservative and a functionally also very innovative legal, religious, and political culture.[28]

Akenson (50) characterizes the spirit of the Mishnah as 'here are the rules; now get on with them.' He allows that this approach 'does not satisfy an audience that places heavy emphasis upon contact with origins and that distrusts anything avowedly new,' whereupon he analyses 'two attempts at pedigree.' The first is tractate Avot's tradition chain and its associated 'spiritual genealogy,' as he nicely puts it. The second is the underpinnings (the 'plinth' [51]) of the later idea of the 'dual Torah,' that is, the claim that rabbinic Oral Torah also was revealed at Sinai, together with the Written Torah. Indeed, these are powerful elements constituting rabbinic attempts to regulate social relations in ways that promote their pre-eminent role, textual anthologies, institutions, and values. But once again, the linear model implies a degree of self-conscious production by virtually autonomous political actors and ideologues.

Regarding the Mishnah's genres, Akenson notes the extent to which aggadic material narrates (and contributes profoundly to the construction of) the rabbis' authority. A characterization of the Mishnah as a collection of laws does not convey the very complex rhetorical features of the legal documents; also, the relationship between the two genres (commonly reduced to law and narrative, for heuristic purposes) is not explained.[29] As well, the Mishnah's rhetorical structure presents enough minority traditions to unsettle the notion that it served merely as a set of operative rules. It is not even clear that it was promoted for this purpose, although that is a plausible inference, and in time it became authoritative.[30]

Akenson captures well some of the ways in which the rabbis promote themselves and (what becomes) their pre-eminent social practice

– textual study – as the natural successors to the priests and the Temple cult. His identification of particularly significant tropes is shrewd. But his narrative may give one the inadvertent impression either that the rabbis came virtually out of nowhere or that they more or less picked up where the Pharisees left off. He endorses the important notion that the rabbis worked hard to promote the venerability of their lineage – their spiritual genealogy, as it were – over and against competing claims (like those of priests, Samaritans, or Yeshua followers).

Relating, however, and not only comparing rabbinic developments to the formation of Christian orthodoxy (and, later, to the early stages in the formation of Islamic orthodoxy) might show how implicated Jewish, Christian, and Muslim scholars were in the wider social contexts of their societies.

Akenson has made a useful contribution to the analysis of sacral nationalism by identifying common themes or symbolic categories in the ideologies of disparate cultures. Comparing such phenomena in non-reductive ways is virtually impossible, but his discussion of biblical and rabbinic cultures would be enriched by diachronically contextualizing developments in rabbinic textual practice and ideology in order to demonstrate how, where, and when the various discursive rules or 'tricks' constituting rabbinic authority claims were constructed (and resisted). Each of these literary tropes has a complex history, and while positivistic reconstructions on the basis of heavily redacted anthologies of rabbinic literature are notoriously problematic, it is at least possible to trace some of the literary record of dominant and counter-traditions. Current scholarship is increasingly cognizant of the importance of locating rabbinic cultural practices in contemporary socio-cultural contexts.[31]

Edward Said's notion of contrapuntal reading underscores the importance of incorporating considerations of power relations in which the dominant and dominated in any social context are situated.[32] Homi Bhabha illuminates how the narration of nation reveals ambivalent attitudes and approaches to national narratives. These performances engender heterogeneity, which opens up the hybridity, the between space, inhabited by the subjects of the national narrative. The result is an unsettling of the serene portrait of an abstract nation-space.[33] Sparke insightfully notes how Bhabha's 'rhetorical elevation of ambivalence abstracts away from the actual organization and violence of power relations' as well as the 'erasure of the state,' but he argues that 'Bhabha offers no account of the historical production of abstract space.'[34]

Akenson's model offers a useful analytical framework for tracking this production; its application here would be strengthened by incorporating contrapuntal, heterogeneous, and contextualized readings of his rabbinic sources.

In the tradition of much contemporary postcolonial scholarship, Akenson's historiographic narrative has a moral;[35] of course, so do sacral nationalisms. Lloyd Kramer has articulated an interesting resemblance between some national myths and some scholarly studies of these myths:

> Nationalists typically describe their nations by emphasizing how they differ from others, so the history of nationalisms could be described on one level as a history of intellectual dichotomies (self/other) that create hierarchies of value. In this respect, much of the historical literature about nationalism replicates the intellectual tendencies of nationalist cultures, because it also categorizes cultures in terms of historical differences and contrasting patterns of 'good' or 'bad' development. (Kramer 1997, 541)

The moral note with which Akenson's chapter concludes finds an echo in Nabil Matar's postcolonial reading of Renaissance cartography, to which this commentary now turns. At many points Matar's analysis is richly textured. I suggest, however, that beneath the serene non-territoriality of the Ottoman Empire's sacred manifesto are a web of untidy power relations, occlusions of subaltern agency, and overlapping territorial claims and regimes.

Ortelius's Map: The Spectre of Comparison

Richard Helgerson analyses, as Matthew Sparke puts it, the phenomenon of state cartography in Elizabethan England: 'the recursive proleptic effects of mapping – the way maps contribute to the construction of spaces that later they seem only to represent ... as if the land itself spoke of the kingdom as a single state.'[36] Matar's study is solidly rooted in this scholarly tradition, but his approach would be strengthened by complicating the cartographic power relationship.[37] While Ortelius's anachronistic imposition of a form of biblical template on a colonialist map is justifiably read as a radically colonizing gesture, in theory it could also be read as a subversive statement – that is, as a subversion of Ottoman hegemony, if one unsettles the picture of the *sanjak* of Syria to disclose a microgeographic view of occupied Palestine (or of occupied

Mt Gerizim in ancient Samaria, to consider another sacral national tradition). The fact that Ortelius's map can *also* be read as an egregious tool of Spanish imperialist ambition – like so many other such maps representing the territories towards which the Spanish ventured violently in this period – does not delegitimize a counter-reading of this *sanjak* as itself a colonized territorial entity, containing a heterogeneous mix of people with attachments to the land and a self-awareness of (competing and highly complicated) notions of indigeneity.

The contrapuntal juxtapositioning of maps derived from radically different cultural contexts invites the viewer to confront different notions of the territories that they depict, but the fundamental spatial and semiotic differences represented by two oppositional maps can lead a viewer to reify one or both of the elements in the opposition. *The more binary one's reading of the opposition between the elements in this pairing, the more that the constructedness of each of the elements in the binary is obscured.*[38] Matar's analysis shows us how the map's biblicizing depiction of a reconstituted tribal confederation in sixteenth-century Palestine can also be read as a romantic conjuring of an imagined terrain of biblical tribes positioned to finally recognize the messiahship of Jesus Christ. He shows how it implicitly marks an erasure of then present-day societies, and he reveals its implication in classic supersessionist theology. He also persuasively connects it to Spanish imperial ambitions, a wider context of Spanish conquests and displacements, and theological notions of restoration in a terrain emptied of Arabs and Turks. Noting that 'Arabic and Turkish writers of the early modern period often mention in their travels and histories the "land of Palestine" (*ard filasteen*) or "the land of Jerusalem" (*ard al-Quds*)' (68), he nonetheless does not interrogate the use of these names as a homogenizing, colonizing erasure of local differences, of competing homogenous nation-space narratives, of other names for these same places. Matar critiques one colonizing cartography but not another, an asymmetry that detracts from the analytical power of his fascinating study.

The interesting point that he is trying to make is undermined by what he implicitly takes to be the real territory ruled by the Ottoman Empire, and which was eclipsed or suppressed by Ortelius' map. He refers to 'the reality of Arabo-Ottoman Palestine' (75). Certainly all three elements in this signifier – 'Arabo-Ottoman Palestine' – can be justified. 'Arabo-' legitimately designates the language spoken by most of the inhabitants of the land in the sixteenth century. 'Ottoman' is a legitimate label for the imperial power ruling the region, and 'Palestine' would have been an intelligible designation to many inhabitants and onlookers. Still, given our postcolonial preoccupations here, the assertion of facticity calls for comment. Notwithstanding the names applied to this place by others in the sixteenth century, including colonizers and colonized, the author asserts that there is an implicitly indisputable, Arabo-Ottoman Palestine 'reality.' Bear in mind that the territory was conquered by the Ottomans only in 1517, whereas 'Palestine,' 'Holy Land,' 'Land of Israel,' and various other signifiers have older (also contested!) lineages. As Matar's analysis demonstrates convincingly, naming 'Palestine' is a political act, but classifying as faith-based one act of naming that contested terrain and calling another 'empirical' is problematic.

Matthew Sparke notes the value in Said's notion of reading contrapuntally 'to break down singularized and unidirectional understandings of the culture of imperialism' (Sparke 1998, 467); as Said puts it, contrapuntal reading facilitates 'a simultaneous awareness both of the metropolitan history that is narrated and of those other histories against which (and together with which) the dominating discourse acts' (Said 1993, 51). Matar's analysis broadens our understanding of how maps are the products 'of contested social practices,' but the inadvertent impression seems to be that the Ottoman maps got it right. All (conventional) maps simultaneously enact erasure and inscription, representing a single layer on a palimpsest of competing colonialist (and anticolonialist) visions.

The fact that contemporaneous Ottoman maps (and the non-Palestine regions of Ortelius's map), to which he makes reference, were grounded in empirical *realia*, while the map's depiction of Palestine seems to have derived from biblical traditions, does not remove Ottoman maps (or the non-Palestine portions of Ortelius's map) from the genre of colonizing discourse. To be sure, comparatively speaking, the Palestine portion of Ortelius's map looks like a poster-child for colonial discourse; but perhaps precisely because of the stark and immediately apparent contrast between the map's two zones (or between Ottoman maps and the Palestine portion of Ortelius's map), Matar seems to impute to these cartographic representations a quality of stable, uncontestable *reality*. The fact that one imperial map is demonstrably less anachronistic than another does not make it 'real'; it only naturalizes one particular empire. If we have appropriately lost our confidence in 'the real,' on what basis can we exchange our nominalist for our realist spectacles when reading only one empire's map? In fact, it may be precisely when a text appears to exhibit a relatively high degree of verisimilitude that its implication in power relations is particularly well hidden. As Philip Alexander observes, 'It is important ... [not] to make too sharp a distinction between theological/mythological cartography on the one hand and real/scientific cartography on the other. *All* maps arguably express a worldview, some more explicitly than others' (Alexander 1992, 978).

Given the theoretical untenability of toponymic essentialism, maps only *appear* to settle things.[39] Matar's study shrewdly highlights the temporal contrasts embedded in Ortelius's representation of the space of the Levant, and especially how a particular biblical cartography[40] is deployed within a Renaissance map ostensibly depicting a sixteenth-century reality. But the sixteenth-century geopolitical reality with which he contrasts Ortelius's cartographic gesture – that Ottoman jurisdiction over the Syrian *sanjak* containing Palestine was backed by imperial power recognized by other great states of the time – calls for comment. The use of administrative terminology (such as 'the Syrian *sanjak*') to signify the contested space of sixteenth-century Palestine does not necessarily reify an Ottoman imperial narrative, but I wonder whether its usage to buttress the verisimilitude of Ottoman maps and the non-Palestine portion of Ortelius's map (contrasted with the 'pious' portrayal of a biblical Palestine) ironically re-enacts Ottoman cartographic imperialism. Matar makes a compelling case that Ottoman maps lack 'theological contortions' *like those in Ortelius's map*, but I fail to see how the absence of theological contortions negates the character of an Ottoman map as a justification of (ex) 'post facto conquest' (68). Maps are inherently 'cartographic inventions,' and at least implicitly, imperial maps justify those conquests.

Cognitive mapping is not necessarily inscribed only in maps.[41] In the final section of his chapter, Matar contrasts two essentialized figures in a binary pairing: biblical territoriality on the one hand and qur'anic non-territoriality on the other. Most Bibles contain maps, he notes; no Qur'an does so. To be sure, the Qur'an is not territorial in the way that the Bible is territorial, but this does not mean that the Qur'an is non-territorial altogether. The Ottoman and other Muslim empires' colonialist adventures were neither the ineluctable consequences of, nor essentially antithetical to, qur'anic spatiality. (I would make the same claim about biblical territorial notions.) Qur'anic and post- or extra-qur'anic spatialities should be differentiated, just as biblical (and post- or extra-biblical) spatialities are not undifferentiated thought complexes. It seems to me that Matar is quite correct to contrast biblical and qur'anic territoriality in important respects; what I question is the absolute distinction that he seems to draw. First, I shall try to unsettle the notion of qur'anic non-territoriality, and then I shall seek to unsettle the notion of biblical territoriality. I claim that the Bible and the Qur'an contain both territorial and non-territorial ideologies, but that neither scripture can be reduced to an essential territorialism or non-territorialism, and that a reifying binary opposition is inadequate.

At the macro-geographic level, the Qur'an represents two fundamental spatial domains: 'the abode of Islam' and 'the abode of war.'[42] This can be seen as a colonizing territorial ideology justifying both prior and subsequent conquests, much as biblical warrants of promised lands, divinely sanctioned wars, and a world under divine rule can be seen as colonizing notions.[43] Characterizing the territoriality of *dar al-Islam* is by no means simple. Using biblical territoriality/ies as the basis for comparison is problematic. Parvin and Sommer suggest a nuanced approach: 'Dar al-Islam is not, then, inherently a territorial concept. Rather, it is a legal construct that has a territorial dimension: a territorial expression of the *umma* (the Islamic community) which itself has a political component' (Parvin and Sommer 1980, 4). Parvin and Sommer suggest that 'this nonsentimental absence of attachment to the soil ... contributes to a dynamism or fluidity in the establishment of territorial extent' (8).[44] Moreover, it was 'the relative isolation of settlements which made vital the control of access routes [that engendered] an expansionist attitude in the context of ensuring protection and maintenance of economic activity' (9). Gardet points to the economic interests of Arab governors as important factors encouraging early Muslim colonization (Gardet 1954, 19). Parvin and Sommer suggest that urbanism was another important factor accounting for the evolution of territoriality in Islam, as colonizers were able to adapt relatively easily to urban centres newly incorporated into their realm (Parvin and Sommer 1980, 10).

As Islam spread, particular sites within urban centres (and beyond) took on great importance, just as various sites took on new importance in the sacred geographies of medieval Christianity and Judaism. Inside the spatial confines of *dar al-Islam*, one can map within a sacred geography cities containing important mosques (Mecca, Medina, al-Quds) as well as larger zones, such as the city of Mecca, and even Arabia as the region containing Mecca and Medina (Firestone 1999, 38).

In addition, an important, predominantly temporal trope in the Qur'an – *jahaliyya* – has territorial implications, just as various biblical tropes have both temporal and spatial aspects.[45] Unredeemed time is implicitly coextensive with unredeemed space. Just as the juxtaposi-tioning of antiquity and early modernity within Ortelius's map flattens past and (then) present to cohere with a particular colonial narrative, so too the periodization of sacred history into unredeemed/redeemed time (and space) through concepts such as *jahaliyya* (and in the Bible more or less similarly through temporal concepts such as pre-lapsarian/post-lapsarian, pre-Sinaitic/post-Sinaitic, pre-Conquest/ post-Conquest, and so on) can function as authorizations for the con-quest of particular places (after or before the fact) in the service of a sacral chronology. God's time, as it were, can be read as an authoriza-tion, if not a demand, for the conquest of God's terrestrial space.

The spatial or territorial implications of concepts that are not ex-plicitly territorial or cartographic can be underestimated. Perhaps we can see Ortelius's erasure of post-biblical Palestinian cartography (and societies) as a corollary to the Qur'an's implicit erasure of pre-Islamic societies by means of the temporal concept of *jahaliyyah*. In the former case the trope is predominantly spatial, in the latter case predominantly temporal; the colonizing force of both tropes is a result of (military and other social forms of power, needless to say, and) a combination of spa-tial and temporal displacement.[46]

As Matar suggests, the Qur'an lacks the sort of place names, specific geographic references, narrative details of itineraries, and other territor-ial tropes that are found in much of the Bible. Perhaps some of these differences can be accounted for in respect of the differences in genre between the two scriptural collections (Humphreys 1989, 276). Just as the Bible need not be our standard for defining the genre of sacred nar-rative, so too biblical cartography(ies) need not be the standard for de-fining sacred geography. Cognitive mapping and territorialisms come in various forms. Angelika Neuwirth has noted that 'toponyms are gen-erally replaced by paraphrastic characterizations or evoked through the particular sanctuaries by which they are distinguished.' She character-izes qur'anic geography as 'a topographia sacra, not profane geography ... where places are represented by emblems' (Neuwirth 2003, 381–2).

The significance of sacred sites in Muslim cultures, then, is not sim-ply a function of explicit naming in the Qur'an. The observation that the Qur'an designs 'a topographia sacra, not profane geography' can also be applied to some biblical maps, particularly in the Pentateuch. The famous lack of an explicit naming of Jerusalem in the Pentateuch can be accounted for in various ways, and Jerusalem's significance and symbology varied throughout antiquity, the Second Temple period, and later, as I discussed above.[47] Mecca, Medina, and al-Quds were not static tropes in Islamic culture. Jerusalem was the pre-eminent sacred site (along with Sinai) for medieval rabbinic Judaism, at least at a symbolic level (as liturgical texts illustrate), but as Matar points out, for the Renaissance period this does not necessarily translate into emigration in large numbers, as attachment to local sites in the 'diaspora' can also be detected.

In both traditions one can find 'a-geographic' emphases that Matar identifies as intrinsic to the Qur'an's nature.[48] Principal themes include the idea that sanctity is rooted in holy, pious, or theologically significant acts, rather than necessarily inhering in places (or people or objects) as such; that human possession of land is contingent on fidelity to God's law; that God owns the earth and humans are mere stewards; that some places are more important than other places because theologically significant historical events are associated with those places (Jerusalem/al-Quds, Sinai, Mecca, Hebron, etc.) or because specific religious practices are tied to those places (pilgrimage/*hajj*, temple cult, tithing, etc.). A biblical geographic trope is a potent factor in Renaissance cartography, as Matar and others have astutely demonstrated, but this does not make biblical geographies proto-colonial any more than biblical gender tropes are proto-heteronormative. Similarly, 'qur'anic' spatial tropes (e.g., *dar al-Islam, dar al-harb*) may be invoked as justification for territorial expansion, but this does not make these tropes proto-colonial. Within the Bible there is a varied and extensive set of geographic tropes; however, the starkly binary opposition between undifferentiated biblical and qur'anic mentalities and geographies is problematic.[49]

Matar appropriately notes that 'the qur'anic repudiation of the land covenant was a repudiation of the henotheism that marked some Israelite, Moabite, and Graeco-Roman localizations of their deities to specific lands' (73). That henotheism was an important element in ancient Israelite, Moabite, and Graeco-Roman cultures is clear. Moreover, the covenantal centrality of the land of Israel in biblical, talmudic, and liturgical literature implicates even diasporic identities within maps encompassing, however tangentially, homeland and diaspora. It bears noting, however, that biblical territorial tropes also are unsettled and resisted across a wide body of biblical and post-biblical rabbinic (and Christian) literature prior to and after the emergence of Islam.[50] Unfortunately, comparing a fairly static portrait of biblical territorial traditions from the first (and second?) millennium BCE (reflecting a negation or devaluation of diasporic cultures) to seventh-century Islamic repudiations of henotheism, while ignoring biblical and post-biblical (rabbinic) diasporic ideological formations, affords an incomplete picture of the many correspondences and differences between and within biblical, qur'anic, and medieval Jewish and Muslim readings of scriptural territorial tropes.

Matar observes that most Bibles contain maps; he adds that no Qur'an does so, which I assume to be correct.[51] I have not undertaken a thorough examination of the presence or absence of maps in Christian Bible editions, but a survey of Hebrew and Jewish Bible editions suggests to me that this distinction is not so clear-cut. Matar's discussion points to the usefulness of maps for following the Bible's elaborate geographical references. For editions of the Hebrew Bible or the Pentateuch, however, one needs to differentiate between, on the one hand, more or less traditional Bibles designed for liturgical use in synagogue or for religious practice at home, and, on the other hand, late modern (twentieth- to twenty-first-century) 'study Bibles.' The former, like editions of the Qur'an, typically lack maps; the latter increasingly contain them.

There is no map in either the 'old JPS' or the NJV, also known as (the) *Tanakh*.[52] Both of these JPS editions *do* contain tables of scriptural readings, and the later version also contains a glossary. The next major versions of the JPS, which combine elements of liturgical and 'study Bibles,' do contain maps.[53] Some of the Bible editions produced by scholars in the Conservative and Reform movements (at least) for synagogue use contain maps; one recent edition does not.[54] My point here is *not* that territorialism is absent from the Bible, from communities of Jewish (or Christian) readers, or from some Jewish editions of the Bible, including several published in late modernity. Rather, I wish to suggest that practical and generic considerations, as well as territorial ideologies, help to explain the presence (and the absence) of maps in some editions of the Bible published within the last century. Furthermore, I hope that I have demonstrated that the presence of maps in a great many editions of the Bible, and the absence of maps in editions of the Qur'an, can be accounted for in various ways.

In retrospect, European colonization of 'the Americas'[55] (and beyond) appears to have been relatively far more destructive than Ottoman colonization, but this should not obscure the postcolonial critic's appreciation of the Ottomans' or other Muslim empires' imperialist and colonialist practices. At the same time, reductive analysis of the rapid expansion of Muslim rule – holding that Islam only expanded through wars of conquest – denies agency to medieval Muslim converts. Matar's discussion might leave a casual reader with the impression that the Qur'an is essentially anticolonial, because it was essentially non-territorial, whereas the Bible is essentially territorial and therefore lends itself more naturally and ineluctably to colonialism.[56]

The task of cultural translation can be complicated further by attempts to reconstruct the history of particular ideas, and in this regard Restorationism is no exception.[57] Matar is careful to note that he uses the term as 'a proper noun peculiar to a distinctly English Protestant idea of Jewish conquest of Palestine in the light of the Abramic covenant' (69), but I wonder whether an understanding of a phenomenon such as sixteenth-century English Protestant Restorationism might be broadened and complicated productively by considering the manifestation of related notions prior to Willet's proposal in 1590 (70).

As Matar suggests, it seems likely that not every European Jew during the Renaissance was keen to emigrate to Palestine. Matar's focus on the supersessionist, conversionary assumptions behind British Protestant Restorationist discourse is illuminating and important. At the same time, I wonder whether, in seeking to trace Restorationism as a Protestant heresy, he overstates the point that there was 'nothing in the political or military status of Renaissance Jews to invoke such a Restoration' (69). There was a substantial migration of Jews to Palestine after 1517 (particularly to Safed, a textile centre that became famous for its Jewish scholar-mystics), which continued for the rest of the century. The catastrophic expulsions of Iberian Jews after the conquest of the Kingdom of Granada, failed efforts to block the establishment of the Inquisition in Portugal, politico-religious conflicts in Europe punctuated dramatically by the sacking of Rome by the army of Charles V, the conquests of Selim I (allusively referred to in Jewish sources as 'the scion of Cyrus'!), rumours about Jewish tribes in Arabia, and other events heightened messianic expectations within Jewish circles in numerous cities and lands. The political status of many Renaissance Jews was exceedingly problematic, and variations on Restorationism might well have struck a chord.[58]

As I have attempted to explain, Matar's observations regarding the colonizing effect of Ortelius's territorial representation of early modern Palestine, through the artifice of a cartographic displacement juxtaposing past and (then) present, is instructive. He has parsed the colonizing, anachronistic displacement of what he calls 'Arabo-Ottoman Palestine' from Ortelius's map. I have posed the question of whether a binary model differentiating an essentially non-territorial (medieval) Qur'an from an essentially territorial (ancient) Bible ironically re-enacts a displacement of alternative (that is, non-Arabo-Ottoman) territorial claims vis-à-vis sixteenth-century Palestine. I have suggested that a representation of an essential territorialism in the Bible needs to be unsettled somewhat by biblical and later counter-traditions resembling more closely what Matar characterizes as the Qur'an's a-geographic nature (or, perhaps, ambivalence about biblical geographic notions, to which Matar quite rightly draws our attention). In addition, I have tried to sketch a somewhat different, tentative way of thinking about qur'anic, Islamic, and Ottoman territoriality, in the hope of complicating what strikes me as an inadvertently reductive, binary opposition between the two elements in his comparison. Notwithstanding the questions that I have raised, Matar's very stimulating analysis makes an important contribution to our understanding of cartography as an instrument of early modern European colonialism.

Text, Territoriality, and Identity for Jews

Toni Morrison has famously written: 'Canon building is Empire building. Canon defense is national defense. Canon debate, whatever the terrain, nature and range (of criticism, of history, of the history of knowledge, of the definition of language, the universality of aesthetic principles, the sociology of art, the humanistic imagination), is the clash of cultures. And all of the interests are vested' (Morrison 1989, 8).

I employ various signifiers in different contexts – 'Tanakh,' 'Hebrew Bible,' 'Old Testament,' 'Hebrew Scriptures,' and 'First Testament,' but in English my personal preference is 'Hebrew Bible.' Levitt's chapter pushed me to reflect on the ideological implications of my use of these various terms in academic discourse (in print and in the classroom), and to consider whether such usage constitutes a colonizing (re)appropriation on the basis of an implied claim to title. Ironically, while Levitt's piece is built on the premise that the nearly complete silence of the decision-makers about the naming decision is highly significant, she too makes an unexplained naming decision. (I also do this regularly.) She does refer to other names, of course, but her consistent practice is to call it the 'Hebrew Bible.'[59] Academic writing about contested signifiers unavoidably employs particular signifiers and not others. It would be confusing to use different signifiers for the same signified, and it seems cumbersome to use compounded or hybridized, multiple signifiers for the same signified, such as *Tanakh*/Hebrew Bible.[60] In this essay I interrogate very tentatively the 'buried network of assumptions'[61] which informs our contributors' and editors' (including my own) analyses. Our fallback terminological decisions are not only convenient, but also significant.

Although the Hebrew Bible and the Old Testament are different books in respect of canon, sequence, and much else,[62] Levitt makes a persuasive argument that in popular cultural contexts, these important differences, not to mention their broader implications, are not widely understood. In view of the massive cultural prestige of 'the Bible' in American culture, her chapter seeks to trace the cultural significance of the Jewish Publication Society's decision to name its landmark 1985 American English translation 'Tanakh.' That edition relegated 'The Holy Scriptures,' which was the title of the earlier JPS translation, to the subtitle.

The full name of the 1985 edition is *Tanakh: A New Translation of THE HOLY SCRIPTURES According to the Traditional Hebrew Text.*[63] The full name of the 1955 edition of the 1917 translation is *THE HOLY SCRIPTURES According to the Masoretic Text. A New Translation with the Aid of Previous Versions and with Constant Consultation of Jewish Authorities.*[64] In the 1955 edition the English title 'The Holy Scriptures' precedes the acronym 'Tanakh' (in Hebrew) on the cover and on the spine. On the cover and spine of the 1985 translation the sequence of the terms 'Tanakh' and 'The Holy Scriptures' is reversed: now 'Tanakh' (in English transliteration) appears above the smaller-font title 'The Holy Scriptures.' Intriguingly, although the Hebrew term 'Tanakh' is found nowhere on the title page of the earlier translation, the Hebrew names for the three divisions of the Tanakh – Torah, Prophets, and Writings – do appear in Hebrew on the title page in a small, unvocalized font immediately preceding the title 'The Holy Scriptures.'[65] Another difference between the names of the two translations is the elaborate subtitle of the earlier edition, which asserts that it was produced with 'the aid of previous versions' and 'constant consultation of Jewish authorities.' Perhaps owing to the Jewish Publication Society's venerable reputation in 1985, as opposed to in 1917, assurances regarding the later translation's scholarly pedigree are found only within the preface.

Using a transliterated Hebrew name for an English language Bible translation aimed at a mass market is a significant act. Levitt is to be commended for seeking to examine this event. As Akenson writes, 'The matter of cultural identity is extremely complex, and most people have multiple identities which are exhibited according to the demands of their immediate context' (45). This makes assessments of particular exhibitions of identity very difficult, but Levitt's aim is even more daunting: her study seeks to explicate the identity implications of an essentially unexplained decision reached by a small group of people at a specific point in time.[66] Like the previous two chapters, her study is a stimulating demonstration of the complexity of postcolonial readings of scripture and its readers. Naming a Bible can be seen, *inter alia*, as a colonizing or anticolonial gesture, and it has territorial implications, albeit in a somewhat different sense than discussed earlier:

> Text, then, becomes a space in which collective identity can be formed without territory, and consequently it can be a metaphor for exile and homelessness. As Heinrich Heine claimed famously about 'the Jews': 'A book is their fatherland, their possession, their ruler … They live between the boundary markers of this book, here they exercise their inalienable civic rights, here nobody can chase them away' (1840). In this context, intertextuality, multilingualism, and translations draw attention to the hybrid space and to movements between spaces/texts. (Fonrobert 2001, 3)

The cultural production of 'standard' Bible editions can be seen as a hegemonic gesture vis-à-vis co-religionists and others. The participation of Harry Orlinsky in the NRSV translation project – a translation that was represented as a 'Standard' version – was both ironic and highly significant vis-à-vis the status of American Jewry. Orlinsky's learning, including his mastery of the Septuagint and the Masoretic traditions, was renowned. His role as the secret 'Mr. Green,' who verified some of the Dead Sea Scrolls, was the stuff of legend. Levitt reasonably considers the impact of his (conflicted) status as a Jewish member of the NRSV project team on his motivation to call for a new Jewish translation, as well as on his support for calling it by a traditional Jewish and Hebrew acronym, *Tanakh*.[67]

Levitt correctly claims that the JPS translation's sequence of books is 'distinctly Jewish,' although it bears noting that this is a convention that emerged out of other, older patterns predating rabbinic Judaism.[68] It occurs to me that while the 1985 JPS translation follows a traditional Jewish sequence, in some ways it shares more qualities with traditional diasporic translations and Western Bible translations than with traditional Jewish Bible editions. The reason is that it omits the classical commentaries, particularly the commentary of Rashi, which was standard in printed editions of the Bible since the 1517 Daniel Bomberg edition.[69] It is organized to be read like a work of literature, a book, rather than as a lectionary source in the synagogue, although it could have been (and occasionally was) used as an English 'Targum' in synagogue ritual. A more effective, although not updated, resource for that purpose, however, was available to English-speaking Jews: the Hertz Pentateuch. Later, the Union of American Hebrew Congregations's *The Torah: A Modern Commentary* was marketed to synagogues, particularly in the Reform movement.[70]

Levitt suggests that the decision to name the text 'Tanakh' without calling attention to the decision itself is emblematic of the underlying ambivalence felt by many American Jews about their place in American culture. She poses thoughtful questions about Orlinsky's identity, and her chapter subjects the surprisingly silent record about the JPS' 1985 naming decision to postcolonial critical inquiry. One of her sources is the JPS' current editor, E. Frankel, who holds the position then occupied by Chaim Potok. Frankel attributes the poor sales of the volume to the inability of Bible purchasers to locate it in bookstores where it may have been improperly shelved. This may well be the case, although a colleague recently pointed out to me that the JPS used to rely heavily on a subscription-based marketing structure, and therefore the volumes may not have been in many bookstores in the first place. I should like to propose some additional factors to account for the mixed commercial success of the 1985 publication, including religious or denominational demographics, economic considerations, and lectionary purchasing practices by synagogues and churches.

The lack of a 'traditional' Jewish commentarial framework (and a Hebrew text) in the 1985 edition may have been an impediment to some Jewish buyers. Both synagogues and individual Jews may have been more inclined to invest in editions of the Pentateuch than in a new English translation of the full Bible. The Pentateuch editions available in 1985 contained an English translation, a vocalized Hebrew text, the supplementary Haftarah portions, a table of scriptural readings for Sabbath and festivals, and a serviceable, explicitly Jewish commentary. There was only so much capacity in the typical North American synagogue budgets, pews, and bookcases. Worshippers could not hold onto a prayer book, a Pentateuch, and an English Tanakh while standing and sitting repeatedly. In time the JPS combined the Pentateuch format, relevant sections of the 1985 translation, and a superb commentarial apparatus into a new series of volumes. I wonder whether the production of a stand-alone English translation lacking either any real commentary or a Hebrew text – precisely when identification with Israel and a resurgence of Hebrew were common in English-speaking Jewish communities – was also a significant impediment to the book's commercial success.

Given that Orlinky is said to be the architect of the decision to use 'Tanakh' as the title, I share Levitt's interest in querying Orlinsky's own naming practices. I was Orlinsky's student for four years between 1982 and 1986, and I do recall that in class he invariably used the name 'Tanakh.' Regrettably, I do not remember that he ever addressed the JPS's naming decision. Outside of class – at least in print – he used a range of different names for the Hebrew Bible. This inconsistency, and particularly his purported championing of the name 'Tanakh' for the JPS translation, is precisely the basis for Levitt's query. In the title of the 1963 paper articulating his call for a new translation, Orlinsky refers to 'the new Jewish version of the Torah.' When referring to the Bible in general (both Jewish and Christian versions), he uses the term 'Bible' or 'Scriptures.'[71] When referring specifically to the Jewish or Hebrew Bible – and to neither the Christian Old (aka Second or Greek) Testament nor the combined Christian Testaments – he uses the term 'Hebrew Bible.' When he needs to differentiate between the Old Testament (OT) and the New Testament (NT) in the context of discussing Christian translations, he uses those terms. In referring to the 1917 edition, he states that the JPSA issued 'an English translation of the Hebrew Bible.'[72] At one point he refers to the ancient Alexandrian Jewish community's 'Greek version of its Sacred Scriptures, the Torah,' which of course he also identifies by the conventional name 'Septuagint.' In a paragraph in which he is comparing the 1917 JPS translation to Protestant and Roman Catholic versions, he refers to 'the 1917 Jewish version' (251). He then refers to the 1962 publication of the 'Torah,' the first component of this new JPS translation: *The Torah, The Five Books of Moses: A New Translation of the Holy Scriptures According to the Masoretic Text* (Orlinsky 1963, 252).[73] In the following sentence he introduces another designation for the full translation – 'the new Jewish version (NJV)' – in order to compare and contrast it with 'the new Protestant and Catholic versions.' He also uses the term 'Hebrew scripture' (256). He often uses the name 'NJV.'[74]

In an academic paper published in the *Journal of Biblical Literature*, the term 'Hebrew Bible' was Orlinsky's preferred academic designation for the series of translations inaugurated by the 1962 translation of the

Torah, the Five Books of Moses.[75] Nevertheless, he used 'Hebrew Bible' and 'Hebrew Scripture' interchangeably, even in two consecutive sentences (Orlinsky 1963, 264). When referring to Christian versions of the First Testament, Orlinsky did not hesitate to employ the term 'Old Testament'; this is the case in the 1963 article as well as in other contexts (Orlinsky 1952). In his 1963 article ('The New Jewish Version') Orlinsky does not once use the term 'Tanakh.' This makes the recent reports of Levitt's witnesses as to Orlinky's pivotal role in the 1985 naming decision especially intriguing.

Orlinsky's discussion of the scholarly value of the new translation is readily apparent; his confidence and pride in the significance of the translation for Christian biblical studies and for Christian culture(s) is remarkable and undisguised. After asserting that 'it is generally agreed that the Jewish philosopher Philo ... laid the ideological foundation for Christianity' and then citing H.A. Wolfson's thesis that (according to Orlinsky) 'another Jewish philosopher, Baruch Spinoza ... was mainly responsible for destroying Philonism and for giving Christianity new direction,' he states that 'it was the Jewish Septuagint version ... that set the norm for a word-for-word reproduction of the Hebrew.' The implication seems to be that Jewish scholarly productions have exercised profound, even revolutionary influence on Christian religious culture. Orlinsky's expectations for the impact of the NJV are anything but modest:

> The translation committee of NJV, reflecting the verve, growing maturity, and optimism of today's great American Jewish community, would like to believe that its new version of the Torah, in its internal and external break with the past, has set a new pattern which authorized Protestant and Catholic translations of the future will tend to follow. (Orlinsky 1963, 264)[76]

Given Orlinsky's documented, undisguised pride in the cultural significance of the (Hebrew) Bible and the NJV translation project for Jews and others, on the one hand, and, on the other hand, the almost complete silence of the historical record regarding this culturally significant but commercially problematic naming decision, Levitt's interest in this cultural moment is understandable. The lack of a paper trail explaining the 1985 decision stands in dramatic contrast with the approach taken twenty years later by the editors of *The Jewish Study Bible*.

In the introduction to *The Jewish Study Bible*, the editors explain that their naming decisions reflect the fact that theirs is a self-consciously

Jewish study Bible. They declare that for Jews there is no other (appropriate) name for the Bible. For their contributors, 'The Tanakh is "the Bible," and for this reason *The Jewish Study Bible* uses the terms "Tanakh" and "the Bible" interchangeably. We avoid the term "Hebrew Bible," a redundancy in the Jewish view. Jews have no Bible but the "Hebrew Bible"' (Berlin and Brettler 2004a, x).

This unabashedly sectarian statement is coherent, but note that the editors boldly articulate what they call 'the Jewish view.' This naming decision and its sweeping justification represent a dramatic shift away from the seeming ambiguity of the JPS's 1985 naming decision.

Naming can indeed be seen as a significant gesture, as all three chapters have illustrated. It can be an important component of colonizing discourse, and it can also be read as evidence of cultural hybridity and resistance to colonization. The effects of any ideological tropes used to promote or justify conquest are best analysed, in my judgment, in combination with a judicious consideration of personal agency and structural functionalism.[77] Even then, historical reconstruction is conjectural. Comparative analysis of putatively colonialist ideologies (or their constituent elements), actors, or institutions in different cultural contexts raises the risk of cultural mistranslation and misrepresentation. Can or should one seek to maintain an ideologically neutral position in respect of ideas, historical actors, or political institutions hypothetically responsible for egregious instances of colonialism? This is not only a question for ethicists.

Akenson's analysis elucidates the potent resonance of particular types of tropes (territory, national name, sacral text, national mythology) as rules of formation in constructing and representing power claims. His theorizing about the discursive rules of sacral nationalism is provocative and useful. Matar provides a fascinating road map with which to identify some of the ways in which maps and names rooted in sacral texts and traditions can be deployed as instruments of power, particularly but not exclusively in a colonial context. His analysis raises important questions about teleologies, essentialist approaches to scriptures, and how to define geography. Levitt presses us to think about some of the ways in which some twentieth-century American Jews may have negotiated their hybridized, postcolonial identity and status as Jews and as Americans by re-enacting patterns reminiscent of age-old discourses about names, translation, and covenantal claims. Totalizing discourse can serve a variety of ends, and the ambitious chapters by Akenson, Matar, and Levitt help to shed light on the nexus between power relations and rhetoric about, inter alia, sacral nationalism, cartography, and canon.

Responses

Nabil Matar

I am grateful to Professor Daum for his comments. They were both challenging and detailed, and I am not sure I can address them all fully. But here are some thoughts:

1. Professor Daum states that maps can operate 'against colonialism,' but I am not sure that it is possible to read Ortelius's map of Palestine in that manner. For a start, while the Ottomans were, of course, imperialists, they did not obliterate contemporary history and ethnography in their maps. Ottoman cartography of the Eastern Mediterranean shows that the new conquerors retained the place names of the regions they conquered, and did not, as Ortelius does in the Palestine map, rename and reshape geography. I am unable to see how Ortelius's map can be counter-read as a statement about Ottoman colonization of a 'territorial entity containing a heterogeneous mix of people with attachments to the land.' On what is this counter-reading to be based? If the intention of Ortelius was to present the past of the regions he mapped, then why are we not shown that in as explicit a manner as he does in the map of Tunisia, which, Ortelius explains, had been conquered by Charles V in 1535? The Ottoman conquest was just a couple of decades earlier. Past imperial action was precisely presented – which is not the case in this map.

One of the surviving Ottoman atlases belongs to the same year as Ortelius's, 1570. *Atlas-i-Hümayan*, the Imperial Atlas, has ten references to the region covered by Ortelius. 'Imperial' that it is, it does not present an alternative geography. An earlier map in the Walters Maritime Atlas similarly shows how the Ottoman cartographer was concerned chiefly with the major cities and the coastal ports that came under the sultan's domination. One reason for this simplicity, even limitedness, as opposed to the detailed anachronisms of Ortelius, is not just the colonial impetus in the latter, but also the Ottoman-Muslim absence of a covenantal understanding of the region. As Ortelius shows the path of the Israelite exodus, he confirms the Judaic covenant he is invoking for an imperializing Spain. The Ottoman cartographers presented the Palestine region in the same manner they presented any other region. It was not any different because for Muslim cartographers, a land-covenant theology was inconceivable.

2. Professor Daum suggests that I 'interrogate' the 'colonizing erasure of local differences of competing homogeneous nation-space narratives, of other names of these same places' (citing the article by Sparke, 'A Map That Roared and an Original Atlas: Canada, Cartography, and the Narration of Nations'). Such imposition of an argument derived from Canada's cartography on Palestine's cartography is quite misleading. The European cartographers of Canada erased 'local differences': they imposed new names, displaced local populations, eradicated tribes, and ultimately de-Indianized the land. The Ottomans were, like the European settlers of Canada, also imperialists. But they did not impose new names, nor did they displace local populations, eradicate tribes, or de-Arabize the land. I wish Professor Daum had presented the concrete evidence (rather than the borrowed theory) which led him to such a view. My reading of Arab travellers in the Middle East in the sixteenth and seventeenth centuries (nearly always pilgrimage accounts to Makkah and Madinah) shows no reaction to Ottoman 'colonizing erasure.' Writers definitely saw themselves as different in language, jurisprudence, and even 'arabicity,' but aside from Maronite and Druze opposition to Ottoman hegemony, I have come across no 'national' reaction to the Ottomans. I think it necessary that statements made about the Arabs and the Ottomans be based on their own literature and not on presumed parallels from European history.

3. The relativization of names, which Professor Daum so cogently presents in the example about Jerusalem, is to be seen not so much in the context of which term is more 'real,' but in terms of Ortelius's own design. Names are, of course, political markers, supporting colonization or challenging it: one who uses 'al-Quds' is allied with a Palestinian interpretation of the city, while one who uses 'Yerushalayim' is allied with an Israeli interpretation. As Professor Daum urges, where the 'real' lies is not just epistemological but also political and historical. Whether such a thesis applies to Ortelius's map of Palestine needs to be carefully examined. When Ortelius (and all cartographers after him) mapped the world, their eyes were on their readers – navigators and merchants and conquerors. Their maps are thus as precise and 'nova' as was possible. The only exception is Palestine. Why did Ortelius choose the old place names for Palestine but not, let us say, for America, and yet insist on describing the Palestine map as 'nova' – something he did not ascribe to his maps of Persia, or India, or Tartaria, or Russia? Why did he not use

'olim' as, for instance, in 'Candia olim Creta,' or as in 'Libyae pars. que hodie Sana appelatur,' to show how change had occurred? The answer, if I may be allowed to repeat myself, is that America was already conquered and the new names ('Hispania Nova') had given legitimacy and apparent permanence to the conquest. Palestine was yet to be conquered, and the old names suggested that it was as ready for conquest as it was at the time of the Israelite exodus. The map is presented as a map of 'nova' Palestine, today's Palestine, which Christian conquest will reduce to its biblical 'reality' of Christian 'terra sancta.'

4. Professor Daum alerts me to the fact that 'the Qur'an represents two fundamental spatial domains: "the abode of Islam" and "the abode of war." Although Professor Daum cites for this statement the magisterial work of F.E. Peters, I must emphasize that neither term appears in the Qur'an. Again, it is important that in discussing Arab-Islamic concepts, Arab-Islamic texts be used accurately. The Qur'an uses (twice) the phrase 'dar al-salam.' And while the phrases 'dar al-harb' and 'dar al-Islam' appear in the writings of later Muslim jurists (from the Abbasid period on), there is no mention of those phrases in either the Qur'an or the Sunna. The phrases therefore have no divine authority in Islam. Nor do they appear on maps: from al-Idrisi to Piri Rayyes to Mutafarreqa, the geography of the world in the Islamic imagination was not depicted in such a dichotomous fashion.

Professor Daum presents many other fascinating observations. I shall, however, stop here and again express my gratitude for the opportunity to respond.

Laura Levitt

In a cover story in *Time Magazine*, chair of the Boston University religion department Stephen Prothero tells the following story, one of his favourite accounts of 'Bible ignorance': 'In 1995 a federal appeals court upheld the overturn of a death sentence in a Colorado kidnap-rape-murder case because jurors had inappropriately brought in extraneous material – Bibles – for an unsanctioned discussion of the Exodus verse "an eye for eye, tooth for tooth ... whoever ... kills a man shall be put to death." The Christian group Focus on the Family complained, "It is a sad day, when the Bible is banned from the jury room." Who's most at fault here? The jurors, who perhaps hadn't noticed that in the Gospel of Matthew Jesus rejects the eye-for-an-eye rule, word for word, in favor of turning the other cheek? The Focus spokesman, who may well have known of Jesus' repudiation of the old law but chose to ignore it? Or any liberal who didn't know enough to bring it up?'[78]

I begin my response to Daum with this story because it speaks to so many of the issues at the heart of my essay. Although we would like to believe that scholars and students of religion appreciate, as Daum suggests, that the Hebrew Bible and the Old Testament are different books, this is clearly not the case. Even scholars of religion have not 'familiarized themselves with differences in respect of canon, sequence, and so on' (Daum). To have done so would have profoundly complicated the argument Prothero makes in the *Time* article. The story the latter tells rests on a very different assumption. It presumes that biblical literacy is about knowing some version of the Christian Bible. This Bible is a single authoritative story that moves from the Old Testament to the New, where the rules of the Old are superseded. Biblical literacy, in other words, depends on knowing that in the Gospel of Matthew the old law is rejected by Jesus, 'an eye for an eye' is transformed into 'turning the other cheek.' Although this is a somewhat pedestrian example it speaks to the broader concerns of my essay and the ambivalent yet passionate desires I see expressed in the decision of the Jewish Publication Society (JPS) to call their 1985 translation of the Hebrew Bible the Tanakh. I also believe it speaks to the question of how a postcolonial reading of this naming decision helps us complicate Jewish desires to be a part of the dominant culture of the United States. It helps us appreciate how the desire to see Jewish culture as a part of this dominant, biblically inflected tradition itself can and often does efface crucial Jewish differences. The naming decision was an effort to do something different in the name of inclusion.

I share Daum's concern about the 'postcolonial implications of naming contested sacred texts,' but for me in the case of the Hebrew Bible, these issues are bound up in efforts to recognize the strangeness of a presumably familiar text. How do we challenge the ways most Americans read the Hebrew Bible? I believe that postcolonial theory enables us to get at this problem. In my reading, the JPS naming decision is symptomatic. It is haunted by what Daum calls 'the spectre of comparison' because the boundaries between what is Jewish and what is Christian are not so clear. American Jews' relationship to the dominant Protestant culture and its identification with the people of the Old Testament – its vision of itself and the nation as the New Israel as a way of telling the American national story – overlaps and intersects with how Jews read the Tanakh in the United States. The question of who is

Israel, the people of the Bible, is at stake, signifying both Jewish otherness and Jewish links to the dominant culture.[79]

The ambivalences I address in my essay are all about how Jews are almost-but-not-quite dominant and the ways this works to produce a kind of cultural mimicry. In other words, the buried network of assumptions I address are how 'sharing' is a misnomer, and what it has taken for American Jews to claim Jewish difference in this most powerful and dangerous site of public belonging, the Bible as a foundational text of Western and American culture. The challenge is that Jews have used this claim to argue for their place within the dominant culture.

Given this, Daum's account of the various Bibles used exclusively by Jews, especially in synagogue contexts, is both fascinating and, in some sense, beside the point. My essay is about the public face of the Jewish Bible, how the Jewishness of the Bible is made a part of public discourse. I am interested in how more specifically Jewish readings and engagements with the Bible are shared, discussed, and acknowledged in American culture, broadly construed. For these reasons I find the 1985 JPS translation significant. I am struck by the lateness of this translation as well as the boldness of the naming decision. And yet despite this effort, there is no sense in the *Time* story that such Jewish claims to the Bible are even an issue in 2007. Biblical literacy is only and exclusively figured in Christian terms.

Ellen Frankel's lament is precisely about this problem. She is not concerned about not reaching Jewish readers and was never particularly interested in the Tanakh as a text for sectarian religious uses; the press publishes other works to meet those needs.[80] She is upset that general readers, non-Jewish readers, non-religious readers who want to read the Bible, will not find the Tanakh with the other versions and translations in the Bible section of their local bookstores. In this respect, my own use of the term 'Hebrew Bible' is, as Daum says, telling. It speaks to precisely what I share with Frankel and the editors and translators of the JPS Tanakh, and that is my desire to talk to mixed and not exclusively Jewish audiences about these issues and the role of the Tanakh and Jewish understandings of the Bible outside of exclusively Jewish religious venues. My essay is about how Jewish culture, more broadly speaking, is and is not a part of how we think about Jewish contributions to the dominant 'Judeo-Christian' culture and what it means to boldly assert that that culture is not necessarily the same as Christian culture.[81]

For all of these reasons I, like Daum, am fascinated by Orlinsky's role in this story. I am struck by the off-handed, unsystematic nature of this naming decision which is, as Daum shows, not a part of Orlinsky's initial arguments for the project. It seems to me that the decision was built on an optimism and enthusiasm that Orlinsky and his colleagues shared about the circulation of this new Jewish translation. It also seems to me that they were extremely hopeful that with this new translation they could interrupt the dominant Protestant understanding of the Bible in public discourse. They appear to have been motivated by the hope that there was finally room at the end of the twentieth century for an unapologetic Jewish translation of the Bible. I think that they believed that this text could become a part of public discourse, especially within the academy and among educated lay readers.

Postcolonial theory demands that we look at the imbricated and the overlapping: impure texts and practices, not those that are more clearly defined as sectarian. This is very much what the JPS Tanakh was all about. My essay uses this text to explore questions of power as they were played out in the case of American Jews who wanted to be Jewish as well as dominant. I take seriously the ways Orlinsky and his colleagues demanded that Jewish otherness be acknowledged within hegemonic US culture. And for this reason their naming decision demanded that Americans see more clearly the Tanakh as a Jewish Bible that both is and is not the same as the Old Testament. And, although it has been over twenty years since the publication of the Jewish Publication Society's Tanakh, its promise for a more complicated understanding of the Hebrew Bible in American culture remains unfulfilled. Perhaps Orlinsky and his colleagues were too optimistic.

NOTES

1 On cultural diversity as a counter-weight to nationalist constructions of pure and indigenous identity, see Ngaboh-Smart 2001 and Chazan 1988.

2 Bruce Willems-Braun's observation is also apt: 'postcoloniality' can too 'easily be taken to assume a historical rupture between past and present'; Willems-Braun 1997, 704. See also Sparke 1998, 466, and Coombe 1995.

3 About the Irish case I shall have very little to say, as it is not in my area of expertise. My comments will focus mostly on his discussions of 'the rabbis.'

4 I realize that Akenson has written at greater length on these matters in other contexts, but out of fairness to the reader who may only confront Akenson's chapter in this collection without the benefit of his more

extended treatment of these issues elsewhere, I confine my remarks to his chapter in this volume.

5 As Lloyd Kramer puts it, Carlton Hayes 'suggested that the new faith frequently gained even greater appeal when it could be fused with traditional religious beliefs and rituals. In every case, however, the nationalist creed requires a language, a literature, and a group of interpreters who sustain the narrative of the nation like theologians or priests sustain the narrative of a religion. Nationalism is a religion, in other words, that relies on the languages and narratives of intellectual elites' (Kramer 1997, 534). See Hayes 1928, 104–5.

6 A.D. Smith (1978) suggested the inadequacy of an 'ideological diffusion' model for the growth of nationalisms, proposing a sociological attention to the role of bureaucracies. On the role of (competing) elites and their respective networks of vertical patronage and horizontal affiliation in the growth of Rabbinic Judaism, see Catherine Hezser's now classic study of Rabbinic society (1997).

7 Akenson aptly writes that 'the matter of cultural identity is extremely complex, and most people have multiple identities which are exhibited according to the demands of their immediate context' (45). On 'counter-traditions' in biblical literature, see Pardes 1992.

8 For a range of approaches to this challenge, see Boyarin and Boyarin 2002; Boyarin 2004; Schwartz 2001; and Mintz 1996.

9 Regarding rabbinic reactions to the calamitous loss of the Temple, see Kraemer 1995.

10 As Daniel Boyarin has written, 'Judaism had survived the end of the monarchy and was developing "diasporic-locative" forms based on the locative force of memory that could have (and ultimately did, after the crisis) survived the destruction of the Temple as well' (Boyarin 2003, 311).

11 For a cogent argument that rabbinic authority was not normative during (at least) the first five centuries following the Temple's destruction, see Schwartz 2002.

12 Boyarin 2003, 310–16.

13 Akenson's reference to the importance of the process of defining and claiming the signifier 'Israel' as a component of the production of rabbinic Judaism is compelling. For a fuller discussion of this issue, see Cohen 1999; for a modification of Cohen's argument, see Boyarin 2003, 312–15.

14 See, for example, Sifre Deut 153. Seth Schwartz (2001, 56) notes that Josephus (Ant. 14.192–5) describes the high priest and his circle as the supreme legal authorities, and Saul Lieberman (1950a, 20–7) pointed out that the most authoritative copies of the Pentateuch were stored in the Temple.

15 Catherine Hezser's important *Social Structure of the Rabbinic Movement* was published in 1997, a year before Akenson's *Surpassing Wonder*. Its absence from his index therefore is understandable, but it would have complicated and enriched his narrative here considerably. On rabbinic tithe entitlements, see, for example, *yMa'aser sheni* 5:5, 56b. On this issue see Levine 1989, 71.

16 Can coincidences between and among these three literary categories, on the basis of which Pharisaism is reconstructed, also be due to other (polemical) factors and dynamics?

17 A.I. Baumgarten pointed out that no rabbinic source 'definitely refers to the party of the Pharisees'; there are positive and negative references to *perushim*, but it is not clear precisely what this term signifies (Baumgarten 1983, 412).

18 See Schwartz 2001 and Himmelfarb 1997. Schwartz notes E.P. Sanders's challenge to the notion that Pharisees promoted observance of biblical purity laws by laypeople (Sanders 1990, 131–254).

19 See the first chapter of Boyarin 1999.

20 2 Kings 17, *Ant.* 9:277–91, Ezra 4, and Elephantine papyri. See Schwartz 1993.

21 *t. Terumot* 4:12.

22 See Strack and Stemberger 1996, 232, Stern 1994, Fonrobert 2001, Lehnardt 2002, Hjelm 2004, Novak 2006, 656, and Kalmin 2006, 93, 220n27.

23 On the Yerushalmi/Palestinian Talmud's literary character, see Rubenstein 2002 and Hezser 1993.

24 There is a great deal of research on the composition of the Babylonian Talmud. For a fine recent study of Babylonian reworking of Palestinian sources and traditions, see Rubenstein 2003.

25 I wholeheartedly agree with his insistence on using a term other than 'Christianity' to describe this phenomenon in the first century; likewise, it seems that we should use signifiers other than 'rabbinic Judaism' or 'the rabbis' to describe the first century.

26 Helpfully, Akenson writes that the rabbis' 'solution [was] worked out over 500 years' (47), but the only significant agency that his narrative seems to note is that of the rabbis themselves, without serious competitors (within or without Jewish communities), absent significant historical events other than the loss of the Temple in 70 CE, and without much consideration of mutually productive interactions with other social groups and ideologies (remnants of the Temple priesthood, supporters of priestly authority, Judeo-Christians, Christians, Muslims, Karaites, etc.). A model of such an approach is Schwartz 2002, 55–69.

27 For a stimulating discussion of rabbinic disputes about tradition and innovation at the tannaitic and amoraic layers, see Fisch 1997.

28 On rabbinic formation as a result of a common, mutual, or interactive dialectics of the production of orthodoxies and heresies, see Boyarin 2004. See also Fisch 1997, Hauptman 1998, Schwartz 2001, 2002, Daum 2001, Eliav 2005, Fraade 1991, Funkenstein 1993, Ilan 1997, and Berger 1998.

29 On the relationship between halakhah and aggadah, see Borowitz 2006. Akenson states that the rabbis, unlike the Christians, used narrative 'not at all in the Mishnah and only sparingly elsewhere' (55). He goes on to speculate that the rabbis avoided narrative because the Christians got there first (56). The first statement could be expanded and the second is insufficient. Early rabbinic aggadic pericopae are generally briefer than the narratives of the Gospels, but there exists an enormous amount of rabbinic aggada, which is woven into a variety of textual frames (and anthologized into relatively large collections).

30 For excellent recent discussions regarding the genre or nature of the Mishnah (anthology? code? textbook? in what sense?), see Elman 2004 and Hezser 2002.

31 See, for example, Schwartz 2001, 2002, and Boyarin 2004.

32 Said 1993.

33 Bhabha 1994, esp. 155. See also Sparke 1998, 467.

34 Sparke 1998, 468.

35 This moral judgment can be detected very near the surface of Akenson's analysis; for example, the term 'tricks' is used to signify the rhetorical elements of sacral nationalism. He closes his chapter with a warning about what he perceives to be the dangers posed by 'monotheism.'

36 Helgerson 1992, Sparke 1998, 466. Jane Jacobs provides a cautionary observation, suggesting that 'emphasis on the hegemonic effect of the map may well overstate the power of the cartographic imagination' (Jacobs 1996, 150).

37 See Sparke 1998, 466.

38 See Daum 2007.

39 Even territorial issues settled in accordance with international law do not therefore constitute essentially real facts removed from the messy domain of power relations and therefore beyond the gaze of the postcolonial critic. See Knight 1985.

40 We should bear in mind that there is no single biblical cartography; on the variety of biblical and early Jewish mapping schemes, see Alexander 1992.

41 I am borrowing the term 'cognitive mapping' from Alexander 1992, 978.

42 See Peters 2003, 150. Crucially, the terms were inferred by exegetes.

43 Or not. I wish to emphasize in the strongest possible terms that I do not
read such structures in the Qur'an as *necessarily* imperialistic. The richly
textured semantic and semiotic range of the term *jihad* is a commonplace,
and Islamic intellectual history – including varieties of non-literal interpretation – is a vast and varied phenomenon, as is biblical exegetical
history in Christianity and Judaism.

44 Parvin and Sommer point to nomadic patterns within pre-Islamic or early
Islamic societies of the Arabian Peninsula as a source for an 'Islamic
notion of undelineated, unbounded territory' (8).

45 Reuven Firestone has suggested: 'In Islamic texts, however, the sense of
jahaliyya in reference to the pre-Islamic period tends to emphasize only the
cruelty, barbarism, and anarchy that Islam wished to be associated with
Arabia before the coming of Muhammad and the Qur'an. Islamic civilization, according to this view, would radically alter Arabian culture'
Firestone 1999, 40.

46 For a stimulating discussion of the entanglements between spatiality and
temporality in biblical narratives, see Sternberg 1990.

47 See Eliav 2005 and Hezser 1997.

48 In some ways these debates replicate long-standing interreligious polemical distinctions, such as body/soul, law/love, letter/spirit, and other
binaries. I wonder to what extent our own postcolonial interrogations of
scripturally rooted territorialisms can be seen as the continuation of such
discussions.

49 Regarding territorialism and diaspora in Jewish thought, see Davies 1982,
125–6, Eisen 1986, Hoffman 1986, Gruen 2002, Boyarin and Boyarin 1993,
and Gafni 1997.

50 For an introduction to some of the diversity in classical Jewish territoriality (and in readings of the same), including biblical texts both resisting and
extending territorial schemas, see Baer 1947, Gafni 1997, Davies 1982,
Hezser 2000, and Boyarin and Boyarin 2002.

51 Maps were not included in the Revelation of the Qur'an; once the
Qur'an's text had stabilized, I assume that adding maps to Qur'an
editions would have been seen by many Muslims as an egregious intru-
sion; similarly, adding a map to a Torah scroll likely would have provoked
consternation among most Jews.

52 Regarding the significance of the NJV title (*Tanakh*), see Laura Levitt's
chapter in the present volume, as well as my discussion of her chapter,
below.

53 In particular, the multi-volume *J.P.S. Torah Commentary* is not practically
designed for liturgical use. A later work of the JPS, *The Jewish Study Bible*,

is a single volume with English only, but it is richly annotated and supplemented, and it also contains maps. See Sarna and Potok 1989–96, Berlin and Brettler 2004b. Two recent (secular) editions of the Pentateuch split the difference: Robert Alter's translation with commentary contains maps (Alter 2004); Richard Elliott Friedman's does not (Friedman 1994).

54   The Reform movement's recent edition of the additional Scriptural portions read or chanted on Sabbaths and festivals (drawn from Prophets and Writings), which seems designed for synagogue and home use, does not contain any maps. Otherwise, however, the work is abundantly supplemented with scholarly material (Plaut and Sperling 1996).

55   It is important to acknowledge that this designation is a colonizing artefact.

56   Were Muslim empires not actually colonialist, because colonialism is reduced to a European phenomenon rooted in biblical territoriality? Matar does not make this tautological claim, but a casual reader might come away with this inadvertent impression. Matar suggests (67) that Ortelius's cartographic representation of an 'exodus-modelled *reconquista* recalled the conquest of America (which Philip II was still overseeing) since, as Steven Salaita has noted, "the conquest of America began with [the conquest of] Canaan" (Salaita 2002, 142).' Matar continues: 'By celebrating the Mosaic conquest of Canaan to the Spanish king, Ortelius's map foreshadowed Spain's conquest of the holy land.' I would add that styling an 'exodus-modelled *reconquista*' of Palestine for Phillip II might also have recalled the very recent Spanish 'reconquista' (the constructedness of which cannot be addressed here), not to mention the Crusades.

57   As Lloyd Kramer suggests, 'There is of course never a single context that accounts for historical texts, just as there is never a single nationalism or a single influence on any specific nationalism' (Kramer 1997, 545).

58   Sixteenth-century Jewish writers expressed ideas similar to those de-scribed by Matar (without, of course, the Protestant Restorationist theology). The theme of redemption was an important one for many Jews after 1391 and 1492. The theme was addressed in incunabula before 1501, as well as in editions of prayer books and the Passover Haggada (Reif 1995, 235–6). There was a controversial attempt to re-establish the sanhed-rin in Safed in the 1520s, an initiative linked to messianism and redemp-tion. The Reubeni-Molcho affair of the 1520s was a failed (messianic?) episode, which attracted attention in Rome, Lisbon, Adrianople, Salonika, and the court of Charles V. Safed was the centre from which theurgic kabbalistic traditions circulated widely to Jews in other lands. On much of this literary activity in the sixteenth century, including the relationship to

Safed, see Zinberg 1974, 5.29–30, 34–85. According to historian Juan Gil, Reubeni was a source for Ortelius (pers. conversation, 2009). Rashi's comment on Genesis 1:1 vigorously defends title to the land. Daniel Bomberg included Rashi's commentary in his 1517 Venice edition of the Bible.

59 There is scholarly work on this subject. See, for example, Brooks and Collins 1990.

60 Not to mention *Tanakh*/(Hebrew Bible)/Old Testament, although of course this is a far more complex issue, which I treat below.

61 This formulation is Gallagher and Greenblatt's (2000, 40); my usage of it was sparked by Keith Whitelam's in his excellent chapter (Whitelam 1989, 288 ff.).

62 On this last subject there is a voluminous literature, including Levenson 1987.

63 On the title page of the 1985 edition the transliterated title 'Tanakh' is followed by the same term in Hebrew letters. In the 1985 edition both the cover and the page opposite the title page contain the Hebrew and transliterated English names of the three divisions.

64 In the 1955 edition of the 1917 translation the entire title is in upper case; in the 1985 edition both 'Tanakh' and 'The Holy Scriptures' appear in upper case.

65 On the title page of the earlier translation the title appears in a much larger font than the lengthy subtitle.

66 As her chapter indicates, the documentary evidence reveals virtually nothing about the thinking behind the decision. Retrospective interpretations are offered.

67 The significance of the post-war period as the historical context in which Orlinsky was able to cross these boundaries merits further consideration.

68 On the evidence regarding the (tripartite or bipartite) structure, sequence, and number of books within the Bible, see Leiman 1991, Sanders 1992, and Brettler 1997.

69 In this sense *The Jewish Study Bible* (2004) seems to me to be more distinctly Jewish, but of course this is not Levitt's topic.

70 For a fine survey of Jewish study Bibles, see Stern 2005.

71 Typical cases are 'readers of the Bible' and 'the bane of the Bible translator' (Orlinsky 1963, 257).

72 According to Orlinsky, even the 1917 version was 'essentially but an extremely modest revision of the English Revised Version of 1885, a revision that probably did not exceed more than a very few percent of the whole' (Orlinsky 1963, 1).

73   Here he uses the very elastic term 'Torah' to refer only to the Five Books of Moses. Most readers are well aware that, in addition to a printed text or translation of the Five Books of Moses, the term can also designate a scroll containing said books, the entire Hebrew Bible/Tanakh, the Written and (classical) Oral Traditions (if qualified by adjectives, such as 'Oral' or its Hebrew equivalent), and even, most loosely, the entirety of inspired Jewish learning (as in the phrase 'Talmud Torah' and its equivalents).

74   Typical is Orlinsky's use of the title *New Jewish Version* (NJV) in a brief scholarly note on Numbers 28:9, 12, and 13, published in *Vetus Testamentum* (Orlinsky 1970). In his review of the *Torah* volume, H.L. Ginsberg, who collaborated with Orlinsky on this project, refers to the new translation collectively as NJPS (Ginsberg 1963). The NJV designation was picked up by others as well. Cf. Goitein 1967–93.

75   Orlinsky 1963, 260–1. For a fine recent discussion of the complexities of these terms and concepts, see Stern 2005.

76   It bears noting that Orlinsky was keenly aware of Philo's cultural and intellectual hybridity, even if he did not employ the now conventional postcolonial term. Cf. Orlinsky 1963, 256. For a discussion of American Jewish biblical scholarship, see Orlinsky 1955, citations on page 2, and Levitt's helpfully more updated citations.

77   I am using 'structural functionalism' to signify an Anglo-American social theory described by Seth Schwartz (2001).

78   Van Biema 2007. See also Prothero 2007.

79   For a fascinating discussion of very different American communities laying claim to the Hebrew Bible, see Goldschmidt 2006.

80   Like some of the study bibles Daum describes; JPS has published a number of those kinds of texts.

81   Here Prothero might have considered, for example, the various ways Jews and Muslims have interpreted the Exodus text in rabbinic literature and Islamic law, building on and reading differently precisely this text.

REFERENCES

Alexander, Philip S. 1992. 'Early Jewish Geography.' In David Noel Freedman, ed., *The Anchor Bible Dictionary*, 977–88. Toronto: Doubleday.

Alter, Robert. 2004. *The Five Books of Moses: A Translation with Commentary*. New York and London: W.W. Norton and Co.

Anderson, Benedict. 1998. *The Spectre of Comparisons: Nationalism, Southeast Asia and the World*. London: Verso.

Aviam, M. 1999. 'Yodfat: Uncovering a Jewish City in the Galilee from the Second Temple Period and the Time of the Great Revolt.' *Qadmaniot* 118: 92–101.

Baer, Yitzhak F. 1947. *Galut*. Trans. Robert Warshow. New York: Schocken Books.

Bahrani, Z. 1998. 'Conjuring Mesopotamia: Imaginative Geography and a World Past.' In L. Meskell, ed., *Archaeology under Fire: Nationalism, Politics and Heritage*, 159–74. London: Routledge.

Baumgarten, A.I. 1983. 'The Name of the Pharisees.' *Journal of Biblical Literature* 102.3: 411–28.

Berger, Michael S. 1998. *Rabbinic Authority*. New York: Oxford University Press.

Berlin, Adele, and Marc Zvi Brettler. 2004a. 'Introduction: What Is "the Jewish Study Bible"?' In Adele Berlin and Marc Zvi Brettler, eds, *The Jewish Study Bible*, ix–xii. Toronto: Oxford University Press.

Adele Berlin and Marc Zvi Brettler, eds. 2004b. *The Jewish Study Bible: Jewish Publication Society Tanakh Translation*. Toronto: Oxford University Press.

Bhabha, Homi. 1994. 'Dissemination: Time, Narrative and the Margins of the Modern Nation.' In Homi Bhabha, ed., *The Location of Culture*, 139–70. New York: Routledge.

Borowitz, Eugene B. 2006. *The Talmud's Theological Language-Game: A Philosophical Discourse Analysis*. Albany: State University of New York Press.

Boyarin, Daniel. 1999. *Dying for God: Martyrdom and the Making of Christianity and Judaism*. Stanford: Stanford University Press.

– 2003. 'The *Diadoche* of the Rabbis; or, Judah the Patriarch at Yavneh.' In Richard Kalmin and Seth Schwartz, eds, *Jewish Culture and Society under the Christian Roman Empire*, 285–318. Leuven: Peeters.

– 2004. *Border Lines: The Partition of Judaeo-Christianity*. Philadelphia: University of Pennsylvania Press.

Boyarin, Daniel, and Jonathan Boyarin. 1993. 'Diaspora: Generation and the Ground of Jewish Identity.' *Critical Inquiry* 19: 693–725.

– 2002. *Powers of Diaspora: Two Essays on the Relevance of Jewish Culture*. Minneapolis, London: University of Minnesota Press.

Brettler, Marc Zvi. 1997. 'Biblical History and Jewish Biblical Theology.' *The Journal of Religion* 77.4: 563–83.

Brooks, Roger, and John Joseph Collins, eds. 1990. *Hebrew Bible or Old Testament?: Studying the Bible in Judaism and Christianity*. Notre Dame: University of Indiana Press.

Burrus, Virginia. 2000. *'Begotten, Not Made': Conceiving Manhood in Late Antiquity*. Stanford: Stanford University Press.

Chazan, Naomi. 1988. 'Patterns of State-Society Incorporation and Disengagement in Africa.' In Donald Rothschild and Naomi Chazan, eds, *The Precarious Balance: State and Society in Africa*. Boulder, CO: Westview.

Cheah, Pheng. 1999. 'Grounds of Comparison.' *Diacritics* 29.4: 2–18.

Cohen, Shaye J.D. 1984. 'The Significance of Yavneh: Pharisees, Rabbis, and the End of Jewish Sectarianism.' *Hebrew Union College Annual* 55: 27–53.

– 1999. *The Beginnings of Jewishness: Boundaries, Varieties, Uncertainties*: Berkeley: University of California Press.

Coombe, Rosemary J. 1995. 'Finding and Losing One's Self in the Topoi: Placing and Displacing the Postmodern Subject in Law: Comment.' *Law & Society Review* 29.4: 599–608.

Daum, Robert A. 2001. 'Describing Yavneh: The Foundational Traditions of Rabbinic Judaism.' PhD diss., University of California, Berkeley.

– 2007. 'Crossing Cruci-Fictional Boundaries: Transgressive Tropes in Chaim Potok's *My Name Is Asher Lev*.' In Paul C. Burns, ed., *Jesus in Twentieth Century Literature, Art, and Movies*, 155–74. New York and London: Continuum.

Davies, W.D. 1982. *The Territorial Dimension of Judaism*. Berkeley: University of California Press.

Eagleton, Terry. 1996. *The Illusion of Postmodernism*. Oxford: Blackwell.

Eisen, Arnold M. 1986. *Galut: Modern Jewish Reflections on Homelessness and Homecoming*. Bloomington and Indianapolis: Indiana University Press.

Eliav, Yaron Z. 2005. *God's Mountain: The Temple Mount in Time, Place, and Memory*. Baltimore: Johns Hopkins University Press.

Elliger, K., and W. Rudolph, eds. 1990. *Torah Neviim Ketuvim: Biblia Hebraica Stuttgartensia*. Stuttgart: Deutsche Bibelgisellschaft.

Elman, Yaakov. 2004. 'Order, Sequence, and Selection: The Mishnah's Anthological Choices.' In David Stern, ed., *The Anthology in Jewish Literature*, 53–80. Oxford: Oxford University Press.

Firestone, Reuven. 1999. *Jihad: The Origin of Holy War in Islam*. New York: Oxford University Press.

Fisch, Menachem. 1997. *Rational Rabbis: Science and Talmudic Culture*. Bloomington: Indiana University Press.

Fonrobert, Charlotte Elisheva. 2001. 'When Women Walk in the Way of Their Fathers: On Gendering the Rabbinic Claim for Authority.' *Journal of the History of Sexuality* 10.3/4: 398–415.

Fraade, Steven D. 1991. *From Tradition to Commentary: Torah and Its Interpretation in the Midrash Sifre to Deuteronomy*. Albany: State University of New York Press.

Friedman, Shamma. 1994. 'The Primacy of Tosefta in Mishnah-Tosefta Parallels.' In *Proceedings of the Eleventh World Congress of Jewish Studies*, 15–22. Jerusalem: Magnes Press.

Funkenstein, Amos. 1993. *Perceptions of Jewish History*. Berkeley: University of California Press.

Gafni, Isaiah M. 1997. *Land, Center and Diaspora: Jewish Constructs in Late Antiquity. Journal for the Study of the Pseudepigrapha: Supplement Series 21*. Sheffield, Eng.: Sheffield Academic Press.

Gallagher, C., and S. Greenblatt. 2000. *Practicing New Historicism*. Chicago: University of Chicago Press.

Gardet, Louis. 1954. *La cité Musulmane: Vie sociale et politique*. Paris: Librarie Politique J. Vrin.

Ginsberg, H.L. 1963. 'The New Jewish Publication Society Translation of the Torah.' *Journal of Bible and Religion* 31.3: 187–92.

Goitein, S.D. 1967–93. *A Mediterranean Society: The Jewish Communities of the Arab World as Portrayed in the Documents of the Cairo Geniza*. Gustave E. von Grunebaum Center for Near Eastern Studies. Berkeley: University of California Press.

Goldschmidt, Henry. 2006. 'The Voices of Jacob on the Streets of Brooklyn: Black and Jewish Israelites in and around Crown Heights.' *American Ethnologist* 33.3: 378–96.

Gruen, Erich S. 2002. *Jews Amidst Greeks and Romans*. Cambridge, MA, and London: Harvard University Press.

Hauptman, Judith. 1998. *Rereading the Rabbis : A Woman's Voice*: Boulder, CO: Westview Press.

– 2005. *Rereading the Mishnah: A New Approach to Ancient Jewish Texts*. Tübingen: Mohr Siebeck.

Hayes, Carlton J.H. 1928. *Essays on Nationalism*. New York: Macmillan.

Helgerson, Richard. 1992. *Forms of Nationhood: The Elizabethan Writing of England*. Chicago: University of Chicago Press.

Hertz, J.H., ed. 1971. *The Pentateuch and Haftorahs: Hebrew Text, English Translation and Commentary*. 2nd. ed. London: Soncino Press.

Hezser, Catherine. 1993. *Form, Function, and Historical Significance of the Rabbinic Story in Yerushalmi Neziqin*: Tübingen: Mohr.

– 1997. *The Social Structure of the Rabbinic Movement in Roman Palestine*: Tübingen: Mohr Siebeck.

– 2000. 'The (in)Significance of Jerusalem in the Talmud Yerushalmi.' In Peter Schäfer and Catherine Hezser, eds, *The Talmud Yerushalmi and Graeco-Roman Culture*, 11–50. Tübingen: Mohr Siebeck.

– 2001. *Jewish Literacy in Roman Palestine*: Tübingen: Mohr Siebeck.
– 2002. 'Classical Rabbinic Literature.' In Martin Goodman, Jeremy Cohen, and David Sorkin, eds, *The Oxford Handbook of Jewish Studies*, 115–40. Toronto: Oxford University Press.
Himmelfarb, Martha. 1997. 'A Kingdom of Priests: The Democratization of the Priesthood in the Literature of Second Temple Judaism.' *Journal of Jewish Thought and Philosophy* 6: 89–104.
Hjelm, Ingrid. 2004. 'What Do Samaritans and Jews Have in Common? Recent Trends in Samaritan Studies.' *Currents in Biblical Research* 3.1: 9–59.
Hoffman, Lawrence A., ed. 1986. *The Land of Israel: Jewish Perspectives*. Notre Dame: University of Notre Dame Press.
The Holy Scriptures. According to the Masoretic Text. A New Translation with the Aid of Previous Versions and with Constant Consultation of Jewish Authorities. Philadelphia: Jewish Publication Society of America, 1917, 1945, 1955.
Humphreys, R. Stephen. 1989. 'Qur'anic Myth and Narrative Structure in Early Islamic Historiography.' In F.M. and R.S. Humphreys Clover, eds, *Tradition and Innovation in Late Antiquity*. Madison: University of Wisconsin Press.
Ilan, Tal. 1997. *Mine and Yours Are Hers: Retrieving Women's History from Rabbinic Literature*. Leiden: Brill.
Jacobs, M.J. 1996. *Edge of Empire: Postcolonialism and the City*. New York: Routledge.
Kalmin, Richard. 2006. 'Midrash and Social History.' In Carol Bakhos, ed., *Current Trends in the Study of Midrash*, 133–59. Leiden: Brill.
Khalidi, W. 1996. 'Islam, the West, and Jerusalem.' Occasional Papers, Georgetown University Center for Contemporary Arab Studies. Washington.
Knight, David B. 1985. 'Territory and People or People and Territory? Thoughts on Postcolonial Self-Determination.' *International Political Science Review / Revue internationale de science politique* 6.2: 248–72.
Kraemer, David. 1995. *Responses to Suffering in Classical Rabbinic Literature*. New York: Oxford University Press.
Kramer, Lloyd S. 1997. 'Historical Narratives and the Meaning of Nationalism.' *Journal of the History of Ideas* 58.3: 525–45.
Lehnardt, Andreas. 2002. 'The Samaritans (*Kutim*) in the Talmud Yerushalmi.' In Peter Schäfer, ed., *The Talmud Yerushalmi and Graeco-Roman Culture 3*, 139–60. Tübingen: Mohr Siebeck.
Leiman, Sid Z. 1991. *The Canonization of Hebrew Scripture: The Talmudic and Midrashic Evidence*. New Haven: Connecticut Academy of Arts and Sciences.

Levenson, Jon D. 1987. 'Why Jews Are Not Interested in Biblical Theology.' In Jacob Neusner, Baruch A. Levine, and Ernest Frerichs, eds, *Judaic Perspectives on Ancient Israel*, 281–307. Philadelphia: Fortress Press.

Levine, Lee. 1989. *The Rabbinic Class of Roman Palestine in Late Antiquity*. New York: Jewish Theological Seminary Press.

Lieberman, Saul. 1950a. *Hellenism in Jewish Palestine*. New York: Jewish Theological Seminary of America.

– 1950b. 'The Publication of the Mishnah.' In *Hellenism in Jewish Palestine*, 83–99. New York: Jewish Theological Seminary of America.

Mintz, Alan. 1996. *Hurban: Responses to Catatrophe in Hebrew Literature*. Syracuse, NY: Syracuse University Press.

Morrison, Toni. 1989. 'Unspeakable Things Unspoken: The Afro-American Presence in American Literature.' *Michigan Quarterly* 28.1: 1–34.

Neuwirth, Angelika. 2003. 'From the Sacred Mosque to the Remote Temple: Surat Al-Isra between Text and Commentary.' In Jane Dammen McAuliffe, Barry D. Walfish, and Joseph W. Goering, eds, *With Reverence for the Word: Medieval Scriptural Exegesis in Judaism, Christianity, and Islam*, 376–407. Toronto: Oxford University Press.

Ngaboh-Smart, Francis. 2001. 'Nationalism and the Aporia of National Identity in Farah's Maps.' *Research in African Literatures* 32.3: 86–102.

Novak, David. 2006. 'Gentiles in Rabbinic Thought.' In Steven T. Katz, ed., *The Cambridge History of Judaism: Volume Four: The Late Roman–Rabbinic Period*, 647–62. New York: Cambridge University Press.

Orlinsky, Harry M. 1952. 'The Hebrew Text and the Ancient Versions of the Old Testament.' In Luther A. Wiegle et al., *An Introduction to the Revised Standard Version of the Old Testament*, 24–32. New York: Thomas Nelson & Sons.

– 1955. 'Jewish Biblical Scholarship in America.' *The Jewish Quarterly Review*, new ser. 45.4: 374–412.

– 1963. 'The New Jewish Version of the Torah: Toward a New Philosophy of Bible Translation.' *Journal of Biblical Literature* 82.3: 249–64.

– 1970. 'Numbers Xxviii: 9, 12, 13.' *Vetus Testamentum* 20, fasc. no. 4: 500.

Pardes, Ilana. 1992. *Countertraditions in the Bible: A Feminist Approach*. Cambridge, MA: Harvard University Press.

Parvin, Manoucher, and Maurie Sommer. 1980. 'Dar Al-Islam: The Evolution of Muslim Territoriality and Its Implications for Conflict Resolution in the Middle East.' *IJMES* 11.1: 1–21.

Peters, F.E. 2003. *The Monotheists: Jews, Christians, and Muslims in Conflict and Competition*. 2 vols. Vol. 1. Princeton: Princeton University Press.

Plaut, W. Gunther, and Bernard J. Bamberger, eds. 1981. *The Torah: A Modern Commentary*. New York: Union of American Hebrew Congregations Press.

Plaut, W. Gunther, and S. David Sperling, eds. 1996. *The Haftarah Commentary*. New York: Union of American Hebrew Congregations Press.

Prothero, Stephen. 2007. *Religious Literacy: What Every American Needs to Know – and Doesn't*. San Francisco: HarperSanFrancisco.

Reif, Stefan C. 1995. *Judaism and Hebrew Prayer: New Perspectives on Jewish Liturgical History*. New York: Cambridge University Press.

Rubenstein, Jeffrey L. 2002. 'Some Structural Patterns of Yerushalmi *Sugyot*.' In Peter Schäfer, ed., *The Talmud Yerushalmi and Graeco-Roman Culture III*, 303–13. Tübingen: Mohr Siebeck.

– 2003. *The Culture of the Babylonian Talmud*: Baltimore: Johns Hopkins University Press.

Said, Edward. 1993. *Culture and Imperialism*. New York: Alfred A. Knopf.

Salaita, Steven. 2002. 'Demystifying the Quest for Canaan: Observations on Mimesis in the New World and Holy Land.' *Critique: Critical Middle Eastern Studies* 11.2: 129–50.

Sanders, E.P. 1990. *Jewish Law from Jesus to the Mishnah*. Philadelphia: Trinity Press International.

Sanders, James A. 1992. 'Canon.' In David Noel Freedman, ed., *The Anchor Bible Dictionary*, 837–60. Toronto: Doubleday.

Sarna, Nahum M. 1995. 'Review of Harry M. Orlinksy and Robert G. Bratcher, a History of Bible Translation and the North American Connection.' *AJS Review* 20.1: 169–72.

Sarna, Nahum M., and Chaim Potok, eds. 1989–96. *The J.P.S. Torah Commentary (Genesis, Exodus, Leviticus, Numbers, Deuteronomy): The Traditional Hebrew Text with the New J.P.S. Translation*. Ed. Ellen Frankel. 5 vols. Philadelphia, New York, Jerusalem: Jewish Publication Society.

Schwartz, Seth. 1993. 'John Hyrcanus I's Destruction of the Gerizim Temple and Judaean–Samaritan Relations.' *Jewish History* 7: 9–25.

– 2001. *Imperialism and Jewish Society, 200 B.C.E. to 640 C.E.* Ed. R. Stephen Humphreys, William Chester Jordan, and Peter Schaefer. Princeton and Oxford: Princeton University Press.

– 2002. 'Rabbinization in the Sixth Century.' In Peter Schäfer, ed., *The Talmud Yerushalmi and Graeco-Roman Culture III*, 55–69. Tübingen: Mohr Siebeck.

Slemon, Steven. 1995. 'The Scramble for Post-Colonialism.' In Bill Ashcroft, Gareth Griffiths, and Helen Tiffin, eds, *The Post-Colonial Studies Reader*, 12–17. New York: Routledge.

Smith, A.D. 1978. 'The Diffusion of Nationalism: Some Historical and Sociological Perspectives.' *British Journal of Sociology* 29.2: 234–48.

Sparke, Matthew. 1998. 'A Map That Roared and an Original Atlas: Canada, Cartography, and the Narration of Nation.' *Annals of the Association of American Geographers* 88.3: 463–95.

Sperling, S. David. 1998. *The Original Torah: The Political Intent of the Bible's Writers*. New York: NYU Press.

Stern, David, ed. 2004. *The Anthology in Jewish Literature*. Oxford: Oxford University Press.

Stern, Elsie R. 2005. 'Teaching Torah in the Twenty-First Century: Three Jewish Bible Commentaries.' *Prooftexts: A Journal of Jewish Literary History* 25.3: 376–402.

Stern, Yissachar (Sacha). 1994. *Jewish Identity in Early Rabbinic Writings*. Leiden: Brill.

Sternberg, Meir. 1990. 'Time and Space in Biblical (Hi)Story Telling: The Grand Chronology.' In Regina M. Schwartz, ed., *The Book and the Text: The Bible and Literary Theory*, 81–145. Cambridge, MA: Basil Blackwell.

Sterne, Lawrence. 1960. *The Life and Opinions of Tristram Shandy, Gentleman*. New York: Signet.

Strack, H.L., and G. Stemberger. 1996. *Introduction to the Talmud and Midrash*. Trans. Markus Bockmuehl. Minneapolis: Fortress Press.

Tanakh: A New Translation of the Holy Scriptures According to the Traditional Hebrew Text. 1985. Philadelphia, New York, Jerusalem: Jewish Publication Society.

Van Biema, David. 2007. 'The Case for Teaching the Bible.' *Time Magazine*, 22 March. Available at http://www.time.com/time/magazine/article/0,9171,1601845,00.html.

White, Hayden. 1987. *The Content of the Form: Narrative Discourse and Historical Representation*. Baltimore and London: Johns Hopkins University Press.

– 1999. *Figural Realism: Studies in the Mimesis Effect*. Baltimore: Johns Hopkins University Press.

Whitelam, Keith W. 1989. 'Israel's Traditions of Origin: Reclaiming the Land.' *Journal for the Study of the Old Testament* 44: 32–6.

Willems-Braun, Bruce. 1997. 'Reply: On Cultural Politics, Sauer, and the Politics of Citation.' *Annals of the Association of American Geographers* 87.4: 703–8.

Williams, R. 1989. 'Does It Make Sense to Speak of Pre-Nicene Orthodoxy?' In R. Williams, ed., *The Making of Orthodoxy: Essays in Honour of Henry Chadwick*, 1–23. Cambridge: Cambridge University Press.

Zinberg, Israel. 1974. *A History of Jewish Literature: The Jewish Center of Culture in the Ottoman Empire*. 12 vols. Vol. 5. New York: Ktav.

Part Two

Confounding Narratives

6

Dominion from Sea to Sea: Eusebius of Caesarea, Constantine the Great, and the Exegesis of Empire

HARRY O. MAIER

'For as many of you were baptized into Christ have put on Christ. There is neither Jew nor Greek, there is neither slave nor free, there is no longer male and female; for you are all one in Christ Jesus. And if you are Christ's, then you are Abraham's offspring, heirs according to promise' (Gal 3:27–9). 'Here there cannot be Greek and Jew, circumcised and uncircumcised, barbarian, Scythian, slave, free, but Christ is all, and in all' (Col 3:11). What have aptly been called the 'utopian declarations' of the apostle Paul helped early Christians to imagine a unity of peoples and cultures transcending traditional ethnic, cultural, and political divisions (Meeks 1977, 209).[1] Paul and his followers formulated the ideals of a trans-ethnic unity of peoples within an imperial context in which, since the time of Alexander the Great, the union of humankind integrated into an overarching cosmopolitan political order had become a utopian political aspiration.[2] It is no accident that Paul formulated a universalizing Christian ideal during the period of the Julio-Claudian Roman imperial dynasty. It, too, offered a vision of lordship in which all the world was under the embrace of a universal order governed by Caesar, a lord who in the extension of Roman *imperium* presented himself as surpassing even Alexander's achievement, and celebrated the completion of the latter's unrealized vision of incorporating the diverse *ethnes* and nations of the world under the banner of a single, civilizing rule.

Augustus's record of achievements recounting his 'subjection of the whole world under the *imperium* of the Roman people' (*Res gestae* inscription) carefully enumerated his military and diplomatic successes to show that his territorial achievement was greater than Alexander's.[3] He displayed the geographical reach of his *imperium* by erecting a now lost Porticus ad Nationes, which included images of all the peoples under his reign, distinguished by dress and ethnographic details.[4] Dio records how the emperor's funeral included a procession of 'all the nations he had acquired, each represented by a likeness which bore some local characteristic' (56.34.3). Long before his death, Augustus ensured that his reign would be remembered as a global achievement of peace and divinely appointed tranquillity. He designed his mausoleum after the tomb of Alexander the Great and incorporated it with other monuments to mark his reign as a global, divinely orchestrated achievement.[5] The mausoleum was erected on the Campus Martius and thus associated with Augustus's divine paternity and power in his successful military pacification of the world. Before it he erected a *horologium* at a right angle to the *ara pacis* (Altar of Peace). The altar celebrated Augustus's achievement of world-wide peace, especially in reliefs personifying pacified subject nations.[6] Its entry was carefully oriented so that on Augustus's birthday (21/23 September) it would be marked by the *horologium*'s gnomon, thus securing a cosmic context for interpreting his geographical achievements and immortalizing them as divinely secured. Augustus commanded that after his death his *res gestae* would be inscribed on bronze tablets and erected as part of the mausoleum; these, with their listing off of peoples and nations pacified under Augustus's *imperium*, furnished the textual backdrop for interpreting the more subtle cosmic and theological themes represented by the burial complex as a whole. This is the imperial context of Paul's utopian declarations of a trans-ethnic union of humankind, where all are brought under the lordship of Jesus Christ through faith in a saving gospel.

Neither Paul nor Augustus could have imagined that three centuries later, imperial celebrations of world-wide domination and scriptural affirmations of a gospel uniting barbarians and Greeks would be joined together to affirm the achievement of a Christian political union of humankind. In treatises celebrating the universal reach of the Christian religion and in panegyric affirming the divinely appointed sovereignty of the emperor Constantine (ca 274/288–337 CE), Eusebius of Caesarea (ca 260–ca 340) joined biblical text to the global span of the Empire to show how God had kept the prophetic promise of salvation extended to all nations.[7] Eusebius celebrated Constantine's reign by invoking political themes borrowed directly from Julio-Claudian celebrations of the *pax Augusta* and interpreted his *imperium* as the fulfilment of biblical prophecy. He heralded Constantine's dominion as making visible Christ's removal of all boundaries separating Jew from Gentile, Greek from barbarian, and uncivilized Scythian from civilized Roman. Under the emperor's divinely inspired leadership, Eusebius affirmed, Constantine integrated the Empire's diverse peoples in a saving unity. Observing the extent of Christ's dominion embodied in Constantine's global rule, uniting 'throughout the whole creation' barbarians and Greeks in 'one combination of souls, and one accordance of doctrine,' Eusebius exclaimed, '"There is no longer barbarian or Greek" [Gal 3:28; cf. Col 3:11]. For everyone fearing God is here a wise person. And now Egyptians, Syrians, Moors, Scythians, Italians, Persians, and Indians, all and at once, have become wise by the doctrines of Christ' (*Theophany* 3.79). He likens the extent of Constantine's Empire to Alexander's dominion (*Life* 1.7), 'diffusing the effulgence of his holy light to the ends of the whole world, even to the most distant Indians, the nations dwelling on the extreme circumference of the inhabited earth' (1.8). 'Holy light' to the ends of the earth: once-savage and immoral barbarians brought providentially under Rome's universal dominion and civilizing influence now submit to the yoke of Christian teaching. Eusebius imagines 'whole myriads ... in every place and city and district in all nations' gathering in churches to receive the biblical instruction and moral training (*Preparation of the Gospel* 1.4). Under the divine establishment of universal Roman rule and appointment of Constantine's Christian *imperium*, the prophecy was fulfilled that '[God] will speak peace among the nations, and his dominion shall be from sea to sea, and from the rivers to the ends of the earth' (Ps 72:8); having arranged worldwide Roman rule, God has fully realized the prophetic promise that '"the fullness of Gentiles shall come in"' (Rom 11:25; *Demonstration of the Gospel* 9.17). Whatever the religious commitments of the historical Constantine, Eusebius offers an imperial portrait that has the emperor playing a scripturally appointed role in establishing the kingdom of God on earth. The political theology of Eusebius of Caesarea testifies to a potent allegiance of traditional Roman title to Empire and Christian interpretation of biblical text to portray a vision of global domination legitimated by reference to saving religion.[8]

A Noticeable Array of Barbarians

Eusebius never tires of acclaiming the global reach of Constantine's *imperium* to the extremities of the world. Recounting the military victories and diplomatic successes of the emperor, he describes how he used to stand near the entry of the imperial palace and observe 'a noticeable array of barbarians in attendance, differing from each other in costume and decorations, and equally unlike in the fashion of their hair, and beard. Their aspect truculent and terrible, their bodily stature prodigious: some of a red complexion, others white as snow, others again of an intermediate color.' He would watch them, dressed in their ethnic costumes, processing in a steady stream and bearing the emperor gifts (*Life of Constantine* 4.7). Here was the visible sign that under Constantine, 'one united Roman Empire as of old' had been formed, incorporating under the emperor's 'peaceful sway the whole world from the rising of the sun to the opposite quarter, both north and south, even to the extremities of the declining day' (*Ecclesiastical History* 10.9.6). Later, when in 336 he delivered his *Oration in Praise of the Emperor Constantine* to help celebrate the thirtieth anniversary of the emperor's accession, he again noted the presence of peoples from distant lands.[9] Gifts from ambassadors of India acclaimed the emperor's global *imperium* (*Life* 4.50). Eusebius the biographer marvelled that during the thirty years of his rule, the emperor extended his sway from 'the Britons of the western Ocean' to the easternmost point of the known world: 'lawless and savage' peoples never subject to Roman rule – among them the Scythians – now submitted themselves to Constantine's civilizing authority (*Life* 4.5–6; also 1.8); even the Persians sued for peace (*Life* 4.8, 57). This is the constant refrain of Eusebius's writings. Again and again he remarks upon how peoples inhabiting the most distant points of the compass are held together under Constantine's reign. 'The nations of the East and the West ..., the people of the Northern and Southern regions,' unite in common pursuit of 'the godly life' in devotion to God, 'acknowledging his only begotten Son their Saviour, as the source of every blessing, and our emperor as the one ruler on earth' (*Oration* 10.6).

In offering such biographical and panegyrical observations, Eusebius was continuing a long tradition of Roman imperial affirmation. Eusebius's portrait of the universal and global reach of the peace, tranquillity, and concord of Constantine's empire borrows heavily from the vocabulary, themes, and imagery used to celebrate the *pax Augusta* as the Golden Age realization of the promise by Jupiter to Romulus's descendants that they would rule with 'no bounds in space or time; ... an empire without end' (*Aen.* 1.282.3). His description of the presence of Indian ambassadors at Constantine's tricennalia is not accidental: the Cumaean Sibyl, promising to Aeneas's descendants 'a golden age in

Latium,' prophesies the advent of 'Augustus Caesar, son of a god ... [who] will advance his empire beyond the Garamants and Indians to a land which lies beyond our stars, beyond the path of year and sun, where sky-bearing Atlas wheels on his shoulders the blazing star-studded sphere' (*Aen.* 6.792–7). Nor is his singling out of the emperor's military and diplomatic successes among the Scythians and Persians coincidental. Horace in his own invocations of the Augustan Golden Age imagined, among the distant peoples seeking the divine favour of Roman rule, 'the Parthian' fearing 'the hosts mighty on land and sea ... The Indians and Scythians, but recently disdainful, ... asking for our answer' (*Carmen saeculare* 52–5). The Roman theology of victory was to relate military successes to a divinely appointed right of the emperor to rule the world, preserved by his care for right religion and promotion of correct morals (Fears 1978). Throughout the generations of imperial dynasties succeeding the Julio-Claudian household, the *pax Augusta* remained the benchmark for measuring political success and envisioning imperial ideals.

This is the tradition that inspired Eusebius's invocation of Constantine's *imperium* as 'one united Empire as of old,' holding the whole world under its peaceful sway. The Augustan Age shaped the imperial imagination for centuries to come by representing in text and iconography the voluntary submission or enforced subjugation of peoples inhabiting the margins of the world known to the Roman *imperium*.[10] Such representations were shrewdly deployed and universally disseminated to emphasize the universal reach and divine appointment of emperors to rule the sea-bounded oval that constituted the ancient picture of the Roman world. On coins and monuments, in state ritual, in epic poetry, philosophical treatises, and historical accounts, the description, representation, and public display of 'barbarians,' the inhabitants of lands at the extremity of Roman civilizing control occupied a central role in cementing firmly in the public imagination the intertwined ideals of Roman global domination, preservation from anarchy, military prowess, moral superiority, and right religion.

In portraying Constantine as a pacifier of nations, Eusebius was joining his voice with a chorus of others who similarly celebrated the Constantinian regime as a divinely willed re-embodiment of past glories, expressed in particular in its successful subjection of peoples inhabiting the imperial frontiers to Roman dominion. This is a recurring theme in panegyric dedicated to Constantine. 'There is no nation on earth so fierce that it does not fear or love you,' acclaims Nazarius in a speech declaimed before the emperor in 321 CE. 'All is quiet without, prosperous within with abundance of rain and a wealth of crops.'[11] The Roman Senate, leaning heavily into a long iconographic tradition, brought this theme to stone when on the triumphal arch it erected to mark Constantine's victory in 312 CE over Maxentius at the Milvian Bridge it included statues of vanquished barbarians, taken from earlier monuments celebrating Constantine's ancestors' military achievements and piety. The reused pieces included statues of subject peoples, narrative reliefs portraying Trajan's victory over the Dacians, and Marcus Aurelius's defeat of invading German tribes, as well as representations of Hadrian offering sacrifices to Roman gods (see figure 6.1).

This was a shrewd redeployment by a pagan Senate of traditional iconography, calculated to win the patronage and allegiance of an emperor whose religious commitments were ambiguous. The sculptures and reliefs of equestrian emperors charging in victory over vanquished barbarians, or bound figures sitting in despondent poses of defeat at the feet of Victory, or – again – statues portraying standing barbarians with hands folded before them – an iconographical commonplace portraying barbarian submission – linked Constantine with the pagan piety and military triumphs of his glorious ancestors. The symbols of fertility and earthy abundance interspersed among them also connected him to the *aurea aetas* of the Augustan dynasty.[12] This imagery urged the Roman public to see Constantine as a Novus Trajanus, Hadrianus, and Marcus Aurelius.[13] It gave visible expression to the open-ended dedicatory inscription celebrating Rome's deliverance 'from the tyrant [Maxentius] and his factions' by Constantine's 'divine inspiration [*instinctu divinitatis*], great wisdom,' and 'with his army and noble arms.'

Constantine's own iconographers promoted similar interpretations of the emperor's reign, again drawing on iconographical themes associated with military triumph that had become commonplace images from the Julio-Claudian period onward.[14] Coins regularly depict subject peoples in the stereotypical seated and downcast pose of submission, with hands bound or in postures of supplication, before the feet of a striding or enthroned Victory or an equestrian Constantine, or below military standards and victory trophies. A particularly striking example issued in 326/7 at Siscia portrays Constantine as Mars or Virtus in full military dress, with spear and thunderbolt, walking on a seated barbarian in eastern non-Roman costume who displays typical downcast posture (*Roman Imperial Coinage* 7.451.208, pl. 13 – see figure 6.2).

Figure 6.1   Relief of vanquished barbarians, Arch of Constantine, Rome, 315 CE
(photo courtesy of Harry Maier).

Another coin, issued in 327 at Thessalonica, portrays a laureate
Constantine with cuirass, holding trophy and spear, standing in victory
over two seated and bowed captives, with the legend GLORIA
CONSTANTINI AUG [Glory of Constantine Augustus] around it (*RIC*
7.520.163, pl. 16). Like emperors from Hadrian onward, Constantine
issued coins with representations of provinces and subject peoples personified as female figures, designed to impress imperial subjects that they
inhabited an *imperium* coterminous with the world, whose frontier peoples
were brought into submission by divinely willed military victories.[15]

Eusebius assumes these representations of Constantinian victory as a
matter of course. But he moves beyond them in conceptualizing a
Christian political theology that takes up older pagan civic ideas centred in the global expansion of Empire, and relating it to a providentially arranged spread of the Gospel. Eusebius's reformulation expresses
faith in the Christian God as the author of the Roman Empire, and the

Figure 6.2 Constantine as Mars or Virtus stepping in victory over a barbarian (*RIC* 7.451 [326/7 CE]) (reproduced from Patrick M. Bruun, *The Roman Imperial Coinage*, vol. 7, *Constantine and Licinius, A.D. 313–337*, ed. C.H.V. Sutherland and R.A.G. Carson; with permission from Spink and Son).

imperial subjugation of the nations as the expression of a divine will exercised through the cosmic governance of Christ made manifest in Constantinian rule. Especially in the *Oration*, he equates barbarian submission to Constantine's *imperium* with barbarian acceptance of the Christian Gospel. The result is a unique wedding of traditional imperial motifs celebrating the Roman order as bringing the world under military subjection with biblical exegesis and Christian theology, to legitimate a Christian Empire as a divinely appointed and prophesied order. A 'noticeable array of barbarians' frequenting Constantine's court is the token of the universal victory of Christianity and God's providential arrangement of history to use the universal reach of empire to achieve the salvation of all peoples.

The Twofold Race of Barbarians

In a classic formulation, Eusebius describes 'two roots of blessing' – that of Roman dominion and of the Christian Gospel – in bringing contending nations and peoples into global unity. Before the advent of Rome's dominion and the redemptive work of Christ, Eusebius comments, the world was torn by faction and warfare, originating in competing political states and the wicked pagan deities or evil spirits governing them (*Oration* 16.2–3, 5). Augustus and Christ, by the providential arrangement of complementary universal political dominion and spiritual triumph, won an earthly and cosmic unity.

> At the same time, one universal power, the Roman Empire, arose and flourished, while the enduring and implacable hatred of nation against nation was now removed: and as the knowledge of one God, and one way of religion and salvation, even the doctrine of Christ, was made known to all humankind; so at the self-same period, the entire dominion of the Roman empire being vested in a single sovereign, profound peace reigned throughout the world. And thus, by the express appointment of the same God, two roots of blessing, the Roman empire, and the doctrine of Christian piety, sprang up together for the benefit of humankind.[16]

Eusebius goes on to observe that before the advent of 'two mighty powers, the Roman Empire ... and the Christian religion' subdued the nations, the world was divided by incessant conflict (*Oration* 16.4–5).

In these passages and others like them, Eusebius draws on old ideas but brings them together into a new unity. His formulation of Rome's dominion as a divinely appointed means of saving factious nations from themselves was a commonplace in pagan praise of Roman rule.[17] The notion of reconciliation, subjection, and unification of conflicting elements is the civic application of neo-Pythagorean ideas of a cosmic/political unity drawn from opposing forces (Chestnut 1978). The view that God orchestrated the rise of Rome as the means of realizing the universal propagation of the Gospel was articulated as early as the second century by Melito of Sardis, in a text Eusebius himself cited in his *Ecclesiastical History* (4.26.7–8). Eusebius's teacher, Origen, interpreted the rise of Augustus and the dominion of the Roman Empire similarly as the providential arrangement of history to achieve a universal propagation of the Christian Gospel.[18] Now, however, Eusebius redeploys these themes to develop a political theology that links them to the rule of a Christian emperor and empire, and places them within a cosmic and theological context centred in notions of imperial conquest and victory.

In his *Oration* Eusebius celebrates Constantine's imperial reach as representing not only military victories and diplomatic successes, but the external sign that 'he has subdued the twofold race of barbarians' (7.13), namely, 'the visible barbarians, [who] like the wild nomad tribes, no better than savage beasts, assail the nations of civilized men, ravage their country, and enslave their cities, rushing on those who inhabit them like ruthless wolves of the desert, and destroying all who fall under their power' and 'those unseen foes, more cruel far than barbarians ... the soul-destroying demons whose course is through the regions of the air ... through the snares of vile polytheism ... enslaving the entire human race' (7.2). Constantine has 'soothed the savage tribes of people by prudent embassies, compelling them to know and acknowledge their superiors, and reclaiming those from a lawless and brutal life to the governance of reason and humanity; at the same time that he proved by the facts themselves that the fierce and ruthless race of unseen spirits had long ago been vanquished by a higher power' (7.13).

Eusebius accounts for pre-Constantinian political faction and global disunity as a consequence of pagan servitude to a pantheon of demonic powers and spirits that unleashed chaos among the nations (*Oration* 7.1–8). Christ by his death and resurrection vanquished these powers, and the disciples extended that victory by taking the Gospel to the whole world (*Oration* 16.8; *Demonstration* 3.5). Now Constantine completes the providential arrangement of history by establishing a Christian Empire extended over the farthest reaches of the world. With Constantine, heavenly and earthly politics join hands; political victories signify heavenly ones:

> As he who is the common Saviour of humankind, by his invisible and Divine power as the good shepherd, drives away from his flock, like savage beasts, those apostate spirits which once flew through the airy tracts above the earth, and fastened on the souls of humans; so this his friend [Constantine], graced by his heavenly favour with victory over all his foes, subdues and chastens the open adversaries of the truth, in accordance with the usages of war. (*Oration* 2.3)

Constantine's Christian Empire is the means by which Rome perfects earlier political conquests and realizes its utopian aspirations of concordant rule and global peace. In *Oration* 16.6–7, Eusebius represents Roman imperial conquest as the first part of a two-stage plan completed with the preaching of Gospel to bring unity to the world. Deploying the well-worn political topos of the state as a properly governed household,

Eusebius acclaims the partnership of Christ and Constantine, realizing under their governance a united humankind. This results, on the one hand, in a unique application of Christian terminology to describe the reign of Constantine, and, on the other, the deployment of imperial ideals and terminology to describe God's providential arrangement of the universe and the realizing of God's saving purposes in the universal global extension of the Gospel. Thus, Eusebius can describe Constantine in semi-divine terms, expressing his rule over the dispersed nations of the earth as an imitation of the divine governance of the universe: 'Invested as he is with a semblance of heavenly sovereignty, [Constantine] directs his gaze above and frames his earthly government according to the pattern of that divine original, feeling strength in its conformity to the monarchy of God' (*Oration* 3.5–5).

Christianizing ancient Hellenistic and Roman imperial political traditions of divine kingship in which earthly rule reflects the divine governance of the universe, he goes on to represent Constantine's earthly monarchy as the reflection and embodiment of cosmic rule.[19] The emperor is 'one, image of the one all-imperial God' (7.12); his 'character is formed after the Divine original of the Great Emperor, ... whose mind reflects, as in a mirror, the radiance of his virtues' (5.4). Likewise, Christ is the 'Supreme Emperor of the human race' (*Oration* 15.11), the 'all-imperial God' (3.8), 'emperor of the universe' (5.2). He rules heaven, 'the Empire beyond' (5.2), by his 'imperial law' (3.6), and the heavens are his 'imperial dwelling places' (1.2). Even as Christ, the heavenly Logos, governs the universe, bringing conflicting physical elements into a harmonious union by his sovereign power (*Oration* 1.4–6; 11.11–16), so he uses Constantine, who regulates himself to live in accordance with the Logos (5.4–8), to draw nations and peoples who would otherwise be in conflict with one another into the concord of saving religion (9.1–19; 17.11–14). The result is an image of imperial rule of earth patterned after the archetypal *imperium* of the Logos in heaven, and an imperial theology that echoes earlier celebrations of Roman rule.[20]

In addition to drawing on Hellenistic ideas of kingship in formulating these ideals, Eusebius reveals his debt to a Roman political theology of victory. Augustan ideology celebrated the emperor as Jupiter's vice-regent, winning divine favour by his *pietas* and so securing an imperial *pax* that mirrored a heavenly concord, the *pax deum*.[21] Constantine and Christ, united in realizing the global reach of a victory over 'the twofold race of barbarians,' is a unique appropriation of this tradition. The adaptation of imperial motifs is already offered in the New Testament account of the peace of Christ ruling believers' hearts (Col 3:15) as a consequence of Christ's triumph over principalities and authorities (2:15) and the inauguration of peace between once hostile Gentiles and God (Col 1:15; 3:11; similarly, Eph 2:11–22; cf. Rom 5:1). Eusebius's teacher, Origen, explicitly linked political peace among the nations to Christ's vanquishing of the demons who bring warfare and strife to earth, and the subsequent unification of all peoples under the rule of the Logos.[22] Eusebian political theology draws these themes out more explicitly. Christ's victory over barbarous demons paves the way for his subduing of barbarian peoples (*Oration* 17.4–14; *Theophany* 3.6–39), initially through the preaching of the Gospel by the disciples (*Oration* 16.8–10; *Theophany* 4.6–9; 5.14–17, 26, 31, 46; *Demonstration* 3.5), and now through the extension of the Christian *imperium* of Constantine to the furthest reaches of the empire (*Life* 1.4–8; 2.28; 4.5–14; *Theophany* 5.52). A cosmic/heavenly peace won through Christ mirrors the earthly peace secured by the emperor. Together they manifest the imperial governance of the Logos over heaven and earth.

    In articulating such a political theology, Eusebius was aware that he was joining himself to powerful ideological currents flowing around him. He celebrated Constantine as himself formulating a theology of empire identical to Eusebius's own. In his *Life of Constantine*, he reports how the emperor wrote and delivered sermons asserting that 'God himself had given him the empire of the world' to advance the universal reign of Christian salvation (4.39); in a much discussed passage, Eusebius quotes Constantine as saying to a gathering of bishops, 'Whereas you are [bishops] of those inside the church, I am appointed by God a bishop of those outside' (*Life* 4.24). Constantine's own *Oration to the Assembly of Saints* offers a vision of imperial episcopacy in attributing his 'brave deeds, victories in war, and triumphs over conquered foes' to Christ (22), and the universal reach of his Empire to the ethical superiority of Christianity over pagan irreligion (22–5). On coins, iconographers similarly represented Constantine's victories as heaven-sent. A dramatic example appears on an issue of 334/5 in Aquileia, where between two military standards and facing soldiers is a long cross. Another from Constantinople in 328/9, portraying the emperor's dominion over the Danubian frontier, depicts Victory seated holding a military trophy with a captive barbarian at her feet; on the obverse, Constantine looks up to heaven. A third from Arles in 336 portrays a military standard with a chi-rho between two soldiers (*RIC* 7.124, pl. 12; 7.32; 7.394). Eusebius was clearly impressed by coins such as these, as indeed he was by the emperor's orations. Commenting on the peace and tranquillity Constantine brought to the world, he notes how Constantine struck coins representing himself 'with the eyes uplifted as in posture of prayer to God' (*Life* 4.15). Such images were the sign of Christ's reign extended over the nations and embodied in the reign of the emperor. In them Eusebius no doubt found support for his theology of victory, celebrating the *pax Constantiniana* as the earthly embodiment of the *pax Christi* established over the principalities, powers, and elemental forces of the cosmos.

The Author of Empire

For Eusebius, Constantine's piety preserves the health and concord of the empire he rules, but it is God, through his divine vice-regent, the all-pervading Logos, who is 'the author of Empire itself, and of all dominion and power' (*Oration* 3.8). It is a short step from God's authorship of empire to seeking prophetic promises of its coming in the book God inspired, the Bible. In taking this step, Eusebius joined his voice with other fourth-century authors, including the younger Augustine, in discovering predictions of global Roman dominion as foreseen in prophetic biblical texts.[23]

Peter Brown has called this late antique way of reading the contemporary advent of a Christian Empire 'the prophetic viewpoint.'[24] Eusebius deployed such a prophetic viewpoint in reading biblical texts, especially Old Testament ones, as predictions not only of the coming of Jesus, but of the advent of a righteous emperor sent by God to conquer pagan idolatry and extend the dominion of God's saving truth from sea to sea. Celebrating Constantine's rule, he exclaims,

> The ancient oracles and predictions of the prophets are fulfilled, more numerous than we can at present cite, and those especially which speak as follows concerning the saving Word. 'He shall have dominion from sea to sea, and from the river to the ends of the earth' [Ps 72:8]. And again, 'In his days shall righteousness spring up, and abundance of peace. And they shall beat their swords into plough-shares, and their spears into pruning hooks, and nation shall not take up sword against nation, neither shall they learn war any more' [Is 2:4]. These words, predicted ages before in the Hebrew tongue, have received in our own day a visible fulfilment, by which the testimonies of the ancient oracles are clearly confirmed. (*Oration* 16.7; see also *Demonstration* 9.17, *Theophany* 3.2)

Eusebius's use of Psalm 72 in the *Oration* is especially remarkable and reveals a significant development in his political theology. A favoured proof text from Justin Martyr onward, most usually in anti-Jewish polemic, it was cited by earlier authors as an Old Testament prediction of the coming of Jesus and world-wide salvation (Justin, *Dialogue with Trypho* 34, 64, 121; Tertullian, *Against Marcion* 5.9; Origen, *Fragment on Psalms* 72.6–8; *First Principles* 2.7.2). Its gravitational hold on the Christian imagination can already be detected in Matt. 2:11, in the story of the Magi bearing the Christ child treasures from the East (cf. Ps 72.10–11). Tertullian makes that connection explicit and goes on to show how the prediction in Psalm 72 of the coming of the Magi is a type for the coming of Gentiles to worship Jesus (*Against the Jews* 9; *Against Marcion* 3.13). As alluded to above, Origen interpreted Psalm 72.8 as predicting the coming of Augustus, and the *pax Romana* as preparation for a world-wide Gospel proclamation (*Against Celsus* 2.30). Origen, the Christian martyr, of course distinguished between the world-wide dominion of a pagan empire and the universal proclamation of the Gospel to all nations. It is this application that dominates Eusebius's earlier treatises. In his *Commentary on Psalms*, the *Demonstration*, and *Theophany*, for example, he follows Origen's reading of Psalm 72:8 as the prophecy of an Augustan world order as the providential preparation for the world-wide dissemination of the Christian Gospel.[25] Like his teacher, Eusebius is guided by a reading of the Bible that forecasts Church and State realizing their respective universal reign on parallel but separate tracks. The all-pervading Logos who planted reason in humans to know him has arranged historical events and empires so that first Abraham would be saved from idolatry and Israel would be drawn to God, then with the incarnation salvation would be more broadly spread; Roman dominion over the nations gave the disciples easy access and quick passage to the nations.

In the *Oration* the earlier distinction is lost and a more dramatic *Reichstheologie* prevails. Now what unfolded on separate paths is joined – Constantine as the Logos's own vice-regent brings God's will to conclusion as universal Empire and Gospel conspire to realize the divinely willed historical plan of salvation. The 'two roots of blessing, the Roman empire, and the doctrine of Christian piety' (*Oration* 16.4) are no longer generally related to Augustus and the Roman *imperium* – the Roman root of blessing is Constantine and the Christian *imperium* he spreads across the world (9.3–19). This later development is already offered in the final book – composed circa 323 – of Eusebius's *Ecclesiastical History*, where Eusebius's prophetic viewpoint leads him to read Constantine's reign in semi-messianic terms: '"Sing to the Lord a new song, for he hath done marvellous things" [Ps 98:1–2] ... "Come and see the works of the Lord, the wonders which he has done upon the earth; he removes wars to the ends of the world, he shall break the bow and snap the spear in half, and shall burn the shields with fire" [Ps 46:8–9] ... These things ... have been clearly fulfilled in our day' (*Church History* 10.1.3, 6). Here Eusebius flirts with the notion that through Constantine history is reaching its divinely arranged ending. In the *Oration* the Constantinian household is equated with the fulfilment of apocalyptic prophecy; the emperor in appointing sons Constantine II, Constantius II, and Constans as Caesars, fulfils Daniel's prediction that in the last days 'the saints of the most high shall take the kingdom' (Dn 7:18; *Orat.* 3.2). Elsewhere, Heilsgeschichte and Reichsgeschichte unite in Eusebius's representation of Constantine as a new Moses, a second David.[26] With the rebuilding of churches destroyed by persecutors and the foundation of new ones, Isaiah's prophecies are fulfilled. 'For in the wilderness, water has broken out, and a pool in thirsty ground, and the dry land shall be watered meadows, and in the thirsty ground there shall be springs of water' (Is 35:6, 7; *Church History* 10.4.32).[27] Constantine is 'our new and excellent Zerubabel' (10.4.36), 'our most peaceful Solomon' (10.4.45).

Barbarians figure centrally in Eusebius's reading of prophetic fulfilment under Constantine. The integration of peoples under Constantine's providentially arranged dominion brings to fulfilment the promise that God 'will transform all races of humankind, both Greek and barbarian, from savagery and barbarism to gentleness and mildness. For he [Isaiah] says, "And the wolf shall feed with the lamb, and the leopard shall lie down with the goat, and the calf and the bull and lion shall feed together"' (Is 6:6; *Demonstration* 3.2). Eusebius draws on a long tradition of Greco-Roman 'orientalism' in his representations of barbarians as wild and immoral peoples. Domesticated and civilized by the combined power of Christ and Caesar, barbarous vice gives way to Roman/Christian virtue: Scythians give up cannibalism; Persians no longer marry their mothers; Bactrians stop feeding one another to the dogs (*Preparation* 1.3). Thus do Christ and Caesar together fulfil Paul's promise that 'the fullness of Gentiles shall come in' (Rom 11:25; *Demonstration* 9.17). Dispersed peoples inhabiting the margins of the empire, joined in common worship of Christ, is the sign of prophetic fulfilment. Now, under the providential arrangement of the Roman Empire, the Word of God having gone out to all creation, especially those subdued barbarians at the world's end, 'there is neither barbarian nor Greek ... Now Egyptians, Syrians, Scythians, Italians, Moors, Persians, and Indians, all and at once have become wise by the doctrines of Christ' (*Theophany* 3.79).

Adapting Pauline usage of Abraham's offspring as the children of faith (Gal 3:6–28), he celebrates the presence of the dispersed nations under the dominion of an imperial Christianity as the realization of God's plan to establish a saving faith that would transcend the limiting, legalistic boundaries of Judaism, to embrace the whole world (*Demonstration* 1.6; *Theophany* 4.5). Here, Constantinian theology joins with supercessionism to affirm that the Hebrew Bible prophetically announces the demise of the Jewish people in the extension of a Christian Empire. This accounts for Eusebius's omission of references to Jews in his adaptations of Pauline formulae celebrating trans-ethnic union in Christ (Gal 3:28; 1 Cor 12:13 and Col 3:11). What in their original context belong to complex arguments about how Gentiles are welcomed into a prior covenant with Israel are now transformed to celebrate a prophetically fulfilled geographical extension of saving Empire to the ends of the earth. There is little need or room for Judaism in this vision of Constantine's empire as the realization of a prophetic expectation that, in God's sovereign arrangement of history, all the nations have come to believe in Christ. 'In days of old,' Eusebius writes, saving religious truths 'were only known to the godly Hebrews.' Now, with the coming of Christ and the extension of his dominion over the farthest reaches of the earth 'no longer as in ancient days [do] some few people easily numbered hold true opinions about God, but many multitudes of barbarians who were once like wild beasts, as well as learned Greeks, are taught simply by his power a like religion to that of the prophets and just men of old' (*Demonstration* 3.3). In the mature Eusebius's *Life of Constantine* and *Oration*, Constantine fulfils prophetic promises in leading the barbarian peoples of the world towards the universal truth of Christian religion, and thereby working with God to transform them into Abraham's offspring.

Victory Monuments

Drawing on a long tradition representing Roman imperial dominion as a divinely willed pacification of hostile forces, Eusebius is fond of representing Constantine's empire as the fruit of conquest. As we have seen, he celebrates the emperor's dominion as the visible token of a Christian victory over a twofold race of barbarians – the peoples inhabiting the margins of Empire and demonic powers. In doing so, he joins forces with imperial iconographers who similarly represented imperial might by portraying the emperor in postures of victory over captive peoples and subdued barbarians. Iconographic representations of conquest and the erection of triumphal monuments and trophies were an important means for emperors to communicate their power and for their subjects to express their allegiance to their ruler. Eusebius, too, offers a monumental view of Constantine's victory and subjugation of peoples. That triumph, however, is not portrayed on triumphal arches. It is rather expressed in the erection of churches. Interpreting the *labarum* in explicitly Christian terms, Eusebius links Constantine's victories under its standard to the triumph of the cross as a symbol expressing the world-wide subjugation of nations. By 'the victorious Sign,' enemies have disappeared, pagans have been silenced, barbarian nations vanquished. In celebration, the emperor crowns his achievement 'by erecting triumphant memorials of its value in all parts of the world, raising temples and churches on a scale of royal costliness, and commanding all to unite in constructing the sacred houses of prayer' (*Oration* 9.12). Eusebius reframes a Roman theology of triumph by celebrating church buildings as the monuments and trophies of imperial victory. Repeatedly, Eusebius portrays Christian churches as monuments or trophies of victory (for example, *Oration* 11.2; 17.4, 14; 18; *Life* 3.33; *Church History* 10.4.16, 20; see also *Demonstration* 1.10; 8.1; *Theophany* 5.42). If in the pagan celebration of *triumphus* conquest was manifested by parading captives in victory procession, now Eusebius celebrates the shared triumph of Constantine and Christ by portraying subject peoples from the furthest reaches of the Empire going to church. Here subjection is not measured by the imprint of an emperor's boot on a subdued people's back, but by the embrace of saving religion. Eusebius's reformulation of the Roman theology of victory to coincide with a world-wide construction of churches represents one of the more dramatic transformations of his imperial heritage.

In appropriating that theology, Eusebius was giving fuller expression to ideas he found already promoted in New Testament texts. He takes up Jesus' Great Commission (Matt 28:10), for example, and uniting it with Phil 2:10–11 (a text that resonates with Augustan themes), he links the preaching of the Gospel with the conquest and subjugation of barbarian nations. Faced with Jesus' command to evangelize the nations,

Eusebius imagines the disciples filled with doubt, and then strengthened by the portrait of conquest and victory outlined in Philippians:

'Go and make disciples of nations!' [Matt 28:19]. How can we do this? For how can we preach to the Romans? And how can we discourse with Egyptians? What diction can we use against the Greeks, being brought up in the Syrian language only? How can we persuade the Persians, the Armenians, the Chaldeans, the Scythians, the Indians, and other nations called barbarians, to desert the gods of their ancestors, and to worship the one creator of all things? These things therefore, the disciples of our Saviour would either have thought, or said. But he who was their lord solved, by one additional word, the aggregate of the things of which they doubts, and pledged them by saying, 'You shall conquer in my name.' (Theophany 5.46, my emphasis)

Significantly, neither the reference to conquering nor that to the name is in Matthew's Great Commission. Nor does Jesus anywhere state, 'You shall conquer in my name.' Eusebius has appropriated a Roman theology of victory in which barbarian conquest is the sign of divinely secured global imperial victory and linked it with a world-wide extension of Christianity. The fulfilment of Jesus' command to evangelize the nations is signified by the erection of ecclesial triumphs of victory: 'Our Saviour without delay erected trophies of this victory [over pagan idolatry and persecution] everywhere ... in every city and village, throughout all countries and even in barbaric wilds, ordaining the erection of churches and sacred buildings to the honour of the supreme God and lord of all' (Oration 17.4). He thus wages 'war after death, to triumph over every enemy, to subjugate each barbarous and civilized nation and city, and to subdue his adversaries with an invisible and secret hand' (17.11). What other king or emperor, Eusebius asks, can match Jesus' ability to pacify the nations and draw them into unity, in worship inside the monuments erected to celebrate his victory (Oration 17.11–14; Theophany 3.6–38)? Constantine, 'our most peaceful Solomon' (Church History 10.4.45), gives architectural expression to this victory and 'fills every place, country and city, Greek and barbarian, with royal dwellings' – 'trophies over his enemies' (Church History 10.4.20). Bible and Empire thus meet, transforming the traditional Roman account of Victory, and linking the Gospel's imperative to an idealized account of world-wide imperial dominion.

Figure 6.3. Joshua vanquishes the Canaanites, after the Column of Trajan. Nave mosaic, Santa Maria Maggiore, Rome, 5th century.

Figure 6.4 Triumphal Arch, Santa Maria Maggiore, Rome, 5th century (from *Art in the Christian Tradition*, a project of the Vanderbilt Divinity Library, Nashville, TN; from the library of Lee M. Jefferson).

Figure 6.5 Adoration of the Magi, Santa Maria Maggiore, Rome, 5th century (from *Art in the Christian Tradition*, a project of the Vanderbilt Divinity Library, Nashville, TN; from the library of Lee M. Jefferson).

A Eusebian theology of victory found its way not only into the treatises we have considered here. It was also expressed iconographically in late Roman Christian art. Though erected almost a century after Eusebius's death in celebration of the Council of Ephesus' affirmation of the Virgin Mary as Theotokos in 431, the late antique mosaics of the Roman basilica of Santa Maria Maggiore portray the theology we have been discussing. Around the nave, Empire and Bible meet in representations of Abraham, Moses, and Joshua as Roman emperors or generals leading the faithful or triumphing over their enemies. The basilica's iconographers in offering these representations of salvation history drew directly from triumphal art; representations of the Egyptians drowning in the Red Sea, as well as Joshua's conquests over Canaanites, for example, are strongly reminiscent of portraits on Trajan's Column of imperial victories over the Dacians (figure 6.3).

Appearing in the already imperially charged architecture of a basilica, this iconography united with space to offer a strikingly pro-imperial message. On the basilica's significantly named triumphal arch, before

Figure 6.6 Adoration of the Magi, 'Dogmatic Sarcophagus' (formerly Lateran 104), ca 320–30 CE, Museo Pio Cristiano, Rome (from *Art in the Christian Tradition*, a project of the Vanderbilt Divinity Library, Nashville, TN; from the library of Lee M. Jefferson).

the apse and altar, iconographers, in imitation of traditional military triumphal art, divided the surface into panels with self-contained narrative representations (figure 6.4). Here they offered representations of barbarians Eusebius would have strongly affirmed. On the north side, the Magi (Matt 2:1–12), dressed in barbarian trousers, submit to an infant Christ dressed in senatorial toga and enthroned as an emperor; on the south side, in a depiction of the Presentation in the Temple (Lk 2:36), Anna appears as veiled Roma offering her worship, and a Hellenistic king comes to give his devotion to the boy emperor Christ (figure 6.5).[28]

In these representations, barbarians, Romans, and Greeks unite together in worship and devotion, their differences transcended through the triumphal incarnation. Especially in their representations of the Magi, the iconographers built on the earlier Constantinian period.

A flagon from the Traprain Treasury (fourth century CE) represents the Magi as Phrygian-capped barbarians offering an enthroned Christ their gifts.[29] The so-called Dogmatic Sarcophagus of the Vatican Museum from the fourth century offers a similar representation. Here Christian art is synthesized with traditional Roman ideals of harmonious marital union as the symbol of imperial concord: on the sarcophagus an aristocratic husband and wife, arms joined, are flanked by biblical scenes. Barbarian gifts offered to the infant Christ and the domestic unity of husband and wife join to express the concordant unity of Christian empire (figure 6.6).

Eusebius's exegesis of biblical text and imperial dominion, seeking to persuade his listeners that Roman title to the world was divinely ordained and was already anticipated in biblical prophecy, is consistent with, if not foundational for, this Christian iconography. Church and empire unite to portray the triumphal achievement of a utopian order as the fulfilment of a prophetic promise of a dominion stretching from sea to sea. Here, there is no longer 'Greek and Jew, barbarian, Scythian.' Here, 'Christ' – and his emperor – 'is all, and in all' (Col. 3:11).

NOTES

1 See also 1 Cor 12:13, and beyond in Eph 2:11–22 and *Ign. Smyrn.* 1.2 for similar affirmations.
2 For detailed discussion, see especially Taylor 1981, 420–556, a summary of which may be found in Taylor 1992, 746–52.
3 For Augustus's listing of territorial achievements in *res gestae* 27–32 and territorial allusions to Alexander, see Nicolet 1994, 16–27. For representations of Roman imperial rule modelled on Alexander's territorial achievements see Heuss 1954; for Augustan invocations of Alexander celebrating imperial expansion and unity of subject peoples, see Wirth 1976 and Klienast 1969.
4 Thus, Servius *ad Aen.* 8.721; for commentary see Smith 1988, 70–7.
5 For the model of the mausoleum, and architectural arrangement with the horologium and *ara pacis*, as well as the complex's symbolic meaning on the Campius Martius, see Nicolet 1994, 16–17.
6 For discussion of the surviving fragments with literature, see Smith 1988, 72–3; for its ideology of *pax* as pacification and subjugation, see Weinstock 1960.

7 In what follows I draw chiefly on Eusebius's *Ecclesiastical History* (composed 312–25 CE); *Life of Constantine* (after 336); *Oration in Praise of Constantine* (335); *Ecclesiastical Theology* (337); *Preparation of the Gospel, Proof of the Gospel* and *Demonstration of the Gospel* (314); *Theophany* (323); *Prophetic Extracts* (before 312); *Commentary on Isaiah* (ca 324); and *Commentary on Psalms* (completed after 325). The numeration and (emended) translations are from Scaff and Wace 1979, Farrar 1920, Gifford 1903, and Lee 1843.

8 For the correct use of the term 'political theology' to describe Eusebius's treatment of the Constantinian order in particular and the Roman order more generally, see the excellently nuanced account of Ruhbach 1976, 252–8.

9 The literary integrity of the *Oration* is debatable, an issue that does not impinge on the discussion offered here; Wallace-Hadrill 1960, 44 defends its integrity.

10 For triumphal art and the use of portraits of subjugated barbarians in Roman iconography see Smith 1988 and Kuttner 1995, 13–93.

11 *Latin Panagyrics* 4.38.3–4; similarly, 17.1–18.6, 35.3–4; see also *Pan.* 6.2.1–5, 10.1–13.5, 7.4.2–4, 14.1–2, 12.2.6–3, and 23.1–25.4.

12 River gods with plant imagery appear over the north and south side arches; for nature personifications and plant imagery in representations of an Augustan Golden Age, see Zanker 1990, 172–83.

13 For full discussion, see Pensabene and Panella 1999 as well as L'Orange 1978, especially 190–1 for linking Constantine with earlier dynasties.

14 For traditional triumphal imagery on coins, as well as its relationship to the Arch of Constantine and other triumphal monuments from the Constantinian period, see Picard 1957, 466–508; also, L'Orange and von Gerkan 1978.

15 For discussion of the iconographic tradition and Constantinian examples see Toynbee 1934, 7–160, esp. 38, 86, 97.

16 See, similarly, *Theophania* 3.1–2 and *Demonstratio evangelica* 3.7.

17 For Rome as civilizing and bringing order to chaos, see Ehrhardt 1961 and Klingner 1979.

18 For example, Origen, *Against Celsus* 2.30; see Peterson 1935, 67–71 for further texts and commentary.

19 For Hellenistic divine kingship ideas in Eusebius, see Baynes 1955, 168–72 and Peterson 1935, 71–82; for application in the cult of the emperor see Chestnut 1978, 1328–32.

20 Thus, Cranz 1952, 56; Opitz 1935; Berkhof 1939, 53–60; Farina 1966, 107–30. For Roman imperial parallels, see Plutarch, *De fort. rom.* 2.316e–317c;

Aelius Aristides, *Or.* 23.76–8; Dio Chrysostom, *Or.* 40.35–41; Ps.-Aristotle, *De mundo* 5 396a32 – 6 401a11; Philo, *Leg.* 8, 15–19; also *1 Clem.* 20.1–11; 61.1–2.

21 For the image of the emperor as Jupiter's viceroy ordering the political realm after the Jovian example of heavenly rule, see Fears 1977, 189–251; Fears 1981.

22 See, for example, *Hom. on Luke* 12, 13; *Against Celsus* 8.65–70.

23 For an excellent survey of authors sharing Eusebius's reading of the Bible as predicting Rome's rise and its spread of the Gospel, as well as the shift in Augustine's thinking, see Markus 1963 and Markus 1970, 27–34, 48–57.

24 Brown 1964, 110.

25 *Comm. on Psalms* 71.7–8 (Migne *PG* 23, 801D–804A); *Demonstration* 9.17; *Theophany* 3.2. See similarly, *Church History* 1.2.23–7, with reference to Dan 7:9–14, and *Comm. on Isaiah* 14.32–15.13; *Prophetic Eclogues* 4.1, all of which comment on Is 2:2–4 as fulfilled in the establishment of a universal *pax romana* at the time of Christ's birth, though in the former case with a veiled reference to Constantine.

26 Constantine as Moses (*Life* 1.12, 20, 38); David (2.5–6; cf. Ps 19:14; 51:13–19).

27 The direct application of the Isaianic prophecy to Constantine similarly represents the later *reichstheologie* commitments of the mature Eusebius; in the *Commentary on Isaiah* (ca 324), roughly contemporary with the composition of the final book of the *Ecclesiastical History*, Isaiah is sometimes read as containing veiled allusions to Constantine's reign; for example, in 15.10 Eusebius exclaims that the promises of Is 2:2–4 are now to be seen 'with our own eyes.' See Hollerich 1999, 19–33, 188–96 for other passages in which there are allusions to Constantine as the one who fulfils Isaiah's prophecies; Hollerich shows (188–96), however, that Eusebius is more inclined to read Isaiah with reference to the geographical extension of the empire under earlier emperors, which is more typical of the earlier period of his political thought. See also, Farina 1966, 139–43, 151.

28 For the adaptation of Roman triumphal iconography in the basilica as a whole, and especially in the triumphal arch, see Deckers 1976, 271–2, 293–310.

29 For discussion and fourth-century date, see Curle 1923, 13–18, 101–12.

REFERENCES

Baynes, Norman H. 1955. 'Eusebius and the Christian Empire.' In *Byzantine Studies and Other Essays*, 168–72. London: Athlone.

Berkhof, Henrickus. 1939. *Die Theologie des Eusebius von Caesarea*. Amsterdam: Uitgeversmaatschappij Holland.

Brown, Peter. 1964. 'St. Augustine's Attitude to Religious Coercion.' *Journal of Roman Studies* 54: 107–16.

Chestnut, G.F. 1978. 'The Ruler and the Logos in Neopythagorean, Middle Platonic, and Late Stoic Philosophy.' *Aufstieg und Niedergang der romischen Welt* 2.16.2: 1310–32.

Cranz, P. Edward. 1952. 'Kingdom and Polity in Eusebius of Caesarea.' *Harvard Theological Review* 45: 47–66.

Curle, Alexander O. 1923. *The Treasure of Traprain: A Scottish Hoard of Roman Silver Plate*. Glasgow: Maclehouse, Jackson.

Deckers, Johannes G. 1976. *Der alttestamentliche Zyklus von S. Maria Maggiore in Rom. Studien zur Bildgeschichte*. Bonn: Rudolf Habelt.

Ehrhardt, A.A.T. 1961. 'Imperium und Humanitas: Grundlagen des römischen Imperialismus.' *Studium Generale* 14: 646–64.

Farina, Raffaele. 1966. *L'impero e l'imperatore cristiano in Eusebio di Cesarea*. Zurich: Pas Verlag.

Farrar, W.J. 1920. *The Proof of the Gospel Being the Demonstratio Evangelica of Eusebius of Caesarea*. London: SPCK.

Fears, J. Rufus. 1977. *Princeps a diis electus: The Divine Election of the Emperor as a Political Concept at Rome*. Rome: American Academy in Rome.

– 1978. 'The Theology of Victory at Rome.' *Aufstieg und Niedergang der romischen Welt* 2.17.2: 737–825.

– 1981. 'The Cult of Jupiter and Roman Imperial Ideology.' *Aufstieg und Niedergang der romischen Welt* 2.17.1: 3–141.

Gifford, E.H. 1903. *Eusebii Pamphilii evangelicae praeparationes*. Oxford: Oxford University Press.

Grabar, André. 1968. *Christian Iconography: A Study of Its Origins*. Princeton: Princeton University Press.

Heuss, A. 1954. 'Alexander der Grosse und die politische Ideologie des Altertums.' *Antike und Abendland* 24: 65–104.

Hollerich, Michael J. 1999. *Eusebius of Caesarea's Commentary on Isaiah: Christian Exegesis in the Age of Constantine*. Oxford: Clarendon.

Klienast, D. 1969. 'Augustus und Alexander.' *Gymnasium* 76: 430–56.

Klingner, F. 1979. 'Humanität und Humanitas.' In *Römische Geisteswelt: Essays zur lateinischen Literatur*, 704–46. Stuttgart: Reclam.

Kuttner, Ann L. 1995. *Dynasty and Empire in the Age of Augustus: The Case of the Boscoreale Cups*. Berkeley: University of California Press.

Lee, Samuel. 1843. *Eusebius of Caesarea on the Theophany or The Divine Manifestation of Our Lord and Saviour Jesus Christ*. Cambridge: Cambridge University Press.

L'Orange, Hans Peter. 1953. *Studies on the Iconography of Cosmic Kingship in the Ancient World*. Oslo: Aschehoug.

L'Orange, Hans Peter, and Armin von Gerkan. 1978. *Der spätantike Bildschmuck des Konstantinsbogens.* Studien zur spätantiken Kunstgeschichte 10. Berlin: de Gruyter.

Markus, Robert A. 1963. 'The Roman Empire in Early Christian Historiography.' *The Downside Review* 81: 340–54

– 1970. *Saeculum: History and Society in the Theology of St. Augustine.* Cambridge: Cambridge University Press.

Meeks, Wayne A. 1977. 'In One Body: The Unity of Humankind in Colossians and Ephesians.' In Jacob Jervell and Wayne A. Meeks, eds, *God's Christ and His People: Studies in Honor of Nils Alstrup Dahl,* 209–21. Oslo: Universitetsforlaget.

Nicolet, Claude. 1994. *Space, Geography, and Politics in the Early Roman Empire.* Ann Arbor: University of Michigan Press.

Opitz, H.-G. 1935. 'Euseb von Caesarea als Theologe.' *Zeitschrift für die neutesta mentliche Wissenschaft* 34: 1–19.

Pensabene, Patrizio, and Clementina Panella. 1999. *Arco di Constantino: Tra archeologia e archeometria.* Rome: Bretschneider.

Peterson, E. 1935. *Der Monotheismus als politisches Problem. Ein Beitrag zur Geschichte der politischen Theologie im Imperium Romanum.* Leipzig: Jakob Hegner.

Picard, G.C. 1957. *Les trophées romains: Contribution à l'histoire de la religion et de l'art triomphal de Rome.* Bibliothèques des Écoles françaises d'Athènes et de Rome, Fasc. 187. Paris: De Boccard.

Ruhbach, Gerhard. 1976. 'Die politische Theologie Eusebs von Caesarea.' In *Die Kirche angesichts der konstantinsichen Wende,* 236–58. Darmstadt: Wissenschaftliche Buchgesellschaft.

Scaff, Philip, and Henry Wace. 1979. *A Select Library of Nicene and Post-Nicene Fathers of the Christian Church.* Grand Rapids, MI: Eerdmans.

Smith, R.R.R. 1988. '*Simulacra Gentium*: The *ETHNE* from the Sebasteion at Aphrodisias.' *JRS* 78: 38–77.

Taylor, Walter Frederick. 1981. 'The Unity of Mankind in Antiquity and Paul.' PhD dissertation. Claremont Graduate School and University Center, Ann Arbor, MI.

– 1992. 'Unity/Unity of Humanity.' In David Noel, ed., *The Anchor Bible Dictionary,* vol. 6: 746–52. New York: Doubleday.

Toynbee, Jocelyn M.C. 1934. *The Hadrianic School: A Chapter in the History of Greek Art.* Cambridge: Cambridge University Press.

Wallace-Hadrill, D.S. 1960. *Eusebius of Caesarea.* Westminster, MD: Canterbury.

Weinstock, Stefan. 1960. 'Pax and the "Ara Pacis."' *Journal of Roman Studies* 50: 44–58.

Wirth, Gerhard. 1976. 'Alexander und Rom.' In O. Reverdin, ed., *Alexandre le Grande: Image et réalité*, 182–210. Entretiens sur l'antiquité 22. Geneva: Hardt.

Zanker, Paul. 1990. *The Power of Images in the Age of Augustus*. Trans. Alan Shapiro. Jerome Lectures 16. Ann Arbor: University of Michigan Press.

7

Unending Sway:
The Ideology of Empire
in Early Christian Latin Thought

KARLA POLLMANN

Introduction: Prophecy and Exegesis

To the Roman race I set limits neither in space nor time:
Unending sway have I bestowed on them.

Virgil, Aeneid 1.278–9[1]

With this divine prophetic promise of Rome's imperial destiny, Jupiter consoles his daughter Venus as she asks anxiously after the future of her son Aeneas and the end of his labours, at a moment when the hero's wanderings over the Mediterranean in search of the new Troy that would be Rome seem to have reached a crisis point.[2] Jupiter sets no bounds of space or time to Roman power: 'unending' (*sine fine*), in Latin as in English, conveys the dimensions of both time and space, removing all limits from the expansion of the race here represented by its founding father.[3] Moreover, the perfect tense of 'I have bestowed' indicates that the splendour of eternal Rome is already a foregone conclusion. The Roman race is justified by right of fate to expand and occupy the whole world and to rule over it, conferring upon its peoples a civilized way of life (*mores*, 'morals,' at *Aen.* 1.264 and 6.852; *iura*, 'laws,' at 1.293). This justification for imperialism would be used over and over again by later colonial powers, the Austro-Hungarian and the British to name but two.[4] All is predestined as divine will or the reflection of a supernatural order.

For this prophecy to become reality, *new* land will have to be occupied, since Aeneas and his band, as refugees from ruined Troy, are without a place to call home. The occupation of land forms a leitmotif in

Jupiter's speech: 'a town and the promised walls of Lavinium' (*Aen.* 1.258–9: *cernes urbem et promissa Lavini / moenia*) form the first stage of the new settlement in Latium, to be followed by the conquest of Italia, a part of what is called Italy today (1.263–5, especially 264: *moresque viris et moenia ponet*), and the moving of the seat of rule from Lavinium to Alba Longa (1.270–1: *regnumque ab sede Lavini / transferet, et Longam multa vi muniet Albam*), twelve miles south-east of Rome, and finally the foundation of Rome itself (276–7). The future conquest of Greece is given particular emphasis (1.283–5), since that is how Troy's ruin will be avenged: Rome will be a second, new-born Troy.[5] Finally, the whole inhabited world will belong to an empire that is limited only by the regions of the sky (1.287–90, cf. 7.98–9).

This Jovian prophecy is echoed in three other prophecies that break through the main narrative level of the legend of Aeneas. At *Aen.* 6.781 Anchises in the underworld prophesies to his son Aeneas: 'Under his [Romulus's] auspices, my son, shall that glorious Rome extend her empire to earth's ends, her ambitions to the skies.'[6] This will occur when the climax of Rome's destiny is reached under the reign of Augustus, as intimated at *Aen.* 6.794–807:

> He [Augustus] will advance his empire beyond the Garamants and Indians to a land which lies beyond our stars, beyond the path of year and sun, where sky-bearing Atlas wheels on his shoulders the blazing star-studded sphere. Against his coming both Caspian realms and the Maeotic land even now shudder at the oracles of their gods, and the mouths of sevenfold Nile quiver in alarm. Not even Hercules traversed so much of earth's extent, though he pierced the stag of brazen foot, quieted the woods of Erymanthus, and made Lerna tremble at his bow; nor he either, who guides his car with vine-leaf reins, triumphant Bacchus, driving his tigers down from Nysa's lofty peak. And do we still hesitate to make known our worth by exploits or shrink in fear from settling on Western soil?[7]

In the sequel, this general statement of unprecedented territorial expansion will be exemplified by various historical instances, at 6.808–59, at 8.626–728 (description of the shield Venus gives to her son Aeneas), and more generally at 12.793–840.[8] It is characteristic of the *Aeneid* that although the Roman race and its origins are important as such, the main emphasis falls on geographical boundaries. The people of Rome must have a distinctive territory that is predestined by the will of the gods or fate: 'But the will of heaven has forced us by its behests to seek out your shores,' as Aeneas himself explains (7.239–40).[9] From that base, further expansion may proceed. The settlement itself must therefore be fortified for protection against external enemies. It is not just 'land,' but a clearly defined area within walls, as for instance at *Aen.* 3.500–1: 'If ever I enter the Tiber and Tiber's neighbouring fields and look on the city walls granted to my race.'[10]

The *Aeneid* is the first poem in European history to make such an imperial claim on behalf of a *nation*.[11] David Quint, in his book *Epic and Empire*, defines the *Aeneid* as an archetypal epic of the imperial victors that universalizes the historically particular (Quint 1993, 8, 52). In archaic and Hellenistic times, such claims of territorial possession were made at most for towns or regions, in 'founder' or *ktistes*-stories,[12] analogous to accounts of the 'first inventor' (*protos heuretes*).[13] The same form of legitimization, but now applied to the whole Roman Empire, is used in the *Aeneid*, especially in books 5–8, where a number of Roman religious and cultural customs are given an aetiological explanation.[14] Moreover, the *Aeneid* follows a specifically aetiological approach by promoting legends of origin as a privileged way of understanding the present. The historical time between this 'history of origins' (*Urgeschichte*) and the present is neglected as essentially irrelevant. And in the attempt to make the present transparent through the past, the past is itself affected; for the past in such a scheme is itself a *projection* of the present – that is, of present interests, needs, and desires.[15]

In the fourth century CE, quarrels about political and cultural hegemony between pagans and Christians gave fresh prominence to such discourses of origins. Under Christian pressure, the pagan Roman elite was more than ever reliant upon a text to define its identity and justify its existence. In this connection, Virgil's *Aeneid* acquired a quasi-sacred status as the fountain of all knowledge – almost a 'pagan bible.' It was used as a textbook in schools, not in order to make pupils read 'good poetry,' as a modern justification might hold it, but because it was considered the perfect tool for instructing young Romans in the knowledge deemed essential for a future leading citizen. By this time, Rome's imperial destiny was both taken for granted – by Romans – and inextricably associated with Virgil's praise of the principate established by Augustus. The rule of the Roman Empire over foreign peoples was a fact, but it was also seen as in need of constant confirmation by imperial panegyric and other media. This already becomes evident when we look at a late-fourth-century Latin commentary on the *Aeneid*, written

by the grammarian Servius and used for teaching purposes. He comments on 1.287 ('Caesar, who shall extend his empire to the ocean, his
glory to the stars')[16] that 'this has either been said for praise or certainly
because it is a historical fact. For as a matter of fact, Julius Caesar also
conquered the British, who live in the Ocean, and, when after his death
his adopted son Augustus held funeral games for him, a star was seen
in the middle of the day.' Augustus later used this omen to declare
Caesar a god, thereby making himself the son of a god[17] and reinforcing
his own claim to absolute power.[18]

Roman Christians confronted with this kind of thinking had essentially two options open to them: they could either reject it completely
and develop a counter-ideology of their own founded exclusively on
the Scriptures, or they could try to adapt and usurp pagan imperial
ideology. As early as Justin Martyr (first to second century CE) Christian
apologists had attempted to give a Christian view of the world in terms
intellectually acceptable to their pagan critics. By bringing their religion
within the pale of pagan intellectual culture, they aimed to make it socially respectable. By the late fourth century, however, the situation had
grown more complex for conscientious Christians, even as their political situation had become increasingly favourable. From being tolerated
at the beginning of the century under Constantine, Christianity had
come to be the official religion of the Roman Empire under Theodosius
(379–95). In less than a hundred years, the Roman state had turned from
persecutor into protector. How were Christians to understand their relationship to such an external power? There was already an apparent
tension within the New Testament, which on the one hand warned the
true believer against the corrupting influences of worldly institutions –
for example, in Revelation 13, where the Beast is identified with Roman
rule – and on the other hand demanded obedience to civil rulers (e.g.,
Romans 13:1–7). In particular, Christians had to weigh carefully the
claims of an empire that was so clearly defined in territorial categories.[19]
In one respect, this feature of Roman ideology could appear to fit well
with the Christian ambition of extending the message of the saviour
Jesus Christ beyond the realm of Israel, which is clear already in some
parts of the New Testament (such as Romans 10:18, Revelation 1–3, 5:13,
and 19–22).[20] Siding with the 'universal' Roman Empire, whose boundaries were reputed to coincide with the whole inhabited world,[21] could
guarantee the spread of the Gospel. The North African writer Optatus,
bishop of Milevis in the fourth century, even went so far as to claim that
'the state is not in the Church, but the Church in the state – that is, the

Roman Empire.'[22] This Christianized Roman ideology, which saw the Roman Empire as the power destined to unify, pacify, civilize, and finally convert the world, culminated in the theology and teleology of empire developed by Eusebius in the fourth century.[23]

As Harry Maier has shown in the previous chapter, Eusebius represented the Roman Empire as God's providential tool to accomplish his plan of bringing Christianity to the world. In performing this role, the Empire would have reached its climax and ultimate perfection. In the *Ecclesiastical History* Eusebius formulates the idea of the progressive development of humanity up to the foundation of the Roman Empire as a preparation for the advent of the Redeemer.[24] He elaborates on this idea in his speech *In Praise of Constantine*:

> At the same time, one empire also flowered everywhere, the Roman, and the eternally implacable and irreconcilable enmity of nations was completely resolved. And as the knowledge of One God was imparted to all people and one manner of piety, the salutary teaching of Christ, in the same way at one and the same time a single sovereign arose from the entire Roman Empire and a deep peace took hold of the totality. Together, at the same critical moment, as if from a single divine free will, two beneficial shoots were produced for humankind: the empire of the Romans and the teachings of true worship.[25]

Eusebius seeks to justify not only the supremacy of both Christianity and the Roman Empire, but also the latter's expansionist, missionary activities on behalf of the former. Christian claims on territory, never well staked in the New Testament, could now be supported by an imperialist agenda of long date.[26] Mutual exclusion and hatred had thus turned into collaboration and enhancement.

The Eusebian ideology of Roman Empire is more or less of a piece with the one expressed in the *Aeneid*, as outlined above.[27] Perhaps not surprisingly, as soon as the socio-political situation allowed it, Virgilian and Christian visions of Roman manifest destiny were merged – the more easily since the *Aeneid* already told a story of losers (Trojans) turning into victors (Rome as a second Troy) that Christians could adapt to their own case.[28] The Virgilian aetiology of the present could now at last be used to Christian advantage. In the Latin-speaking West, where Virgil's presence was most pervasive, the work of harmonization was taken up by Prudentius, an imperial high magistrate who became a Christian around 400 and was also possibly the greatest Christian poet of Late Antiquity. He pursues the task in two distinct literary-rhetorical genres: by apologetic argument, notably in his tirade *Against Symmachus*, and by allegorical narrative, in *The Fight of the Human Soul* (*Psychomachia*). We shall concentrate on *Against Symmachus*, since it is there that he deals most directly with issues of territorial possession.[29]

Spiritualizing Roman Empire: The Poetry of Prudentius

In 381, the altar and statue of the goddess Victory were removed from the senate house in Rome – a stronghold of paganism – by order of the emperor Gratian (d. 383). A few years later Quintus Aurelius Symmachus, a leading pagan aristocrat, orator, and high magistrate, made a plea to Gratian's successor, Valentinian II, for the restoration of these symbols. Without the altar of Victory, Symmachus argued, Rome would lack the divine protection in battle that had made it great. This and other traditional arguments against Christianity were rebutted by Ambrose, bishop of Milan, in a series of letters to the same emperor. Those letters, in turn, provided a model for Prudentius's hexameter poem in two books, *Against Symmachus*. Prudentius adds his own ideas and arguments. Book 1 aims to put Symmachus's demands and their refutation into a wider historical context. It is clear from internal evidence that the poet did not compose his 'reply' to Symmachus until 402–3 – that is, roughly twenty years after the original incident.[30] As S. Döpp (1980) has shown, the motive for writing the poem at so late a date was the victory of General Stilicho at the battle of Pollentia in 402 against the Goths. That victory could now be conveniently used – though not, it is true, without some potential risk[31] – against the pagan party, as proof that the Christian God was indeed a powerful protector of the Roman Empire. The poem is thus considerably more than a rhetorical exercise in turning prose arguments into poetry. It is a heartfelt expression of Prudentius's personal concerns, including a plea in favour of the imperial family and a vision of Rome reborn as a Christian polity.

Prudentius sets forth an imperial theology of the type represented pre-eminently by Eusebius. For this purpose, however, he reaches back to the very beginning of Roman history – a technique already reminiscent of another hexameter poem, the *Aeneid*. To justify the present Christian order of things, he has to prove both that pagan belief was bad for Rome, and that Rome's destiny and ultimate prosperity lay in the adoption of Christianity.[32] As a first step he demonstrates, partly with reference to pagan sources, that Rome's venerable state gods were in fact no more than outstanding human beings (a theory known as euhemerism),[33] and that the religious foundations of the Roman Empire reposed on 'legend or error.'[34] Then he makes it appear that the success of the Roman race was owed all along to the will of the Christian God: 'Happy had they been had they known that all their successes were ordered by the governance of the God Christ, whose will it was that kingdoms should run their appointed courses and the triumphs of Rome should grow from more to more, and that He should enter the world in the fullness of time' (*Against Symmachus* 1.287–90).[35] At 1.455–65 Rome's missionary goal to civilize other nations is expressed in the very terms formulated by Virgil in *Aeneid* 6.851–3 (especially 6.852: 'to crown peace with morals,' *pacique imponere mores*). Now, however, this scheme of thought is used to make the adoption of Christianity appear as a necessary consequence of the peace in the Roman Empire. Rome, a civilized and civilizing world power, must adopt the only suitable – indeed, the only civilized – religion, namely Christianity, which had made Constantine invincible (1.467ff.).[36] Here Prudentius follows Eusebius, who in his *Life of Constantine* 1.28–32 reported Constantine's famous vision and the dream in which he had been told that he would conquer his rivals if he adopted Christianity.[37] For Eusebius, there was a direct connection not only between the peace under Augustus and the birth of the saviour of the world, but also between the acceptance of Christianity and the victory and rule of Constantine.[38] In this latest new age, according to Prudentius, there will be even greater expansion: 'And do we still hesitate to believe that Rome, O Christ, has devoted herself to you and placed herself under your government, and that with all her people and her greatest citizens she is now eagerly extending her earthly realm beyond the stars of the great firmament?' (1.587–90).[39] Admittedly there is some ambiguity in the phrasing of this proposition as a rhetorical question – a point to which we shall return.

The most striking instance of Prudentius's Christianized imperialism is his adaptation of the Virgilian quotation given at the beginning of this chapter: 'No bounds indeed did [the emperor Theodosius] prescribe, no limits of time did he set. Unending sway he teaches, so that the valour of Rome should never grow old nor the glory she had won know age' (1.541–3).[40] A careful comparison with the Virgilian model reveals some crucial alterations. The addressee of the original, namely the Roman race (*his*, 'to this people') is suppressed and replaced by the affirmative 'indeed' (*denique*). Instead of *metas rerum* ('limits in space'), Prudentius keeps only 'limits' and replaces *rerum* with *statuit* ('he prescribed'), doubling the verb that he already shares with Virgil (*ponere*, 'to set'). The whole statement is transferred from the first person, with Jupiter speaking, to the third person. The poet himself makes the statement, but it is referred to Theodosius, who as a Christian emperor occupied the position of earthly rule. Thus, Prudentius 'corrects' or improves upon the mistaken 'theology' of the pagan original text and brings out what he takes to be its true historical meaning, a meaning hitherto hidden from the (non-Christian) reader. One could think of this as a kind of euhemerism applied in favour of the Christian faith, whereby Jupiter is declared to be not a god, as in pagan superstition, but an outstanding human individual (Theodosius).

The textual comparison can yield more still. Virgil's present tense for Jupiter's act of (not) setting limits (*pono*, 'I set') is doubled by Prudentius by a perfect (*statuit*, 'he prescribed') for one dimension and a present tense (*ponit*, 'he sets') for the other, though the latter is probably a poetic variation – for the sake of the metre – and is meant to be understood as a perfect as well. In other words, the Virgilian prophecy has been fulfilled; it is a fait accompli. However, in the following line the 'divine' perfect of the Virgilian original (*dedi*, 'I have bestowed') is replaced by a present (*docet*, 'he teaches'), which cannot so easily be seen as a poetic variation. It is more plausible to take this present tense at full value, with the sense that the 'unending sway' is not an already God-given historical fact that cannot be altered or lost anymore. Instead, the Christian emperor is introduced as a teacher or persuasive agent whose pedagogical aspirations continue through the ages and constitute an enduring admonition: 'unending sway' would thus be a permanent challenge and appeal, to which every Christian is expected to respond. It would also imply that the 'sway' is never fully achieved, but forever to be enlarged. Finally, because of the changed historical situation in relation to Virgil, Prudentius has to add a qualifying statement at 1.542–3 ('so that the valour of Rome should never grow old nor the glory she had won know age'), for which there is no Virgilian equivalent,[41] and which emphasizes or explains the force of the present tense of *docet*. The continuing endeavours of the Roman Empire ensure its constant rejuvenation despite its historically advanced age.[42] At the same time, Prudentius adds a spiritual dimension to Virgil's political statement, implicitly associating Rome's claim to earthly hegemony with (biblical) prophecies of the eternal kingdom of God (Döpp 1988, 341; Lühken 2002, 180–1).

Like Virgil, Prudentius has a *territorial* concept of the Roman Empire.[43] He also formulates a *telos* for Roman history that is understood as linear and progressive, not as cyclical (Smolak 1999, 132–9). In traditionally Roman fashion, a clear link is established between military and political success and adherence to the right religion – now meaning Christianity. Spiritual disposition and the political state of the Empire are analogous in Prudentius. In the same way that the pacified Roman Empire enabled Christianity to come into the world, so also the pacified soul of the human individual enables the Christian faith to enter (2.628–32). Christianity thus lays claim both to the domain of the human soul and to the territory of the Empire, and these claims are interrelated in a socio-morphous psychology and a bio-morphous idea of the state.[44] Interestingly, Prudentius reinforces this point by citing what he saw as the failure of pagan religion in this respect, pointing out that traditional Roman religion was not strong enough to withstand external influences, since the more Rome extended her sway, the more alien gods entered her realms (2.343–69).

It is perhaps not so remarkable, given his ostensibly pagan addressee (or target), that Prudentius uses the Bible only very sparingly to support his case in *Against Symmachus*.[45] The main exception occurs at 2.1020–63, at the climax of this work. Symmachus had argued that the Roman famine of 383 CE had been caused by the anti-pagan decrees of the emperor Gratian in the previous year, which had provoked the revenge of the pagan gods. Among other arguments against this, Prudentius paraphrases the parable of the sower whose seed fell partly on fertile ground, where it bore rich fruit, and partly on stony ground, where it yielded nothing (Mt 13:1–23; Mk 4:1–20; Lk 8:4–15). Of particular interest to us here is how Prudentius uses this parable and the exegesis already provided by Jesus himself in the New Testament to spiritualize (or allegorize) the notion of the land.[46] By his framing of the paraphrase of the biblical analogy Prudentius makes it clear that material and earthly possessions are irrelevant for a Christian. In his preliminary remarks at 2.1018–19 he already opens up an eschatological dimension: 'For to those whose hope is shaped for eternity every good thing which this present life brings is slight.' Then, looking back at the paraphrased passage at 2.1035–9, he writes: 'With these rules [i.e., to sow only on fertile land] does God encourage the farmer, and he lets the Father's heavenly law sink into his ear and understanding, so managing the corn-land both in soul and field that his heart shall be no less well-conditioned through cultivation within than his smiling acres when they display their harvest.' On the one hand, Prudentius advocates a new Christian lifestyle in which there will be holdings of fertile land. On the other hand, by allegorizing the parable and referring its contents to an eternal realm he allows the possibility of not taking 'land' literally at all, but instead as a figure of speech for immaterial things of ultimate value. We have moved on from the synecdochic analogy of the human soul and the political territory of the Empire to the metaphorical analogy of the soul and agricultural land. Although even under the Christian God the agricultural harvest cannot always be guaranteed, the Christian faith is nonetheless superior, since it alone prepares the psychological ground for coping with such disasters. The claim on the territory of the soul is thus finally more important than the claim on the soil.[47]

When the Goths sacked the city of Rome in 410 CE, the naive identification of the Christian God as Rome's right divinity and as guarantor of her military supremacy was doomed. Scholarship has often treated Prudentius as a conservative Roman patriot who could not reconcile his Roman and Christian pieties. Bastiaensen rightly rejects such a view as inaccurate, because it does not take into account the evidence from *all* of his poetry (Bastiaensen 1993, 128–9). Prudentius never canonized the terrestrial Rome as the ultimate Christian reality. Virgil's permanent political hegemony is replaced by the expectation of belonging to the eternal, supra-political kingdom of God, a transcendental conception that is clearly marked, for example, at *Crowns of Martyrdom* 2.548–60, where he envisages a 'Roman' heaven for the martyred Laurentius.[48] An eschatological dimension is likewise indicated at *Against Symmachus* 2.756–9, in a speech of the personified Roma to the Christian emperor Theodosius: 'To you, our emperor, a living glory is due, a living reward for your merit, since you have sought after honour that is deathless. As ruler of the world you shall be made partner with Christ for ever, for under his leadership you draw my realm to the heavens.'[49]

Prudentius's point of view is consistently and consequentially Christian. The emperor Augustus may have played a providential role in history, he concedes, but venerating him as a deity is an abominable paganism (*Against Symmachus* 1.245–50).[50] Similarly, a careful distinction is to be made between the despicable worship of Roma as a deity (1.218–22) and the acceptable poetic usage of Roma as a personification (2.80, 650).[51] Despite providence, there is a discontinuity or partial non-coincidence between the religious and earthly dimensions of the Roman Empire (1.408–505). For this reason, statements or rhetorical questions such as the one at 1.587–90 (already discussed above),[52] especially concerning 'the extension of the earthly realm beyond the lofty stars,' are somewhat ambiguous. They could be understood as an emulation of the pagan panegyrical motif of praise for the extent of an empire, as is, for instance, the case in *Aen.* 1.287 (quoted above), 6.795–6, and 7.99, 272.[53] However, this poet's general insistence on the heavenly, eternal dimensions of the Roman Empire, especially obvious in book 2 of *Against Symmachus*,[54] makes it more likely that these phrases have a more subtle function in the overall argument and that their ambiguity is calculated to further a Christian concept of empire that would outstrip the boundaries of pagan discourse by turning a rhetorical device into an eschatological trope. In like manner, the construction of the temple at the culminating point of Prudentius's poem *The Fight of the Human Soul* serves as a reminder to the reader of the ultimately eschatological reality of the heavenly Jerusalem (910–15).[55] When Prudentius speaks about his self-awareness, motivation, and aims as a Christian poet, as he does especially in the preface and the epilogue to his collected poems, politics do not in fact play a role at all. Rather than simply blowing the trumpet of imperial ideology and triumphalism, he seems chiefly concerned to spiritualize them.[56] One could fairly say that this attitude discloses at least a lingering ambivalence towards the traditional values of the Roman Empire.

After Roman Empire: Augustinian Hermeneutics

The Lord appeared to Abram and said: 'I will assign this land to your heirs.'

Genesis 12:7[57]

The similarity between the situation evoked by this biblical verse and that expressed in the Virgilian lines cited at the beginning of this chapter is certainly striking. Once again a god is giving assurances for a future generation. In this case, however, he is talking not to another deity but directly to the human being chiefly concerned. Unlike Aeneas, Abra(ha)m has a certain prophecy to rely on, which is then repeated in the course of his travels.[58] It is true that Aeneas also receives intermittent signs from the gods, but these serve mainly as corrections and clarifications to help him find his way, whereas in the Old Testament, God's later statements merely reconfirm his earlier announcement. Of course, there are other differences too. Here it is not unending power in space and time that is promised, but land[59] – and land that has not yet been bestowed.

Erich Auerbach once famously distinguished between the modes of description used respectively by the Bible, especially (but not only) the Old Testament, and in classical epic, as exemplified by Homer.[60] We can perhaps make a similar distinction here between the style of this and surrounding verses from Genesis and the corresponding passage in book 1 of the *Aeneid*: on the one hand, the abruptness and suggestiveness of the biblical pronouncement; on the other hand, the fully externalized description, uniform illumination, and display of unmistakeable meanings in the pagan epic. Auerbach goes on to argue that these different modes of description reflect different modes of storytelling; the more circumstantial style of the pagan epic is suitable for legends, whereas the more opaque style of the Old Testament befits a discourse that 'comes closer and closer to history as the narrative proceeds.'[61] These claims would need careful qualification in the present case, since Virgil clearly aimed at a certain kind of historical truth, albeit presented in a legendary form, and the 'meaning' of the *Aeneid* became (and still is) the object of much debate. Conversely, the purportedly factual or historical narrative of the Old Testament has repeatedly been 'dehistoricized' in order to make its content more immediately relevant to a later reader. But Auerbach was right to point out that the universal-historical claims of the Old Testament were a problem. They were so especially to early Christians, and to none more so than Augustine of Hippo (354–430).

Scholarship frequently contrasts Augustine's position on this subject with Prudentius's.[62] Typically, one or the other is seen as the more 'progressive.' One reason for the continuing lack of consensus may be Prudentius's ambivalence towards the Roman Empire, on which we have touched above (Näf 1995, 92–5). Another may be that Augustine's attitude towards the Roman Empire undergoes a significant change. Around 400/1, that is, precisely at the time when Prudentius is thought to have been producing most of his poetry, Augustine altered his opinion of the role of the Roman Empire in God's plan for human history and salvation, shifting from a religio-political enthusiasm for the post-Constantinian Christian Empire and 'Christian times' (*tempora Christiana*) that was shared by many of his contemporaries, to a more sceptical view of the Empire as in itself devoid of religious significance and merely instrumental in God's purposes. Instead of standing at the culmination of God's plan for the salvation of humankind, the Empire thus becomes theoretically dispensable.[63] Augustine paradigmatically changed the evaluation of the empire from sacralization to secularization.

Augustine also deals with the famous prophecy from book 1 of Virgil's *Aeneid*.[64] He does so first in a sermon delivered in Carthage in 410 or 411, where he interprets these words as a flattery of the Romans, which Virgil put into the mouth of Jupiter so as not to take responsibility himself for a false prophecy.[65] The other, and more important, instance is at *City of God* 2.29, where he exhorts the Romans to abandon worship of the false pagan gods:

> Do not hearken to your degenerate descendants who cast aspersions on Christ and Christians, denouncing the times as bad, since the times *they* are looking for are not of peaceful living but of carefree sinning. You never approved such a goal even for your earthly fatherland. Lay hold without delay on the heavenly fatherland, which will cost you only the slightest toil, and you will reign in it truly forever. For there you shall have no fire of Vesta, no Capitoline stone, but *the one true God sets limits neither in space nor time; unending sway will he bestow* [emphasis added].[66]

Augustine is very close to Prudentius in his manner of adapting the Virgilian phrase. But here it is the one true God, rather than the emperor Theodosius (as in Prudentius), who replaces Jupiter as agent of the prophecy. With *ponit* ('he sets') Augustine keeps the present tense of the Virgilian original (*pono*, 'I set'), only changing it, like Prudentius, into the third-person singular. But at the same time, crucially modifying – or perhaps even correcting[67] – Prudentius, he transforms the Virgilian perfect-tense *dedi* ('I have bestowed') and the Prudentian present-tense *docet* ('he teaches') into an even more challenging future *dabit* ('he will bestow'), transforming the Christian poet's paraenetic statement into a clearly eschatological one.[68]

Augustine regards the Roman Empire neither as perpetual (*Serm.* 81.8, PL 38.504-5; 105.9, PL 38.622), nor as having a special role in history,[69] nor as distinguished by a special moral quality in comparison with other empires (*City of God* 19.21, 24). Occasionally he detects a divine will behind the pacification of the world by the Romans (*City of God* 18.22), but generally he is very critical of such earthly 'empires of peace.'[70] Since he is determined to separate the Church and her mission from any worldly institution,[71] he does not approve of religious colonization either. It is thus hardly surprising that he never uses Genesis 12:7 as a title for Christian territorialism. Instead, he spiritualizes the passage and refers it to the individual Christian soul or sees it as a past fact in the history of Israel. A particularly expansive passage from his commentary on the Psalms will make his position clear:

But if in this passage the Old Testament is to be understood with respect to the land of Canaan – for thus the context of the Psalm runs, 'and he stated this to Jacob himself as a law and to Israel itself as an eternal covenant, saying, Unto thee will I give the land of Canaan, the allotment of your inheritance' [Ps 104:10–11] – how is it to be understood as everlasting, since that earthly inheritance could not be everlasting? And for this reason it is called the Old Testament, because it is abolished by the New. But a thousand generations do also not seem to signify anything eternal, since they involve an end ... Hence it seems to me that we ought not to understand this passage as referring to the Old Testament, which as is said through the prophet was to be cancelled by the New: 'Behold, the days come, says the Lord, when I will make a new covenant with the house of Jacob ...' [Jer 31:31] ... The command then is faith, that the righteous should live by faith; and an eternal inheritance is set before this faith. 'A thousand generations,' then, are, on account of the perfect number, to be understood for all; that is, as long as generation continuously succeeds generation, so long is it commanded to us to live by faith. This the people of God observe, the children of promise who succeed by birth, and depart by death, until every generation be finished; and this is signified by the number thousand; because the cube of the number ten, ten times ten times ten, amounts to a thousand ... This is everlasting inheritance. (*Enarr. in Psalm.* 104.6–7, CCL 40.1539–40)[72]

Conclusion

The aim of the preceding remarks has been to give a glimpse of early Christian views of the relation between empire and Christianity, as they emerged from the encounter between traditional Roman (especially Latin) political teleology and a biblical revelation. It should by now be clear how little truth there is in the claim that the idea of divinely ordained conquest was a novelty of the Christian (and Islamic) West.[73] The longevity of that idea in the medieval and modern world is testimony, in the first instance, to the overpowering impact of pagan Roman imperial ideology. If it was easy for Christians of the early centuries, as a persecuted minority, to hate that pagan ideology, the temptation to associate with it increased after the establishment of Christianity as a 'state religion' in the late fourth century. Yet the ambivalence of Christian thinkers on these matters is not solely a reflection of the changing political situation of Christianity. It is also a sign of tensions inherent in Christian thought and the Christian view of history from the start. In other words, it is a hermeneutical problem.

My particular aim in this essay has been to show that in some respects the differences between Prudentius and Augustine are not as great as scholarship has generally suggested. Both, as we have seen, could spiritualize territorial claims. Both in their different ways thus bear witness to a figure of thought – and of exegesis – that is characteristic of Christianity in its double allegiance to history and eternity.[74] In *Against Symmachus* Prudentius uses a biblical framework in order to rewrite pagan Roman imperial ideology. In his eyes, Rome is justified in ruling over the whole world as her territory, but her rule has to be severed from pagan religion. Because rule and religion were closely related in Roman thought, the poet seeks to usurp both the cultural and the political hegemony of Rome for Christian ends. This Christian 'takeover' is seen as, on the one hand, completing Rome's earthly destiny in an ideal and predestined way and, on the other, as extending Rome's 'geographical' reach into a supra-geographical eternity. By applying Christian hermeneutics to Roman ideology Prudentius at once pleads for a historical discontinuity (false gods have to be abandoned) and argues that the Roman Empire is perfected and fulfilled with Christianity. He thus runs the risk of an ambivalent result. Rome as *the* colonial power of the day is potentially undermined by a Christianity that ultimately claims an eternal territory and wishes to challenge the short-term territorialism of pagan political thought. Meanwhile, Christianity is compromised by association with an originally pagan claim to hegemony, by postulating the Christian faith as the only possible one for the world. Thus, Christian intolerance and religious imperialism stand in sharp contrast to pagan religious tolerance and syncretism. The two poles of world usurpation and world denial between which Christianity moves reflect in a way the liminal state of the Roman Empire at the time of Prudentius and Augustine, as having turned from prosecuting Christianity to accepting it as state religion.

As a poet, Prudentius could make use of the established 'master narrative' (Quint 1993, 15) of the *Aeneid* in a way that extended its meaning into Christian times. Augustine in his prose work the *City of God* used different literary and rhetorical means to make an abrupt parting with both pagan and Christian poetry. According to David Quint, 'The *Aeneid* ascribes to political power the capacity to fashion human history into narrative … and attaches political meaning to narrative form itself' (Quint 1993, 8–9). Both Prudentius and Augustine would have agreed with the second half of this statement, Prudentius approvingly,

Augustine disapprovingly. However, they would have coincided in their disagreement with the first half: for them, it is not political power, but God's power as depicted in the Bible – and as apprehended in biblical hermeneutics – that alone has the capacity to fashion human history into narrative. Both writers pursued this hermeneutical insight in their respective genres, Prudentius using poetry for variously apologetic and allegorical purposes, Augustine constructing a kind of prose epic or anti-epic in the *City of God*. And yet, despite the latter's best efforts, the reception-history of that work shows that later generations could still use it to lay claim to earthly empires.[75]

NOTES

1   *his ego nec metas rerum nec tempora pono: / imperium sine fine dedi.* Translations of the *Aeneid* are taken from the Loeb edition by H. Rushton Fairclough, revised by G.P. Gould, sometimes with modifications.
2   For good discussion and comparisons with analogous events in the *Iliad* and the *Odyssey*, see Schmidt 2001, 66–9.
3   Austin 1971 on 1.278f. paraphrases *metas rerum* with 'fortune,' which misses the territorial implications of the phrase. See Servius on *Aen.* 1.278: *metas ad terras rettulit, tempora ad annos*; 6.794–5 is clearer about the geographical extension of the Roman Empire.
4   See the stimulating and wide-ranging account by S. Howe (2002), especially 9–15. It will be one of the aims of this essay to show that Howe is wrong to claim (14) that the idea of divinely ordained conquest is peculiar to the Christian and Islamic West, and that it is originally a pagan (or, to speak less tendentiously, pre-Christian) Roman concept. For an excellent analysis of the relevant passages in Virgil's *Aeneid*, see Gärtner 1996a (here 1147–8), the best concise survey of the reception of 'Roman imperialism' in Late Antiquity known to me.
5   Cf. *Aen.* 3.504–5.
6   *En huius, nate, auspiciis illa incluta Roma / imperium terris, animos aequabit Olympo.*
7   *super et Garamantas et Indos / proferet imperium; iacet extra sidera tellus, / extra anni solisque uias, ubi caelifer Atlas / axem umero torquet stellis ardentibus aptum. / huius in aduentum iam nunc et Caspia regna / responsis horrent diuum et Maeotia tellus, / et septemgemini turbant trepida ostia Nili. / nec uero Alcides tantum telluris obiuit, / fixerit aeripedem ceruam licet, aut Erymanthi / pacarit nemora et Lernam tremefecerit arcu; / nec qui pampineis uictor iuga flectit habenis*

/ Liber, agens celso Nysae de uertice tigris. / et dubitamus adhuc uirtutem
extendere factis, / aut metus Ausonia prohibet consistere terra?

8 Of course, Virgil was not the only one arguing along those lines; see, e.g.,
Horace, *Odes* 3.3.18ff. and cf. Austin's commentary on the *Aeneid* 100. My
investigation concentrates on Virgil for two reasons: his epic is the most
powerful literary expression of Roman imperial ideology and we possess
particularly rich sources for the way he was interpreted in Late Antiquity.

9 *sed nos fata deum vestras exquirere terras / imperiis egere suis.*

10 *si quando Thybrim vicinaque Thybridis arva / intrare gentique meae data moenia*
cernam.

11 In Homer's *Iliad*, the poem with which 'European' literature may be
imagined to begin, the main theme (as already recognized by Herodotus
1.1–5) is the fight between Europe and Asia, but no claim for conquest is
made, as the Greeks return to their home after their final victory.

12 See Dougherty 1993.

13 See Thraede 1962.

14 Cf. Schmidt 2001, 76–7.

15 Cf. Schmidt 2001, 78–9, tracing this mechanism of *Geschichtshermeneutik*
back to an archaic, mainly oral form of historiography, which was strictly
speaking outdated in the Augustan Age.

16 *imperium Oceano, famam qui terminet astris.*

17 Cf., e.g., *Aen.* 6.792: *Augustus Caesar, divi genus,* and numerous other
instances also in other sources. Quint (62) notes the irony that the living
Caesar had been a scandal to Augustus and his poets, whereas the dead
and apotheosized Caesar was a source of divine authorization and
guidance.

18 Donatus, in his commentary on the *Aeneid* from the beginning of the fifth
century, explains the function of the phrase as to praise Augustus's
achievements (*Interpretationes Vergilianae* vol. 1, 63–4).

19 Cf. Thraede 1991, 388n27.

20 Note already in the Old Testament, e.g., Sirach 10:4: 'The power of the
earth is in the hand of the Lord, and in due time he will set over it one that
is profitable.'

21 Despite the fact that other, non-Roman, empires were known: see Gärtner
1996a, 1146–7.

22 Optatus, *Against the Donatists* 3.3.5: *Non enim respublica est in ecclesia, sed*
ecclesia in republica, id est in imperio Romano. Cf. Brennecke 1992.

23 See Kofsky 2000, esp. 215–19 and 286–7; Buchheit 1985; and Smolak 1999,
137 on the beginnings of 'Rome teleology,' which according to Eusebius,
Ecclesiastical History 4.26.1–11, go back to Melito, bishop of Sardis, who

lived around 170 CE. In Latin literature the idea is first found in Ambrose: see Klingner 1965, 659.

24 Eusebius, *Ecclesiastical History* 1.2.17–27: 'Then, at last, when all men, even the heathen throughout the world, were now fitted for the benefits prepared for them beforehand, for the reception of the knowledge of the father, then again that same divine and heavenly Logos of God, the teacher of virtues, the minister of the father in all good things, appeared at the beginning of the Roman Empire through man' (trans. K. Lake).

25 Eusebius, *In Praise of Constantine* 16.4, trans. H.A. Drake, with modifications.

26 See Gärtner 1996a, 1176–8 on the slightly earlier Lactantius, who changed his opinion from initial distance from the Roman Empire to final acceptance of the coexistence of proper piety and prosperity within the community.

27 Already Eusebius, in chapters 19 and 20 of his *Oration on the Emperor Constantine*, quotes from Virgil's fourth eclogue and refers the prophecies made there to Christ and his church; cf. Benko 1980.

28 Quint 11, 51–79.

29 Although less explicitly, these notions occur also in the *Fight of the Human Soul*: see Smolak 2001, 132–6.

30 See Shanzer 1989, esp. 443, 458–60.

31 Because any subsequent military reverse would put everything in doubt again – as occurred when the Goths sacked Rome ten years later. See the section on Augustine, below.

32 These devices were presumably designed to win over pagan members of the senatorial class: see Cunningham 1976, esp. 58; Rohmann 2002; and Döpp 1999.

33 After the person who supposedly first elaborated it. See Winiarczyk 2002.

34 See *Against Symmachus* 1.180: *vel fama vel error*; for the whole argument see 1.164–244.

35 *felices, si cuncta Deo sua prospera Christo / principe disposita scissent, qui currere regna / certis ducta modis Romanorumque triumphos / crescere et inpletis voluit se infundere saeclis.* See above for the same argument in Eusebius and also *Against Symmachus* 2.35–6, 583–755, and Prudentius, *Crowns of Martyrdom* 2.413–40, where the Christian God is consistently named as the true cause of Rome's successes throughout history; Peebles 1951, 60–1; and Garuti 1996, 155–6.

36 Buchheit 1985, 194–6.

37 Cf. Cameron and Hall 1999, 38–9 and 204–13, who also mention (209) the quite different version in Lactantius, *Deaths of the Persecutors* 44.5; also Kofsky 2000, 47.

38 Kofsky 2000, 48, 215–19, 287.

39 *et dubitamus adhuc Romam tibi, Christe, dicatam / in leges transisse tuas omnique volentem / cum populo et summis cum civibus ardua magni / iam super astra poli terrenum extendere regnum?* For the adoption of the reading *et dubitamus adhuc* ('and do we still hesitate') from Virgil, *Georgics* 2.433 and *Aen.* 6.806, see Döpp 1988, 338.

40 *denique nec metas statuit nec tempora ponit, / imperium sine fine docet, ne Romula virtus / iam sit anus, norit ne gloria parta senectam.* Garuti in his translation (114) supplies the subject of the verbs as 'il principe'; cf. Garuti 1996, 161–2; Paschoud 1967, 225–6 proposes 'le premier empereur chrétien,' i.e., Theodosius, as does Döpp 1988, 341.

41 For *Romula virtus* in the same metrical position see Silius Italicus 16.254 in an expansionist context: the Romans, having successfully conquered Spain, ask the Numidian king Syphax for his alliance. For *gloria parta* see Cicero, *Republic* 2.5. Döpp 1988, 341 rightly emphasizes the spiritualization of these moral values in Prudentius.

42 In *Against Symmachus* 2.80ff. and 649ff. Prudentius gives the personified Roma a speech likewise emphasizing her youthful vigour despite old age; see also 1.511–23 and 550–60. For a similar view of Roma in Claudian, see Gärtner 1996b.

43 See also Thraede 1991, passim, esp. 388–93, for part of the following.

44 This goes back to Plato and Cicero: see Smolak 2001, 133–4.

45 Cf. Partoens 1999, 162. Remarkably, Genesis 12:7 nowhere appears. See the section on Augustine below.

46 See Mt 13:19–23 and Herzog 1966, 23–5. We find significantly little Virgil here: Mahoney 1934, 103, 107, 119, 122.

47 This is where Augustine will be even more consequential in his argumentation. See 188–9 above.

48 2.555: *aeternae in arce curiae*; 559: *Roma caelestis*, which both point at a transcendental perspective on the city of Rome. See Fux 2003, ad loc., with useful information. It is important to notice the use of Roman political terminology in eschatological contexts, as also at *Fight of the Human Soul* 839: *nomina apostolici ... bis sena senatus*. Again, this does not imply a divinization of Roman institutions, but rather their radical discontinuity with the ultimate Christian reality, as in the *eschaton* these institutions will be completely revalorized; thus Fux 2003, 227.

49 *Vive tibi, princeps, debetur gloria, vivum / virtutis pretium decus immortale secuto. / regnator mundi Christo sociabere in aevum, / quo ductore meum trahis ad caelestia regnum*; cf. Gärtner 1996a, 1186.

50 Garuti 1996, 156–7, with relevant material; also Fishwick 1990.

51 This is also true of virtues, which can be used as personifications (as in the *The Fight of the Human Soul*) but must not be worshipped as deities; see above 185.

52 Cf. Döpp 1988, 338 and Lühken 2002, 178–9, 272, who highlight the optimistic reaction to Theodosius's successful Christianization of the Empire, but without noting the areas of ambiguity.

53 Cf. Horsfall 2000 on *Aen.* 7.272 for further parallels.

54 E.g. 2.756–9, 1018–9, 1062–3.

55 Smolak 2001, an otherwise excellent article, does not emphasize this sufficiently.

56 For the Epilogue see Smolak 2002, 325–34. This imperial ideology is less prominent in Latin poets of the following century. It does not occur at all in Dracontius, and is depoliticized in Avitus, e.g., *Spir.* 1.175: *progeniem sine fine dedi* ('I have bestowed issue without end') as God's promise to Adam and Eve: see Pollmann 2001, 116–17. But in medieval times the *translatio imperii* was a standard feature.

57 *apparuitque Dominus Abram et dixit ei: semini tuo dabo terram hanc.*

58 As Augustine points out at *City of God* 16.18.

59 See Westermann 1981, 180–1.

60 In chapter 1 of his *Mimesis: The Representation of Reality in Western Literature*, entitled 'Odysseus' Scar,' 3–23. See the differentiated evaluation in de Jong 1999, 154–64.

61 Auerbach 1953, 19.

62 Cf. Smolak 1999 as a typical instance.

63 The classic account of this change is R.A. Markus, *Saeculum: History and Society in the Theology of St Augustine.* Cf. Hollerich 1999, 312.

64 For this and some of the following, I am indebted to the excellent summary of Gärtner 1996a, 1189–90; see also Tornan 2006, 150f, 224–6.

65 *Serm.* 105.10, PL 38.622–3: *qui hoc terrenis regnis promiserunt, non ueritate ducti sunt, sed adulatione mentiti sunt. poeta illorum quidam induxit Iouem loquentem, et ait de Romanis, his ego nec metas rerum, nec tempora pono: imperium sine fine dedi* [*Aen.* 1, 278ff.]. *non plane ita respondet ueritas.*

66 *non audias degeneres tuos Christo Christianisue detrahentes et accusantes uelut tempora mala, cum quaerant tempora, quibus non sit quieta uita, sed potius secura nequitia. haec tibi numquam nec pro terrena patria placuerunt. nunc iam caelestem arripe, pro qua minimum laborabis, et in ea ueraciter semperque regnabis. illic enim tibi non Vestalis focus, non lapis Capitolinus, sed Deus unus et uerus nec metas rerum nec tempora ponit; imperium sine fine dabit.*

67 Smolak 2001, 145–6 sees a connection between this passage in the *City of God* and Prudentius's *Fight of the Human Soul*, but does not include the

Against Symmanchus in his argumentation. It appears likely from Smolak 2001, 147 that Augustine knew at least some of Prudentius's writings.

68 See also the future tense in Gen 12:7. Augustine uses the earthly Roman Empire as a point of comparison with the eternal celestial one also, e.g., at *Epist.* 138.3 (CSEL 44.144) and *Epist.* 220.8 (CSEL 57.437).

69 Including the history of salvation: *City of God* 17.13, where Augustine emphasizes that due to the mutability of human affairs, no earthly reign can guarantee this promised peace, but only the heavenly, i.e., eschatological, Jerusalem.

70 *City of God* 1, preface, criticizing Virgil, *Aen.* 6.853 ('To spare the fallen and subdue the proud') as inflated self-praise. For a more general discussion see *City of God* 19.12.

71 See esp. *City of God* 19.17.

72 Cf. with other arguments and contexts, but never imperialistic, *Quaest. in Hept.* 1.28; *Trin.* 2.19 and 2.37; *City of God* 16.18.

73 Above, n. 4.

74 Similar results, based partly on different evidence, can be found in Rösler 1886, 447–79, Heim 1992, 257–92, and Pietsch 2001.

75 For an example see Vessey 1999.

REFERENCES

Auerbach, Eric. 1953. *Mimesis: The Representation of Reality in Western Literature.* Trans. W.R. Trask. Princeton: Princeton University Press.

Austin, R.G. 1971. *P. Vergilii Maronis Aeneidos, liber primus, with a commentary by R.G. Austin.* Oxford: Oxford University Press.

Bastiaensen, A.A.R. 1993. 'Prudentius in Recent Literary Criticism.' In J. den Boeft and A. Hilhorst, eds, *Early Christian Poetry: A Collection of Essays*, 101–34. Leiden: Brill.

Benko, S. 1980. 'Virgil's Fourth Eclogue in Christian Interpretation.' *Aufstieg und Niedergang der römischen Welt* 31.1: 646–705.

Brennecke, H.C. 1992. 'Ecclesia est in re publica, id est in imperio Romano (Optatus 3.3). Das Christentum in der Gesellschaft an der Wende zum "Konstantinischen Zeitalter."' *Jahrbuch für Biblische Theologie* 7: 209–39.

Buchheit, V. 1985. 'Prudentius über Gesittung durch Eroberung und Bekehrung.' *Würzburger Jahrbücher* 11: 189–224.

Cameron, A., and S. Hall. 1999. *Eusebius: Life of Constantine. Translated with Introduction and Commentary.* Oxford: Oxford University Press.

Cunningham, M.P. 1976. 'The Contexts of Prudentius' Poems.' *Classical Philology* 71: 56–66.

de Jong, I. 1999. 'Auerbach and Homer.' In J.N. Kazazis and A. Rengakos, eds, *Euphrosyne: Festschrift D.N. Maronitis*, 154–64. Stuttgart: F. Steiner Verlag.

Donatus. 1905. *Interpretationes Vergilianae*. Ed. H. Georgii. Leipzig: B.G. Teubner.

Döpp, S. 1980. 'Prudentius' Gedicht gegen Symmachus. Anlaß und Struktur.' *Jahrbuch für Antike und Christentum* 23: 65–81.

– 1988. 'Vergilische Elemente in Prudentius' Contra Symmachum.' *Hermes* 116: 337–42.

– 1999. 'Prudentius' Gedicht *Contra Symmachum* in der religiösen Auseinandersetzung seiner Zeit.' In G. Binder and K. Ehlich, eds, *Religiöse Kommunikation: Formen und Praxis vor der Neuzeit*. Trier: Wissenschaftlicher Verlag.

Dougherty, C. 1993. *The Poetics of Colonization: From City to Text in Archaic Greece*. New York and Oxford: Oxford University Press.

Fishwick, D. 1990. 'Prudentius and the Cult of Divus Augustus.' *Historia* 39: 475–86.

Fux, P.-Y. 2003. *Les sept passions de Prudence*. Fribourg: Éditions Universitaires Fribourg.

Gärtner, H.A. 1996a. 'Imperium Romanum.' *Reallexikon für Antike und Christentum* 17: 1142–98.

– 1996b. 'Roma redet.' *Acta Antiqua Academiae Scientiarum Hungaricae* 37: 277–84.

Garuti, G. 1996. *Prudentius Contra Symmachum. Testo, traduzione e commento*. Rome: Japadre.

Heim, F. 1992. *La théologie de la victoire*. Paris: Beauchesne.

Herzog, R. 1966. *Die allegorische Dichtkunst des Prudentius*. Munich: Beck.

Hollerich, M.J. 1999. 'John Milbank, Augustine, and the "Secular."' In M. Vessey, K. Pollmann, and A. Fitzgerald, eds, *History, Apocalypse, and the Secular Imagination: New Essays on Augustine's 'City of God.'* Bowling Green, OH: Philosophy Documentation Center.

Horsfall, N. 2000. *Virgil, Aeneid 7: A Commentary*. Leiden: Brill.

Howe, S. 2002. *Empire: A Very Short Introduction*. Oxford: Oxford University Press.

Klingner, F. 1965. 'Rom als Idee.' In *Römische Geisteswelt*, 645–66. Munich: H. Ellerman.

Kofsky, A. 2000. *Eusebius of Caesarea against Paganism*. Leiden: Brill.

Lühken, M. 2002. *Christianorum Maro et Flaccus: Zur Vergil- und Horazrezeption des Prudentius*. Göttingen: Vandenhoeck and Ruprecht.

Mahoney, A. 1934. 'Vergil in the Works of Prudentius.' PhD dissertation. Washington: Catholic University of America.

Markus, R.A. 1989. *Saeculum: History and Society in the Theology of St Augustine*. 2nd ed. Cambridge: Cambridge University Press.

Näf, B. 1995. *Senatorisches Standesbewußtsein in spätrömischer Zeit*. Fribourg: Universitätsverlag, Freiburg.

Partoens, G. 1999. '"Deus agricolam confirmat." L'élaboration de la parabole du semeur dans les Livres Contre Symmaque de Prudence.' In J. den Boeft and M.L. van Ploo-van de Lisdonk, eds, *The Impact of Scripture in Early Christianity*, 161–86. Leiden: Brill.

Paschoud, F. 1967. *Roma aeterna: Études sur le patriotisme romain dans l'Occident Latin à l'époque des grandes invasions*. Neuchâtel: Institut Suisse de Rome.

Peebles, B.M. 1951. *The Poet Prudentius*. New York: McMullen.

Pietsch, C. 2001. 'Aeternas temptare vias. Zur Romidee im Werk des Prudentius.' *Hermes* 129: 259–75.

Pollmann, K. 2001. 'Das lateinische Epos in der Spätantike.' In J. Rüpke, ed., *Von Göttern und Menschen erzählen: Formkonstanzen und Funktionswandel vormoderner Epik*, 93–129. Stuttgart: F. Steiner.

Quint, David. 1993. *Epic and Empire: Politics and Generic Form from Virgil to Milton*. Princeton: Princeton University Press.

Rohmann, D. 2002. 'Das langsame Sterben der Veterum Cultura Deorum: Pagane Kulte bei Prudentius.' *Hermes* 131: 235–53.

Rösler, A. 1886. *Der katholische Dichter Aurelius Prudentius Clemens*. Freiburg: Herder.

Schmidt, E.A. 2001. 'Vergils Aeneis als augusteische Dichtung.' In J. Rüpke, ed., *Von Göttern und Menschen erzählen: Formkonstanzen und Funktionswandel vormoderner Epik*, 65–92. Stuttgart: F. Steiner.

Shanzer, D. 1989. 'The Date and Composition of Prudentius' *Contra orationem Symmachi libri*.' *Rivista di Filologia e di Istruzione Classica* 117: 441–62.

Smolak, K. 1999. 'Res publica res populi Dei. Ciceros *De re publica* bei Augustinus (civ. 19) und Prudentius (*Symm*. 2).' *Wiener Humanistische Blätter, Sonderheft: Zur Philosophie der Antike*, 109–39. Vienna: Wiener Humanistische Gesellschaft.

– 2001. 'Die Psychomachie des Prudentius als historisches Epos.' In M. Salvadore, ed., *La poesia tardoantica e medievale: Atti del Convegno Internazionale di Studi*, 121–44. Turin: Edizioni dell'Orso.

– 2002. 'Überlegungen zum *Epilogus* des Prudentius.' In *FS Ch. Gnilka*. *Jahrbuch für Antike und Christentum Ergänzungsband* 33, 325–34. Münster: Aschendorffsche Verlagsbuchhandlung.

Thraede, K. 1962. 'Erfinder II.' *Reallexikon für Antike und Christentum* 5 (1962): 1191–278.

– 1991. 'Concordia Romana in der Antwort des Prudentius auf die dritte Relatio des Symmachus.' In E. Dassmann and K. Thraede, eds, *Festschrift E. Dassmann*, 380–94. Münster: Aschendorffsche Verlagsbuchhandlung.

Tornan, C. 2006. *Zwischen Rhetorik und Philosophie.* Berlin and New York: Walter de Gruyter.

Vessey, M. 1999. 'The *Citie of God* (1610) and the London Virginia Company.' In M. Vessey, K. Pollmann, and A. Fitzgerald, eds, *History, Apocalypse, and the Secular Imagination: New Essays on Augustine's 'City of God,'* 257–81. Bowling Green, OH: Philosophy Documentation Center, 1999.

Westermann, C. 1981. *Genesis. 2. Teilband. Biblischer Kommentar.* Neukirchen: Neukirchener Verlag.

Winiarczyk, M. 2002. *Euhemeros von Messene: Leben, Werk und Nachwirkung.* Munich and Leipzig: K.G. Saur.

8

'The Ends of the Earth': The Bible, Bibles, and the Other in Early Medieval Europe

IAN WOOD

Missionary Histories?

Although evangelization has not been a constant feature of its history, Christianity always had and has the potential to be a missionary religion. After all, St Matthew's Gospel provided the commission for all missionaries (28:19): 'Go ye therefore, and teach all nations, baptising them in the name of the Father and of the Son, and of the Holy Ghost' (KJV). In addition, the Gospels and Acts provided narratives of mission, and the Epistles spiritual and pastoral advice. It may therefore be a little surprising to realize how novel it was for Bede (ca 673–735) to make Christianization one of the dominant themes of his *Ecclesiastical History of the English People*.[1] None of the earlier narrators of barbarian history had made so much of the acceptance of the Christian religion. Gregory of Tours, who saw the conversion of Clovis as a defining moment in history,[2] did not spend time describing the conversion of other rulers: neither did Fredegar, nor the author of the *Liber historiae Francorum* (Book of the History of the Franks). The Christianization of the Goths is passed over quickly by Jordanes, no doubt because of the embarrassment of their becoming 'Arians rather than Christians' (*Ariani potius quam Christiani effecti*).[3] And Isidore of Seville does no better, although Reccared's conversion to Catholicism was an event of central importance to him and to the Visigothic church in Spain. Writing half a century after Bede, Paul the Deacon, presumably for reasons not unlike those inhibiting Jordanes and Isidore, does not pause on the initial Christianization of the Lombards. Nor indeed does he deal clearly with their ultimate switch from Arianism to Catholicism, despite his interest in the Lombards as a Christian nation, attached to the cult of John the Baptist.

In the ninth century an account of the Christianization of the Bavarians and Carantanians, the *Conversio Bagoariorum et Carantanorum*, was drawn up by the diocese of Salzburg as a response to the claims made by the Greek missionary Methodius.[4] It is, however, largely a list of church foundations and dedications, aimed at making a legal point about ecclesiastical jurisdiction. Among medieval narrative historians it is, perhaps, Adam of Bremen, writing in the late eleventh century, who comes closest to Bede in emphasizing mission – although he does so for different reasons. Like the author of the *Conversio*, his concern was to defend the jurisdictional claims of the archbishops of his diocese, but he pursued his aim over a much wider canvas, and with a broader sense of narrative.[5] At the same time, his sense of the world of mission was very different from Bede's, as we shall see. The two historians and their differences provide a chronological framework for the argument I wish to present. Having looked at issues raised by their narratives, I will conclude by making some comments on the Bible as a physical object carried by individual missionaries.

Mission and Eschatology: Bede as Historian and Exegete

Bede's history, of course, is a *historia ecclesiastica*. Even so, previous ecclesiastical historians had placed more emphasis on issues other than mission, not least that of persecution. The history of the Anglo-Saxon church up to Bede's time was admittedly such as to force the issue of Christianization to the fore: Christianity was received not just by one, but by several Anglo-Saxon kingdoms. Indeed, Bede actually skimped on its reception in some of them. One is hard put to understand from his account when and how Wessex was Christianized. Even so, Bede's history contains substantial narratives on the Christianization of Kent, Northumbria, the Middle Angles, Essex, Mercia, the Isle of Wight, and the South Saxons – to say nothing of his comments on missions to the Picts or the Frisians. With so many kingdoms accepting Christianity, it was relatively easy to see Anglo-Saxon history as an ongoing tale of Christianization. Yet, our familiarity with Bede's narrative perhaps blinds us to the novelty of that narrative in the early eighth century.

Even among hagiographers, few had devoted as high a proportion of their texts to Christianization as did Bede: the *Life of Wilfrid* by Stephanus (ed. Colgrave, 26, 41–2) and, more particularly, the Whitby *Life of Gregory the Great* – both of them, significantly, Northumbrian – put some emphasis on mission.[6] And certainly the seventh-century *Lives* of

Patrick are deeply concerned to present a narrative of Christianization, albeit a fanciful one.[7] From the continent, however, the haul of such narratives from before the late eighth century is small. The earliest *Life of Amandus* may have concentrated on mission, but it only survives in fragments (Riedmann 1976, 262–89). Historical and hagiographical narratives in which Christianization is given the same prominence as it is in Bede's *Historia ecclesiastica* tend to be later in date, and indeed have usually been influenced by his text.

To emphasize the novelty of Bede's choice of mission as a dominant theme in the history of a people is obviously not to claim that a missionary ideology itself was new. Gregory the Great had developed one, not least in his sending of Augustine to Kent in 596 (Markus 1997, 177–87).[8] Before him in the late 420s and 430s, Pope Celestine seems to have had a similar missionary concern, as suggested by his sending Palladius to the Irish. His ideas were shared by Pope Leo and, within the same circle, by Prosper of Aquitaine, who wrote the tract *De vocatione omnium gentium* (On the Calling of all the Nations) (Charles-Edwards 1993, 1–12). This papal vision, in which Britain and Ireland regularly appear as a group of islands at the ends of the earth, was well known to Bede (O'Reilly 2005, 124–8). Nor had missionary ideology in the fifth and sixth centuries been confined to the popes and their associates. In the early sixth century Avitus of Vienne certainly encouraged Clovis to evangelize the peoples subject to the Franks.[9] A hundred years later Amandus, himself a missionary among the Basques, Bavarians, and Slavs, as well as the peoples of north-eastern Francia, seems to have combined the Irish ascetic tradition of the 'pilgrimage for Christ' (*peregrinatio pro Christo*) with Gregory the Great's pastoral concerns to create his own missionary ideology (Fritze 1969). What Bede did was to draw on such ideas and make them central to a narrative, to an extent that no one had done before.

Although the narrative of early Anglo-Saxon history was easily presented as a history of Christianization, it is clear that Bede's decision to emphasize that aspect was not dictated solely by the material before him. Christianization as a theme had long influenced the Northumbrian monk, all the more so because he drew no strict distinction between pastoral care and mission to the heathen.[10] The way Bede presents it, Cuthbert's pastoral work as a preacher in the recently Christianized world of Northumbria is not an obviously different activity from Aidan's initial mission to Oswald's heathen subjects. Indeed, the overlap between pastoral care and mission to the pagan in regions which were not totally alien to the preacher was such that it is easy to read the actions of a reformer such as Boniface as being directed more towards the heathen than was actually the case (Wood 2001a, 58–60). A distinction between pastoral care and mission becomes much more apparent after Bede's time, when the mission fields differed culturally and socially from the world in which the missionaries themselves were trained. As we shall see, this distinction seems to have been particularly important in the ninth, tenth, and eleventh centuries.

In considering the development of Bede's missionary interest, it is telling that he chose relatively early in his career, perhaps as early as 709, to write a commentary on the Acts of the Apostles. Moreover, his is the earliest commentary on Acts to have survived. There had been eastern commentaries, but that of Diodorus of Tarsus no longer exists, and that of Theodore of Mopsuestia survives only in fragments. John Chrysostom's homilies on Acts were probably unknown in the West.[11] More than any other book of the New Testament, the Acts of the Apostles is a narrative of Christianization. Its importance for the enlargement of the Christian mission to the gentiles was not lost on Bede, who pauses more than once to emphasize the fact. For instance, the events of Pentecost lead to the comment that 'at the same time he indicated that the holy church, when it had spread to the ends of the earth was to speak in the languages of all nations.'[12] The eschatological tone recurs in a comment on 3:1: 'Then labouring continuously until evening, they embued many thousands of people with the word of faith, because the teachers of the church, coming at the end of the world, also preach first to ailing Israel and afterwards to the gentile world. For they are the laborers whom the householder brought into the vineyard at the ninth and the eleventh hour.'[13] The vision of Peter (Acts 10) naturally leads to further such comment.[14] In addition, Peter's earlier insistence on finding a twelfth apostle to replace Judas prompts the observation that 'since at the end of the world it is believed that the Jewish people who crucified the Lord are to be reconciled to the church, as the fiftieth day drew nigh the full number of apostles was restored.'[15] Thus, the replacement of Judas comes to symbolize the future integration of the Jews into the Church at the end of time.

Bede's eschatological emphases in his commentary on Acts are scarcely surprising. After all, one of his earliest works is his *Explanatio Apocalypsis* of 703–9 (Bonner 1966). As has been noted, however, his reading of the Apocalypse is essentially Augustinian, in that it stresses the individual's moral development rather than any millenarian doctrine (McGinn 1995,

70–1). It is equally notable that he did not portray the evangelization of the English, living as they did at the limit of the earth, as being likely to herald the immediate end of the world. But then Bede knew that the continental cousins of the Anglo-Saxons had yet to be Christianized. Others, for instance Victorinus of Pettau (Lumsden 2001, 15–16), had seen the Christianization of similarly placed peoples in a more eschatological light. So too, Patrick set a millenarian interpretation on his work at the edge of the world.[16] As we will see, others followed suit in the ninth century. By contrast, Bede specifically deviated from earlier interpretations of the Apocalypse in not associating the breaking of the first seal with the history of mission.[17]

That a commentary on Acts should prompt comment on mission is not in itself remarkable. More so is some of Bede's commentary on books of the Old Testament, where apparently less relevant text is used as a springboard to discuss evangelization. Diarmuid Scully singled out Bede's concern with salvation history in his commentaries on the *Book of Tobit* and the *Canticle of Habbakuk*. Thus, the verse in *Tobit* 'Then when everything that was to be taken on the journey had been made ready, Tobias bade farewell to his father and mother, and they both set off together' prompts comment on the apostles' preaching first to the Jews, and then to the gentiles.[18] Immediately thereafter, mention of Tobit's dog calls to mind Gregory the Great's identification of dogs as preachers, for they barked 'loudly on the Lord's behalf.'[19] Mission is similarly central to Bede's *De templo* (On the Temple), written shortly before the *Ecclesiastical History*, which is largely a commentary on 3 Kings (as Bede, who counted the books of Samuel as 1 and 2 Kings, calls 1 Kings), chapters 5 to 8. The builders of the temple are presented throughout as ministers of the word sent to Jews and gentiles alike,[20] for just as Hiram king of Tyre provided craftsmen for building the temple, so non-Jews had a role to play 'in the building of the Church.' In short, mission was central to Bede's thought before he ever turned to write his *Ecclesiastical History*. He raises the issue as often in his discussions of the Old Testament as in those of the New.

That the Bible was central to mission goes without saying. The chief purpose of mission was to spread the Word contained in the Bible. What is striking about Bede's commentaries and about his *Ecclesiastical History* is not that the Bible could prompt consideration of mission, but rather that it was the Old Testament that prompted him to write so often about Christianization. Given such emphasis, it is not difficult to see why Boniface, like Bede, as concerned with reform as with mission, should write to acquire copies of the latter's biblical commentaries. The Northumbrian's emphasis on preaching among both Christians and pagans was perfectly attuned to the West Saxon's work of reform and pastoral care, as well as his missionary intentions.

The Limits of Ethnography: Adam of Bremen

A little over a century after Bede, another writer interpreted mission in a manner more reminiscent of Victorinus of Pettau and Patrick. As Rimbert considered Anskar's achievement in Sweden, he recalled the words of Isaiah: 'Listen, O isles unto me; and hearken ye people, from far; The Lord hath called me from the womb; from the bowels of my mother hath he made mention of my name. And he hath made my mouth like a sharp sword; in the shadow of his hand hath he hid me, and made me a polished shaft; in his quiver hath he hid me; And said unto me, Thou art my servant, O Israel, in whom I will be glorified.'[21] The quotation continued, including a phrase already used by earlier theorists of mission:[22] 'I will also give thee for a light to the Gentiles, that thou mayest be salvation for them unto the end of the earth' (Is 49:6).[23] Immediately afterwards Rimbert repeated, with variation, parts of the quotation, but with some significant glosses: '"Listen, O isles," because almost the whole of that land is made up of islands, and, added to that, "Thou wilt be salvation for them unto the end of the earth," because the end of the world in the northern parts lies in the regions of the Suedes.' An image of islands, which had been important for Bede's reading of mission in the British Isles, was now applied to Scandinavia. But the potentially eschatological sense of the quotation is subsequently enhanced by a slip of the pen, when Rimbert refers to Isaiah as the even more apocalyptic Jeremiah.

Two centuries later Adam of Bremen paraphrased Rimbert's account. When, however, he came to this passage it was not Isaiah, but Ezekiel who came to mind, and he substituted the words 'And I will send a fire on Magog, and on them that dwell carelessly in the isles: and they shall know that I am the Lord.'[24] In light of the fact that Anskar's mission was ultimately a failure, this may seem a rather curious prophecy to cite. Clearly, one of the factors that led Adam to cite Ezekiel in place of Isaiah was the reference to islands common to both prophets. Just as Bede has emphasized the insular nature of Britain, Rimbert saw Scandinavia as a world of islands, and so too did Adam.[25] Indeed, the fourth book of his *Gesta Hammaburgensis ecclesiae pontificum* (Acts of the Bishops of the

Church of Hamburg), which is essentially a geographical description of the northern missionary territories of the archbishops of Hamburg-Bremen, is entitled *Descriptio insularum Aquilonis*, 'Description of the Islands of the North.' The opening sentence of the book states that the province of the Danes is almost entirely divided into islands: *Provintia Danorum tota fere in insulas dispertita est.*[26]

A number of issues converge in these passages. Scandinavia – like Britain – is thought to be at the northern edge of the world. It is a world of islands, and thus calls to mind prophecies of Isaiah and Ezekiel. Ezekiel's words cover the destruction of Gog and Magog. Their presence enhances the implicit eschatology of missionary activity at the physical limits of the world, for apocalyptic writings such as the *Pseudo-Methodius* had linked Gog and Magog with the arrival of the anti-Christ. Further, there is more than one missionary injunction in Matthew's Gospel. Chapter 24 contains the verse 'And this gospel of the kingdom shall be preached in all the world for a witness unto all nations; and then shall the end come' (14). The other command in the penultimate verse of the Gospel continues with the words 'Teaching them to observe all things whatsoever I have commanded you; and, lo, I am with you always, even unto the end of the world' (Mt 28:20). This too was a passage cited by Adam in his account of Rimbert.[27] Like Patrick, these two writers related mission at the geographical limits of the earth to the eschatological end of the world. As we have seen, Bede had not dwelt on this point, even though earlier writers had linked mission with the end of the world.

The threat of the apocalypse was a constant, but it was mitigated by Christ's words that no man knew when it would come (Mt 24:34–5, 42). Perhaps for this reason, defining the physical limits of the earth could become an immediate concern. This was a problem that had not impinged much on the consciousness of missionaries active within the Roman world, or just beyond what had once been its frontiers: they rarely had to deal with the absolute edge of humanity or with a completely alien Other. Romans had been used to a plethora of religions. Even Germanic paganism would have been relatively familiar to soldiers who had served on the frontiers of the Western Empire – not that it seems to have been a particularly exotic religion, being concerned most with geographical and natural features: the cult of individual gods does not appear to have been dominant, except perhaps in wartime. Germanic paganism would have been even less alien to the members of the successor states that emerged in the Roman West in the

.course of the fifth and sixth centuries. By contrast, all the accounts of Slav religion suggest that it was very different in its organization, being dominated by the images of gods housed within large temple complexes (Słupecki 1994).[28] The only Germanic site which may have equalled Arkona or Rethra was eleventh-century Uppsala, and one may wonder to what extent the cult there had been influenced by Slavonic practice as well as Christianity.[29] To writers of the ninth, tenth, and eleventh centuries, the Slav lands and central and northern Scandinavia were a very much more alien world than Germania had been to their predecessors.

The New Testament, concerned as it was with the holy land and, in Paul's journeys, with the Mediterranean world, had little to offer on the issue of the physical limits of the earth, although the Old did give some guidance: there were, for instance, the islands of Isaiah and Ezekiel which, as we have already noted, could be interpreted as lying at the edge of the world, and could further be identified with the island world of Scandinavia. It was, however, possible to bring other information to bear in order to grapple more fully with the problem of identifying the limits of the earth.

Adam of Bremen once again provides a useful introduction to the problem. Although he lived in a place which had never been Roman, what lay beyond his immediate horizon was infinitely more alien. As we have seen, in his account of Anskar's work in Sweden he called up Ezekiel's prophecy on Gog and Magog, with its apocalyptic overtones. In his geographical description of the Northern world in book 4 of his history he placed the Riphean Mountains to the east of the town of Sigtuna. There in the high snows could be found Amazons, Cynocephali, Cyclopes, Ymantopodes, and cannibals.[30] This was not simply bookish knowledge – though it was that too: Adam had heard it from Sven Estridson, the king of Denmark himself. If anyone in the southern Baltic knew of the realities beyond Sigtuna it should have been Sven, for the kings of Denmark had interests in the northern world.

On the other hand, everything that Adam tells us about the monstrous peoples, other than what he has to say on their geography, betrays classical learning. According to Adam, in order to procreate, the Amazons have sex with merchants. Their male children are *cynocephali*, and their female most beautiful women.[31] Curiously Adam, unlike most authors, does not define *cynocephali* as dogheaded: he comments rather that they are beings whose heads are on their chests: *Cynocephali sunt, qui in pectore caput habent.*[32] On the whole, however, he seems to have derived his information from Solinus (himself following Pliny), and Martianus Capella, where features he ascribes to his northern Amazons are associated with the African Blemmyes,[33] although he adds a comment from the Alexander Romance of the Archpriest Leo.[34] The information on the Ymantopodes, who hop on one leg, is also derived from Solinus, as Adam clearly states, although once again in the original source they are to be found in Africa.[35]

Adam, or Sven, if he really was the source of information, was not the first to transfer some if not all of these marginal peoples to the Baltic. Otto the Great had told the Arab traveller Ibrahim ibn Ya'qub that the Cynocephali lived to the west of the Rus (Jacob 1927, 14, 17). Earlier still the cosmographer known as Aethicus Ister, writing perhaps in Bavaria and probably in the early eighth century, had placed them on an island called Munitia, which certainly lay in the north, although exactly where is unclear.[36] Although the *Cosmography* of Aethicus has been seen as a humorous work, it undoubtedly had a serious intent. Drawing on traditions such as those preserved in *Pseudo-Methodius*, sections of the *Cosmography* have an eschatological flavour. In addition, the author's image of the North as a largely insular world is not unlike that offered by Rimbert and Adam. The similarities raise interesting questions on the extent to which some of the cosmographer's ideas on the marginal world of the North may have been relatively common.

More important from the point of view of missionary history, the nature of the Cynocephali had been discussed at length by Ratramnus of Corbie and Rimbert, the hagiographer of Anskar and bishop of Hamburg-Bremen.[37] Rimbert had been told that he was likely to meet Cynocephali in his missionary endeavours, and he wished to know whether he should convert them or not: in short, were they humans or animals? Ratramnus, faced with this question, offered an extraordinarily comprehensive response. From the information given by Rimbert, he established that the social habits of the Cynocephali indicated that they had a rational nature. He then turned to earlier information: to the fact that St Christopher was a Cynocephalus, and to Isidore's description of the Cynocephali, *gygantes* and *ciclopes*, as *monstra hominum*: in other words, monstrous yet human. They could thus be compared with Pigmies, Hippopods, and Macrobii. Ratramnus admits that not all that is born of woman is human, but concludes that Rimbert's account of cynocephalic society clinched the matter in favour of their humanity. His informant had said that they possessed domestic animals, and this must suggest a rational soul because of God's subjection of animals to men. Ratramnus's case is extremely sophisticated, using concepts of society and reason rather more than claims to authority. Certainly the Bible is cited twice: once because of its acknowledgment of the existence of giants (Gn 6:4), and once because of God's concession to man of authority over the animals (Gn 1:28). Nevertheless, it does not determine the case for the humanity of the Cynocephali.

It is important to note that this discussion of the monstrous involves beings that were thought to be close at hand. Nothing could be further from the truth than the modern assumption that in the medieval imagination monsters only existed far away.[38] In the ninth century they were regarded as being just around the corner. Their very proximity is central to their place in missionary thought. Why the Cynocephali in particular should have been transferred in the imagination from Africa to the Baltic is unclear, although there is evidence for the wearing of dog-like masks in the region (Hägg 1984, 69–72). More important is the intellectual use to which knowledge of the Cynocephali was put. Being part human and part animal, they provided an ideal case study into the location of the limits of humanity. The issue was not whether they existed, but whether or not they were human: if they were, they were to be the object of mission; if they were not, they were to be killed. Rimbert's consideration of the Cynocephali thus needs to be treated in the context of his appreciation that the islands of the Baltic represented the limit of the world. More than a simple geographical limit was being established: the limits of humanity were being scrutinized.

Bede and Adam of Bremen make an interesting pair: both are concerned with missionary history at the edge of the known world. For Bede, mission was an essential aspect of salvation history, above all of the salvation of his own people and of their continental cousins. For Adam it was central to the history of his diocese and the jurisdiction of its bishops. At the same time, the contrast between their visualizations of the edge of the world is an interesting one. Bede did not imagine a host of monstrous races just over the horizon. Perhaps he knew too much about Britain and Ireland to visualize spaces for the Cynocephali and their like. For Adam, however, as for Sven Estridson, Otto the Great, and Rimbert, the monstrous races were near neighbours. So too did Bruno of Querfurt envisage some of Adalbert of Prague's persecutors as being dog-headed. He did so shortly before following in Adalbert's footsteps, and thus he must have expected to encounter such monsters himself. The introduction of the Cynocephali and their ilk into the discourse of mission must mark a change in missionary horizons. I would suggest that this change is related to the fact that Scandinavia and the Slav lands seemed more alien to churchmen than did the territories that had once been within the Roman Empire or had bordered it. Interestingly, Helmold of Bosau, who in the later twelfth century wrote what was in many respects a continuation of Adam of Bremen's history, was much less troubled by what lay beyond the confines of Germany. By his day the Slav lands were relatively familiar.

Books for Missionaries

Just as the Bible could prompt a missionary to envisage his work in alien territory within a millenarian context, so too could it offer reassurance in several ways. One should not forget that the Bible, or rather an individual book thereof, was a physical object that the missionary carried with him. Christopher de Hamel, writing a history of the illuminated manuscript, categorized some of the great Bibles of the sixth to eighth centuries as 'Books for Missionaries' (de Hamel 1986, 11–37). One might quarrel with the appropriateness of the phrase for some of the examples that de Hamel provides, but not with the linkage of missionaries and books. Missionaries certainly carried the scriptures with then, albeit not the great illuminated Bibles that have survived from the eighth and ninth centuries.

It is striking how often books, and particularly Bibles, even very costly productions, are referred to in missionary narratives.[39] After his murder, Kilian was buried with his books.[40] According to the second *Life of Boniface*, a Utrecht text of the ninth century, the saint, attacked by pagans while evangelizing in Frisia, was killed trying to defend himself with a Bible.[41] The earlier, eighth-century *Life of Boniface* by Willibald recalls that the saint's murderers ransacked his coffers, in which there were numerous books and relics (*librorum volumina et reliquiarum capsas*).[42] Whether or not the story of Boniface defending himself with a Bible is true, we have his own request to abbess Eadburg of Thanet for a deluxe manuscript of the Petrine epistles, written in gold, 'for the honour and reverence of the holy scriptures before the eyes of the worldly in preaching, and because I have a particular desire always to have with me the writings of him who directed me on this path.'[43] Anskar had with him about forty books when he set out for Sweden with Witmar in 829: they were all lost following a pirate attack.[44] The library that Louis the Pious had given him was also to be destroyed, during the Viking sack of Hamburg.[45] The theft of a book after the murder of the missionary Nithard prompted a chain of divine vengeance in which most of the thief's family died.[46] Rimbert, himself a missionary and Anskar's successor as bishop of Hamburg-Bremen, who recorded these episodes, was also remembered in his *Vita* for his collection of books.[47] At the end of the tenth century, Adalbert of Prague was said to have been holding a manuscript the first time he was assaulted by the Prussians.[48] Bruno of Querfurt, who wrote the second *Life of Adalbert*, also recorded in his *Life of the Five Brothers* that, in their search for treasure, the thieves who martyred the five so-called brothers, Benedict, John, and their companions, found only a missal.[49]

Given that the hagiographers of missionaries showed such interest in biblical and liturgical books, it is perhaps not surprising that monasteries and churches with which those missionaries were associated claimed to have works they had owned or even written. The earliest are the Augustine Gospels, reputedly brought from Rome to Canterbury by the Gregorian mission (Webster and Backhouse 1991, 17–19). Cuthbert – a pastoral figure, if not a missionary – was buried with the Stoneyhurst Gospels (ibid., 121). Fulda boasts the book with which Boniface supposedly defended himself, although the story of that defence was first recorded at Utrecht, where the book in question was thought to be a Bible. What Fulda preserved was a copy of Isidore's *Synonyma* cut through by a blade.[50] One may wonder whether Utrecht deliberately choose to describe the book as a Bible, or whether the monks of Fulda, intent on creating a relic, drew the line at violating a Bible with the blow of a sword. The monastery of Werden claimed to have a copy of the epistles of Paul, transcribed by Liudger himself.[51]

Missionaries thus were associated with books, and they took them on their travels. If Willebald and Rimbert are to be believed, they could take large numbers of them: a coffer or more in the case of Boniface's journey to Dokkum, forty volumes in Anskar's first visit to Sweden. These were high-profile missions, with significant political backing. Later missionaries who wished to be less visible, thinking they would have more influence if they went native, must have carried fewer volumes. But some books were of course necessary. A priest needed liturgical as well as biblical texts (although not necessarily the whole Bible), to perform the liturgy for himself and his companions. For a missionary this may have had a psychological value over and above that of ritual performed in the safety of a monastery or a cathedral church. In writing to Eadburg, Boniface talks of the consolation of books and the help of vestments (*solamine librorum sive vestimentorum adiuvamine*).[52] He is, of course, deliberately singling out objects like those with which Eadburg had supplied him. Nevertheless, his comment is a plausible indication that missionaries did find consolation in books and vestments.

The latter, indeed, are commented on in the hagiography of mission. Kilian was buried with his vestments, along with his books.[53] Missionaries deliberately put on vestments for major confrontations. In the short *Passion* of Adalbert of Prague, apparently written in his foundation of Meseritz soon after his death, the martyr set out for the town of Cholin after celebrating mass, having taken off his chasuble and put on the rest of his vestments (*abstracta tantum casucula, reliquo episcopalis vestimenti ornamenti indutus*).[54] Bruno of Querfurt underwent an ordeal by fire wearing his episcopal clothing.[55] Liturgical objects could serve as well. When Adalbert set out for Prussia he took with him his crosier (*sumpto baculo*).[56] We should remember too that Boniface's coffers, on his last journey to Dokkum, contained relics as well as books.[57] The consolation that books, clothes, and relics brought to Boniface and his like was surely in part psychological: objects and rituals helped to create a sense of familiarity and security, particularly when a missionary was afield in a hostile world.

Bibles as physical objects thus had a part to play in the world of the missionary. They were, of course, central to forming a missionary's attitudes. Increasingly surrounded by such beings as Cynocephali, in the imagination at least, it is not surprising that missionaries in the field clung to those things with which they were familiar: their Bibles, their vestments, and their liturgical objects. The Bible's message thus situated a missionary's work on the edge of the world, but at the same time it provided reassurance.

Bede, more than most, had seen the Bible as a missionary text and the history of his people as one of Christianization. For missionaries in the north, the New Testament had its limitations: above all it did not portray the alien world in which they had to work. There the Old Testament was more useful; so too was information that could be gleaned from cosmographical and apocalyptic sources on the monstrous races. The growing awareness of these races, which can be seen in a comparison between Bede and Adam, is an indication of the change that had taken place in the history of mission between the eighth and eleventh centuries. Bede had put mission at the forefront of historical interpretation, but in his imagination the missionaries he portrayed were operating in a known world – even if Augustine and his companions, as they left Rome in 596, would not have agreed. They did, after all, attempt to turn back, having reached southern Gaul. By the time of Rimbert, and still in the time of Adam, churchmen were facing up to the fact that not all the world was familiar. In this respect they were rather closer to their sixteenth-century successors active outside Europe than they were to those who worked in the successor states of the Roman Empire, even in the Anglo-Saxon kingdoms of the seventh century.

NOTES

1 See Wood 2001a, 25–6. The present essay takes up a number of themes set out in this book, carrying the ideas further into the eleventh century.

2 Gregory, *Liber historiarum* 2: 29–31, ed. B. Krusch and W. Levison, in *Monumenta Germaniae historica, Scriptores rerum Merovingicarum* 1, 1 (Hannover, 1951).

3 Jordanes, *Getica*, 25: 132, ed. T. Mommsen, in *Monumenta Germaniae historica, Auctores antiquissimi* 5 (Berlin, 1882).

4 *Conversio Bagoariorum et Carantanorum*, ed. F. Losek, in *Monumenta Germaniae historica, Studien und Texte* 15 (Hannover, 1997).

5 Adam of Bremen, *Gesta Hammaburgensis ecclesiae pontificum*, ed. W. Trillmich, in *Quellen des 9. und 11. Jahrhunderts zur Geschichte der hamburgischen Kirche und des Reiches* (Darmstadt, 1961). For a useful survey of opinions see the introduction by Tim Reuter to the new edition of F.J. Tschan's translation of *History of the Archbishops of Hamburg-Bremen* (New York, 2002), xi–xxi.

6 Stephanus, *Vita Wilfridi* 26, 41–2, ed. B. Colgrave, in *The Life of Bishop Wilfrid by Eddius Stephanus* (Cambridge, 1927); B. Colgrave, ed., *The Earliest Life of Gregory the Great* (Kansas City, 1968).

7 L. Bieler, *The Patrician Texts in the Book of Armagh* (Dublin, 1979).

8 The literary, patristic, and papal background to Bede's missionary ideas are set out in O'Reilly 2005.

9 D. Shanzer and I.N. Wood, *Avitus of Vienne: Letters and Selected Prose* (Liverpool, 2002), 362–73.

10 Essentially the same point is expressed differently in Thacker 1983.

11 L.T. Martin, trans., *The Venerable Bede, Commentary on the Acts of the Apostles* (Kalamazoo, 1989), xviii.

12 Bede, *Commentary on Acts* 2:3a, trans. Martin.

13 Ibid., 3:1.

14 Ibid., 10.

15 Ibid., 1:16.

16 Patrick, *Epistola ad milites Corotici* 11; Patrick, *Confessio* 40, ed. D.R. Howlett, in *The Book of Letters of Saint Patrick the Bishop* (Dublin, 1994): McGinn 1995, 66.

17 Bede, *Explanatio Apocalypsis*, PL 93, col. 146; Lumsden 2001, 48.

18 Bede, *In Tobiam* 10, ed. D. Hurst, *Corpus Christianorum Series Latina* 119B (Turnhout, 1983); trans. S. Connolly, *Bede, On Tobit and On the Canticle of Habakkuk* (Dublin, 1997).

19 Bede, *In Tobiam* 11: Gregory the Great, *Homiliae in Evangelia*, 40 (PL 76) and *Moralia in Job*, ed. M. Adriaen, in *Corpus Christianorum, Series Latina* 143A (Turnbout, 1979–85) 1014: Connolly, *Bede, On Tobit*, 46n52.

20 E.g., Bede, *De templo* 1, 2.3.

21 Isaiah, 49:1–3: Rimbert, *Vita Anskarii* 25, ed. Trillmich, in *Quellen des 9. und 11. Jahrhunderts zur.*

22 On earlier uses of this quotation, see O'Reilly 2005, 121.

23 The text is not that of the Authorised Version.

24 Adam of Bremen, *Gesta Hammaburgensis ecclesiae pontificum* 1.26 (28), citing Ezekiel 39:6.

25 For Bede's vision of Britain as a world of islands, cf. O'Reilly 2005.

26 Adam of Bremen, *Gesta Hammaburgensis* 4.1. See also 3.73.

27 Ibid., 1.42 (44).

28 Helmold of Bosau, *Chronica Slavorum* 1: 2, ed. H. Stoob (Berlin, 1963).

29 One should, however, note the possibility that Adam's description of the temple may have been a propagandist fiction: see Janson 2000, 83–8.

30 Adam of Bremen, *Gesta Hammaburgensis* 4.25.

31 Ibid., 4.19.

32 Ibid.

33 Solinus, 31, 5, 52, 27, ed. T. Mommsen (Berlin, 1895); Martianus Capella, *Philologia* (= *De nuptiis Philologiae et Mercurii*) 4.624, ed. A. Dick (Stuttgart, 1969); also Solinus, 30, 6; 15, 4.

34 Archpriest Leo, *Alexanderroman* 3.25, ed. A. Hilka (Halle, 1920).

35 That Adam knew the works of Solinus and Martianus Capella at first hand is implied by his direct mention of them: Adam of Bremen, *Gesta Hammaburgensis* 2.22 (19); 4.12, 19, 20, 21, 25, 35 (34), 39 (38).schol., 116 (115), 130 (125), 152 (146), 153.

36 Aethicus Ister, *Cosmographia* 2, ed. O. Prinz, in *Monumenta Germaniae historica*, Quellen zur Zeitgeschichte des Mittelalters 14 (Munich, 1993) 114–16.

37 Ratramnus = *Ep. Variorum* 12, ed. E. Dümmler, in *Monumenta Germaniae historica, epistolae* 6 = *Epistolae Karolini aevi* 4 (Berlin, 1925): Wood 1987, 64–6; Wood 2001b, 214–15; Wood 2001a, 252–3.

38 See, for instance, Williams 1996, 13–14.

39 What follows is an expanded restatement of a point made in Wood 2001a, 260–1.
40 *Passio Kiliani* 11, ed. W. Levison, in *Monumenta Germaniae historica, Scriptores rerum Merovingicarum* 5 (Hannover, 1910).
41 *Vita altera Bonifatii* 16, ed. W. Levison, in *Vitae Sancti Bonifatii, Monumenta Germaniae historica, Scriptores rerum Germanicarum* 57 (Hannover, 1905).
42 Willibald, *Vita Bonifatii* 8, ed. Levison, in *Vitae Sancti Bonifatii* 57.
43 *ad honorem et reverentiam sanctarum scriptuarum ante oculos carnalium in predicando, et quia dicta eius, qui me in hoc iter direxit, maxime semper in praesentia cupiam habere*; Boniface 1916, esp. 35.
44 Rimbert, *Vita Anskarii* 10.
45 Ibid., 16.
46 Ibid., 18.
47 *Vita Rimberti* 11, ed. G. Waitz, *Monumenta Germaniae historica, scriptores rerum Germanicarum* 55 (Hannover, 1884).
48 John Canaparius, *Vita Adalberti* 28, ed. G.H. Pertz, *Monumenta Germaniae historica, scriptores* 4 (Hannover, 1841): Bruno, *Passio Adalberti* 24–5, ed. Pertz, *Monumenta Germaniae historica, Scriptores* 4.
49 Bruno, *Vita quinque fratrum* 13, ed. M. Kade, *Monumenta Germaniae historica, Scriptores* 15, 2 (Hannover, 1888).
50 *799, Kunst und Kultur der Karolingerzeit*, vol. 2 (Paderborn, 1999), 472–3.
51 Ibid., 2.483–5.
52 Boniface, ep. 35.
53 *Passio Kiliani* 11.
54 *Passio Adalberti* 2, ed. G. Waitz, in *Monumenta Germaniae historica, Scriptores* 15, 2.
55 Wibert, *Historia de predicatione Episcopi Brunonis cum suis capellanis in Prussia et martyrio eorum*, ed. G.H. Pertz, in *Monumenta Germaniae historica, Scriptores* 4; also Peter Damian, *Vita Romualdi* 27, ed. G. Tabacco, in *Fonti per la storia d'Italia* 94 (Rome, 1957).
56 *Passio Adalberti* 2.
57 Willibald, *Vita Bonifatii* 8, ed. Levison.

REFERENCES (secondary sources only)

Bonner, G. 1966. *Saint Bede in the Tradition of Western Apocalyptic Commentary.* Jarrow: St Paul's Church.

Charles-Edwards, T.M. 1993. 'Palladius, Prosper, and Leo the Great: Mission and Primatial Authority.' In D.N. Dumville, ed., *St Patrick, A.D. 493–1993*, 1–12. Woodbridge: The Boydell Press.

de Hamel, C. 1986. *A History of Illuminated Manuscripts*. Oxford: Phaidon.

Fritze, W.H. 1969. '*Universalis gentium confessio*: Formeln, Träger und Wege universalmissionarischen Denkens im 7. Jahrhundert.' *Frühmittelalterliche Studien* 3: 78–130.

Hägg, I. 1984. *Die Textilfunde aus dem Hafen von Haithabu*. Neumünster: K. Wachholtz.

Jacob, G. 1927. *Arabische Berichte von Gesandten an germanische Fürstenhöfe aus dem 9. und 10. Jahrhundert*. Berlin: W. de Gruyter.

Janson, H. 2000. 'Adam of Bremen and the Conversion of Scandinavia.' In G. Armstrong and I.N. Wood, eds, *Christianizing Peoples and Converting Individuals*, 83–8. Turnhout: Brepols.

Lumsden, D.W. 2001. *And Then the End Will Come: Early Latin Christian Interpretations of the Opening of the Seven Seals*. New York: Garland.

Markus, R. 1997. *Gregory the Great and His World*. Cambridge: Cambridge University Press.

McGinn, B. 1995. 'The End of the World and the Beginning of Christendom.' In M. Bull, ed., *Apocalypse Theory and the Ends of the World*. Oxford: Blackwell.

O'Reilly, J. 2005. 'Islands and Idols at the Ends of the Earth: Exegesis and Conversion in Bede's *Historia Ecclesiastica*.' In S. Lebecq, M. Perrin, and O. Szerwiniak, eds, *Bède le Vénérable entre tradition et postérité*, 119–45. Villeneuve d'Ascq: CEGES, Université Charles-de-Gaulle, Lille III.

Riedmann, J. 1976. 'Unbekannte frühkarolingische Handschriftfragmente in der Bibliothek des Tiroler Landmuseums Ferdinandeum.' *Mitteilungen des Instituts für Österreichische Geschichtsforschung* 84: 262–89.

Słupecki, L.P. 1994. *Slavonic Pagan Sanctuaries*. Warsaw: Institute of Archaeology and Ethnology, Polish Academy of Sciences.

Thacker, Alan. 1983. 'Bede's Ideal of Reform.' In P. Wormald, ed., *Ideal and Reality in Frankish and Anglo-Saxon Society: Studies Presented to J.M. Wallace-Hadrill*, 130–53. Oxford: Blackwell.

Webster, L., and J. Backhouse, eds. 1991. *The Making of England: Anglo-Saxon Art and Culture, AD 600–900*. London: British Museum Press.

Williams, D. 1996. *Deformed Discourse: The Function of the Monster in Medieval Thought and Literature*. Exeter: University of Exeter Press.

Wood, I.N. 1987. 'Pagans and Christians in Ninth-Century Scandinavia.' In B. Sawyer, P. Sawyer, and I.N. Wood, eds, *The Christianization of Scandinavia*. Alingsås: Viktoria Bokförlag.

– 2001a. *The Missionary Life*. London: Longman, 2001.

– 2001b. 'Missionaries and the Christian Frontier.' In W. Pohl, I. Wood, and H. Reimitz, eds, *The Transformation of Frontiers from Late Antiquity to the Carolingians*. Leiden: Brill.

9

Promised Lands, Premised Texts (Commentary on Part Two)

MARK VESSEY

In a book published in time for the Columbus quincentenary of 1992, Stephen Greenblatt recounted the history of the colonization of the New World as a tale of contrived and reported wonders. On his reading of the documents, European ethnographic amazement served to fill out an otherwise manifestly defective claim to land title in the New Indies and beyond. Columbus could write in his letter to Luis de Santangel: 'To the first island which I found, I gave the name *San Salvador*, in remembrance of the Divine Majesty, Who has marvelously bestowed all this.' Greenblatt comments:

> The marvel of the divine gift is at once a legitimation and a transcendence of the legal act. Roman law procedures dictate the principal gesture of appropriation [viz., the planting of a flag and reading of a proclamation], but [those procedures] are supplemented by an incommensurable and marvelous assurance, the assurance in effect of the biblical promise: 'If you diligently keep all these commandments that I now charge you to observe, by loving the Lord your God, by conforming to his ways and by holding fast to him, the Lord will drive out all these nations before you and you shall occupy the territory of nations greater and more powerful than you. Every place where you set the soles of your feet shall be yours.' (Deut 11:22–4) (Greenblatt 1991, 52)[1]

It is certain that Columbus had such promises in mind. In this case, however, the quotation is the modern scholar's rather than the admiral's. It comes at the end of a paragraph and is not elaborated upon; nor is there much further discussion of biblical precedents in the rest of the book, which instead concentrates its energy on appropriative 'speech-acts' outside an explicitly prophetic context. The main exception is a passage at the end of the same chapter, citing a dream in which Columbus heard himself hailed by a voice that recalled God's great mercies to him: 'What did He more for the people of Israel when He brought them out of Egypt? Or for David, whom from a shepherd He made to be a king in Judaea?' For Greenblatt, such assurances are a sign of Columbus's mounting desperation in later years: 'For a moment at least – a moment at once of perfect wonder and of possessive madness – Columbus has become king of the Promised Land' (Greenblatt 1991, 85). Those are the last words of the chapter. Though fascinated by Columbus's reliance on the technique of renaming or 'christening' foreign lands in order to take possession of them, Greenblatt did not inquire further into the 'biblical' mentality that manifestly underwrote such gestures. Already at the outset he explained that he would favour *petites histoires* over *grand récit*, on the grounds that 'the discourse of travel in the late Middle Ages and the Renaissance is rarely if ever interesting at the level of sustained narrative and teleological design' (2).

Teleology is unsurprising by definition. Small wonder, then, that for all his desire to turn the ethnographic gaze back on the colonizing observer, Greenblatt should have expended only gentle irony on the mad logic by which the emissary of a fifteenth-century Spanish Christian monarch once claimed lands in the Far West on the strength of Yahweh's covenant with the ancient Israelites. As late as 1992, it would appear, the devices for so prodigious a transfer of title were still too native to a certain kind of Western self-understanding for them to make a truly compelling subject for inquiry. Nearly two decades later, as the memory of Columbus recedes again into a wider historico-political horizon, there may be better reasons to explore the process by which such mighty engines of the westering colonial imagination were set in train.

On a hint from Tzvetan Todorov, Greenblatt quoted Samuel Purchas, whose ponderous digests of the records of European navigation and exploration of exotic realms, published in England late in the reign of James I (1603–25), partly at the behest of the East India Company, helped confirm his countrymen's dawning sense of an imperial calling. Purchas, like others of his time, considered that European adventurers enjoyed an advantage over 'barbarous' or 'savage' peoples by virtue of their mastery of *writing* systems. As he explains in a chapter on 'the diversity of Letters used by the divers Nations in the World' in *Hakluytus Posthumus or Purchas His Pilgrimes*:

By writing Man seemes immortall, conferreth and consulteth with the Patriarkes, Prophets, Apostles, Fathers, Philosophers, Historians, and learnes the wisdome of the Sages which have been in all times before him; yea by translations or learning the Languages, in all places and Regions of the World: and lastly, by his owne writings surviveth himself, remaines (*litera scripta manet*) thorow all ages a Teacher and Counsellor to the last of men: yea hereby God holds conference with men, and in his sacred Scriptures, as at first in the Tables of Stone, speakes to all. (Purchas 1625, 486; cited in Greenblatt 1991, 10)

As Greenblatt points out, while Purchas's 'overweening cultural confidence and religious dogmatism' may have fallen out of fashion in more recent times ('at least in academic circles'), his notion of the 'litterall advantage' has continued to be influential. In *The Conquest of America*, Todorov went so far as to argue that 'the crucial difference between European and American peoples was the presence or absence of writing.' Greenblatt would discount Todorov's claims for the instrumental value of the Europeans' supposedly superior 'technology of symbolism' (11–12),[2] and offer an alternative account of the conquest, focusing on what he called 'representational technology' or 'representational machinery.' Adapting Marxist economic theory and extending his own earlier work on the cultural politics and poetics of Renaissance England, he casts his analysis in terms of 'the reproduction and circulation of mimetic capital.' Even though, he concedes, 'the Roman Empire and Christianity provided impressive precedents, in the modern world-order it is with capitalism that the proliferation and circulation of representations (and devices for the generation and transmission of representations) achieved a spectacular and virtually inescapable global magnitude' (6).

Attractive as Greenblatt's argument for the role of new 'representational' technology in the colonial process unquestionably is, especially in the light of Benedict Anderson's generally well-received claim for the importance of 'print-capitalism' in the formation of modern discourses of nationhood,[3] it may nonetheless underestimate the narrative and symbolic resources already laid up by 'the Roman Empire and Christianity.' Purchas, in the passage quoted, opened his catalogue of the wonders of writing by imagining Europeans of his time in conversation with biblical patriarchs, prophets, and apostles, and closed it with them in conference with God himself in his Scriptures, 'as at first' in the tables of the law given to Moses. Was this not in fact the 'conference' that would have *had* to take place before Columbus could 'legitimately' take possession of a Caribbean island for Spain by claiming the divine promises of the Book of Deuteronomy? In order to cast his early-seventeenth-century witness as the forerunner and misleader of Todorov, Greenblatt takes him to refer straightforwardly to the European possession of alphabetical literacy. Purchas, however, may in the long run prove more eloquent as the exponent of an unselfconscious (if recognizably Protestant) faith in the advanced – but ancient – technology of the Bible.

The engraved title page of *Purchas His Pilgrimes* already spoke for the whole volume (figure 9.1). The outermost panels of its upper register display a double supernatural sanction for British nationhood under Tudor and early Stuart rulers. On the left, the reigning monarch James I and his son, the future Charles I, appear before a map of the realm, surrounded on three sides by texts from the Old Testament (in the 'King James Version'). The easiest verse to read is the one in English at the foot: 'He shewed his word unto Jacob [Jacobus, i.e., James], and he hath not dealt so with any nation' (Ps 147:19–20). On the right is an effigy of the late Queen Elizabeth, attended by the since-deceased Prince Henry, undergirded by two tags from Virgil's *Aeneid*, the first of which ('O quam te memorem virgo!') implicitly deifies Elizabeth,[4] while the second, in elegant Roman capitals, assimilates Britain's national destiny to that of Rome as partly foreseen by Aeneas on his visit to the underworld: the all-but-terminal *nec ultra* of truncated epic prophecy silently summons the *plus ultra* of transatlantic discovery and conquest.[5] The symmetry of biblical and classical schemes of predestination would have been instantly resolved by viewers at the time, already used to James I's idea of himself as Solomon and Augustus reborn in one. No less revealing of sixteenth-century English Protestant sensibilities is the panel between those just described, with its two small lower sections commemorating the providential defeats of the Gunpowder Plot in 1605 and of the Spanish Armada in 1588. Above these scenes is one of an army in the field, glossed by a reference to Numbers 9:17: 'And when the cloud was taken up from the tabernacle, then after that the children of Israel journeyed: and in the place where the cloud abode, there the children of Israel pitched their tents.' Still higher up, centred in the place of greatest honour, is a model of the New Jerusalem laid out as a walled town full of buildings in a contemporary style of architecture. A caption beneath the cloud combines phrases from two verses of

Figure 9.1 Engraved title page of *Hakluytus Posthumus or Purchas His Pilgrimes* (reprinted with permission of the Rare Book and Manuscript Library of the University of Illinois at Urbana-Champaign).

Hebrews 11 (13, 15) to call in the promises made to Abraham and the patriarchs ('They were strangers and pilgrims on the earth,' 'God hath prepared for them a Citty'), while a simple citation framing the city itself ('Ap[ocalypse] 21') signals the assurance of their imminent if not present fulfilment.

In a 'Preface to the Reader,' Purchas disclaimed any professionally theological purpose, presenting himself, after Richard Hakluyt, as a humble transcriber and translator of other men's eye-witness accounts. Yet he still expressed a hope that he and his fellow scribbling pilgrims might 'minister individuall and sensible materials (as it were with Stones, Brickes and Mortar) to those universall Speculators for their Theoricall structures,' by which he meant theologians and works of theology (Purchas 1625, sig. ¶4v). Although Purchas himself was only a Bachelor of Divinity, there is already a speculative theology at work in his geographical history of the world, just as there was traditionally assumed to be in the sacred, universal, and natural history of the Christian Bible, of which his twenty extracanonical books on 'God's Wonders in Nature & Providence' were simultaneously exegesis, interpolation, and nationalistically tendentious application. History and divinity were laid out there together like a textual analogue of Solomon's temple or a great city. The method employed is essentially that of the literal or scriptural 'conference' outlined in the chapter on writing. *Purchas His Pilgrimes* is a semi-portable typographic device, designed to enable the early modern reader to commune with approved sages and historians of all times, from Moses and Solomon to the latest-returned travellers, and to hear them collectively deliver the charter of a far-flung British 'city of God' on earth. The machine-code of that program for translating ancient into modern nations is already compiled on the same title page, in the carpet pattern of thirty medallions commemorating famous navigators, explorers, and conquerors from Noah and Abraham, Ulysses and Aeneas, to Alexander the Great, Julius Caesar, the Apostles, Constantine, the Crusaders, Columbus, and finally Sebastian Cabot, 'Grand Pilot of England.' The absence of Moses from the portrait gallery would be surprising, did we not infer from the Old Testament citations on the same page that he was already taken for the primary compiler (before Hakluyt and Purchas) of the narrative scenography of divine history. More exactly, he was taken for its first *secondary* author, according to the subsequent transcriber Purchas, who also wrote in his chapter on writing: 'It is, I see not how probably by some affirmed, that *Moses* first received Letters [i.e., the alphabet] in the Two Tables of the Law written by the finger of God' (176). That chapter closes with another, matching instance of divine inscription, as Purchas recalled 'that which *Eusebius* in the life of *Constantine* recordeth written by Divine hand, which some say was the Crosse, but his description appeareth rather to have beene the two first letters of Christs name, [*chi*] and [*rho*] combined, with promise of victory to the pious Emperor, not in that signe (of the Crosse) but in Christ himselfe, to whom be glory for ever, *Amen*' (179). 'Amen' would have been the final word of the first book, the last committed to the press in 1625, only Purchas decided to append a set of comparative alphabetical tables, beginning with 'the *Phoenician* or *Samaritan* Letters, which some say were the *Mosaicall* and first *Hebrew*,' and ending with a transliteration of Gothic into Old English (1808–86). It would be hard to find a more strictly literal illustration than this of the encompassing narrative-representational device by which the sacred texts of one people were to be converted into a title deed for another far removed from it in time and space. As Purchas confirmed by his citation of Eusebius, the device in question was no patent invention of Englishmen in the reign of King James, any more than the 'King James Version' of the Bible could be considered such. It too was a work of many nations and generations. The foregoing essays by Maier, Pollmann, and Wood provide snapshots of that work in progress.

Signs and Sights of Empire: The Constantinian Regime

What was the sign of victory, inscribed by the hand of God, that Constantine was supposed to have seen? According to the historian Eusebius,

> About the time of the midday sun, when day was just turning, he said he saw with his own eyes, up in the sky and resting over the sun, a cross-shaped trophy formed from light, and a text attached to it which said, 'By this conquer.' Amazement at the spectacle seized both him and the whole company of soldiers which was then accompanying him. (1.28)[6]

The following night, Christ appeared to Constantine with the same sign and ordered him to make a copy of it; on waking, the emperor summoned craftsmen for the purpose.

> It was constructed to the following design. A tall pole plated with gold had a transverse bar forming the shape of a cross. Up at the extreme top a

wreath woven of precious stones and gold had been fastened. On it two letters, intimating by its first characters the name 'Christ,' formed the monogram of the Saviour's title, rho being intersected in the middle by chi. These letters the emperor also used to wear upon his helmet in later times. From the transverse bar, which was bisected by the pole, hung suspended a cloth, an imperial tapestry covered with a pattern of precious stones fastened together, which glittered with shafts of light, and interwoven with much gold, producing an impression of indescribable beauty on those who saw it. This banner then, attached to the bar, was given equal dimensions of length and breadth. But the upright pole, which extended upwards a long way from its lower end, below the trophy of the cross and near the top of the tapestry delineated, carried the golden head-and-shoulders portrait of the Godbeloved Emperor, and likewise of his sons. This saving sign was always used by the Emperor for protection against every opposing and hostile force, and he commanded replicas of it to lead all his armies. (1.31)[7]

The precision of this description of Constantine's standard, the *labarum* (which also appears on his coinage), attests at once to the performative 'reality' of late Roman court and military ceremonial and to the rhetorical-discursive norms according to which the ideology implicit in that ceremonial were reproduced and disseminated through texts such as Eusebius's. Not just the prestige of the emperor – or, in this period, the imperial college of emperors – but the very unity and integrity of the empire itself can be shown to have depended in large measure on the production, maintenance, and circulation of visual and verbal signs of divinely sanctioned authority.[8] With the 'conversion' of Constantine, the Roman empire of signs began to acquire distinctively Christian registers, both of narrative and of imagery.[9] While the first Christian emperor played an important personal role in this process, he was also subject – as Roman emperors always had been – to the representations made of and on behalf of him by others, whether officially appointed or not. Although Eusebius has often been called a 'court theologian,' the phrase is anachronistic and the terms of his relationship with Constantine remain a topic for scholarly conjecture. What is not in doubt is the early and long-term impact of his massive literary oeuvre on the collective identities eventually claimed for Christian peoples or nations, Roman and post-Roman. Eusebius's contribution to the discourse of Christian 'nationhood' has been well studied of late.[10] Another, very promising line of inquiry has highlighted his resourceful use of textual and bibliographic media for the narration – and visualization – of Rome's emergence as an elect (Christian) nation in succession to the ancient Hebrews.[11] Such work provides a rich setting for Maier's essay, which places Eusebius's presentation of Constantine as universal ruler in the double context of biblical prophecy and Roman monumental iconography.

In the sequel to the passage quoted above from the *Life of Constantine*, Eusebius relates how Constantine summoned certain religious experts who informed him that the god of his vision was 'the Onlybegotten Son of the one and only God' and 'began to teach him the reasons for his coming, explaining to him in detail the story of his self-accommodation to human conditions' (1.32). We are given to understand that Constantine underwent a process of Christian catechesis, which traditionally began with a narrative of sacred history based on the Old and New Testaments. Soon thereafter, Eusebius says, he took up study of the 'divinely inspired writings' themselves. The next chapter describes his victory over Maxentius at the Milvian Bridge in 312 CE, in language borrowed from the biblical account of the drowning of Pharaoh's army in Exodus 15. These are the first biblical allusions in the *Life*, announcing a figure of thought that is one of the most conspicuous features of Eusebius's sacral-imperial propaganda. *Mutatis mutandis*, Constantine was another Moses. The emperor's noonday vision and its subsequent divine exegesis were the equivalents of Moses' experience at Horeb (Ex 3:2–4). In both cases, astonishment was the prelude to enlightenment and a conviction of divine calling to be the leader of a 'people.' Apart from its strictly Roman antecedents, Eusebius's description of Constantine's standard and the process of its manufacture recalls the biblical account of the making of the Ark of the Covenant.[12] Such intertextual gestures define 'the prophetic viewpoint,' as Maier calls it, adopting a phrase of Peter Brown's. This was (and is) a way of seeing events and persons of the present or recent times that instantly endows them with the prestige – and, as it were, the presumptive normativity – afforded by a prior script(ure). Under the name of 'figuralism' or 'typology,' it is commonly taken to be one of the most potent of all Christian exegetical-representational techniques, recognized both for its capacity to impart high 'seriousness' to everyday reality and for its (sometimes baneful) efficacy in the creation of collective identities.[13]

As the language of 'figure' or 'type' implies, not the least of the attractions of this mode of discourse is its appeal to the visual-imaginative sense. Focusing on imagined correspondences between historically separated events, scenes, persons, and/or objects of narration, it is literally a way of *seeing* things – and of making things seen – in and through *texts*. (The co-intricacy of verbal and non-verbal effects is already apparent in Eusebius's account of Constantine's 'vision' of the cross with its accompanying text, and again in the exegesis of the *chi-rho* figure surmounting the *labarum*.) The emphasis on visuality may also extend to the application of biblical passages whose only historical reference is to a future now claimed as the present. Thus, in the passage Maier quotes from Eusebius's oration in praise of Constantine, things predicted long ago in the Hebrew of the Old Testament are said to have been made manifest ('visible,' *horomena*) in deeds of the present time. The oration itself is part of this process of coming-to-appear. The link between prophecy and fulfilment needs to be visibly made. The orator (or writer) is the one who enables the hearers (readers) to see.

This theory and technique of prophetic-historical validation was neither particular nor exclusive to Christians as interpreters of the Old and New Testaments. The same kind of claims, reinforced by comparable scenic or visual effects of language, were the stock-in-trade of Roman imperial discourse. Long before Constantine, imperial orators were mining the Sibylline Oracles for prophecies suitable to the current political situation.[14] The 'prophetic viewpoint' was already central to Virgil's *Aeneid*. It is most graphically displayed in the ekphrasis of Aeneas's shield in book 8 of the poem, with its depictions of future Roman world empire. That work of divine art is said to be beyond verbal elucidation (*non enarrabile textum*, 8.625), yet is still lingeringly expounded by the poet.[15] Maier instructively situates Eusebius's Christianization of the Virgilian prophecy of Roman 'empire without end' in a long tradition of *aggiornamento* of the ideal of the *pax Augusta*. In the opening and closing sections of his essay he also sketches a parallel between the monumental fabric of Augustan Rome and Constantine's program of Christian building. Public buildings and their decoration were an established medium of Roman imperial communication. How close was the relation between the visuality of Christian exegetical discourse and the visible monuments of Christian-imperial power?

According to Eusebius, upon his triumphal entry into Rome after the defeat of Maxentius, the emperor Constantine

> announced to all people in large lettering and inscriptions the sign of the Saviour, setting this up in the middle of the imperial city (*mesei tei basileuousei polei*) as a great trophy of victory over his enemies, explicitly

inscribing this in indelible letters as the salvific sign of the authority of Rome and the protection of the whole empire. He therefore immediately ordered a tall pole to be erected in the shape of a cross in the hand of a statue made to represent himself, and this text to be inscribed upon it word for word in Latin: 'By this salutary sign, the true proof of valour, I liberated your city, saved from the tyrant's yoke; moreover the Senate and People of Rome I liberated and restored to their ancient splendour and brilliance.' (*Life of Constantine* 1.40, trans. Cameron and Hall; cf. *Ecclesiastical History* 9.9.10; *In Praise of Constantine* 9.8–11)

In his next breath, the biographer recalls the rejoicings not just of the 'liberated' inhabitants of the city of Rome but of all the Western 'nations' as they recognized the 'common good of mankind which by God's grace had dawned in Constantine.' The conquest of the East, and of the Roman 'barbarians' who disturbed its peace, still lay ahead, but already the saving power of Constantine's god was radiating from the imagined centre of the old Roman world. Eusebius was never at Rome, but in every account he gave of this statue of Constantine he stressed either its central position in the city or its prominence to view, or both. Although the archaeological evidence is hard to interpret, the likeliest identification of the artwork in question is with a colossal statue that once stood in the western apse of a huge basilica in the Roman Forum, the construction of which was begun by Maxentius and completed under Constantine. This basilica, a triumphal arch next to the Colosseum, and an equestrian statue (probably also in the Forum) would have formed the most conspicuous 'Constantinian' sites and sights of the central urban space of Rome. The basilica was not a church. In fact, none of the Constantinian public works in the *centro storico* was designed specifically for the Christian community or for an identifiably Christian purpose. Constantine's church building at Rome was confined to private property at the periphery of the urban complex and to areas outside the city walls.[16] If Linda Safran is right, the eyes of the massive statue of Constantine in the Basilica Nova looked out eastwards past the ancient, 'pagan' Temple of the City to the Colossus of the Sun commissioned by Nero, which later gave its name to the nearby Flavian Amphitheatre, or Colosseum. 'By taking [all this] in with his gaze,' Safran suggests, 'Constantine in the basilica is visibly tied to the destiny of the *urbs aeterna,* as symbolized by the Colossus' (Safran 2006, 52). It was not by any stretch of the imagination a Christian way to look, or to be seen looking.

By returning in our mind's eye to ground on which Eusebius never set foot and to which Constantine returned only twice after 312, and for visits of barely two months in each case (in 315 and 326), we may be led to nuance slightly Maier's deft assimilation of Augustan and Constantinian visual-monumental regimes. The century that separates Constantine's Roman church endowments from the typological mosaics of the basilica-church of Santa Maria Maggiore was an eventful one both politically and architecturally, and we must be careful not to retroject the visibly Christian city of a later time onto its predecessor structures. It has been justly observed that 'Eusebius shows an unusual awareness of the importance of visual representation' (Eusebius 1999, 316). His desire to make Constantine's Roman statue, *labarum* in hand, the focal point of an already presumptively universal Christian polity makes perfect sense both in the light of traditional Roman imperial discursive regimes and in the context of his own attempt to place Christ, rather than Augustus, at the centre of all human history.[17] For all that, Eusebius could not have had much confidence in the actual effects on public consciousness of the modest innovations made by Constantine to the decor of the Roman Forum. Compared with the sculptural program of the Augustan Altar of Peace with its incised narrative of the *res gestae*, the recycled reliefs and deliberately bland inscription of the Arch of Constantine – on which the emperor is said to have triumphed over his enemy 'by divine inspiration' (*instinctu divinitatis*, an unobjectionably classical phrase) – were feeble instruments of propaganda. In his new capital of Constantinople (founded in 330), the emperor would have more scope for demonstratively Christian building, though even there the changes to the old Severan city would at first be minimal. Eusebius, in any case, was a verbal artisan. He concentrated all his efforts on visual programs that could be elaborated in words or, as we now say, texts. To this end, as Maier's essay once again shows, the Christian scriptures with their rich store of narrative and figural elements were an especially precious resource. Since God had revealed himself to the ancient Hebrews in the writings of his historians, prophets, and poets, what better means than these could there now be for inspiring in *all* peoples the wonder and obedience that his name ought to command?

We could even say that the Greek Eusebius took for granted the demise or supersession of the civic scenery of Rome, and with it that of all the provincial cities that claimed Rome as their architectural model, as the primary canvas of imperial representation. As new converts to the

Christian religion were expected to step out of the public concourse of the ancient city into the private, verbally and visually storied space of a church building, Eusebius, almost the last Christian apologist of Roman times, ushered his readers into a self-enclosed textual domain, full of brightly lit images and ideologically loaded narratives. So far as this analogy holds, it will be Virgil's explanation of the reputedly in-explicable artwork of Aeneas's shield, rather than Augustus's 'careful enumerat[ion] of his military and diplomatic successes' (Maier, 149 above) on the Altar of Peace, that most nearly prefigures the Eusebian exegesis of empire.

Still, it is only an analogy. As a Greek, Eusebius did not stake much on exegesis of Rome's principal Latin poet of empire. Constantine, who had been brought up in the western half of the Empire, probably gave him his cue to read Virgil's Fourth Eclogue as a Messianic prophecy. Lactantius, his Latin contemporary, was far more energetic in this line of work (Courcelle 1957). For the flowering of a Virgilian-Christian prophetic and (post-)imperial discourse, we must turn to Latin writers of the later fourth and early fifth centuries.

'My Kingdom Is Not of This World': Poetics of Transcendence

The formative role of Virgil's poetry, especially the *Aeneid*, in Western discourses of empire and colonization has been closely observed by literary historians in the present era of postcolonial critique. Beside David Quint's *Epic and Empire*, cited by Pollmann in her essay, we should set Richard Waswo's fiercely disabusing account of the long-term impacts of the founding legend of the Roman 'nation' in Italy by the Trojan Aeneas, considered as the archetype of 'the stories we tell ourselves about the places we take over, whose inhabitants are timeless, culture-less, and therefore hopeless' (Waswo 1997, 352).[18] If there is a weakness to these large-scale studies by literary comparatists, it is their relative neglect of the period of late antiquity. After brief mention of Constantine, Waswo presses on to the Frankish chroniclers. Quint goes straight from Augustan Rome to the 'Renaissance imperialism' of Camões' *Lusíadas*. Current scholarship on the late antique reception of Virgil and the Christian refashioning of Roman imperial discourse provides resources for a more careful assessment of the Latin, Western sequels to the Eusebian theology of empire, such as is offered here by Pollmann in regard to Prudentius and Augustine, writers pivotal for what would later pass as 'the Christian tradition,' but who composed their works

– one exclusively in verse, the other almost entirely in prose – at a time before anything so settled or unitary as a 'Christian tradition' could properly be said to exist.[19]

'The rule of the Roman Empire over foreign peoples was a fact, but' – Pollmann reminds us – 'it was also seen as in need of constant confirmation by imperial panegyric and other media' (178). Prudentius's contemporary and fellow poet, Paulinus of Nola, composed a panegyric (not extant) in praise of the most Christian emperor Theodosius. Augustine, too, had been employed for a time as a court propagandist; it was part of his job as public rhetor in the imperial capital of Milan, an appointment made by the senator and urban prefect Symmachus, later targeted in Prudentius's poem. Fluency in praising the emperor was something young Roman males learned at school, along with their Virgil. Extant Latin panegyrics from the period are thick with Virgilian allusions and quotations, mainly from the *Aeneid*.[20] That poem, writes Pollmann, was 'almost a "pagan bible."' Almost, but – it seems important to add – not quite, or not yet. The Christian sense of the Bible as an encompassing narrative and unified code of life was still nascent in the fourth century; Augustine, Prudentius, and their generation would do much to reinforce it, and their ingrained habits of reference to normative authors of classical culture, such as Virgil, undoubtedly helped them in that direction. But we risk skewing our 'book history' by crediting non-Christian Roman culture with a pre-existent 'bible' to which the Christian scriptures would then have formed a strategic counterpoise. (The best exhibition of the quasi-biblical use of Virgil in a non-Christian context, Macrobius's *Saturnalia*, though ostensibly reflecting conditions at Rome in the 380s, was not actually composed until half a century later, after Augustine's *City of God*.) The idea that the routines of Graeco-Roman literary pedagogy – above all, those of the grammarian's school – constituted the essential disciplinary model for Christian recourse to the textual authority of Scripture has proved all but irresistible to modern scholars in quest of the origins of medieval and later forms of 'textuality.' Yet if the grammarian was such a key exponent of imperial ideology, we may wonder why his profession was not better rewarded at the time.[21] Instructive as they are, the excerpts chosen by Pollmann from Servius's commentary on the *Aeneid* cannot by themselves demonstrate the socio-political importance of grammar in the late empire. As her reference to 'panegyric and other media' already suggests, it was the *mise en oeuvre* of such products of grammatical exegesis by other specialists that gave them their real power. The lexis and morphology of Roman imperialist discourse might be taught in the schoolroom; its syntax could only be grasped in the public performance – the ceremonial or ritual – of empire, as repeatedly played out against the backdrop of Roman civic architecture and monuments.[22]

We saw earlier what little effect Constantine's conversion had had on the centre of the city of Rome itself. When the historian Ammianus Marcellinus described the entry of Constantius II into Rome in 357, he could do so without needing to mention a single Christian building (*History* 16.10.13–17). It was this emperor who first ordered the removal of the Altar of Victory from the Roman senate house. As a site for traditional ('pagan') offerings of incense and libations for the health of empire and emperor, the altar was a rallying point for those unsympathetic to the 'new' religion. It was subsequently restored, then taken down again on the order of the emperor Gratian in 382. Controversy ensued. There was a further restoration some years later, then another removal.[23] Just what risk there was of yet another restoration when Prudentius composed his poem *Against Symmachus* in 402–3 is open to debate, but it is in any case striking to see how central a place this particular monument still held in the Christian imagination of a non- or pre-Christian Rome. In the climactic section of book 1, as Pollmann points out, Prudentius set forth a recognizably Eusebian view of Rome's Christian imperial destiny, including an account of Constantine's victory at the Milvian Bridge and subsequent triumphal entry into Rome. He did so in distinctly Virgilian accents, preparing the reader for his 'improved' version of the Virgilian vision of Rome's greatness, a vision no longer attributed to Jupiter but instead to the Christian emperor Theodosius (379–95). Much of the burden of narrative and ideology is in fact carried by a speech that the poet put in the mouth of Theodosius, as if spoken by him to the city of Rome. At the end of his speech, the emperor addresses the city in its ritual and material being, at the same time appealing to its (Christian) elite: 'I would now have you set aside your childish festivals, absurd ceremonies, and offerings unworthy of so great a kingdom. You leading citizens, wash the marbles that are spattered with a sickly stain. Let your statues, the works of great artists, stand clean; let these be our country's fairest ornaments, and let no base usage pollute the monuments of art [*monumenta artis*] and turn it into sin'[24] (1.499–505). What *are* these monuments? If Prudentius had in mind any specifically Christian program of decoration, it does not emerge clearly from his lines. Nor is there any hint of iconoclasm; even if non-Christian religious observances could be banished from the city, it was unrealistic to think of Rome being cleared of all its non-Christian statuary. (The statue of Victory remained in the senate house until the Gothic sack of 410.) The wished-for cleansing is surely metaphorical, not to say abstract. Little if anything may change on the ground, but in the mind's eye of the poet, and potentially that of his readers too, the fabric of Rome will lose its threateningly pre-Christian face as its monuments – formerly the visual and plastic expressions of a civic ideology indissociable from the cult of the emperor – are at last revealed as works of pure art, signifying only themselves and their makers' skill.

It would appear, then, that the spiritualization of Roman territorial claims that Pollmann detects in Prudentius was accompanied by a no less conscious aestheticization of the original, and still highly contested, urban scene of Roman power. Like other developments presaged in *Against Symmachus*, this physical transformation of the Eternal City may be best understood in eschatological terms, as something occurring towards the end of time. It would then again invite comparison with the post-Roman-imperial imaginings of Augustine, especially as they are revealed in the work of his *De civitate dei* that English readers cannot help calling the *City of God*, despite the literal impossibility of making the Latin *civitas* ('body politic') a synonym for *urbs* ('city-space').[25] As Augustine goes beyond Prudentius in treating the Roman Empire as 'theoretically dispensable' (Pollmann, 187), so he is (even) quicker to dissolve the material reality of the Roman city. Rome, Milan, and Trier – all imperial capitals – are virtually featureless in the *Confessions*, as is Carthage, capital of Africa Proconsularis.[26] The *City of God* may have been begun in response to responses to the Gothic sack of Rome in 410, but we search its pages in vain for any remotely graphic, let alone ekphrastic, representation of the city itself. 'Late antique Rome is scarcely present in Augustine's text,' writes Gillian Clark (Clark 2007, 124).[27] In its place, she suggests, Augustine in the early part of the *De civitate dei* raised a 'city of books,' a 'textual Rome' which he then promptly demolished in order to clear imaginative space for his alternative vision of a Christian society unconfined by walls or indeed by any physical limits.

Even this attractive metaphor of a 'textual' city may understate the case. *Pace* Clark, the *City of God* is not much like a city. True, it is full of materials taken from books in which Rome – place, race, and empire – was celebrated, beginning with Virgil's *Aeneid*, but these fragmentary intertexts are laid out in Augustine's work without the contextual support of any of the performances of 'civic theology' (a term he adopted from Varro) that, in his own time, still made their message compelling to audiences and spectators. As Clark also observes, Augustine in the *City of God* takes no account of the ways in which Roman history and traditional Roman religion were actualized in the day-to-day life of late antique cities. Whereas the antiquarian Varro, as Augustine quotes Cicero saying, had brought Romans of the late Republic 'back home' to their own city (*nostra urbe*) by carefully researching their ancestral customs,[28] Augustine sought to alienate readers of the late Empire from their hereditary 'built' environment, projecting them instead into a long-term narrative of sacred community derived from the Bible. As provisionally fixed by that narrative, which formed the historical axis for Augustine's 'universal' hermeneutic (Pollmann 2005), their present coordinates as members of the *civitas dei* would be chronographical as well as eschatologically determined, rather than topographical or geographical (*City of God*, books 11–22).

Augustine's post-Roman history of the world does indeed have a powerful visual dimension, but it is a visuality deliberately divorced from the spectacles of empire, an apocalypse without stage-machinery, a panegyric of the *civitas dei* unenhanced by any other media. By the time his reader reached the reference to a 'kingdom without end' with which the *City of God* ends (22.30), all earthly realms and cities should have vanished from sight. And yet, as Pollmann notes in closing, this very work would later be invoked as a charter for colonization. Its weakness was its strategically Old Roman intertextuality. As long as Virgil (and Livy and others) survived, Augustine's 'prose anti-epic' could always be read against the grain. Rome would not be unbuilt in a day.

There Be Monsters: New Technology, New Ethnographies

'As long as the Colossus stands, Rome stands too; when the Colossus falls, Rome falls too; when Rome falls, the world falls too.' The saying appears in an early medieval collection, possibly of Anglo-Saxon provenance, once falsely attributed to Bede.[29] On all possible datings of the fall of (ancient) Rome, the prophecy proved false. More important than any physical shocks administered to the Eternal City during later antiquity were the alterations made to 'classical' ways of seeing the world, including ethnography. By the late second century, Christian intellectuals were revising conventional Greek and Roman accounts of the peopling of the earth, in light of the genealogy and geography of Genesis 10–11. Reference has already been made in passing to Eusebius's contributions. In Latin, Jerome's deployment of material from Josephus's *Jewish Antiquities* in his *Hebrew Questions on Genesis* was decisive, but only for a time. Like Augustine and other Christian writers still confident of the solidity of Roman institutions, Jerome was culturally conservative, eager to harmonize biblical and classical traditions wherever possible, thereby saving both. As Hervé Inglebert has shown, a more radical stance was taken by Isidore of Seville, writing in the seventh century in the former Roman province of Hispania, which had long since passed under Visigothic rule. Unlike his Latin predecessors, Isidore conceded that classical ethnography might *fail* to capture the current state of the nations. He took it for granted, however, that the latter was fully covered by a divine dispensation, even if human beings did not yet perfectly understand the terms in which God had revealed his purposes in the Bible (Inglebert 2001, 181–4). His reflections on the division of peoples and languages in book 9 of his *Etymologies* – a work that goes further than most in reinscribing universal Romanity as transcendent Latin textuality[30] – have served as a reference point for modern discussion of issues of ethnicity and the ideological construction of nationhood ('ethnogenesis') in early medieval Europe.[31] After Isidore, and often reliant upon him, one other early medieval Latin author stands out as a theorist of Christian religion and nationhood: he is Bede, author of the *Ecclesiastical History of the English People* and of a body of biblical exegesis that would be a staple for Christian missions beyond the shores of that island.[32] By choosing Bede as the initial focus of his essay, Ian Wood brings us to the frontier with a new, northern world where no Roman legionary had ever trod.

Wood makes a compelling case for Bede as the first serious exponent of *Kirchengeschichte als Missionsgeschichte* ('ecclesiastical history as missionary history').[33] The process of Christianization was a theme for Bede to a degree that it had not been for any other early medieval narrator of a non-Roman national history, or even for Eusebius. He brought to its treatment a complex of concepts, images, and micronarratives drawn from his reading of biblical texts and other Christian writers, including Augustine (of Hippo) and Gregory the Great, the pope who had sent another Augustine to convert the English. While Bede's special interest in the Acts of the Apostles, a work previously neglected by Latin exegetes, strikes Wood as natural enough in the circumstances, his readiness to exploit Old Testament passages for the sake of 'missionary ideology' is certainly more remarkable. Even with help from Gregory the Great, it requires a special effort to see Tobit's barking dog as a figure of evangelical zeal (Wood, 204). Yet such allegorical tricks of sight – and, in this case, hearing – are commonplace in Bede's writings. Another notable instance is his characterization of the cowherd Caedmon as a 'clean animal' (cf. Lv 11:3, Dt 14:6) in virtue of his capacity to 'chew over' the biblical exegesis supplied to him by the monks of Whitby, then reproduce it as part of a rendition of the whole of salvation history in English alliterative verse (*Ecclesiastical History* 4.24).[34] Caedmon is Bede's lay, illiterate, vernacular double; the cowherd's purely aural/oral compositional facility mimics the historian-exegete's own prowess as a 'technocrat of the written word.'

The emergence of such a technocracy in early medieval Europe has been interpreted by Peter Brown as a sign of the 'imaginative triumph, in late antique culture, of the notion of Sacred Scriptures.' For this to occur, Brown suggests, a long-standing elite prejudice in favour of the power of the spoken word – in 'live' oratorical performance or poetic recitation – had to yield to a more visual orientation, of a type specifically encouraged by (monastic) biblical *lectio*. Brown locates the shift from oral-performative *praesentia* to static-textual *pictura* in the generations on either side of 600; this would be the watershed separating the age of Augustine and his contemporaries from that of Bede. He is given his cue by two letters of Pope Gregory the Great to Bishop Serenus of Marseilles, written in 599 and 600, in which Gregory recommended the use of pictures as a way of instructing the unlettered, especially those whom he called the *gentes*, meaning peoples outside the bounds of (Christian) Roman civilization.[35] It is tempting, in the light of this analysis, to consider Bede's vividly *figural* biblical exegesis as more than just a resource for his missionary ideology – to regard it, indeed, as the primary medium of his writerly evangelism. Bede's zoomorphic imagery of Christian preachers was a way of populating an imaginary 'biblical' world coextensive with his own. If Gregory was right, it could also be a means of salvation for peoples hitherto shut out from the gospel of Christ.

In taking this hint from Brown, however, we should allow for the likelihood that he himself slightly overestimated the inbred resistance of late Roman elites to the *literally* pictorial dimension of books and, consequently, that there may be less of a gulf between Augustine's, Prudentius's, or Eusebius's technology of the biblical word and Bede's. Brown cites Quintilian's disdain for lawyers who brought visual aids to court and infers from other evidence that no self-respecting ancient reader of Homer would ever have wished to see a map of Odysseus's travels. The visual appeal of verbal ekphrasis was presumably enough for such refined souls. Perhaps it was, some of the time. But recent re-. search on Roman cartography and 'map consciousness' suggests that the pictorial and textual sensibilities of educated, affluent late Roman men and women may have been less dissociated than Brown's historical scheme implies.[36] And there is another factor to be borne in mind. If Christian book culture of the early Middle Ages appears more heavily reliant on illustrations, diagrams, and other non-verbal effects than we take the high literary culture of the late classical period to have been, that may be because Christian technicians of the word – authors, scribes, artists – drew on a wider range of bibliographic models. The Christian preference for the spine-hinged *codex* form of book over the roll or *volumen* traditionally used for literary works in the ancient Graeco-Roman world would be the most obvious indicator of such openness to innovation.[37] It is clear, in any case, that the Northumbrian scriptorium where Bede and his fellow monks produced the deluxe copy of the Vulgate known (from its later resting place) as the Codex Amiatinus, along with other large-format, single-volume, illuminated bibles, was already able to draw on a considerable 'technological' legacy.[38] Although, as Wood reminds us (210), that was patently not the kind of book that Boniface and others carried with them to remote mission fields, the reassurance that such men obtained from their own bibles and the confidence that they placed in them as objects with which to awe the 'nations' of the unconverted will have owed something to their conviction of the power of the Christian book – that is to say, of Christian *exegesis* and Christian book-*making* – to achieve an all-encompassing representation of the created world and of human history. Even away from home, the missionary never found himself outside the book.

Seen against this mental landscape, the monsters that Wood finds appearing in missionary histories of a later date than Bede's take on a life they could not have had in the classical sources from which they ultimately came, or even in the *City of God* 16.8, where Augustine had paused in his account of the descent of the nations from Adam and Eve to consider whether the 'monstrous races' mentioned by classical writers really existed and, if so, whether they were human. (Characteristically, he declined to settle either question. He did, however, confidently affirm that barking is not a human trait.) Encouraged by certain Old Testament texts, writers such as Rimbert and Adam of Bremen could speculate on their own proximity to the physical ends of the earth. Combining those references with certain New Testament passages, they could take a further step and wonder about their own proximity to the end of time. Personal or reported experience of a 'completely alien Other' (Wood, 206) in northern lands, taken with a dash of Old Testament prophecy and a much larger dose of classical cosmography, would then lead them to a question never posed by Bede but inescapable for Christian travel writers, explorers, and missionaries of later centuries, about the limits of humanity itself. In an essay that complements Wood's on this point, Scott Bruce has shown how, in making the argument to Rimbert (and against Augustine) for the essential humanity of the *cynocephali*, Ratramnus of Corbie set special store by the *Life of St Christopher*. Christopher was a dog-headed but otherwise human-seeming creature to whom God, in answer to his prayers, gave the power to speak what his rational mind already conceived, and who had died a martyr's death. If Christopher could be saved, so could others of his canine kind. By replacing a race of monsters 'with a race of rational beings descended from Adam and receptive to the message of the Gospel,' these Carolingian thinkers 'opened up a new field of missionary activity' (Bruce 2006, 56).

The monsters that populate the edge of the known world in the histories of Adam of Bremen are the verbal, textually visible equivalent of the painted ones ringing Northern European world maps (*mappaemundi*) of a somewhat later date. In the Hereford Map (ca 1300) the circular depiction of the world, its places, and races is surmounted by – as if drawn up towards – an image of Christ as judge at the end of time. The telescoping of biblical history onto planar geography was a well-established device: examples can be found in Western book illustration from as early as the time of Bede, in manuscripts of the *Commentary on the Apocalypse* of Beatus of Liébana – but without monsters (Edson 2005).[39] The monsters came later, in Christian maps as in Christian historiography. Once there, they were hard to displace.[40] More than four centuries after Adam of Bremen's conversations with King Sven of Denmark about dog-headed men and other prodigies of the far north, Columbus would write to Ferdinand and Isabella expressing surprise at finding no monstrous human beings in what he took for the Indies. The shock was only momentary. Within a few years of the landfall, Europeans were routinely representing these 'Indians' as monsters, in both texts and images (Friedman 2005, 57–8).[41]

The enlargement of imaginary-discursive resources marked in Wood's essay by the passage from Bede's dog-like evangelists to Adam of Bremen's *cynocephali* is surely an important one. Bede had access to the same classical geographies and cosmographies as later writers of his clime, and Augustine already gave him a licence to interpret any and all marvels (*miracula*) and monsters (*monstra*) as signs of God's will (*City of God* 21.8). Bede as a historian is prodigal with marvels, but real monsters remained beyond his ken. Caedmon's horizon was still narrower, in this respect, than that of the *Beowulf* poet. Would it be making too much of the difference in question to suggest that it is properly with Bede – rather than, say, with Gregory the Great – that we touch the limit of a process of re-*mediation* that partly characterizes 'The Transformation of the Roman World'?[42]

The 'Roman world' had always been a projection of the city of Rome, just as Roman nationality had always been an extension of the citizenship (*civitas*) of the same. Rome, almost uniquely in history, was a city that defined a cosmos (Edwards and Woolf 2003). The means of that projection, extension, and definition were partly military, but mainly civil. From the time of Augustus, the media of Roman civility or civilization – legal, bureaucratic, ceremonial, cultic, monumental, rhetorical – had as their primary function the confirmation of the emperor's prestige and the communication of his will (or, following the reforms of Diocletian in the late third century, the communication of the notionally consensual will of several sharers in the imperial office) (Millar 1992, Ando 2000).[43] To begin with, but less so as time went on, the emperor could be found at Rome. Upon Diocletian's creation of an imperial college and the strategic devolution of Rome's role as capital to cities closer to the northern and eastern frontiers, the mediation of the sacred presence (*praesentia*) of the emperor(s) to the regions inevitably became a more complex affair, as attested by the wealth of panegyrical writing – as well as by new and renovated public buildings – from this period. The Roman technology of imperial awe kept evolving. Nero might commission a colossal statue of himself at Rome and count on its fame to spread; Constantine felt obliged to found a 'new Rome' – and even then his publicists had their work cut out. We saw how Eusebius sought to capture Constantine's Roman triumph for readers who, like him, may never have visited the Eternal City. Prudentius's and Augustine's adjustments of the Virgilian prophetic view point in the same direction. The multimedia effects of Roman imperial ideology were being replaced – or replicated, on new terms – by a Christian technology of awe that drew its resources from the Scriptures and wherever else it found them. Like its Roman equivalent, this Christian technology projected a world and a supranational nationality. Central to both, in early medieval cartography as in Augustinian eschatology, was the city of Jerusalem.

Bede's indifference to monsters can be read as a sign of the perfect sufficiency for his purposes of the Roman-Christian media that he so expertly managed. It no longer mattered whether the Colossus still stood. No Christian world depended upon it. Even so, the Christian world as Bede knew it was one whose psychological limits had been set by the Roman Empire: he knew the monsters that the Romans knew, and – to repeat a critical distinction made by Wood – they were *not* just round the corner. When Boniface and other English missionaries set off with Bede's biblical-exegetical works as support for their missions, they took with them a world- and nation-shaping apparatus of essentially *late Roman* manufacture. It would be for them and their successors to extend its range without compromising its awful efficiency.

Responses

Harry O. Maier

The conspiracy of text and image joined together to justify the imperial reach of empire is seductive. Eusebius's 'prophetic viewpoint' is indeed a realized eschatology. The fifth-century mosaics of Santa Maria Maggiore put into full effect his application of biblical text to the contemporary achievements of empire. As Vessey points out, those who a century earlier stepped outside the 'verbally and visually storied space of a church building' into the urban space of the Roman city described by Ammianus Marcellinus and others could still only see through a glass dimly. Eusebius's commentaries, history, and orations were at best a vade mecum to see how imperial image and biblical narrative could conspire together to make visible a world as yet to be fully realized. So it is important not to get carried away with Eusebius, or at least not to retroject the prophetic viewpoint inherent in the iconographical program of the fifth century onto the fourth. On those streets a Virgilian (not to mention Horatian) iconographic code, hallowed by the Julio-Claudians and imitated by every dynasty thereafter, was still *the* picture language of the Roman Empire, and it was through that lens that imperial achievement continued to receive its prophetic *focus imaginarius*. Outside the walls of the Christian basilicas that he erected on his private estates, Constantine shrewdly deployed a visual code that was elastic and polysemous. If Eusebius urges us to interpret Constantine and his imperial achievements as the fulfilment of Christian expectation, the emperor's coins and monuments express a surplus of meaning that spills over any strict Christian narration. The seduction of Eusebius is the way he so deftly weaves the visual media of empire with the exegesis of biblical narrative. In bringing biblical text to monument he magnifies the vision of his teacher Origen, but in doing so he fails to communicate a fuller picture.

The later church historian Socrates testifies to the demands for a more elastic prophetic viewpoint than the one implied in Eusebius's writings. When in 391 Theophilus the bishop of Alexandria destroyed the local Temple of Serapis, he reports that 'there were found in it, engraven on stone, certain characters which they call hieroglyphics, having the form of crosses.' Alexandrian Christians immediately seized upon the image as a prophetic indication that the ancient priests of Serapis anticipated the coming of Christ and the full realization of their religious devotion in Christianity, whereupon 'a very great number of the pagans embraced Christianity, and confessing their sins, were baptized.' Other devotees of Serapis where happier to live and let live: 'For the Christians who affirm that the cross is the sign of Christ's saving passion, claimed this character as peculiarly theirs; but the pagans alleged that it might appertain to Christ and Serapis in common; "for," said they, "it symbolizes one thing to Christians and another to heathens"' (*Church History* 5.17). Socrates, a historian more inclined to incredulity than his predecessor Eusebius, was suspicious of the Christian prophetic viewpoint assumed at Alexandria. How, he asked, could the priests of Serapis have foreseen the mystery of the Passion, when the incarnation 'was "a mystery hid from the ages and from generations" as the apostle declares [1 Cor 2:7, 8].' The episode is instructive for our attempts to assess the merger of imperial image and historical narration in the interpretive framework of Eusebius of Caesarea. We can expect that Constantine found himself in an ambiguous situation, not unlike the devotees of the cult of Serapis. Alistair Kee outlines a compelling case for the polysemous nature of the *labarum*, which Christians such as Eusebius and pagans such as the aristocracies on whose allegiance Constantine relied for the successes of dynasty could alike have interpreted as they wished (Kee 1982, 1–50, 117–75). On the imperial coinage it appears in iconographical programs fully at home in the imperial theology of victory and so would have been susceptible to diverse interpretation. Even as he kept his patronage of Christianity out of the public domain, so Constantine's imperial artists kept the iconographical imagery associated with the emperor's reign open to interpretation, however much it was weighted towards the Christian side.[44] There is no unambiguous public Christian iconography associated with Constantine's reign, or that of his sons. The imagery remains decidedly polysemous. The contribution of a church historian such as Eusebius is to place that imagery within his own prophetic point of view. Eusebius, like the Christians at the Sarapeum at Alexandria, believed the best story was one of prophetic promise and fulfilment, and for this he and they had the Bible with its typological codes. Others either unconvinced or inclined towards more traditional appropriations had their own rich heritage on which to draw, as was the case, for example, with Constantine's panegyrists who drew from the stock of rhetorical commonplaces on display, for example, in Aelius Aristides' Twenty-Sixth Oration in praise of Rome, or Pliny the Younger's panegyric to Trajan.

Thus, I would now argue, Socrates' story of the pagan response to the discovery of crosses at the Serapeum encourages a more nuanced account of the conspiracy of text and image in laying claim to territory. The purpose of the combination of biblical text, commonplaces in political oration, epic and civic poetry, and imperial iconography was to persuade the diverse peoples of a vast empire of the divine right of emperors to rule them. In the Constantinian period, imperial iconographers deftly deployed imagery to allow enough room for Christians and pagans alike to bring their respective narratives and religious traditions to make that reign compelling. By the time the cycle of mosaics at Santa Maria Maggiore was complete, the Eusebian vision had triumphed, but that is indeed the story of a later generation. From the time of Constantine onward, biblical and Roman imperial texts, separately or together, furnished the prophetic viewpoints and picture-language in which Christians and non-Christians alike were to discover *their* place in the territorial assignment of empire.[45]

Ian Wood

The question of whether Bede or Gregory the Great marks the end of the 'Transformation of the Roman World' is an interesting one. Of course, like all debates about periodization, it is ultimately a theoretical exercise; yet if followed through carefully it can help us think more deeply about our material. Taking two 'patristic' figures as alternative limits may, if we think in too linear a way, lead us to forget some of the oddities of the intervening period. Bede can easily be seen as the last of the Church Fathers: that would appear to be how the Carolingians saw him, though the distance in time between, say, Bede and Hrabanus

Maurus was not very different from the gap between Gregory and Bede (Hill 2006). Looking at history-writing one might again wish to draw the limit with Bede, or with another Gregory, the sixth-century bishop of Tours. But then one would be left with Paul the Deacon as an obvious successor, who actually looked back, particularly in his *Romana*, to Jordanes. More importantly, between Gregory of Tours and Bede there is Isidore, and the extraordinary compilation ascribed to Fredegar, a work whose great strangeness is disguised by our tendency to read 'Fredegar book 4' and to ignore the previous three books, where we are already in a saga-telling world. It is a world, as Peter Brown used to remind his undergraduate students in the 1970s, whose horizons are a good deal wider than those of Gregory of Tours. Those horizons also involve playing games with the memory of Alexander the Great – Fredegar's Theodoric the Ostrogoth is presented as a Macedonian (!), and if we are not yet in the world of Pseudo-Methodius, we are very close to it, and that by the 660s. We are even closer to it when we turn to Aethicus Ister, which, whenever and wherever it was written, was attracting attention in early eighth-century Bavaria. And with Aethicus we are certainly dealing with an author who was every bit as interested in the monstrous as was the author of the *Passio Christopheri*. So none of our posited limits is entirely secure. As Vessey notes, Scott Bruce has emphasized the importance of the story of the dog-headed Christopher to Ratramnus of Corbie in the ninth century. The *Passion of Christopher* was in fact attracting attention a century earlier. Although manuscripts of the *Passion* are well attested from the tenth century onwards, the text already appears in the so-called Homiliary of Burchard of Würzburg, of the last quarter of the eighth century. With the *Passion*, Aethicus Ister, and Ratramnus, we are clearly beyond the boundaries of what would normally be thought of as Late Antiquity, but we need to think hard to determine where we place Fredegar. Is he already way beyond the pale? And if so, what are we to make of the fact that his fantasies involve an admittedly distorted classical world: that of Alexander and even of Troy, as seen through the eyes of Dares?

NOTES

1   Greenblatt is citing *Select Documents Illustrating the Four Voyages of Columbus*, trans. and ed. Cecil Jane, 2 vols. (London: Hakluyt Society, 1930–2), i. 2.

2 Todorov 1984. See also Marchitello 1997, ch. 4: 'Possessing the New World: Historicism and the Story of the Anecdote.'

3 Anderson 1991. For discussion of some of Anderson's claims, see above 20–31.

4 Virgil, *Aeneid* 1.327–8, 'By what name shall I know you, maiden?' The line is there spoken by Aeneas to his mother Venus, who is disguised as a huntress. The same tag had supplied one of the emblems for 'Aprill' of Edmund Spenser's *Shepheardes Calender* (1579), an eclogue glorifying Elizabeth.

5 *Hunc tantum nobis fata ostendere, nec ultra esse sinunt* ('This one the fates let us see this much, but no further'). The text adapts and slightly scrambles *Aeneid* 6.869–70, where the reference was to Marcellus, the short-lived nephew and adopted son of Octavian. *Plus ultra* had originally been the *impresa* of the Habsburg ruler Charles V, the last Holy Roman Emperor to be crowned in Italy: see Rosenthal 1971.

6 Translations are from Eusebius 1999, 83–4.

7 In the parallel but partly divergent account given by Lactantius, *On the Deaths of the Persecutors* 44, Constantine is told in a dream to inscribe the *chi-rho* figure on his soldiers' shields.

8 Ando 2000, esp. ch. 7; MacCormack 1981; L'Huillier 1992.

9 Cameron 1991.

10 Lieu 2004, passim; Johnson 2006. Such studies are part of a general awakening of scholarly interest in questions of ethnicity and collective identity in the later ancient world. See also Stroumsa 1999, 57–84; Miles 1999; Mitchell and Greatrex 2000; Lieu 2002; Boyarin 2004; and Buell 2005. Eusebius is also a major focus of Jacobs 2004.

11 Mendels 1999; Grafton and Williams 2006, esp. ch. 3 ('Eusebius's *Chronicle*: History Made Visible').

12 See the commentary of Cameron and Hall, Eusebius 1999, with Rapp 1998, 292–7.

13 Auerbach 1984, 11–76, an essay first published (in German) in 1944; Auerbach 1953; White 1999; Dawson 2002.

14 Potter 1994.

15 Hardie 1986, 336–76; Quint 1993, 21–31.

16 Krautheimer 1980, ch. 1, emphasizing the 'limitations set [by the local aristocracy] upon his program of visibly Christianizing Rome ... Close to the city walls and hidden among other palace buildings, the new churches were hardly visible to Rome's casual visitor' (31). See further Curran 2000, 76–114, and for a more optimistic assessment of the impact of Constantine's conversion on the fabric of the city, Humphries 2007, 21–58, esp. 26–33.

17 See now esp. Johnson 2006, ch. 6: 'Rome among the Nations.'

18 For complementary perspectives on Virgil as the poet par excellence of Western 'civilization,' see Ziolkowski 1993 and Kennedy 1997. Writing shortly before the 9/11 attacks on the United States, Joseph Farrell noted how 'the rise of American power both in world politics and in the more circumscribed world of Latin literary studies, [had been] paralleled by a marked increase in the amount of Vergil scholarship produced,' then surmised that 'we have got tired of the Vergilian hegemony ... just as we have tried to rid ourselves of the binary politics of the Cold War and have had to accustom ourselves to a world in which there is only one superpower, for better or worse, but many lesser centers of residual or emerging power as well' (Farrell 2001, 17, 24).

19 See also Heim 1992, Inglebert 1996, MacCormack 1998, and Rees 2004.

20 See, e.g., the Index of Ancient Authors in Nixon and Rodgers 1994.

21 The high honours paid to Servius in the fiction of Macrobius's *Saturnalia* are an exception to prove the rule: Kaster 1980; see also ch. 3 of Kaster 1988. In his *Chronicle* for the year 354 Jerome recalled the rhetorician Marius Victorinus and his own grammar teacher Aelius Donatus; only the former is said to have been honoured with a statue at Rome. If Donatus ever attained the senatorial rank of *vir clarissimus*, it would have been upon his appointment as orator of the city: Kaster 1988, 275–8.

22 On this point see now the important study by Humphries (2007).

23 A blow-by-blow account of the contest can be found in Croke and Harries 1982, ch. 2.

24 Trans. adapted from the Loeb edition, Prudentius 1969–71, 1.389.

25 Whole books have been based on this (calculated?) misprision, e.g. Ward 2000, esp. 226–38: 'Augustine's City of God,' immediately followed by a section on 'Millennial Manchester.'

26 The only urban monument specifically mentioned in the whole of the work, a statue of the orator Marius Victorinus at Rome (see also above, n. 21), may have been taken from a book: Vessey 2005, 239–45.

27 The Augustinian eclipse of the physical city – the Rome of Roman history and Virgilian epic – in favour of a biblically grounded opposition of two kinds of community (*civitas*) is captured by MacCormack 1998, ch. 5 ('"The High Walls of Rome": The City on Earth and the Heavenly City').

28 *City of God* 6.2, citing Cicero, *Academica* 1.3.9; cited by Clark 2007, 127.

29 *Patrologia Latina* 94.543B; cited by Safran 2006, 56.

30 See Henderson 2007.

31 Pohl 1998, esp. 23–25. This is in the first of several volumes from the European Science Foundation research project 'The Transformation of the

Roman World' that bear on questions of nationhood. The modern scholarly literature on ethnogenesis during and immediately after the Migration Period is now substantial and by no means univocal. For a rapid introduction, see Geary 2002.

32 See Tugene 2001.

33 See also Wood 2001, esp. 42–5.

34 Wieland 1984 explores the various registers of this imagery, including a possible allusion to the iconography of St Luke, traditionally represented as a calf.

35 Brown 1999, 26–7, 18 (texts of Gregory the Great). See also the response by Wood in the same volume.

36 See, e.g., Talbert 2004. The forensic context for Quintilian's remarks on visual aids is laid out in Bablitz 2007, 193.

37 See now in general Grafton and Williams 2006.

38 See, e.g., Gorman 2000 and Chazelle 2006.

39 See also Kline 2005.

40 Bildhauer and Mills 2003 is concerned mainly with Northern European evidence from the later Middle Ages.

41 For subsequent developments, see Goddard's essay (ch. 10) below.

42 This was the title of the European Science Foundation research project co-directed by Ian Wood; see above, n. 31.

43 For the changed situation after the turn of the fourth century, as the eastern and western halves of the empire began to follow different courses, see Millar 2006.

44 For the *labarum* as decidedly and unambiguously Christian, see Barnes 1981, 48–9, and for a more nuanced and correct account that allows for the polysemous nature of the device and its associations with imperial theologies of victory on Roman standards and military iconography, see Ando 2000, 261–9.

45 On the place and function of the cycle of mosaics in the Theodosian period, and that of other contemporary basilicas in a Christian state cult, see Elsner 1998, 221–35 and Grabar 1968, 31–56. For the visual language of imperial iconography see Grabar 1968, xli–l, as well as the more recent account by Hölscher 2004.

REFERENCES

Anderson, Benedict. 1991. *Imagined Communities: Reflections on the Origin and Spread of Nationalism*. Rev. ed. London: Verso.

Ando, Clifford. 2000. *Imperial Ideology and Provincial Loyalty in the Roman Empire*. Berkeley: University of California Press.

Auerbach, Erich. 1953. *Mimesis: The Representation of Reality in Western Literature*. Trans. Willard R. Trask. Princeton: Princeton University Press.

– 1984. *Scenes from the Drama of European Literature* (1944). Minneapolis: University of Minneapolis Press.

Bablitz, Leanne. 2007. *Actors and Audience in the Roman Courtroom*. London: Routledge.

Barnes, Timothy D. 1981. *Constantine and Eusebius*. Cambridge, MA: Harvard University Press.

Bildhauer, Bettina, and Robert Mills, eds. 2003. *The Monstrous Middle Ages*. Cardiff: University of Wales Press.

Boyarin, Daniel. 2004. *Border Lines: The Partition of Judaeo-Christianity*. Philadelphia: University of Pennsylvania Press.

Brown, Peter. 1999. 'Images as a Substitute for Writing.' In Evangelos Chrysos and Ian Wood, eds, *East and West: Modes of Communication*, 15–34. Leiden: Brill.

Bruce, Scott G. 2006. 'Hagiography as Monstrous Ethnography: A Note on Ratramnus of Corbie's Letter Concerning the Conversion of the Cynocephali.' In Gernot R. Wieland, Carin Ruff, and Ross G. Arthur, eds, *Insignis Sophiae Arcator: Essays in Honour of Michael W. Herren on His 65th Birthday*, 45–56. Turnhout: Brepols.

Buell, Denise Kimber. 2005. *Why This New Race: Ethnic Reasoning in Early Christianity*. New York: Columbia University Press.

Cameron, Averil. 1991. *Christianity and the Rhetoric of Empire: The Development of Christian Discourse*. Berkeley: University of California Press.

Chazelle, Celia. 2006. 'Christ and the Vision of God: The Biblical Diagrams of the Codex Amiatinus.' In Jeffrey F. Hamburger and Anne-Marie Bouche, eds, *The Mind's Eye: Art and Theological Argument in the Middle Ages*, 84–111. Princeton: Princeton University Press.

Clark, Gillian. 2007. 'City of Books: Augustine and the World as Text.' In William E. Klingshirn and Linda Safran, eds, *The Early Christian Book*, 117–38. Washington: Catholic University of America Press.

Courcelle, Pierre. 1957. 'Les exégèses chrétiennes de la quatrième Eclogue.' *Revue des Études Anciennes* 61: 294–319, repr. in *Opuscula Selecta: Bibliographie et recueil d'articles publiés entre 1938 et 1980*. Paris: Études Augustiniennes, 1984.

Croke, Brian, and Jill Harries. 1982. *Religious Conflict in Fourth-Century Rome: A Documentary Study*. Sydney: Sydney University Press.

Curran, John. 2000. *Pagan City and Christian Capital: Rome in the Fourth Century*. Oxford: Oxford University Press.

Dawson, John David. 2002. *Christian Figural Reading and the Fashioning of Identity*. Berkeley: University of California Press.

Edson, Evelyn. 2005. 'Mapping the Middle Ages: The Imaginary and Real Universe of the *Mappaemundi*.' In Leif Søndergaard and Rasmus Thorning Hansen, eds, *Monsters, Marvels and Miracles: Imaginary Journeys and Landscapes in the Middle Ages*, 11–25. Odense: University Press of Southern Denmark.

Edwards, Catherine, and Greg Woolf, eds, 2003. *Rome the Cosmopolis*. Cambridge: Cambridge University Press.

Elsner, Jas. 1998. *Imperial Rome and Christian Triumph*. Oxford: Oxford University Press.

Eusebius. *Life of Constantine*. 1999. Trans. Averil Cameron and Stuart G. Hall. Oxford: Clarendon Press.

Farrell, Joseph. 2001. 'The Vergilian Century.' *Vergilius: The Journal of the Vergil Society* 47: 11–28.

Friedman, John Block. 2005. 'Monsters at the Earth's Imagined Corners: Wonders and Discovery in the Late Middle Ages.' In Leif Søndergaard and Rasmus Thorning Hansen, eds, *Monsters, Marvels and Miracles: Imaginary Journeys and Landscapes in the Middle Ages*, 41–64. Odense: University Press of Southern Denmark.

Geary, Patrick J. 2002. *The Myth of Nations: The Medieval Origins of Europe*. Princeton: Princeton University Press.

Gorman, Michael. 2000. 'The Diagrams in the Oldest Manuscripts of Cassiodorus' *Institutiones*.' *Revue Benedictine* 110: 27–41.

Grabar, André. 1968. *Christian Iconography: A Study of Its Origins*. Princeton: Princeton University Press.

Grafton, Anthony, and Megan Williams. 2006. *Christianity and the Transformation of the Book: Origen, Eusebius, and the Library of Caesarea*. Cambridge, MA: Harvard University Press.

Greenblatt, Stephen. 1991. *Marvelous Possessions: The Wonder of the New World*. Chicago: University of Chicago Press.

Hardie, Philip R. 1986. *Virgil's Aeneid: Cosmos and Imperium*. Oxford: Clarendon Press.

Heim, François. 1992. *La théologie de la victoire: De Constantin à Théodose*. Paris: Beauchesne.

Henderson, John. 2007. *The Medieval World of Isidore of Seville: Truth from Words*. Cambridge: Cambridge University Press.

Hill, J.M. 2006. 'Carolingian Perspectives on the Authority of Bede.' In Scott DeGregorio, ed., *Innovation and Tradition in the Writings of the Venerable Bede*, 227–49. Morgantown: West Virginia University Press.

Hölscher, Tonio. 2004. *The Language of Images in Roman Art*. Trans. Anthony Snodgrass. Cambridge: Cambridge University Press.

Humphries, Mark. 2007. 'From Emperor to Pope? Ceremonial, Space, and Authority at Rome from Constantine to Gregory the Great.' In Kate Cooper and Julia Hillner, eds, *Religion, Dynasty, and Patronage in Early Christian Rome, 300–900*, 21–58. Cambridge: Cambridge University Press.

Inglebert, Hervé. 1996. *Les Romains chrétiens face à l'histoire de Rome: Histoire, christianisme et romanités en Occident dans l'Antiquité tardive*. Paris: Institut des Études Augustiniennes.

– 2001. *Interpretatio Christiana: Les mutations des savoirs (cosmographie, géographie, ethnographie, histoire) dans l'Antiquité chrétienne (30–630 après J.-C.)*. Paris: Institut d'Études Augustiniennes.

Jacobs, Andrew. 2004. *Remains of the Jews: The Holy Land and Christian Empire in Late Antiquity*. Stanford: Stanford University Press.

Jane, Cecil, trans. and ed. 1930–2. *Select Documents Illustrating the Four Voyages of Columbus*. 2 vols. London: Hakluyt Society.

Johnson, Aaron P. 2006. *Ethnicity and Argument in Eusebius' Praeparatio Evangelica*. Oxford: Oxford University Press.

Kaster, Robert. 1980. 'Macrobius and Servius: *Verecundia* and the Grammarian's Function.' *Harvard Studies in Classical Philology* 84: 219–62.

– 1988. *Guardians of Language: The Grammarian and Society in Late Antiquity*. Berkeley: University of California Press.

Kee, Alistair. 1982. *Constantine versus Christ: The Triumph of Ideology*. London: SCM.

Kennedy, Duncan F. 1997. 'Modern Receptions and Their Interpretative Implications.' In Charles Martindale, ed., *The Cambridge Companion to Virgil*, 38–55. Cambridge: Cambridge University Press.

Kline, Naomi Reed. 2005. 'The World of the Strange Races.' In Leif Søndergaard and Rasmus Thorning Hansen, eds, *Monsters, Marvels and Miracles: Imaginary Journeys and Landscapes in the Middle Ages*, 27–40. Odense: University Press of Southern Denmark.

Krautheimer, Richard. 1980. *Rome: Profile of a City, 312–1308*. Princeton: Princeton University Press.

L'Huillier, Marie-Claude. 1992. *L'Empire des mots: Orateurs gaulois et empereurs romains, 3e et 4e siècles*. Paris: Les Belles Lettres.

Lieu, Judith M. 2002. *Neither Jew nor Greek? Constructing Early Christianity*. Edinburgh: T. & T. Clark.

– 2004. *Christian Identity in the Jewish and Graeco-Roman World*. Oxford: Oxford University Press.

MacCormack, Sabine G. 1981. *Art and Ceremony in Late Antiquity*. Berkeley: University of California Press.

– 1998. *The Shadows of Poetry: Vergil in the Mind of Augustine*. Berkeley: University of California Press.

Marchitello, Howard. 1997. *Narrative and Meaning in Early Modern England: Browne's Skull and Other Histories*. Cambridge: Cambridge University Press.

Mendels, Doron. 1999. *The Media Revolution of Early Christianity: An Essay on Eusebius's Ecclesiastical History*. Grand Rapids: Eerdmans.

Miles, Richard, ed. 1999. *Constructing Identities in Late Antiquity*. London: Routledge.

Millar, Fergus. 1992. *The Emperor in the Roman World (31 BC–AD 337)*. 2nd ed. London: Duckworth.

– 2006. *A Greek Roman Empire: Power and Belief under Theodosius II (408–450)*. Berkeley: University of California Press.

Mitchell, Stephen, and Geoffrey Greatrex, eds. 2000. *Ethnicity and Culture in Late Antiquity*. London: Duckworth and the Classical Press of Wales.

Nixon, C.E.V., and Barbara Saylor Rodgers, eds. 1994. *In Praise of Later Roman Emperors: The Panegyrici Latini*. Berkeley: University of California Press.

Pohl, Walter. 1998. 'Telling the Difference: Signs of Ethnic Identity.' In Walter Pohl and Helmut Reimitz, eds, *Strategies of Distinction: The Construction of Ethnic Communities, 300–800*, 17–69. Leiden: Brill.

Pollmann, Karla. 2005. 'Augustine's Hermeneutics as a Universal Discipline!?' In Karla Pollmann and Mark Vessey, eds, *Augustine and the Disciplines: From Cassiciacum to 'Confessions,'* 206–31. Oxford: Oxford University Press.

Potter, David. 1994. *Prophets and Emperors: Human and Divine Authority from Augustus to Theodosius*. Cambridge, MA: Harvard University Press.

Prudentius. 1969–71. Trans. H.J. Thomson, ed. Loeb Classical Library. 2 vols. London: Heinemann.

Purchas, Samuel. 1625. *Hakluytus Posthumus or Purchas His Pilgrimes. Contayning a History of the World, in Sea voyages & lande-Travells by Englishmen and others*. London: W. Stansby for H. Fetherstone.

Quint, David. 1993. *Epic and Empire: Politics and Generic Form from Virgil to Milton*. Princeton: Princeton University Press.

Rapp, Claudia. 1998. 'Comparison, Paradigm and the Case of Moses in Panegyric and Hagiography.' In Mary Whitby, ed., *The Propaganda of Power: The Role of Panegyric in Late Antiquity*, 277–98. Leiden: Brill.

Rees, Roger, ed. 2004. *Romane Memento: Vergil in the Fourth Century*. London: Duckworth.

Rosenthal, Earl. 1971. '*Plus Ultra, Non Plus Ultra*, and the Columnar Device of the Emperor Charles V.' *Journal of the Warburg and Courtauld Institutes* 34: 204–28.

Safran, Linda. 2006. 'What Constantine Saw: Reflections on the Capitoline Colossus, Visuality, and Early Christian Studies.' In *Millennium: Jahrbuch zu*

Kultur und Geschichte des ersten Jahrtausends n. Chr. / Yearbook on the Culture and History of the First Millennium C.E. 3: 43–73.

Stroumsa, Guy. 1999. *Barbarian Philosophy: The Religious Revolution of Early Christianity.* Tübingen: Mohr Siebeck.

Talbert, Richard. 2004. 'Cartography and Taste in Peutinger's Roman Map.' In Richard Talbert and Kai Brodersen, eds, *Space in the Roman World: Its Perception and Presentation*, 115–41. Münster: Lit Verlag.

Todorov, Tzvetan. 1984. *The Conquest of America: The Question of the Other.* Trans. Richard Howard. New York: Harper & Row.

Tugene, Georges. 2001. *L'idée de nation chez Bède le Vénérable.* Paris: Institut d'Études Augustiniennes.

Vessey, Mark. 2005. 'History, Fiction, and Figuralism in Book 8 of Augustine's *Confessions*.' In Dale B. Martin and Patricia Cox Miller, eds, *The Cultural Turn in Late Ancient Studies: Gender, Asceticism, and Historiography*, 237–57. Durham, NC: Duke University Press.

Ward, Graham. 2000. *Cities of God.* London: Routledge.

Waswo, Richard. 1997. *The Founding Legend of Western Civilization: From Virgil to Vietnam.* Hanover, NH: Wesleyan University Press.

White, Hayden. 1999. *Figural Realism: Studies in the Mimesis Effect.* Baltimore: Johns Hopkins University Press.

Wieland, Gernot. 1984. 'Caedmon, the Clean Animal.' *American Benedictine Review* 35: 194–203.

Wood, Ian. 2001. *The Missionary Life: Saints and the Evangelisation of Europe, 400–1050.* Edinburgh: Longman.

Ziolkowski, Theodore. 1993. *Virgil and the Moderns.* Princeton: Princeton University Press.

Part Three

Colonial and Postcolonial Readings, Premodern Ironies

10

The Amerindian in Divine History: The Limits of Biblical Authority in the Jesuit Mission to New France, 1632–1649

PETER A. GODDARD

The Bible furnishes an essential resource for missionary activity. The directive to win souls to Christ is a central message of the New Testament, and the Scriptures attest to the techniques and success of the Apostles in promoting the Christian faith. The Bible also provides believers with the necessary confidence in understanding the course of history and the progressive unfolding of God's plan for humanity: a divine history, as it was understood. Jesuits, by far the most enterprising of the Catholic missionary orders in the early modern world, shared this traditional sense of the centrality of biblical authority.[1] In their important seventeenth-century mission to New France, however, their actual reliance on the literal sense of the Bible and the divine history it provided was minimal. In their own spirituality, Jesuits were Christ-centred and dependent on direct revelation. In their understanding of history, they promoted the classical model of human development known as the 'stadial' theory, which sees human society advancing through stages, with the Christian stage, in this case, at the apex. In such a perspective, Huron and Algonquian people become representatives of fallen humanity, their lives shaped by their distance from and profound ignorance of divine revelation. As this essay will make clear, the Jesuits' desire to transform Amerindian peoples through education and their sense of the difficulty of invoking biblical texts for literal guidance in such an alien context led them to confine the Bible, for the most part, to an exhortatory role. While the Bible may have been important for the morale of the missionaries themselves, and undoubtedly had a certain symbolic power for their converts, its role in shaping the overall ideology of the New France mission was quite limited.

The Bible in the New France Mission

In contrast to the Spanish 'spiritual conquest' of Mesoamerica in the previous century, seventeenth-century French initiatives in the northern part of the New World did not trumpet their divine purpose or justification. Millennial dreams of empire would have been a luxury to a nation that had only emerged from a half-century of religious war as recently as 1598. To be sure, the concept of mission to the New World was already well rooted in the Catholic reform movement. Such missions were understood to constitute the principal activity of religious orders, including the Jesuits, the Capuchins, and the Recollects. While the Jesuits were a new kind of religious organization, emphasizing active forms of spiritual life, the Capuchins and the Recollects were reform branches of the great missionary order of St Francis. Rarely, however, did these missionaries superimpose on descriptions of their own activity a moral purpose or even a geography derived directly from biblical precedents. Surveying the wind-bent forests of the north shore of the Gulf of St Lawrence in 1534, Jacques Cartier – the French discoverer of Canada – had identified the northern New World as the land God had given to Cain (Cartier 1924, 60). A century later neither the missionaries themselves nor their supporters back home apparently felt any need to linger over such (discouraging!) parallels (Bastiensen 1989, 375–82).

Nor do biblical considerations seem greatly to have influenced other men's calculations of colonial prospects in the early modern world. Conquistadors, traders, and explorers, whether wonder-struck or simply shortsighted, were 'neither keen advocates nor avid readers' of the Bible (Sugirtharajah 2001, 48). As the example of Cartier suggests, theirs was an entirely conventional understanding of the biblical myth, quickly overtaken in practice by the drive for profit and dominion. Such men, even when literate and able to make historical comparisons, made little attempt to relate what they encountered – and indeed precipitated – in the New World to the great motifs of biblical narrative.

Despite the increasing importance in France's confessional debates of preaching from Scripture, Jesuit missionaries were themselves notably circumspect in their deployment of the Bible. In Catholic orthodoxy, the biblical Word was not considered a sufficient guide to Christian faith and practice. Even, and perhaps especially, on the colonial frontier, we observe a certain prudence on the part of the Roman Catholic authorities with regard to the scriptural principle, especially after the Council of Trent (1545–63) decreed 'ultra-restrictive' measures concerning biblical translation and interpretation (Chédozeau 1989, 341). The Bible was, after all, 'the religion of Protestants,' as William Chillingworth would later call it, and a dangerous instrument in the wrong hands. The council ruled that Bible-reading among the laity was to be limited to those with 'capacity' to read the Holy Scripture (guided by Catholic tradition) and 'permission' from a cleric who could attest to it. The Society of Jesus followed the Council of Trent in this qualified enthusiasm for biblical studies. While frequently skirting heterodoxy in the early decades, Jesuits maintained the emphasis on direct communication with God that had been one of the marks of the late medieval *devotio moderna*. In their famous *Spiritual Exercises*, the scriptural Word was complemented and even supplanted by the 'interior word' (Loyola 1909).[2] There may have been a further institutional factor at work. The missionary vocation, which the Jesuits had embodied since their founding in 1540, was understood to be one of action. Though based on Christ's injunctions in the Gospels (e.g., Mt 24:14, 28:18–19), missionary activity was not itself an obvious locale for sustained reflection on Scripture. Missionaries were too busy themselves with spreading the good news, not with biblical debate or theological conference.

Missionaries to New France quickly found these assumptions reinforced by their experience of the work of God among the Amerindian peoples newly incorporated in the Christian sphere. Paul Le Jeune, writing in 1639 of the exemplary life and death of the Algonquian convert Ignace Amiskouapeo, presents this illiterate individual's extraordinary grace and Christian perfection as evidence of the 'living book, which is Jesus Christ.' He goes on:

> If the Savages could derive these thoughts and these sentiments from any other source than from the living book … I would doubt it if they are speaking sincerely; but they have neither printed book nor writing in their possession – and if they had these, they would understand nothing therein, for they have no intercourse with any man on earth who could give them these ideas. (*JR* 1639, 98–9; *MNF* 4.316–17)

Hearts formerly the repositories of barbarism had been newly filled by God himself. The faith of these new Christians was 'pre-biblical,' deriving from Christ alone. That religious inclinations should be found in such unlikely settings was proof in itself that the 'finger of God was here' (*JR* 1644–5, 153; *MNF* 6.400).

Jesuits in New France did of course invoke the biblical example of reaching out to unbelieving peoples. Algonquians and Hurons were likened to the Samarians and Macedonians who had sought and received the missionary St Paul, with the difference that they were considered as supplicants rather than interlocutors (*JR* 1633, 211–12; *MNF* 2.484). Predictably perhaps, after consoling passages from the Psalms, the other biblical books most commonly cited in the missionary accounts are Paul's letters and the Acts of the Apostles. The Pauline epistles and Acts detailed early Christian expansion, imbuing readers with a sense of their religion's inevitable progress. They did so, however, without dwelling on the mystical elements of the faith which the Jesuits specially affected. Indeed, the preoccupation with mission at the expense of spiritual reflection would become a matter of concern to leading members of the Society in the seventeenth century, who feared that headlong embrace of the project of conversion might eclipse the primary union with God which lay at the heart of their vocation (see de Guibert 1994, 558–95).

As Christian educators, Jesuits relied less on the Bible to teach 'Christian doctrine' than on the catechism. In the innovative catechetical literature of the sixteenth century, doctrine was boiled down to a simplified form, while the Bible was invoked more often for embellishment or illustration than as a primary text to be studied and understood. Tremendous investment in the development of catechisms by Jesuits such as Peter Canisius in Germany and Étienne Binet in France was not matched by equal fervour in biblical scholarship. John O'Malley has noted the early Jesuits' praise for, but relative lack of interest in, new Latin translations of Scripture (O'Malley 1993, 115–19, 256–68). Examination of Jesuits' biblical references suggests that they continued to place their faith in the 'Vulgate' or traditional text of the Latin Bible rather than, say, in the more contemporary Latin Douai Bible. Their corporate culture was not one of vigorous Bible-reading, nor did the Bible direct the course of their diverse educational and missionary activity.

We can observe the restricted role of the Bible as a resource for spiritual education in a typical mission setting, as described by François du Peron in a letter to his brother, also a Jesuit, from the Huron country in 1639. After a number of years of proselytizing, the missionaries had attracted a core group of neophytes, eager to learn the faith and to break with their traditional culture. Yet the work of teaching remained great, as did the missionaries' own needs for spiritual nourishment. Du Peron found little opportunity for Bible study or for using the Bible in the training of new converts (the 'savages' of this translated account, from his letter to Joseph Imbert du Peron, 27 April 1639):

> The importunity of the savages – who are continually about us in our cabin, and who sometimes break down a door, throw stones at our cabin, and wound our people – this importunity, I say, does not prevent our observance of our hours, as well regulated as in one of our colleges in France. At four o'clock the rising bell rings; then follows the orison, at the end of which the masses begin and continue until eight o'clock; during this period each one keeps silent, reads his spiritual book, and says his lesser hours. At eight o'clock, the door is left open to the savages, until four in the evening; it is permitted to talk with the savages at this time, as much to instruct them as to learn their language. In this time, also, our Fathers visit the cabins of the town, to baptize the sick and to instruct the well; as for me, my employment is the study of the language, watching the cabin, helping the Christians and catechumens pray to God, and keeping school for their children from noon until two o'clock, when the bell rings for examination of conscience. Then follows the dinner, during which is read some chapter from the Bible; and at supper Reverend du Barry's *Philagie of Jesus* is read; the *Benedicite* and Grace is said in Huron, on account of the savages who are present. We dine around the fire, seated on a log, with our plates on the ground.[3]

Catechism was at the centre of instruction in these challenging circumstances. The Bible was an edifying text, but not the main vehicle of mission practice.

When the missionaries do invoke biblical authority in their day-to-day activity and in the reports that they presented in the annual mission *Relations*, their citations tend to be aphoristic and slogan-like, and generally of an exhortatory nature. Nor do Jesuit writers generally cram their discourse with biblical proof-texts. An injunction to economy, befitting men of action in a hostile environment, worked against extensive biblical quotation. Memorized Latin phrases crop up, in exclamatory rather than explanatory contexts. Now and again the quotation sounds more or less biblical – a Latinism inserted to add a ringing quality to the prose.[4] An interesting exception to this pattern can be found in accounts of the suffering of fellow Jesuits. The experience of Isaac Jogues, who was mutilated by his Iroquoian captors over several weeks in 1645, is rendered in a memorial in vivid biblical language, the onset of torture, for example, being related to the looming passion of

Christ described in Matthew 24:8: 'All this is but the beginnings of birth pangs' ('Narré de la prise du Père Isaac Jogues,' *MNF* 4.273).

As appears from the letter of du Peron already cited, the Bible as a physical object, teaching vehicle, and symbol, was certainly present in the New France mission field. Missionaries carried Bibles, read them, and proffered them as sacramentals, auxiliaries to worship which helped to convey spiritual power. The Bible was a symbol of connection to the temporal and higher powers which sustained the Jesuit mission and, in an environment of limited intercultural dialogue, whether written or spoken, a prime means of reinforcing the mission. 'All our power,' writes du Peron, 'lies at the end of our tongues, in the exhibition and production of our books and writings, the effects of which they never cease to wonder at. This is the only thing that avails us with these people, in lieu of all other motive of credibility' (*JR* 16.135; see Dening 1980, 173–4). Such reference to the symbolic power of the Word, as opposed to a literal subordination to it, appears to have been a strength of Catholic preaching in non-European locales. (Protestant missions were more prone to insist on familiarity with the Bible as a condition of conversion to the new faith.)

Similar observations can be made regarding biblical translations for an Amerindian audience. Unlike in China, where a literate population made such media necessary for missionary work, no large-scale enterprise of translation was attempted for the peoples of the northern American forests (Dehergne 1986, 211–18). The idioms of Hebrew and Aramaic – of ancient Semitic, desert civilizations – not surprisingly proved difficult to translate into this context. Biblical language consequently had little impact on Iroquoian and Algonquian languages, in sharp contrast to the effect which biblical translation had on European vernaculars in the early modern period. The limited character of biblical reference in the mission itself is confirmed by the tendency to quote Scripture in Latin rather than the vernacular, and consequently to avoid any extended parallels.

In short, if North America was a land of biblical promise, the biblical references of French Jesuits gave little or no explicit sign of it.

A New Understanding of Divine History

Encounters alike with the 'New World' and with the 'New Science' challenged classical and Christian structures of authority in the early modern period, and Jesuits were often centrally involved in these contests. Chief among traditional sources of religious authority was of course the Bible, the holy text which informed and guided Christian belief and practice. The Bible also provided, in narrative form, a historical framework for Christian life. Old Testament and New furnished what Northrop Frye calls a 'typology' or pattern for understanding events past, present, and to come. In principle, every Christian had access to this authoritative resource for discerning the pattern in his or her spiritual, or even worldly, life. Whether in fact he or she chose to use it, however, depended upon the prevailing intellectual currents. The standard history of biblical criticism maintains that the great watershed separating the modern from the traditional understanding of the world was crossed by Baruch Spinoza in the late seventeenth century, and that it was his work that opened vistas to the Enlightenment. For Spinoza, the Bible was no longer to be understood as a literal guide to the present but was reduced to serving as a source of pious encouragement and speculative history – or, as Frye would later argue, of creative imagination in the modern era (Frye 1982; Frei 1974, 40–2).[5] I would like to suggest, however, that a similar divide may have been crossed somewhat earlier and in places far less hospitable to profound thought than the philosopher's study.

A Jesuit understanding of 'divine history' is brought into sharp relief in their mission to the Huron and Algonquian peoples of early Canada. Two features stand out. One is the relatively muted recourse to biblical authority in everyday mission life – for good reasons, as we have seen – and in reportage from the mission. The other is an alternative (i.e., non-biblical) view of divine history, one which emphasized not literal precedents, but rather the metaphors of human development.

We have already argued that Jesuit use of the Bible conformed to the restrained use of Scripture in reformed Catholicism. Not only were biblical citations present merely in aphoristic, Latin form, but their frequency declined over time. By the end of the period examined here, biblical citation had been pushed aside as missionaries struggled to reinvent the mission following the collapse of the Huron mission centre at Ste Marie. Nevertheless, as befitted an order made up of products of a powerful humanist program in the schools and colleges, Jesuit missionaries also subscribed to a world-view in which the Bible was of primary importance. Missionaries to Canada issued from the most learned milieux of seventeenth-century Catholic Europe. Men such as Paul le Jeune were graduates of an impressive Jesuit curriculum, and had taught in demanding Jesuit colleges back in France before embarking to the mission fields. In their former lives, many would have participated in the rich discussion arising from contact between Christian traditions and emerging knowledge both of the non-European world and of the new science. And yet it is here that we see, in contrast to the conservatism of their approaches to the Bible in the mission itself, some bold steps away from reliance on the biblical scheme of history which had for so long shaped Christian understanding.

In their mission enterprise, these Jesuits deployed insights from the groundbreaking works of Spanish Jesuit José de Acosta. His *De procuranda Indorum salute* or 'On Obtaining the Salvation of the Indians' (1588) and *Historia natural y moral de las Indias* (1599) set forth a means of comprehending both the diversity and the spiritual condition of New World peoples.[6] Acosta located the genealogy of Amerindian peoples in biblical history: they were descendants of Noah's son Japhet and had wandered across Asia to the New World. The 'newness' of such people in European eyes was a function of the distance they had travelled, a distance analogous to the passage of time (Pagden 1982, 192–6). The deplorable spiritual condition of Mesoamerican peoples, Acosta argued, resulted from their having forgotten their roots. Their history, like their culture itself, was an index of their degeneration. Accordingly, in 1634 the pioneering Jesuit missionary Paul Le Jeune appraised the Amerindian predicament as a reflection of their departure from the main trajectory of Christian history:

> I believe that souls are all made of the same stock, and that they do not materially differ; hence, these barbarians having well formed bodies, and organs well regulated and well arranged, their minds ought to work with ease. Education and instruction alone are lacking. Their soul is a soil which is naturally good, but loaded down with all the evils that a land abandoned since the birth of the world can produce. (Le Jeune 1635, 101)

By and large, Jesuits in New France shared this framing of the mission in divine history. But Le Jeune's conviction of the essential unity of mankind was coupled with a sense that these peoples, 'abandoned since the birth of the world,' lay beyond divine history as it was plotted in Scripture. An additional analysis would be needed for the Amerindians in the state in which they were discovered in the vast northern woods. A biblical concept of the unity of all peoples was useful, to Le Jeune and others, primarily to sustain the sometimes contested claim for the fundamental humanity of these New World peoples.

(Although one might imagine that this would never be in doubt for a missionary, it is striking how often missionaries in New France and elsewhere felt obliged to defend it.) In Le Jeune's view, however, the sacred history of the Bible needed to be supplemented from another source. The heritage of classical antiquity, with its more fully developed model of history based on the experience of the Greek cities and its more accurate world-picture, could potentially help illuminate the history of 'pagan' America. Welcoming a Montagnais convert in 1639, Le Jeune remarks: 'May God forever be blessed by Angels and man, by Scythians and Barbarians, as well as Greeks' (JR 16.133). Besides the likely echo of St Paul (Col 3:11), there is here a scheme of comparison that owes as much to classical ethnography as to any biblical narrative.

Essentialized Christianity and Naturalized History

In New Spain a century earlier, the Bible had been interpreted in the tradition of medieval apocalypticism, as a prediction of the coming end of the world. The Franciscan Jerónimo Mendieta, in his *Historia Eclesiástica Indiana* (completed 1596) envisioned the establishment of a New Jerusalem in the smouldering Valley of Mexico. His fellow friars hoped for a reign of miracles which would shape an exemplary Amerindian Christianity, and hence herald the end of the world. Understood in this apocalyptic sense, the mission was intermediary between a corrupting Europe and an uncorrupted America. Amerindian innocence would trump European civilization and instruct the world in its conduct for the last days.[7] Such moods do not necessarily last very long, though this one did serve to inflate the claims of conversions made by the Franciscans. It also allowed the inscription of Mesoamerican geography with the markers of divine history: no less a person than the Devil himself had his Jerusalem in Tenochtitlán and his Rome in Cuzco. However, these Franciscan delusions marked the passing of the notion of a mass conversion of Amerindians as the harbinger of millennial change. Jesuits in New France would be much more reluctant to delineate their enterprise in such boldly biblical terms.

For them, only the embryonic French colony at Québec, and not the Amerindian territories stretching beyond, could be characterized as a 'Jerusalem blessed by God' (Le Jeune 1635, 5). In contrast to Protestant missionaries in territories claimed by England and later the United States, the Bible did not provide these Jesuits with a map on which the course of the mission could be directly plotted and a 'moral geography' imposed (DeRogatis 2003). French Jesuits, like French colonists generally, arrived in the New World mission field after furrows had already been ploughed, often in a messianic way, by the pioneer Franciscans. This was the case in New France, where in 1632 Jesuits inherited a sketchy Recollect attempt to penetrate the Great Lakes' interior and create a Christian Utopia among the Hurons. The Huron mission was a major project of the Jesuits until the Hurons themselves were overrun by their Iroquois enemies and the mission destroyed in 1649. After that, the focus shifted from a laborious process of settlement, school-, and hospital-building alongside populous Iroquoian communities, to a new style of mission whose ambitions were strictly proportional to the freight capacity of birchbark canoes plying the Upper Great Lakes in search of nomadic Algonquian peoples.

Louis Châtellier has described the contemporary drive in missionary Christianity in Catholic Europe as a discovery of the 'religion of the poor,' an essentialized Christianity which broke with the doctrinal straitjacket of conservative orthodoxy, affirmed at the Council of Trent, through dialogue with popular forms of observance (Châtellier 1993, 120).[8] Jesuits in the *pays d'en haut* or 'upper country' (the French term for the vast Canadian interior) were working in territory largely untouched by biblically based notions of Christianization. In time, the missionaries produced a *métissage* of Christianity and Amerindian religion which marked their own entry, in North America at least, into what could now be described as the liberating space of cultural relativism. 'Although they live in the woods, they are none the less men,' the missionary Paul Ragueneau noted. This was something that Jesuits were all the more disposed to affirm of the nomadic hunters of the great north and west, following the bitter failures of their mission among the settled Iroquoians at mid-century (*JR* 1645–6, 29.263). The same rupture would signal the beginning of a new identification of Amerindians as peoples with their own histories, as distinct from one inscribed upon them by colonists. Thereafter, missionaries would approach their hosts with a new instinct for compromise and diplomacy, no longer so inclined to dismiss Amerindian practices as backward superstition.[9]

While the Bible's account of the original dispersal of peoples may have served to underline the essential unity of mankind and its origins in divine creation, its version of history (despite the best efforts of Protestant exegetes) remained troublingly void of details relevant to the situation of the northern New World. Awareness of the lacunae and ambiguities of the biblical record inspired a seventeenth-century intellectual cottage industry, the chief figures in which were Menasseh ben-Israel, Richard Simon, and Isaac de la Peyrère.[10] Peyrère's great contribution was to show how non-Christian histories, such as those of the Chinese and the inhabitants of Greenland, implied a longer chronology than the one supposedly sketched out in Old Testament.

Among Jesuits, this conundrum led to the groundbreaking work of Joseph-François Lafitau, entitled *Moeurs des sauvages ameriquains comparées aux moeurs des premiers temps* (1724).[11] This treatise, which established a history for the Amerindians related, but not subjugated to, the biblical narrative, and which also found room for comparisons between Iroquoian and Algonquian rituals and the practices of pagan Greeks and Romans, is a milestone in the development of a theory of cultural relativism. Lafitau's was the greatest of all Jesuit syntheses of New World history. Meanwhile, in New France, missionary interpretations of divine history had already taken a turn away from biblical literalism towards a view which presented the Amerindians primarily as 'poor,' but censured them for the depravity which such poverty – in its moral and cognitive dimensions – typically entailed.

At their settlement in the Huron territory, the Jesuits mounted what was in effect a display of the tools of Christian knowledge. Among devices used to confound not just superstition but virtually the entire world-view of the Huron spectator, was a terrestrial globe. The Jesuit source is silent as to its specific didactic purpose, but the general intent is clear: Huron mythology must give way to a divine history which can be plotted spatially as well as temporally, and which would include Amerindian lineages within it. This said, the Jesuits do not simply recount a 'true' version of history for the benefit of prospective converts. Instead, their refutation of Amerindian religion and cosmology proceeds on the grounds of rationality. Christianity could be delineated as a set of 'maxims.' At issue here was not the specifically Christian concept of rationality as the property of a mind made in God's image, but another, more pragmatic rationality – that of the correspondence of Amerindian claims with *natural* facts. Rather than seeking to explain a range of natural (e.g., meteorological, astronomical, psychological) phenomena in relation to the Bible, as previous generations of missionaries had sought to do, the Jesuits staked their claim to superior knowledge on an increasingly confident natural philosophy (*JR* 12.27, 153; 38.85).

How, then, did they account for the condition of the *sauvage* as he and she were found in the forest vastness of the northern New World? This sorry state was explained as a function of historical development – or

264 Peter A. Goddard

rather, the lack of it. Observing the rescue of European survivors of a shipwreck, who had been marooned on Sable Island for a period of years, Marc Lescarbot said of the walrus-hide draped figures: 'Here is how savages are formed' (Lescarbot 1609, 20). Jesuits largely shared this view. The appalling condition of the Amerindians was a result of a long-term decline, one which had not only left them in spiritual darkness and in thrall to the Devil, but had also condemned them to poverty and misery. Paul Le Jeune, seeing Montagnais for the first time, noted their lack of material goods and the simplicity of their lifestyle, which he construed as a measure of want, rather than as the elegance of a design: 'At the best, all their riches are only poverty. Their gold and silver, their diamonds and pearls, are little white grains of porcelain which do not seem to amount to much.' And he added that 'it would not take a great many years to learn all of their crafts' (*JR* 5.53, 25).

Le Jeune's remarks, while ludicrous as ethnography, contain the germs of a secular as well as divine history. He observed that the Amerindians seemed like people from an earlier time, a time through which Christian Europe had already passed: 'Before the faith was received in Germany, Spain or England, those nations were not more civilized' (*JR* 5.32).[12] Like the many comparisons of Algonquians and Iroquoians with French peasantry (in which the Amerindians usually come out ahead), this opinion – that the Amerindians were at a particular stage of development – reflects the Aristotelian, classically-oriented cast of mind of these missionaries and their rationalist conviction of the knowability of all nature. Theirs was a stadial theory of human development.

The twist, of course, is that in the case of the Amerindians, there was less evidence of progress than of decline. All that was left them were shadows alike of the knowledge of their divine origins and of the order and restraint which had once obtained among them and had at that time reflected God's rule. Jesuits proposed that these people had a past that was common to humanity in general, while their present was illustrative of the state universally obtaining when people lived without acceptance or knowledge of their God: 'These are the most forlorn people in the world' (*JR* 24.75). The prevalence of language referring to the darkness which envelops Amerindian culture, especially Amerindian religion, confirms the sense of distance from a land of revelation now co-located with Europe itself.

This idea that the forests of Canada were a land which God had forgotten could also fuel a rhetoric of the diabolic: *here* was where the Devil had his Empire (*JR* 14.2–3). However, I am not inclined to read too much significance into such largely formal utterances. There are simply too many instances where Jesuits identify the true enemy as the ignorance and seclusion in which these peoples live, and where they present their mission as one of instruction rather than of exorcism. Nonetheless, the depiction of Canada as a vacancy somehow beyond God's oversight undoubtedly did leave scope for imagining the ploys of humanity's arch-adversary. Jesuit writers, faced with the abyss separating their culture from that of the indigenous people, were not above adding the trope of diabolism to mundane descriptions of the hardships of mission. To speak of Amerindian ritual as devil worship was to underline the forsakenness of a land which had, so to speak, fallen off the divine map.

It seems reasonable to conclude, therefore, that the biblical account of the dispersal of peoples was a truism which failed to stimulate much serious inquiry, still less debate, among the Jesuits in New France. Instead, they located these barbarian and *sauvage* peoples in a stadial model, and adopted a secular history to argue for their prospects of conversion. If the barbarians of Europe had managed it, why could not the Amerindians? Conversion to Christianity was a shortcut to civilization. By assisting the conversion of the Amerindians, the missionaries would be enabling them to become full members of a world community.

Yet if the biblical divine history left a gap where such peoples ought to have been, the Bible as repository of the Church's moral teachings nonetheless remained crucial in the framing of mission. It was the basis for preaching separation from the ways of the wicked, renunciation of the body, and the coming-together in a transcendent community. These themes resonate in Jesuit pastoral theology. Here is not the place to expound on the links between seventeenth-century Jesuit theology and the model used for instruction and conversion of the Amerindians in New France. It is worth noting, however, that much of that theology was more practical than arcane. As disseminated in vernacular publications, it was meant to serve as a step-by-step guide to conversion. The Jesuits' conception of conversion was no longer essentially monastic. Instead, they aimed to convert individuals to a higher level of observance and godliness while in the world. This imperative produced a pastoral theology overwhelmingly centred on the individual convert, whose 'interior reformation' would result in a life that was devout, reasonable, and correctly oriented. The high point of this movement in Jesuit pastoral theology, at least as measured by the intensity of publications, roughly coincided with the peak of enthusiasm for the Canadian mission among the Jesuits of France. Connections between the movement's proponents and those who went as missionaries to New France are not hard to discern, since the mission from 1632 to 1649 was staffed by a number of students who owed their training to this milieu.[13]

At the heart of Jesuit pastoral theology was an analysis of the sources of disordered conduct (i.e., sin) among Christians and non-Christians alike. The soul was a scene of conflict between animal and reasonable impulses. When the former overwhelmed the latter, sin was the inevitable result. For our purpose, the crucially 'biblical-historical' feature of this allegory is the insistence that the postlapsarian state was characterized by unbridled passion and disorder. (In fact, the Garden of Eden suspiciously resembles the early modern ideal of the absolute state.) As François Loryot put it in 1609, before the Fall, the passions were subjected to Reason in an 'enclosure of a peaceful obedience.' After the original transgression, however, 'they took up arms of revolt, and led a war so cruel against their Queen & sovereign mistress,' namely Reason (Loryot 1609, 47). A more radical interpretation of the passions of fallen, corrupted humanity is found in the writings of the influential if esoteric Jesuit pedagogue and mentor Louis Lallement.[14] According to Lallement, fallen humanity possesses not even a glimmer of redemption, so dominated is it by a vicious nature. Such a view lay somewhat outside the generally more positive appraisal of human nature upheld by Jesuits since the founding of the order, but for a time in the seventeenth century it was ascendant, and elements of it seem to have filtered into the mission culture of New France.

The *Relations* strongly favour a stereotype of the Amerindian as unrestrained, unregulated, disobedient, and wanton. Much space is taken up with portraits of a population whose members experience the daily effect of distance from God. 'It is enough to say that they are completely savage,' wrote Charles Lalemant in 1627, mapping out a prospective mission to the interior. 'From morning to night they have not other care than to fill their stomach ... Vices of the flesh are common to them, such that one marries several women, and leaves them whenever he feels like it, to take others. Cleanliness is unknown among them' (*JR* 4.199). Savagery was the very state of incontinence which prevailed in the soul dominated by the base animal instincts, cut off from the reasonable part – and even more so from any communion with God. This was an east-of-Edenic state: one of instability, wandering, mere subsistence, and ignorance. The long journey these people had supposedly taken did not, in this case, excuse their waywardness. Whatever 'historical' explanations may have been to hand, the primary focus was on sin and the failings of the individual.

The promulgation of this stereotype of the inconstant, brutal, and untamed pagan was nonetheless clearly strategic. The bleak description of the Amerindian condition formed part of a conversion narrative which emphasized the transforming effects of God's grace. To stress the subject's depravity before conversion was to underscore the awesome power of his or her assent. It is little wonder that such close-up and inherently dramatic scenarios held more appeal for Jesuits in the forests of New France than the elaborately biblical histories worked out a century earlier by Spanish intellectuals who could always retreat to a Mexican convent or a chair in Salamanca to collect their thoughts.

Conclusion: 'Religion of the Soul' and the Limits of Biblical History

A half-century of steady reportage and writing about their mission in New France did not in the short run elicit any general acclaim for the project of Amerindian conversion, either within Jesuit ranks or from the public of *dévots* who were presumably the primary public for the *Relations* back home. In some cases, absolutely the wrong conclusions were drawn. From the safety of his perch in France, the Jesuit François Annat declared in 1644: 'Old France could have been like the New, if God hadn't viewed it more favourably. Who does not feel obliged to thank God for having made our condition better than that of the savages?' (Annat 1644, 95). This was hardly the message the Jesuits in Canada had meant to convey. Their goal had been to describe the workings of a mission which transformed God's most abandoned people into Christians sharing the same boon of grace as the French themselves. Indeed, the cloak of righteousness to be donned was often of a French cut, the prescriptions for conversion as cultural as they were religious, designed to promote a model of 'civilized' comportment which was likewise the object of pedagogical and disciplinary programs within Europe itself. Aristotle, rather than Abraham, was the authoritative guide to this civilizing process.

It is a regrettable paradox that the universalist message of missionary Christianity, the 'good news of the kingdom' (Mt 24:13), proved less resonant in regard to the Amerindian population of New France than an easily misappropriated discourse of the *sauvage*. Missionaries hardly intended to condemn these peoples: God would be the judge of all that. Unfortunately, their strident denunciation and ridiculing of Amerindian practices (a rhetoric which may have owed something to the tone of Jesuit anti-Huguenot polemic) too easily confirmed for armchair travellers in France the essential beastliness of these creatures of the forest gloom. And once the mission could be construed primarily as a charitable project directed at such poor wretches, it lost the urgency which a stronger representation of the case for 'biblical-historical' continuities could have provided.

Ironically, from the point of view of standard postmodernist critiques of biblical and other *grands récits*, the disparity between a colonial master-narrative supported by the Bible and the perceived realities of the New France mission may have contributed to the limbo in which peoples of the colonial frontier found themselves in the face of European expansion. More readily conceived as savage exemplars of fallen humanity than as wandering children of a God who had never lost sight of all his peoples, the Amerindians of New France would not benefit from any ascribed biblical genealogy. The Jesuits approached them as individual pagans, accountable for their sins, answerable for the state of their souls, and given only slim allowance for their 'savage' practices. An alternative, fully historical theory of cultural difference, present in a germ in Acosta but not taken up systematically until Lafitau in the eighteenth century, was slow in coming. Paul Le Jeune's optimism – that all men were of the same stock and shared the same divine destiny – was overtaken in the short run by a one-sided description of peoples who appeared to have spent their entire history outside the Garden of Eden and whose way back to a common humanity was blocked by their own ignorance and backwardness. A biblical narrative premised on a hopeful future gave way to a bleak, stadial view of history in which the Amerindian lost out.

NOTES

1   The Society of Jesus (Jesuits) was established in 1540, and quickly spread throughout the Catholic world and beyond as a major educational and missionary order. Its French Province sent missionaries to the French colony of New France in 1625, and established a mission among the Hurons of the southern Georgian Bay area of Lake Huron in 1634. The mission to the Hurons involved the greatest share of mission resources, and was the site of the Jesuits' greatest successes but also of their greatest defeat, the destruction of the Huron people and the mission at the hands of

the Iroquois in 1649. The Jesuits produced a steady stream of reportage from New France; their *Relations* were published annually from 1632 to 1673. A facsimile reproduction of the *Relations* from New France is found at www.canadiana.org, while a modern critical edition is found in *Monumenta Novae Franciae*, hereafter *MNF*. An English translation is available in *The Jesuit Relations and Allied Documents* (Thwaites 1896), hereafter *JR*. See Campeau 1987, for religious history, and for an ethno-historical interpretation which stresses the Amerindian response to the missionary enterprise, see Trigger 1987.

2 Rule 11 of the 'Rules to Have the True Sentiment of the Church' prescribes 'positive and scholastic' authority as the means to a 'true understanding of sacred scripture.' In discussing scriptural passages, the *Spiritual Exercises* adopt a catechetical approach, offering 'points' of emphasis or summary but rarely the passages themselves. Much of the *Exercises* concerns the individual's unmediated approach to God.

3 François du Peron to Joseph Imbert du Peron, 27 April 1639, in *JR* 15.165.

4 E.g., editor Lucien Campeau notes the spurious but convincing-sounding *Dominus est, faciens quod in oculis suis placitum fuerit* in a 1645 letter from Charlies Garnier, in the Huron country (*MNF* 6.258).

5 Frye argues that Spinoza's *Tractatus theologico-politicus* (1670) ushered in a new era in which Scripture ceases to be seen 'primarily as a source of natural or speculative or historical knowledge' and serves instead 'to inculcate piety and obedience to God.'

6 'Adamite' and monogenetic theories of origins in sixteenth- and seventeenth-century European thought are discussed in Gliozzi 2000.

7 See Phelan 1970.

8 'L'ancienne mission tridentine était peut-être en train de changer pour devenir une force de rénovation et, parfois, de contestation à l'intérieur de l'Église romaine' ('The old Tridentine missionary impulse was possibly in the process of changing to become a force for renewal and, in some cases, contestation within the Roman Church').

9 Richard White's concept of the 'middle ground' certainly applies to later seventeenth-century missionary activity, as the Jesuits found themselves strategic partners in the increasingly far-flung French empire (White 1991).

10 See LaPlanche 1985 and 1994.

11 Translated by William Fenton as *Customs of the American Indians: Compared with the Customs of Primitive Times* (Lafitau 1724).

12 Le Jeune's first, unpublished *Relation*, entitled 'Relation briesve d'un milieu d'un bois, 16 aoust 1632,' to Estienne Charlet, assistant provincial, offered a more pointed version of this passage: 'Il est vray, les sauvages

sont barbares; mais quelle barbarie n'a point esté en Allemagne, en Espagne, en Angleterre, et mesme dans les Gaules, avant que la foy y fust receu? Quelle manie dans l'Aegypte d'adorer les oignons, des crocodils, etc. Et cependant, on y a veu par après tant d'âmes sainctes' ('True, the natives are barbarians. But what barbarism was there not in Germany, in Spain, in England, and even in the ancient provinces of Gaul before the faith was received there? What folly among the Egyptians to worship onions, crocodiles, etc. And yet in time we have seen so many saintly souls appear there') (*MNF* 2.289). Reference to primitive Gauls was purged from the *Relation* dispatched a few weeks later to the provincial Jacquinot.

13 See Goddard 1998.

14 See Champion 1781.

REFERENCES

Annat, François. 1644. *Le libellé intitulé 'Théologie morale des Jésuites' contredit & convaincu en tous ses chefs*. Paris: no publisher.

Bastiensen, Michel. 1989. 'Bible, missions et iranologies: Le cas du *Gazophylacium*.' In Jean-Robert Armogathe, ed., *Le grand siècle et la Bible*, 375–82. Paris: Beauchesne.

Campeau, Lucien. 1987. *La mission des jésuites chez les Hurons, 1634–1650*. Montreal: Bellarmin.

Cartier, Jacques. 1924. *The Voyages of Jacques Cartier*. Ed. H.P. Biggar. Ottawa: F.A. Acland.

Champion, Pierre, ed. 1781. *La vie et doctrine spirituelle du Père Lous Lallemant* [1694]. Paris: Estienne Michallet.

Châtellier, Louis. 1993. *La religion des pauvres: Les missions rurales en Europe et la formation du catholicisme moderne, XVIe–XIXe siècle*. Paris: Aubier.

Chédozeau, Bernard. 1989. 'Les grandes étapes de la publication de la Bible catholique en français.' In Jean-Robert Armogathe, ed., *Le grand siècle et la . Bible*. Paris: Beauchesne.

de Guibert, Joseph. 1994. *The Jesuits: Their Spiritual Doctrine and Practice*. Trans. William J. Young. Chicago: Institute of Jesuit Sources.

Dehergne, Joseph. 1986. 'Travaux des jésuites sur la Bible en Chine.' In Yvon Belaval and Dominique Bourel, eds, *Le siècle des Lumières et la Bible*, 211–18. Paris: Beauchesne.

Dening, Greg. 1980. *Islands and Beaches: Discourse on a Silent Land: Marquesas 1774–1880*. Honolulu: University Press of Hawaii.

DeRogatis, Amy. 2003. *Moral Geography: Maps, Missionaries, and the American Frontier*. New York: Columbia University Press.

Frei, Hans. 1974. *The Eclipse of Biblical Narrative: A Study in Eighteenth and Nineteenth Century Hermeneutics*. New Haven: Yale University Press.

Frye, Northrop. 1982. *The Great Code: The Bible and Literature*. Toronto: Academic Press Canada.

Gliozzi, Giuliano. 2000. *Adam et le Nouveau Monde. La naissance de l'anthropologie comme idéologie coloniale: Des généalogies bibliques aux théories raciale (1500–1700)*. Trans. Arlette Estève and Pascal Gabellone. Lecques: Théétète.

Goddard, Peter A. 1998. 'Augustine and the Amerindians in Seventeenth-Century New France.' *Church History* 67: 662–81.

Lafitau, Joseph-François. 1724. *Moeurs des sauvages ameriquains comparées aux moeurs des premiers temps*. Trans. William Fenton as *Customs of the American Indians: Compared with the Customs of Primitive Times*. Toronto: Champlain Society.

LaPlanche, François. 1985. 'Tradition et modernité au XVIIe siècle: L'exégèse biblique des protestants français.' *Annales: Economies, sociétés, civilisations* 40: 463–88.

– 1994. *La Bible en France entre mythe et critique (XVIe–XIXe siècle)*. Paris: Albin Michel.

Le Jeune, Paul. 1635. *Relation de ce qui s'est passé en la Nouvelle-France en l'année 1634*. Paris: Cramoisy.

Lescarbot, Marc. 1609. *Histoire de la Nouvelle France*. Paris: Millot.

Loryot, François. 1609. *Fleurs des secretz moraux concernant les passions du coeur humaine*. Paris: Chez Ioseph Cotteraux.

Loyola, Ignatius. 1909. *Spiritual Exercises*. Trans. Elder Mullan. New York: P.J. Kenedy and Sons.

Monumenta Novae Franciae. 1967–. Ed. Lucien Campeau. 9 vols. Rome: Monumenta Hist. Soc. Jesu.

O'Malley, John W. 1993. *The First Jesuits*. Cambridge, MA: Harvard University Press.

Pagden, Anthony. 1982. *The Fall of Natural Man: The American Indian and the Origins of Comparative Ethnology*. Cambridge: Cambridge University Press.

Phelan, J. Leddy. 1970. *The Millennial Kingdom of the Franciscans in the New World*. 2nd ed. Berkeley: University of California Press.

Sugirtharajah, R.S. 2001. *The Bible and the Third World: Precolonial, Colonial and Postcolonial Encounters*. Cambridge: Cambridge University Press.

Thwaites, Reuben Gold, ed. 1896. *The Jesuit Relations and Allied Documents: Travels and Explorations of the Jesuit Missionaries in New France, 1610–1791.* 73 vols. [1896–1901]. Repr. New York: Pageant Book Co., 1959, 73 vols. in 36.

Trigger, Bruce. 1987. *The Children of Aataentsic: A History of the Huron People to 1660.* Montreal: McGill-Queen's University Press.

White, Richard. 1991. *The Middle Ground: Indians, Empires, and Republics in the Great Lakes Region, 1650–1815.* Cambridge: Cambridge University Press.

11

Joshua in America:
On Cowboys, Canaanites,
and Indians

LAURA E. DONALDSON

Introduction: Joshua in America

On a cold December night in 1763, the Paxtung Rangers – also known as the 'Paxton Boys' – brutally murdered the Indian inhabitants of Conestoga, Pennsylvania: three elderly men, two women, and a young boy, 'the rest being out among the neighbouring White People, some to sell the Baskets, Brooms and Bowls they manufactured, and others on other Occasions' (Franklin 1967, 58). Two weeks later, the Boys completed their vengeful quest by storming the Lancaster prison, where the surviving Conestogan remnant had been housed for safekeeping. By all accounts, the ensuing bloodbath was especially horrific. One eyewitness relates that when he entered the prison yard, he immediately recognized the body of Toshetaquah, or Will Soc, a well-known Sussquehannock man:

> Across him and [his] squaw lay two children, of about the age of three years, whose heads were split with the tomahawk, and their scalps taken off. Towards the middle of the jail yard, along the west side of the wall, lay a stout Indian, whom I particularly noticed to have been shot in his breast; his legs were chopped with the tomahawk, his hands cut off, and finally a rifle ball discharged in his mouth, so that his head was blown to atoms, and the brains were splashed against and yet hanging to the well, for three or four feet around. This man's hands and feet had also been chopped off with a tomahawk. In this manner lay the whole of them, men, women and children spread about the prison years; shot, scalped, hacked and cut to pieces. (William Henry, quoted in Dunbar 1957, 29)

The perpetrators of these atrocities were a group of Scotch-Irish Presbyterians from a beleaguered frontier town southeast of Lancaster, and the victims a mixed community of Sussquehannock, Delaware, and Senecas who still proudly displayed the wampum belt recording their 1701 treaty with William Penn. A local traveller named Thomas Wright encountered the Boys on their way home from Conestoga. After Wright expressed revulsion at the deed, a member of the company asked whether he believed in the Bible, and whether the Scriptures did not command the destruction of the 'heathen' – a retort reiterated much more provocatively by Benjamin Franklin, the mayor of nearby Philadelphia.[1] 'But,' exclaims Franklin, 'it seems that these People think they have a better Justification; nothing less than the *Word of God*. With the Scriptures in their Hands and Mouths, they ... justify their Wickedness, by the Command given *Joshua* to destroy the Heathen' (Franklin 1967, 63). The testimony of both Wright and Franklin explicitly connects the Paxton Boys to the ancient Mediterranean practice of the *charam*, or the ritual 'devotion to destruction' of one's enemies. In the Hebrew Testament, the *charam* appears in such passages as Deuteronomy 7:2 and 1 Samuel 15:3, and is manifested in Yahweh's command that the Israelites kill every Canaanite 'man and woman, child and infant, ox and sheep, camel and donkey' (1 Sm 15:3). Although historians have offered alternative explanations for the events that unfolded in 1763 – the government's failure to protect frontier communities, preferential treatment of the Indians by Pennsylvania's Quaker leaders, rage induced by the gruesome discovery of squatters' bodies in the town of Wyoming, and even the lingering effects of social disorganization – the theological underpinning of the *charam* is nonetheless crucial for understanding the Paxton Boys' massacres.

I emphasize the theological because the founder of the Paxtung Rangers was none other than the 'fighting (Presbyterian) parson' John Elder, who advocated ridding the eighteenth century's western frontier of all Native inhabitants.[2] As both originator and chaplain of the group, the Reverend Elder surely made abundant use of the widespread Puritan metaphor likening American Indians to 'red Canaanites,' and consequently bears some responsibility for the Boys' deadly interpretation of this North American biblical trope. Not surprisingly, the killings at Conestoga and Lancaster inspired a vigorous public debate over the *charam*. For example, one pamphlet addresses those who have 'cannived [*sic*] at, or do approve of, the late Massacre of the Indians at *Lancaster*,' and approvingly cites Jacob's remorse over the murder of

Shechem's family as a rebuttal of the Paxton Boy's position (Anonymous 1957, 93). 'The Paxtoniade,' a satirical poem published under the pseudonym of 'Christopher Gymnast,' introduces the character of O'Haro, who is chosen by the Boys as their leader because he has been an 'Elder' in the community for over thirty years – a name that is most certainly a sly pun on the actual John Elder. O'Haro/John Elder inspires his troops to nefarious deeds by appealing to the *charam* as well as the metaphorical construction of American Indians as red Canaanites: 'Now, Sirs, I ween it is but *right*, / That we upon these *Canaanites*, / Without delay should Vengeance take, / Both for our own, and the K----K's sake: / Should totally destroy the *heathen*, / And never till we've kill'd em leave 'em; / Destroy them quote frae out the Land; / and for it we have God's Command' (Gymnast 1957, 169). The author lampoons O'Haro's belief by making him enunciate the *charam* in exceedingly bad poetic rhyme: 'Seeing then we've such good cause to hate 'em /what I intend's to exterpate 'em: / To suffer them no more to thrive, / And leave nor Root nor branch alive' (ibid., 170). Whether or not the Boys actually used the *charam* as a justification for Indian killing, it nevertheless possesses a long-standing rhetorical importance in this key episode of United States history.

The biblical hermeneutics of the Paxton Boys also speak urgently to more recent controversies, and particularly to another public debate waged over its interpretation by Michael Walzer and the late Edward Said. In 1985, Walzer published *Exodus and Revolution*, which represents the Israelite exodus from Egypt as a liberatory journey forward, 'not only in time and space. It is a march toward a goal, a moral progress, a transformation' (Walzer 1985, 12). Edward Said's rebuttal of Walzer appeared in *Grand Street* the following year, and this launched a series of contentious critical debates that still reverberate some twenty years later. Said, a Christian Palestinian and renowned colonial discourse theorist, entitled his response 'A Canaanite Reading' to foreground the ways in which Walzer's book gave moral credibility to the extermination of the Promised Land's indigenous inhabitants. My essay intervenes in this biblical and political controversy by displacing it into a North American framework. My hope is that the geo-political disorientations produced by this displacement create a space hospitable to previously unconsidered perspectives on the Exodus and its legacies. For example, the essay's first section interrogates William Albright's so-called Conquest Hypothesis – also called the 'American' hypothesis – and its close relationship to the North American eugenics movement.

This section also investigates why, given this disconcerting relationship, both Walzer and Said uncritically accept its premises in their highly polemical debate.

In 1989, Robert Allen Warrior, an Osage graduate student at Union Theological Seminary, extended Said's critique to include Native North Americans – although he curiously fails to note either Said or Walzer in his much-anthologized essay 'A Native American Perspective: Canaanites, Cowboys and Indians.' Warrior argues that the Exodus story constitutes an 'inappropriate' model for thinking about the liberation of indigenous peoples and contends that American Indians 'obviously' identify with 'the people who already lived in the promised land,' and he calls for a reading strategy that puts Canaanites – biblical and otherwise – at the centre of Christian theological reflection and political action (Warrior 1995, 283). It is hard to disagree with this statement, since contemporary Native peoples share much with our ancient indigenous counterparts. Like the Canaanites, we have experienced military occupation, land expropriation, disproportionate incarceration, arbitrary termination, forced labour, and diasporic removal. However, the question of identification among the colonized is much more complex than Warrior admits, and in this essay's final section I explore the possibility of multiple American Indian identifications through the Jewish rabbinical practice of Midrash, or the interpretation of the Hebrew Testament through storytelling. More particularly, in collaboration with Hopi/Miwok poet Wendy Rose, I construct a Native North American Midrash on Exodus 1:8–13. Before this storytelling can happen, however, one needs to understand the enabling conditions for the production of the Conquest Hypothesis and its relationship to modern eugenics theory.

Breeding Better Bibles

The Number of purely white People in the World is proportionably very small ... And while we are, as I may call it, *Scouring* our planet, by clearing America of woods, and so making this Side of our globe reflect a brighter Light to the Eyes of Inhabitants in Mars or Venus, why should we in the Sight of Superior Beings, darken its people? Why increase the sons of Africa, by Planting them in America, where we have so fair an opportunity, by excluding all Blacks and Tawneys [American Indians], for increasing the lovely White? (Franklin 1967, 234)[3]

Benjamin Franklin published his concerns about 'the increase of man-kind' only three years before he confronted the scriptural problem of the Canaanite conquest quite literally in the streets: after the killings at Lancaster and Conestoga, he and other citizens of Philadelphia dis-suaded the Paxton Boys from liquidating the local Indians hiding in the City of Brotherly Love. Although Franklin rejected Indian-killing as a strategy for 'increasing the lovely White,' his anxiety resonates strongly with a different problem of Joshua in America: the eugenicist overtones of William Foxwell Albright's 'Conquest Hypothesis.' Albright, the long-time chair of Johns Hopkins University's 'Oriental Seminary,' argued for the substantial veracity of the biblical conquest account, and his hypothesis dominated scholarship on the subject for many years. Albright's famed biblical colloquium at Hopkins included graduate students such as George Mendenhall, David Noel Freedman, George Wright, and John Bright, who disseminated his ideas and subse-quently developed their own status in the field. In *From the Stone Age to Christianity: Monotheism and the Historical Process* (1940, 1957), Albright opposed the prevailing 'peaceful immigration' view of German schol-ars Martin Noth and Albrecht Alt and instead asserted that 'the Israelites proceeded without loss of time to destroy and occupy Canaanite towns all over the country' (1957, 278). He further suggested that the Israelite annihilation of the Canaanites was no worse than the modern massacre of Armenians by the Turks or the reciprocal massacres over the centur-ies of Protestants and Catholics (83). For Albright, this comparison es-pecially applied to 'we Americans,' who had less right to judge the ancient Israelites because of 'our' own behaviour in exterminating 'scores of thousands of Indians' and crowding the rest into the 'great concentration camps' (280) known as reservations. And, he adds, the fact that this was inevitable does not make it any more edifying to con-temporary North Americans.

One cannot dismiss Albright's apology for the *charam* as merely an unfortunate attitude held by many during the first half of the twentieth century (and after). As Keith Whitelam observes, however, Albright was eulogized as the icon of objective historical scholarship even through the 1980s – a view that helped to cloak the involvement of biblical studies in the larger project of historical colonialism (Whitelam 1996, 88). Albright's resolutely 'Orientalist' representation of the Canaanites is a particularly instructive example of this mystification. In this characterization, a people manifesting 'orgiastic nature worship' and a 'cult of fertility in the form of serpent symbols and sensuous nudity' is replaced by Israel, 'with its pastoral simplicity and purity of life, its lofty monotheism and severe code of ethics' (Albright 1957, 281). Constructing the Canaanites as the opposite of rational, Western monotheism dehumanizes them, and their eradication becomes just another consequence of colonial/imperial progress (Whitelam 1996, 84). Indeed, Albright contends, the annihilation of the Canaanites was actually 'fortunate' since it prevented the fusion of two radically disparate peoples: 'It was fortunate for the future of monotheism that the Israelites of the Conquest were a wild folk, endowed with primitive energy and ruthless will to exist, since the resulting decimation of the Canaanites prevented the complete fusion of the two kindred folk which would almost inevitably have depressed Yahwistic standards to a point where recovery was impossible' (1957, 281). The full implications of this remarkable statement only become clear when it is placed within the larger context of North American eugenics.

Coined in 1883 by British scientist Francis Dalton – whom Albright extols in *From the Stone Age* as a 'great geneticist' (1957, 122) – the term *eugenics* originated in a Greek root meaning 'good in birth' or more accurately, 'well born.' Influenced by his uncle, Charles Darwin, Dalton pioneered the 'science' of improving human stock by giving the more 'suitable' races a better chance of prevailing quickly over the less suitable (Kevles 1995, xiii), a goal now closely associated with the ideologies of Nazism and other white-supremacy groups. For decades after its emergence in the late nineteenth and early twentieth centuries, however, eugenics did not necessarily connote an extremist point of view, but rather, one espoused by many middle-class, educated, and otherwise temperate citizens. As a case in point, women's rights advocate Margaret Sanger, anarchist Emma Goldman, socialist George Bernard Shaw, and sexual psychologist Havelock Ellis all embraced the eugenics movement in the name of social progress. Nancy Gallagher notes in her fascinating study, *Breeding Better Vermonters*, that eugenics appealed to progressive intellectuals' trust in the ability of science to solve human problems and of professional experts to provide reliable information (Gallagher 1999, 3). The popularity of eugenics in the United States quickly led to the establishment of groups such as the Race Betterment Society (established by John Harvey Kellogg with cereal profits), the American Eugenics Society, and the Eugenics Society of Northern California (whose founder, Charles Goethe, donated his wealth to California State University, Sacramento and his name to that institution's arboretum). Eugenics even influenced

American popular culture through the AES's highly successful sermon contests and its competitions for identifying the nation's most eugenically 'fit' families. And, as unlikely as it may seem, the AES Fitter Families initiative provides an important clue to understanding Albright's evolutionary history of Canaanites and Israelites.

An outgrowth of the Better Babies movement, the Fitter Families Contest began at the 1921 Kansas Free Fair, and soon spread to state fairs across the country. The Fitter Families competitions were featured in the 'human stock' section of various state fairs, and contestants provided the family's complete eugenic history in addition to undergoing a barrage of medical, psychological, and intelligence tests. As Dr Florence Brown Sherbon explained to attendees of the 1928 Race Betterment Conference, the site of the contest was no coincidence:

> We feel that the agricultural fair was the logical place for this movement to have its origin. It [eugenics] is simply an extension of scientific plant and animal husbandry to the next higher order of creation and we are thereby creating the science of human husbandry. It is just as simple as that. The families we found were willing to come along with the baby. They came to the fairs for this all-round extensive examination, which does not pretend to draw any more line between heredity and environment than is drawn by the stock judge when he judges and examines stock and takes into consideration the heredity, the feeding and the care of the product. (Sherbon 1928, 120)

Breeding better families thus involved 'positive' eugenic practices that selected and facilitated desirable qualities as well as 'negative,' or dysgenic, policies discouraging the reproduction of the undesirable.[4] Albright's concern about preventing the fusion of Canaanite and Yahwistic peoples lends itself to a similar eugenicist rhetoric: the allegedly positive psychological, religious, and cultural characteristics he assigns to the Israelites must be vigilantly protected from interbreeding with the much more negative profile of the Canaanites. However, his dysgenic belief that 'there is a point beyond which racial mixture cannot go' ultimately betrays the racist underpinnings of the Conquest Hypothesis. This emerges most dramatically in comments that appear in both the first (1940) and second (1957) editions of *From the Stone Age to Christianity*:

> It is significant that after the first phase of the Israelite Conquest we hear no more about 'devoting' the population of Canaanite towns [to

destruction], but only of driving them out or putting them to tribute (Jud. 1, *passim*). From the impartial standpoint of a philosopher of history, it often seems necessary that a people of markedly inferior type should vanish before a people of superior potentialities, since there is a point beyond which racial mixture cannot go without disaster. When such a process takes place – *as at present in Australia* – there is generally little that can be done by the humanitarian – though every deed of brutality and injustice is infallibly visited upon the aggressor. (1957, 280; emphasis added)

In this statement, Albright adopts a eugenicist rationale for the annihilation of the Canaanites even as he apologizes for the *charam*'s abuses. However, it is his offhand comparison between the biblical plot and the racial politics of pre–Second World War Australia that offers one of the most revealing perspectives on the eugenicist underpinnings of the Conquest Hypothesis.

The twentieth-century North American eugenicist movement regarded the white settler colonies of Australia, South Africa, Canada, and the United States as 'inner dikes' against the world's 'rising tide of colour,' and the former British colony of Australia became a test case in this regard. From the time of its establishment, Australia vigilantly maintained an Anglo-European identity through a systematic repression of Aboriginal peoples as well as an extremely restrictive immigration policy. In the interval between the world wars, however, the edifice of 'White Australia' began to crumble: 1925 witnessed a path-breaking conference on Aboriginal citizenship and land rights, and other South Asian peoples threatened to breach Australia's previously unassailable immigration walls. The eugenics community regarded this state of affairs as nothing short of alarming. According to Lothrop Stoddard, a Harvard-trained historian and one of the North American eugenics movement's most prominent voices, 'the Australians, 5,000,000 whites in a far-off continent as large as the United States, defy clamoring Asia and swear to keep Australia a white man's land. Says Professor Pearson: "We are guarding the last part of the world in which the higher races can increase and live freely, for the higher civilization. We are denying the yellow race nothing but what it can find in the home of its birth, or in countries like the Indian Archipelago, where the white man can never live except as an exotic"' (Stoddard 1921, 282). In his widely read *The Rising Tide of Color against White World-Supremacy*, Stoddard called upon 'the lusty young Anglo-Saxon communities bordering the Pacific-Australia, New Zealand, British Columbia, and our own coast' to 'set their faces like flint against the Oriental' and 'emblazon across their portals the legend: "All White"' (281). Albright does not exactly emblazon 'All White' across the portals of the Hebrew Bible, but his parallel between the dangers of race-mixing in Australia and in the Hebrew Testament uncannily echoes the racialist proclamations of his contemporary Stoddard: he laments the 'necessary' disappearance of Australia's Aboriginal people and the 'humanitarian' abuses of policies allowing only whites to enter the Land Down Under, while simultaneously asserting the dysgenic effects of race and culture mixing.

Albright's appeal to eugenicist arguments raises many troubling issues about the Conquest Hypothesis and its collusion with white-supremacist ideologies; it also throws Walzer's and Said's failure to detect and question what is perhaps the Hypothesis' most important enabling context into stark relief. What, then, is a more critically responsible paradigm for reading the Exodus, and how might it transform our reading of the story? In collaboration with both Rabbi Akiva ben Joseph and Wendy Rose, I offer one possible model in the final section of my essay: a Native North American Midrash on Exodus 1:8–13.

Builder Israelites and Mission Neophytes:
A Native North American Midrash

Now a new king arose over Egypt, who did not know Joseph. He said to his people, 'Look, the Israelite people are more numerous and more powerful than we. Come, let us deal shrewdly with them, or they will increase and, in the event of war, join our enemies and fight against us and escape from the land.' Therefore they set taskmasters over them to oppress them with forced labor. They built supply cities, Pithom and Rameses, for Pharaoh. But the more they were oppressed, the more they multiplied and spread, so that the Egyptians came to dread the Israelites. The Egyptians became ruthless in imposing tasks on the Israelites. (Ex 1:8–13, NRSV)

Said Rabbi Akiva: 'Pharaoh's police would strangle the Israelites in the walls of the buildings, between the bricks. And they would cry out from within the walls and God would hear their moaning.' (*Pirke d'Rabbi Eliezer*)

They built the mission with dead Indians.
They built the mission with dead Indians.
They built the mission with dead Indians.

They built the mission with dead Indians.
                    Wendy Rose, 'Excavation at Santa Barbara Mission'

Michael Walzer consigns his comments on Canaanite genocide to the last chapter of *Exodus and Revolution*: 'Read the text as it stands, however, and there is clearly *no tension* between the concern for strangers and the original conquest and occupation of the land – for the Canaanites are explicitly excluded [by the narrator] from the world of moral concern. According to the commandments of Deuteronomy, they are to be driven out or killed – all of them, men, women, and children – and their idols destroyed … That is straightforward enough, and it hardly matters that the conquest seems to have had in fact a very different character: more like a gradual infiltration than a systematic campaign of extermination' (1985, 142). In this extraordinarily troubling passage – comparable, in my mind, to Albright's eugenicist argument for the conquest – Walzer casually dismisses the issue of biblical *charam* and his indirect reference to the historical model of gradual infiltration cannot disguise the moral glossing of his statement. Indeed, scholars other than Said have chastised Walzer for these sentiments. According to Mark Walhout, for example, Walzer's excluding of the conquest must seem suspicious to those who embrace it as one of the Exodus story's main stages. This would encompass not only 'colonizing literalists' such as Afrikaners and radical Zionists, but also those whose land has been colonized, such as the Zulu and the Palestinians: 'For the colonizer, the biblical conquest of the Promised Land is part and parcel of a national-religious ideology that was central to the founding of a modern state. For the native inhabitant, on the other hand, it is the suppressed subtext of Canaanite experience that is the key to the Exodus narrative and to the self-understanding of an oppressed people' (Walhout 1994, 206). The history of colonialism as well as biblical criticism on the Exodus disputes any characterization of the conquest as marginal in Western politics.

Given Walzer's trivializing of Canaanite suffering, it can hardly be surprising that Said complains about the supposed oppression of the Israelites in Egypt: 'Walzer spends no time at all on what brought the Jews to Egypt (in Genesis) nor on the great degree of wealth and power which because of Joseph they achieved there. It is quite misleading to refer to them as an oppressed people when Genesis 46 and 47 tell in some detail of how "they had possessions therein, and grew, and multiplied exceedingly"' (Said 1986, 91). Said argues that, because they were foreign, Jews became easy targets for 'local rage and frustration' when a famine caused hardship in Egypt. This oppression is 'hardly comparable with that of American Blacks or contemporary Latin Americans' (91). Perhaps not – and yet it does seem uncannily similar to the persecution often endured by immigrants to North America when they have defied the odds and done very well in their adopted countries. The anxiety that this success engenders in dominant cultures has often provoked severe and violent reprisals. Said's refusal to acknowledge the possibility of Israelite oppression mimics Walzer's position in its obstinate misunderstanding. This mutual failure of empathy must surely preclude the emergence of any productive hermeneutic or political action. It is precisely at this point that the rabbinical practice of Midrash – and I would hope, my own non-rabbinical signifying on the Exodus – can make a meaningful intervention.

From the Hebrew root *darash*, which means, 'to search, investigate or study,' Midrash is an interpretive method that focuses on discrete biblical verses rather than entire books or story cycles. Jacob Neusner usefully distinguishes among three midrashic levels: the first explains the meanings imputed to particular Scriptural verses; the second states important propositions or syllogisms of thought in conversation with verses or sustained passages of Scripture; and the third retells biblical stories so that they are imbued with new immediacy (Neusner 1989, 3–4). My Midrash on Exodus 1:8–13 emphasizes the latter two levels since it proposes a 'syllogism of thought' – or, more particularly, experience – between the builder Israelites and California mission Indians. In so doing, it also manifests the tendency of Midrash to exceed its identified text. *Midrashim* always 'seems to be ... going too far, saying not only what the text does not say but also what the text, taken by itself, does not appear to warrant' (Bruns 1987, 629). Daniel Boyarin extends this point by comparing the practice to strong readers fighting not for originality, but 'to find what they must in the holy text. Their own intertext – that is, the cultural codes which enable them to make meaning and find meaning, constrain the rabbis [and other readers] to fill in the gaps of the Torah's discourse' (Boyarin 1990, 16). I am fighting to find the suppressed stories and identifications among Israelites, Canaanites, and American Indians in the holy text of the Exodus, and I begin with the assertion that the Egyptians made the lives of the Israelites 'bitter with hard service in mortar and brick' (Ex 1:13).

The experience of Israelites and American Indians congeals within the walls of their oppressors. Under their respective masters – urbanized

Egyptians and black-robed Franciscans – they become literal building blocks for a colonial edifice, and their anguished voices cry out from the bricks. Rabbi Akiva ben Joseph's[5] poignant evocation of the Israelites' moaning (quoted in the epigraph to this section) interprets Exodus 1:8–13 by interrogating what happens when the Egyptians force the *'Apiru* to build the royal supply cities of Pithom and Rameses. According to the Exodus *Midrashim*, 'at first he [Pharaoh] made them shepherds …; then he made them builders, as it is said, "He built store-cities – to inhibit them from procreating"' (Rabbi Chama bar Chanina, as cited in Zornberg 2001, 38). Days spent in too many hours of punishing work, diets bordering on starvation, no medical care, and harsh living conditions all conspired to prevent the Israelites from engaging in, or conceiving from, life-affirming sexual acts. Lest one miss the genocidal implications of this conclusion, the *Yalkut Shimeoni Shemoth* offers a further imaginative gloss: 'Said Rabbi Joshua ben Levi: When the angel, Michael saw that the angels of the nations were supporting the Egyptian case, he made a sign to the angel Gabriel, who flew to Egypt in one swoop, and extracted from a building one brick with its clay and with one baby that they had wedged into the building' (as cited in Zornberg 2001, 39). Overwork and starvation consequently turn into something more sinister and active – the murder of future Israelite generations. Rabbi Joshua's scriptural signifying noted that the angels were apparently arguing about whether Yahweh should save not only his people, but also their cruel Egyptian masters. The archangel Michael abruptly resolved the debate by examining the effects of the building program: Israelite babies 'wedged' into the walls of the Pharaoh's storehouses. From the Hebrew verb *lehashkia*, *wedged* here means to be submerged, to become part of a larger whole, to be merged, and mixed up beyond recognition (Zornberg 2001, 40). The *'Apiru* become entombed within Egyptian walls and, as a diasporic people, also face the spectre of losing their distinctive faith and identity: genocide as culturecide, assimilation as death.

These midrashic explorations of the Exodus forge a scriptural imaginary that links American Indians with both Canaanites and Israelites. Like the Israelites, Native North Americans were forced to become builders, but for the *padres* instead of the Egyptians. These Native 'neophytes,' as they were called, constructed the missions and provided all the labour for their maintenance. Like the Israelites, mission Indians also faced starvation, disease, and extremely harsh working conditions. As David Stannard notes in *American Holocaust: The Conquest of the New World*, the average living space for mission Indians was only seven by two feet per person (less than that allotted to Africans on slave ships bound for America). Further, like the Israelites in Rabbi Chama bar Chanina's Midrash, Native neophytes were not only inhibited from procreating, they also experienced death rates that exceeded their birth rate by a ratio of two to one (Stannard 1992, 137). According to Stannard, the mission system drove tens of thousands of American Indians to early and agonizing deaths. Yet such historical data can only take one so far; to enter more deeply into the connection of mission Indians to the builder Israelites, we need the creative inventions of poetry and storytelling – and, particularly, Wendy Rose's poetic articulations of the Chumash 'men and women asleep in the wall' of Santa Barbara Mission.

Before she discovered her vocation as a poet, Rose studied anthropology at the University of California, Berkeley, where she also worked at the Hearst Museum of Anthropology. She begins her 1993 poem 'Excavation at Santa Barbara Mission' with the double-edged metaphor of an archaeologist's trowel that simultaneously becomes her artist's brush: 'My pointed trowel / is the artist's brush / that will stroke and pry / uncover and expose / the old mission wall' (Rose 1993, 6). The wielder of these instruments bears a striking resemblance to Rose who, in addition to being an anthropologist and poet, is also a talented painter whose pen and ink drawings frequently illustrate her poetry collections. The metaphorical edges of the trowel / artist's brush cut deeply because, as Rose once remarked in an interview, the business of the Indian anthropologist is to protect rather than expose, 'to use the exploiter's tools to deflect attempts at exploitation' (Hunter 1983, 72). Rather than protecting her Indian subjects against exploitation, however, the narrator of the poem represents herself as cannibalistically consuming them instead: 'Beneath the flags / of three invaders, / I am a hungry scientist / sustaining myself / with bones of / men and women asleep in the wall' (Rose 1993, 7–8). This verse evokes the human bones discovered within Santa Barbara Mission's adobe walls – bones that most likely belonged to the Chumash, the Native people whose ancestral California homelands encompassed the lands claimed by the mission. Although no one knows exactly why the bones were placed in the walls, their presence in the poem precipitates a crisis within the anthropologist/narrator: are they merely artefacts to be exhumed or respected remnants of a complete human life?

In a Westernized society dominated by the processes of commodity fetishism,[6] it is hard for anyone – anthropologist or artist, Native or non-Native – to escape the capitalist nexus of consumption and desire.

This sobering insight causes the narrator to resolve the ethical crisis of the bones in the walls by discarding her scientific objectivity and recognizing 'how helpless I am / for the deeper I go / the more I find / crouching in white dust, listening to the whistle / of longbones breaking / apart like memories' (Rose 1993, 7). The narrator's ideological decomposing allows the bones to begin recomposing: 'So many bones / mixed with the blood / from my own knuckles / that dig and tug / in the yellow dust' (7–8). The poet/anthropologist consequently (and painfully) acknowledges an inability to escape the outcomes of her actions: ethically, intellectually, and artistically, she becomes *lehaskia*: mixed up, merged with, and wedged into the entombed Native bones.

In *The Sacred Hoop*, Paula Gunn Allen (Laguna Pueblo/Lebanese) asserts that it is impossible to exaggerate the impact of genocide in the minds of Native poets and writers. 'We are the dead,' she writes, 'and the witnesses to the death of hundreds of thousands of our people, of the water, the air, the animals and forests and grassy lands that sustained them and us not so very long ago' (Allen 1986, 155). Further, according to Gunn Allen, American Indian women's poetry addresses the stark facts of extinction with a vigour and resilience that is not merely a lamentation, but which instead directs our attention to 'a kind of hope born of facing the brutal and bitter facts of our recent history and present condition' (160). 'Excavation at Santa Barbara Mission' manifests this hope when the bones enact a reverse consumption of the narrator's blood and, in so doing, re-infuse themselves with the marrow of her life. This happens when the narrator exhumes bone fragments and associates them with functional and beautiful items (Tongson-McCall 1996, 20): 'Marrow / like lace, piece of skull, / upturned cup, fingerbones / scattered like corn / and ribs interlaced / like cholla' (Rose 1993, 6). This process of interlacing and recomposing similarly describes the persona of the narrator as she sheds her anthropological skin to uncover the Native poet who memorializes, rather than exhumes (and consumes), the terrible witness of the bones buried within the mission walls.

The final stanza of 'Excavation at Santa Barbara Mission' – 'They built the mission with dead Indians / They built the mission with dead Indians / They built the mission with dead Indians / They built the mission with dead Indians' – produces an anti-genocidal moment of recognition for the narrator as well as reader/listeners. Only a direct confrontation of colonization and its consequences allows any healing to emerge from such catastrophe. The ending's fourfold refrain – one repetition for each of the four sacred directions – also affirms the nascent identity and transformed epistemology of the narrator. Most American Indian songs make meaning through repetitive structures of intensification rather than Euro-American rhyme or metre schemes. These repetitions often have an entrancing effect and help to induce a holistic state of consciousness within the singer and her audience: 'One suits one's words and movements (if one is a dancer) to the repetitive pattern. Soon breath, heartbeat, thought, emotion, and word are one. The repetition integrates or fuses, allowing thought and word to coalesce into one rhythmic whole' (Allen 1986, 63). The poem's final chant works to inculcate within readers/listeners a deep integration of its disturbing message even as it administers a curative for Santa Barbara Mission's abyssal truths.

In her 1993 collection *Going to War with All My Relations*, Rose explicitly thematizes this process of anti-genocidal healing when she proclaims in the poem immediately following 'Excavation at Santa Barbara Mission' that 'there will be / no archaeology / to my bones' (9). Indeed, reanimating Native remains imprisoned in Euro-American museums and colonized as artefacts constitutes a major goal of her postcolonial *resistance poetry*. I describe Rose's work in terms of resistance to acknowledge how such poems as 'Excavation at Santa Barbara Mission' function as a potent semantic weapon in the ongoing struggle for decolonization (see Harlow 1987, ch. 2); the resistance is postcolonial because the poems critically engage with the legacies of Anglo-European colonialism and, as evidenced by the narrator of 'Excavation at Santa Barbara Mission,' manifest the ambivalence so characteristic of colonial subjectivities. Perhaps most importantly, Rose's poetry emulates its rabbinical counterparts by filling in the gaps of how the texts represent their subjects. If the practice of Midrash fractures the magisterial story of the Exodus into multiple and contradictory narratives (Zornberg 2001, 4), mine, in collaboration with Rose, refracts it through the experiential prism of not only the Canaanites, but also the builder Israelites. Unlike the analyses of Walzer and Said, my Midrash on the Exodus allows the recognition not only of Canaanite oppression, but also of Jewish subjugation. In contrast to Robert Warrior's construction of a 'natural' link between Canaanites and American Indians, my Midrash discerns more intricate patterns of identification among Israelites, Canaanites, and American Indians. Through it all, I have tried to liberate both discursively and poetically those stories that remain wedged into the numerous equivalents of Egyptian walls.

Relocating Joshua from the biblical plains of Jericho to the landscapes of Turtle Island implies a journey that would rival the Israelites' forty years' wandering for its circuitousness. After her own immersion in the 'passion and patience,' as well as the powerfully divisive opinions, engendered by such desert journeys, writer Terry Tempest Williams poignantly asks: 'How are we to find our way toward conversation?' (2001, 3). Her answer? Stories. For Williams, stories bypass rhetoric and pierce the heart. They provide us with 'a wash of images and emotion that returns us to our highest and deepest selves, where we remember what it means to be human, living in place with our neighbors' (3). I hope that this essay has offered stories that have bypassed the oppositional Exodus rhetoric of Israelite versus Canaanite and pierced the reader's heart: that of the Paxton Boys and their Native victims, of Albright's dysgenic biblical mixing, and of builder Israelites and mission Indians. In these narratives, one encounters no easy solutions, but rather, the taking of risks –most especially, the risk of connection and living side by side with our most unlikely neighbours. Perhaps, after all is said and done, it is precisely such risk-taking that most vividly evokes the ancient Exodus promise of liberation.

NOTES

1 This anecdote is cited in Francis Parkman's *The Conspiracy of Pontiac*. Parkman relates that he drew the account of the massacre from the narrative of Matthew Smith, the leader of the Paxton Boys' assault on Conestoga. According to Parkman, Smith's description was published by Mr Redmond Conyngham of Lancaster in the *Lancaster Intelligencer* for 1843. Mr Conyngham states that he procured it from the son of Smith, for whom his father had written it. See Taylor 1991, 705.

2 On 13 September 1763 Elder wrote a letter to Governor John Penn, suggesting 'the propriety of an immediate removal of the Indians from Conestoga' by the military. Penn refused, stating that he 'could not remove them without adequate cause' and that the government was pledged to their protection (Pennsylvania Archives, 8th series, VI, 5482–3; as quoted in Dunbar 1957, 22).

3 Although Franklin's actual statement ends by evoking 'the lovely White and Red,' he does not reference people of colour or American Indians with the latter. Indeed, in the passages immediately preceding the one quoted he includes in the category of the 'tawny' Africans, Asians and Native Americans.

4 Such dysgenic attempts eventually led to forced sterilizations of women of colour and those who were mentally or physically challenged, as well as restrictive immigration policies.
5 Rabbi Akiva Ben Joseph (50–135 CE) is credited with developing exegetical practices crucial to rabbinic Judaism, including that of the *Mishnah*.
6 For a more extended discussion of 'consuming' American Indians, see my essay 'On Medicine Women and White Shame-ans: New Age Native Americanism and Commodity Fetishism as Pop Culture Feminism' (1999).

REFERENCES

Albright, William Foxwell. 1957. *From the Stone Age to Christianity: Monotheism and the Historical Process*. 2nd ed. Baltimore: Johns Hopkins University Press. Original ed., 1940.
Allen, Paula Gunn. 1986. *The Sacred Hoop: Recovering the Feminine in American Indian Traditions*. Boston: Beacon Press.
Anonymous. 1957. 'A Serious Address to *Such of the Inhabitants of* PENNSYLVANIA, As have cannived [*sic*] at, or do approve of, the late Massacre of the Indians at *Lancaster*; or the Design of Killing those who are now in the Barracks at PHILADELPHIA.' In J.R. Dunbar, ed., *The Paxton Papers*. The Hague: Martinus Nijhoff.
Boyarin, Daniel. 1990. *Intertextuality and the Reading of Midrash*. Bloomington and Indianapolis: Indiana University Press.
Bruns, Gerald L. 1987. 'Midrash and Allegory.' In R. Alter and F. Kermode, eds, *The Literary Guide to the Bible*. Cambridge, MA: Belknap Press of Harvard University.
Donaldson, Laura E. 1999. 'On Medicine Women and White Shame-ans: New Age Native Americanism and Commodity Fetishism as Pop Culture Feminism.' *Signs* 24: 677–96.
Dunbar, John R. 1957. 'Introduction.' In J.R. Dunbar, ed., *The Paxton Papers*. The Hague: Martinus Nijhoff.
Franklin, Benjamin. 1967. 'A Narrative of the late Massacres, in Lancaster County, of a Number of Indians, Friends of this Province, by Persons Unknown, With Some Observations on the Same.' In L.W. Labaree, H.C. Boatfield, and J.H. Hutson, eds, *The Papers of Benjamin Franklin: January 1 through December 31, 1764*. New Haven and London: Yale University Press / American Philosophical Society.
Gallagher, Nancy L. 1999. *Breeding Better Vermonters: The Eugenics Project in the Green Mountain State*. Hanover and London: University Press of New England.

Gymnast, Christopher. 1957. 'The Paxtoniade: A Poem.' In J.R. Dunbar, ed., *The Paxton Papers*. The Hague: Martinus Nijhoff.

Hunter, Carol. 1983. 'A MELUS Interview: Wendy Rose.' *MELUS* 10 (3): 67–87.

Kevles, Daniel J. 1995. *In the Name of Eugenics: Genetics and the Uses of Human Heredity*. 2nd ed. Cambridge, MA: Harvard University Press.

Neusner, Jacob. 1989. *Invitation to Midrash: The Working of Rabbinic Bible Interpretation*. San Francisco: Harper & Row.

Rose, Wendy. 1993. *Going to War with All My Relations*. Flagstaff, AZ: Entrada Books. Cited above with the author's kind permission.

Said, Edward. 1986. 'Michael Walzer's "Exodus and Revolution": A Canaanite Reading.' *Grand Street* 5 (2): 86–106.

Sherbon, Florence Brown. 1928. 'A Unique Experience.' Paper read at Third Race Betterment Conference, 2–6 January, Battle Creek, Michigan.

Stannard, David E. 1992. *American Holocaust: The Conquest of the New World*. New York and Oxford: Oxford University Press.

Stoddard, Lothrop. 1921. *The Rising Tide of Color against White World-Supremacy*. New York: Charles Scribner's Sons.

Taylor, William R., ed. 1991. *Francis Parkman: The Oregon Trail / The Conspiracy of Pontiac*. New York: Library of America.

Tongson-McCall, Karen. 1996. 'The Nether World of Neither World: Hybridization in the Literature of Wendy Rose.' *American Indian Culture and Research Journal* 20 (4): 1–40.

Walzer, Michael. 1985. *Exodus and Revolution*. New York: Basic Books.

Walhout, Mark. 1994. 'The *Intifada* of the Intellectuals: An Ecumenical Perspective on the Walzer–Said Exchange.' In Susan Van Zanten Gallagher, ed., *Post-colonial Literature and the Biblical Call for Justice*, 198–217. Jackson: University of Mississippi Press.

Warrior, Robert Allen. 1995. 'A Native American Perspective: Canaanites, Cowboys and Indians.' In R.S. Sugirtharajah, ed., *Voices from the Margin: Interpreting the Bible in the Third World*, 277–88. Maryknoll, NY: Orbis.

Whitelam, Keith W. 1996. *The Invention of Ancient Israel: The Silencing of Palestinian History*. London and New York: Routledge.

Williams, Terry Tempest. 2001. *Red: Passion and Patience in the Desert*. New York: Pantheon.

Zornberg, Avivah Gottlieb. 2001. *The Particulars of Rapture: Reflections on Exodus*. New York: Doubleday.

12

Premodern Ironies: First Nations and Chosen Peoples

JACE WEAVER

In May 1862, Cherokee journalist, poet, and novelist John Rollin Ridge published an article in the *Hesperian* with the modest and unprepossessing title 'The North American Indians: What They Have Been and What They Are – Their Relations with the United States in the Existing National Crisis – The Modification of Their Character by the Infusion of White Blood and the Contact of Civilization – Their Probable Destiny.' In it he related the story of one of the first Christian missionaries to go among the Cherokee.

The missionary gathered the people of the town in the council house and began telling them the biblical story. According to Ridge, 'With great gravity did they sit and listen, while the venerable minister went on to simplify to their comprehensions the general principles of the great moral code which is founded upon the golden rule.' His explication, given in halting Cherokee, particularly pleased one old war chief, the veteran of many battles, and the old man would nod his approval and even repeatedly interrupted the pastor to say things like, 'You hear what this good man says. It is the truth that he is telling you. See that you do not forget it.' At length, after many such interjections, the missionary finally got to the story of Jesus. Now the old warrior in the corner seemed to grow agitated. He glanced around him and began to rock back and forth. When the speaker got to the crucifixion, the chief could contain himself no longer. He leapt to his feet and cried, 'White Chief, lead us on the war-path! Show us the murdering dogs of whom you speak. We will revenge the death of this good man!' The missionary was forced to explain that the events of which he spoke took place a very long time ago in a place very far away and that those involved were not immediately available to have revenge taken upon them.

Ridge concludes, 'Upon this explanation, the ardor of the chief at once abated, and he subsided into such a total indifference regarding the new religion, that he could never again be induced to attention to it whatever' (Ridge 1862, 102–3).

The story needs little in the way of interpretation. Native religious traditions are empirical, based on observation of phenomena around them, and experiential in the most immediate sense. The old war chief of Ridge's account had no time for a religion that did not affect his immediate existence and whose efficacy was based on chronologically and geographically remote and unverifiable events.

In his 1862 essay, Ridge relates the previous story as historical fact. Permit me another one that I have good reason to suspect is apocryphal. Yet it, too, has what I like to term truth that transcends mere fact. A missionary was preaching at a camp meeting to a group of Christian Indians. On this particular occasion he was preaching of the kingdom of heaven. He described it in the most glowing of terms, a place of great beauty, streets paved with gold, sweet music. When he finished, he asked the converts, 'How many of you want to see the kingdom?' Every hand went up except that of one chief in the front row. Irritated, the preacher decided that he had not done a good enough job of putting his message in terms his tawny audience could understand. He tried again. The kingdom was a place of rolling meadows and woodlands where game was abundant, and no one had to work hard, and everyone was happy. He then asked again, 'Now, who wants to see the kingdom?' Every hand went up, except that of the one lone chief. The evangelist was now nearly beside himself. In a desperate attempt to get that last hand raised, he described the alternative – hell – a place of fire and brimstone and endless thirst and torture. Confident of the desired result, he asked once more, '*Now* how many of you want to go to the kingdom?' Every hand shot up except that one man's. The missionary looked him straight in the eye and said, 'What's the matter, Chief? Don't you want to go to the kingdom?' The old man replied calmly, 'Yes, perhaps eventually, but the way you're carrying on, you sound like you're loading up the wagon right now.'[1]

The two stories taken together illustrate forcefully the tremendous agency of Native peoples. Too often, when people talk about the missionary experience of Natives, Native agency is effaced. Even in the book *Missionary Conquest* by George Tinker, Indians are not actors but are merely acted upon; they are not self-determined but are rather selves determined (Weaver 1998, 3–5; Tinker 1993). There are, thankfully, exceptions: whether it be John Rollin Ridge's essay, or Homer Noley's book *First White Frost*, or John Webster Grant's *Moon of Wintertime*, Native agency is clearly visible, by conversion and acceptance of the new and strange message or, like the chiefs in our two stories, by some form of rejection.

Of course, even when Natives did convert to Christianity, it was often a very different form of conversion than what the White missionaries envisioned. Missionaries wanted Indians to swap one religion for another and, in the process, to trade one culture for another as a necessary corollary. Instead, the phenomenon of religious dimorphism has always been strong among Natives. Religious dimorphism is the simultaneous practice of two separate forms of religion. It is not syncretism. There is no blending of Christian and Native practices. It is simply a matter of 'This is what I do when I go to ceremony, and this is what I do when I go to church.' The two are kept distinct and separate, except insomuch as they are practised by the same individual.

Anthropologist Joseph Epes Brown calls this same phenomenon 'nonexclusive cumulative adhesion' (Brown et al. 2007, 20), a term I have always liked, believing that is something you could get people to go to the barricades for: 'We want bread and roses, too! We're striking for nonexclusive cumulative adhesion!' Who could argue with that? Actually, the missionaries who came to convert Natives had a great argument with religious dimorphism – when they knew about it. More often than not, Indians have kept the fact of it hidden from their would-be Christian overseers, and simply practised it: 'This is what I do when I go to ceremony, and this is what I do when I go to church.' And for Natives in that situation, there is no tension in such a confession of faith. It is, in a sense, very postmodern. And, of course, since it was an option not available before the Conquest, very postcolonial as well.

There was Native agency in the conversion story. Indians vexed missionaries by asking prickly questions that the evangelists had assumed were beyond Natives' limited intellectual capabilities. If Natives were to practise only monogamy and if marriage was eternal, what of the man who was widowed and remarried? With whom would he be in heaven? If Jesus was the only means of going to heaven, what about all their relations who had died before the missionaries came with news of this Jesus? Or, conversely, consider the Mohawk from Kanawake who said that the missionaries claimed they brought God to the Indians: Poor, weak god, he mused, can't go anywhere by himself, always needs someone to carry him around. Or, as a Huron once famously asked a Frenchman who was extolling the virtues of France and French culture, 'If France is so wonderful, why did you leave it to come to my country?'

'Premodern Ironies.' I am aware that, unlike in situations of religious dimorphism, there is a built-in metaphorical tension between the two words of my title. Irony is a quintessential stance of late modernity – even postmodernity. Can one have genuinely premodern ironies? As I was imagining this title and the lecture (and chapter) that has flowed from it, I thought of the editor of *Vanity Fair*, Graydon Carter, who, in the wake of the September 11 attacks, proclaimed irony dead. Fortunately for those of us who make at least part of our livings trafficking in irony, including myself *and* Graydon Carter, reports of irony's demise were premature. The publication of W.H. New's book, based on his 2002 Sedgewick Lecture at the University of British Columbia, *Grandchild of Empire: About Irony, Mainly in the Commonwealth*, would seem to endorse my strategic resort to irony. So heartened, I remembered my favourite scene from Betty Louise Bell's novel *Faces in the Moon*. In one of the final passages, the novel's heroine, a largely deracinated Cherokee woman, goes to the library to research her family. When faced with a patronizing librarian who asks with bemusement, 'Who do you *think* you are?' the woman replies, 'I am your worst nightmare. I'm an Indian with a pen' (Bell 1995, 192). At a conference at Union Theological Seminary, George Tinker transposed the line to tell the postmodernists in the audience, 'I'm your worst nightmare, a premodern with a word processor.' So maybe the two old chiefs in our two stories were their would-be missionizers' worst nightmares: premoderns with indigenous wit enough to assert their own agency.

Those familiar with my work probably know two things: first, that I have a deep-running scepticism about the postcolonial and its cousin postmodernism; and second, that I have a long-standing, on-again, off-again, love-hate relationship with Reinhold Niebuhr.[2] To understand the irony of the relationship between postcolonial studies and postmodernism (which provides the former with its 'philosophical and theoretical grounding' and is likewise 'anti-foundational') one must look back to the late nineteenth century, when two great rationalizing sciences arose, sociology and anthropology. Sociology purported to study that which was normative in society. Anthropology studied the Other and advised colonial masters in the manners and mores of native peoples, that the latter might be more effectively controlled. It is for that reason that Claude Lévi-Strauss calls anthropology the handmaiden of colonialism (cited in Said 1994, 149). In like manner, in the late twentieth century, two related systems of critical thought grew up to explain the world: postmodernism and postcolonialism. I am wary of these systems that (and I think it is more than simple coincidence) – just as the peoples of the Two-Thirds World begin to find their voices and assert their own agency and subjectivity – proclaim the end of subjectivity.

Here I must pause for a moment of confession. Although in my work I am often critical of anthropologists as well as postmodern and postcolonial theorists, I am actually tainted by them all. One cannot study Native American religious traditions without at least some knowledge of the disciplinary mechanisms of anthropology. After all, my anthropology professor at Columbia was none other than Margaret Mead. I am also a graduate with a baccalaureate from the University of Paris, where I was first exposed not only to Lévi-Strauss, but also to theorists of the postmodern condition such as Jacques Derrida and François Lyotard. I have been especially critical of Derrida from a postcolonial standpoint, but I must admit to falling for the siren song of postmodernism on occasion. Gerald Vizenor, the foremost Native exponent of postmodernism, sees the postmodern as the tribal. He also takes a sort of postcolonial turn in his book *Manifest Manners* when he points out that English, the language of boarding and residential schools and colonial oppression, was also the language that permitted the spread of the Ghost Dance (Vizenor 1994, 105–6). I believe that postmodern and postcolonial theories can be useful tools in analysing literature. I enjoy postmodernism's wordplay, its sense of irony, its jouissance. Vizenor is a master of these devices, as he gives the figure of Trickster a decidedly postmodern spin, 'associating trickster's resistance to definition and his shape-shifting abilities with postmodern ideas about the infinite signification of language' – as another Native scholar puts it (Womack 1999, 239). I in turn played with this idea in my piece 'Trickster: The Sacred Fool' in *Other Words* (246–57), where I analyse both the Jacob cycle and the Jesus event in the Bible as trickster stories with their transgressions and boundary crossings and transformations. Ultimately, however, I fault postmodernism and postcolonialism for being ahistorical, universalizing, and depoliticizing. Their common error is that they mistake having deconstructed something theoretically with having displaced it politically or in reality. And one cannot just tear down constantly – simply deconstruct – without offering something constructive in its place.

Native identity is not 'free-wheeling,' to borrow Jacqueline Rose's phrase (Rose 1996). It is real and grounded – grounded first, literally, in the ground, in a sense of place, and grounded, second, in a web of relations to family, to tribal nation, and to the rest of creation that brings us back to the earth and to place.

Craig Womack, a Muscogee scholar of literature, argues for privileging Native voices in the study of Native literature. He writes:

> The postmodernists might laugh at claims of prioritizing insider status, questioning the very nature of what constitutes an insider and pointing out that no pure Creek, or Native, viewpoint exists, that Natives and non-Natives are constantly deconstructing each other. In terms of a reality check, however, we might remind ourselves that authenticity and insider and outsider status are, in fact, often discussed in Native communities, especially given the historical reality that outsiders have so often been the ones interpreting things Indian. Further, it seems foolhardy to me to abandon a search for the affirmation of a national literary identity simply to fall in line with the latest literary trend. The construction of such an identity reaffirms the real truth about our place in history – we are not mere victims but active agents in history, innovators of new ways, of Indian ways, of thinking and being and speaking and authoring in this world created by colonial contact. (Womack 1999, 5–6)

Writing about a poem by Joy Harjo, a fellow Muscogee and one of our best Native poets today in the United States, a poem that involves Choffee the Rabbit, the Muscogee trickster and culture hero, Womack says:

> Harjo's poem ... concedes the value of a little ambiguity by recognizing Rabbit's insistence on remaining undefined, the power of mystery over definition, the role of the gamble in modern life, the arbitrariness of time as a construct, the need for laughter, not just seriousness. Muskogeans would not abandon the Lower World's [i.e., this world's] chaos in favor of the Upper World's [the spirit world's] cycles and order; neither does the poet ignore the creative power of shape-shifting in certain contexts ...
>
> Further ... Choffee provides the context for an important strategic move Harjo makes by using the idea of the Muscogee world to decenter the assumption that things European are normative. If one is always reacting *against* Eurocentrism, then Europe is still the center. If one argues, for example, that Creek warfare in the eighteenth century was not any more

barbaric than the Spanish Inquisition, one maintains that Europe is still the moral barometer by which everything is gauged. Harjo rejects such a center ... and this is the positive side of Rabbit's disruption, his tendency to throw things off balance, to confuse centers and margins, inside and outside. (252)

As I hear those words again, I appreciate anew why Vizenor chose Trickster as his icon of Native postmodernism – decentring, shape-shifting, disrupting, forcing laughter. It all sounds very postmodern. Such characteristics are why, in *Other Words* and in my work with Clara Sue Kidwell, Homer Noley, and George Tinker on *A Native American Theology*, I insisted on Trickster as a new (yet at the same time quite ancient) category of theological discourse (Kidwell, Noley, and Tinker 2001, 113–25). Yet there remains one important difference between Trickster and postmodernism or postcoloniality – namely, cultural context. In discussing Harjo's Choffee poem, Womack concludes, 'In other words, the Muscogee world is not the opposite of the Western world, *it is a world that must be judged by its own merits, in its own terms*. This is the argument of this study, that Native literatures deserve to be judged by their own criteria, in their own terms, not merely in agreement with, or reaction against, European literature and theory' (Womack 1999, 242; emphasis added). I would certainly contend that the argument can be extended to other cultural elements beyond just literature.

Yet it is here at this juncture of Trickster and laughter that Reinhold Niebuhr, certainly no postmodernist and no postcolonial critic, can re-enter our conversation. I value Niebuhr not for his historiography, which I have repeatedly shown to be deficient with regard to North American indigenes, but for his conceptualization of irony. Niebuhr delineates three types of events in history: the pathetic, the tragic, and the ironic. Pathos is that element of history that inspires pity, but deserves neither admiration nor contrition. Suffering resulting from purely natural causes is the clearest example of pathos. Tragedy is the conscious choice of evil for the sake of good. For Niebuhr, writing at the height of the Cold War, that the United States supposedly had to have and threaten to use nuclear weapons in order to preserve itself and its allies was tragic. Irony 'consists of apparently fortuitous incongruities of life which are discovered, upon closer examination, to be not merely fortuitous.' It is distinguished from the pathetic in that humans bear responsibility for it. It is distinguished from the tragic in that the responsibility rests on unconscious weakness rather than conscious choice. Irony, unlike pathos or tragedy, must dissolve when it is brought to light. It elicits laughter. American history for Niebuhr is ironic: there is a gap between the ideal of the United States' self-image and the reality of its history and existence (Niebuhr 1952, vii–viii; Weaver 2001, 142).

Natives have been representing themselves in print for almost 250 years and have striven to bring to light, in hopes of dissolving them, the ironic histories, readings, and philosophies that have been imposed upon them by the dominant culture. Without falling into the post-modernist/postcolonial naivety of believing that theoretical decon-struction necessarily means ultimate efficacy, they have asserted their own subjectivity and have attempted to spell out their own histories, readings, and intellectual discourse in a way that affirms their personhood.

It cannot be denied that Natives on this continent have been sub-jected to ironic readings of the Bible that attacked both their dignity and their subjectivity. Permit me to discuss just a handful of such readings, many of which have been covered at length in my essay 'From I-Hermeneutics to We-Hermeneutics' in *Native American Religious Identity:Unforgotten Gods*. First there was the long-running debate over the humanity of Natives and how to reconcile this with the biblical wit-ness, a dispute which glowed white-hot from 1493 to 1512, when it was decided that Natives were indeed human beings. But even thereafter the argument raged as to whether they were descendants of Ham or Shem. In that debate irony was piled upon irony. I would describe this as an example of the 'consistency of racism.' The so-called curse of Ham was used (and is still used in conservative theological circles) to justify scripturally the enslavement of Africans and the subjugation of African-Americans. One can find things written about Indians that sound iden-tical to things written about Blacks. One can find things the English said and wrote about the Irish that sound as if they could have been said about Indians or Blacks.

A second ironic reading is the equating by missionary biblical exe-getes, in their effort to undermine Native cultures, of Trickster with Satan. This is simply unfair and untrue, though the Satan of the Book of Job is congruent with Trickster. Trickster is not immoral or evil. He is simply amoral.

Yet another irony, which Homer Noley exposes quite expertly in *First White Frost*, is the exploitation of the parable of the wheat and the tares, in which the wheat is interpreted as true Native converts to Christianity and the tares are those who either practise religious dimorphism or refuse to convert. Biblical interpretation was thus used not to unite in a spirit of welcome and brotherhood, but to divide Natives one from another – friend from friend, relative from relative (Noley 1991, 169–204). Yet Jesus asks in the Gospel of Thomas, 'I am not a divider, am I?'

By far the ironic reading that subjected Natives to the most opprobrium and which, consequently, has received the most attention is viewing the Native population of North America as the Canaanites inhibiting occupation of the Promised Land by God's new Israel. From this trope I draw my subtitle here, 'First Nations and Chosen Peoples.' Alfred Cave has done an excellent job of demonstrating that this comparison, which identifies Indians with the Canaanites, and other biblical language spurred and justified the colonial enterprise. Merely one example would be Sir George Peckham's view that Natives would either be exterminated or forced, like the Gibeonites, to submit 'as drudges to hewe wood and carie water.' This belief did not cease with the end of the formal colonial period, but persisted well into the nineteenth century and, among some, continues even to today (Cave 1988, 282).

This is the characterization that caused Robert Warrior, an Osage from Oklahoma, to argue that Native persons must read the Bible with Canaanite eyes – from a Canaanite perspective. He articulates this in his now famous and widely anthologized article 'Canaanites, Cowboys, and Indians' (already discussed by Laura Donaldson in the previous chapter). There is much to recommend Warrior's declaration. How can a people conquered, occupied, and deprived of their homelands accept the religion of their colonizer? Unless, as Warrior states, the biblical witness can be redeemed, no Native Christian theology of liberation is possible. William Baldridge, a Cherokee and former Baptist clergyman, attempted to respond to Warrior's challenge, suggesting the Cyro-Phoenician or Canaanite woman who seeks healing for her child from Jesus as a liberative model of an indigene living with the religion of one's oppressor. Though I believe it to be promising, Warrior rejected Baldridge's suggestion for valid reasons.[3]

I would like to suggest a story – actually, a network of related stories – not, as with Baldridge, from the Greek scriptures, but from the Hebrew scriptures, as another liberative location. The interpretation rests upon close textual reading of the passages. It also partly depends upon evidence external to the text itself (and therefore probably would not satisfy Warrior). We know from historical and archaeological evidence that the *eisode*, the entrance into and conquest of Canaan, was not as total as the biblical witness would have us believe. Though the Hebrew accounts talk of a total extermination of the Canaanites, we know this simply did not happen. One piece of textual evidence for this is the previously mentioned story of the Gibeonites. The Gibeonites persisted, and their presence in the Promised Land had to be explained by the Chosen People. So it was imagined that they had submitted, and they were recast in the Israelite mind as hewers of wood and drawers of water. A second example is more peculiar to me: it is the story of Zelophehad's daughters.

The daughters make their entrance in Numbers 27. Moses and Eleazar have just completed the census of the Israelites. It is on the basis of this accounting that lands will be allotted upon entry into Canaan. Just as Moses and Eleazar finish, five women step out of the crowd:

> Then the daughters of Zelophehad came forward ... The names of his daughters were: Mahlah, Noah, Hoglah, Milcah, and Tirzah. They stood before Moses, Eleazar the priest, the leaders, and all the congregation, at the entrance of the tent of meeting, and they said, 'Our father died in the wilderness; he was not among the company of those who gathered together against the Lord in the company of Korah, but died for his own sin; and he had no sons. Why should the name of our father be taken away from his clan because he had no son? Give us a possession among our father's brothers.'

The daughters are justifiably worried. Because their father died without a male heir, and because daughters are not allowed to inherit, they will be left with no place in the Promised Land. Confronted by them, Moses does not know what to do; he consults his god.

> Moses brought their case before the Lord. And the Lord spoke to Moses, saying: 'The daughters of Zelophehad are right in what they are saying; you shall indeed let them possess an inheritance among their father's brothers and pass the inheritance of their father on to them. You shall also say to the Israelites, "If a man dies, and has no son, then you shall pass his inheritance on to his daughter. If he has no daughter, then you shall give his inheritance to his brothers. If he has no brothers, then you shall give his inheritance to the nearest kinsman of his clan, and he shall possess it. It shall be for the Israelites a statute and ordinance, as the Lord commanded Moses."' (Nm 27:1–11 [RSV])

So God says that, of course, all persons have the right to share equally in his promise. A general rule is then promulgated.

The story of Zelophehad's daughters, however, does not end there with that victory. After the *eisode*, when Joshua and Eleazar are actually carrying out the apportionment of lands in Canaan, they once again forget about Zelophehad's daughters. It is then incumbent upon the daughters to again step forward and demand the promise be fulfilled, and it is (Jo 17:1–6).

The story of Zelophehad's daughters no doubt has many things to tell us about equality, about solidarity, about persistence. But how is it relevant to Warrior's challenge concerning the exodus/*eisode* model? I have argued elsewhere that it has direct meaning for the story of the Canaanites and hence for a Native theology of liberation:

> The names of the five daughters (Mahlah, Noah, Hoglah, Milcah, and Tirzah) were, in fact, the names of five towns in northern Canaan in the land of Hepher [listed as the father of Zelophehad in both Numbers and Joshua]. The names were taken from Numbers 26, where they were meant as towns, and reinterpreted for purposes of the allotment story. The Hepherites were not destroyed or dispossessed. Neither were they reduced to hewers of wood and drawers of water like the Gibeonites [supposedly were]. Rather, they formed a religio-political alliance with the Israelites. (Weaver 2001, 245)[4]

The story of Zelophehad's daughters in Numbers and Joshua is the account of the maintenance of Hepherite cultural and territorial integrity – an integrity that, according to 1 Kings 4:10, survived at least until the time of Solomon. Like the Gibeonites, the Hepherites perdured, and their persistence had to be explained. They were depicted as the daughters of Zelophehad who by direct divine sanction enjoyed equally the promise of Yahweh. 'American Indians are thus,' I conclude, 'the Hepherites, Zelophehad's daughters, sharing a god with, and living in the midst of, a foreign people, yet preserving their own identity and self-determination' (ibid.).

Just because I struggle as a Native Christian to redeem or preserve the biblical witness *for* Native Christians does not mean that I accept all of orthodox Christian dogma or scripture. To do so would run the risk of what I have termed 'Apple Piety' (Weaver 2000b, 181).[5] Rather, Natives, as all other Christians, must exercise their own subjectivity and self-determination, and decide for themselves what Christianity and the Bible are for them. One example might be the Christian doctrine of the atonement. Traditionally, there are two ways of understanding the atoning sacrifice of Jesus on the cross: the substitutionary theory of atonement and the moral influence theory. Neither of these speaks to Native peoples. Native religious traditions are not salvific. Neither creation nor humanity is conceived of as fallen, so there is no concomitant need for supernatural redemption. I do not believe that Native communities, assaulted and deeply damaged by more than five hundred years of colonialism, can believe that God in any way wanted or needed the death of Jesus in order to be 'reconciled' with humanity. Rather, many Natives aver that the crucifixion was simply the work of human beings and that when it occurred God wept. Then, as Psalm 2 states, God laughed with derision at the folly of humanity. God asked, 'Is that all there is? Is that the best you can do?' Then came, in response, the resurrection (cf. Weaver 2000b, 182).

Conversely, however, if I argue against the deployment and applicability of postmodernism and the postcolonial in the case of America's indigenes, this does not mean there are no aspects of Native cultures that lend themselves to postmodern or postcolonial interpretation and use. I have already mentioned the ambiguity of Trickster. I also said that Native people recognize no tension in their easy-going religious pluralism or dimorphism. It is part of the polycentric nature of Native cultures. Such polycentrism can be illustrated by two final examples.

There is a story told of an anthropologist who went to do fieldwork in a particular Native community. Her host began by showing her their council fire in the middle of the village. He explained that the fire was the centre of the universe and then related the tribe's creation story that proved it. The next day, he took her to a neighbouring, related village. In the centre of the village was a council fire. The elder from the second village announced that the fire was the centre of the universe, and her original host nodded in agreement. Confused, the anthropologist said, 'You said *your* fire was the centre of the universe. Now you agree when he says *his* fire is. How can they both be the centre?' The man casually replied, 'When we're there, *that's* the centre of the universe. When we're here, *this* is the centre of the universe.'

The other story is variously attributed, but it is most often said to involve Red Jacket, a Seneca who, in the early nineteenth century, had several celebrated disputations with Christian missionaries. It is said that a missionary came to the village and gathered the residents around him. He then proceeded to tell the biblical story from creation through resurrection. When the evangelist had finished, Red Jacket replied, 'It is a good story. Let me tell you ours.' The Indian began to tell the Iroquois creation myth. The missionary leapt to his feet, crying, 'I give you eternal truths, and all you offer are lies and blasphemy!' Unfazed, Red Jacket shot back, 'Sir, you are obviously not well schooled in the art of courtesy. We listened to your story and believed it. Can you not listen to our story and believe it as well?'

I find it hard to believe that one can get more postmodern or more postcolonial than that.

NOTES

1 Cf. Ameringer 1940.

2 My scepticism concerning postcolonialism can be seen, among other places, in my edited volume *Native American Religious Identity: Unforgotten Gods* (1998), 1–25, in my book *Other Words: American Indian Literature, Law, and Culture* (2001), 280–304, and in my essay 'Indigenousness and Indigeneity' (2000a), 221–35. My interest in, and ambivalence about, Niebuhr is reflected in my article 'Original Simplicities and Present Complexities: Reinhold Niebuhr, Ethnocentrism, and the Myth of American Exceptionalism' (1995), subsequently revised as 'American Indians and Native Americans: Reinhold Niebuhr, Historiography, and Indigenous Peoples,' for a volume published in Canada (O'Meara and West 1996, 19–30), and later in *Native American Religious Identity*, 15–16, and *Other Words*, 140–53.

3 For Warrior's argument, his dialogue with Baldridge, and my response, see Weaver 2001, 242–5.

4 The chapter in which this appears is entitled 'A Biblical Paradigm for Native Liberation.'

5 'Apple' is a Native expression, equivalent to 'Oreo' for African-Americans, signifying Red on the outside and White on the inside.

REFERENCES

Ameringer, Oscar. 1940. *If You Don't Weaken*. Reprint. New York: Greenwood Press, 1969.

Bell, Betty Louise. 1995. *Faces in the Moon*. Norman: University of Oklahoma Press.

Brown, Joseph Epes, Marina Brown Weatherly, Michael Oren Fitzgerald, and Elenita Brown. 2007. *Spiritual Legacy of the American Indian: Commemorative Edition with Letters While Living with Black Elk*. Bloomington, IN: World Wisdom.

Cave, Alfred A. 1988. 'Canaanites in a Promised Land: The American Indian and the Providential Theory of Empire.' *American Indian Quarterly* 12.4: 277–97.

Grant, John Webster. 1984. *Moon of Wintertime: Missionaries and the Indians of Canada in Encounter since 1534.* Toronto: University of Toronto Press.

Kidwell, Clara Sue, Homer Noley, and George E. Tinker. 2001. *A Native American Theology.* Maryknoll, NY: Orbis Books.

New, W.H. 2003. *Grandchild of Empire: Of Irony, Mainly in the Commonwealth.* Vancouver: Ronsdale Press.

Niebuhr, Reinhold. 1952. *The Irony of American History.* New York: Charles Scribner's Sons.

Noley, Homer. 1991. *First White Frost.* Nashville: Abingdon Press.

O'Meara, Sylvia, and Douglas A. West, eds. 1996. *From Our Eyes: Learning from Indigenous Peoples.* Toronto: Garamond Press.

Ridge, John Rollin. 1862. 'The North American Indians.' In David Farmer and Rennard Strickland, eds, *A Trumpet of Our Own: Yellow Bird's Essays on the North American Indian.* San Francisco: Book Club of San Francisco, 1981.

Rose, Jacqueline. 1996. *States of Fantasy.* New York: Oxford University Press.

Said, Edward. 1994. *Culture and Imperialism.* New York: Vintage Books.

Tinker, George. 1993. *Missionary Conquest.* Minneapolis: Fortress Press.

Vizenor, Gerald. 1994. *Manifest Manners: Postindian Warriors of Survivance.* Hanover, NH: Wesleyand University Press.

Weaver, Jace. 1995. 'Original Simplicities and Present Complexities: Reinhold Niebuhr, Ethnocentrism, and the Myth of American Exceptionalism.' *Journal of the American Academy of Religion* 63: 231–48.

– 1996. 'American Indians and Native Americans: Reinhold Niebuhr, Historiography, and Indigenous Peoples.' In Sylvia O'Meara and Douglas A. West, eds, *From Our Eyes: Learning from Indigenous Peoples.* Toronto: Garamond Press.

– 1998. 'From I-Hermeneutics to We-Hermeneutics: Native Americans and the Post-Colonial.' In Jace Weaver, ed., *Native American Religious Identity: Unforgotten Gods*, 1–25. Maryknoll, NY: Orbis Books.

– 2000a. 'Indigenousness and Indigeneity.' In Henry Schwarz and Sangeeta Ray, eds, *A Companion to Postcolonial Studies*, 221–35. Oxford: Blackwell Publishers.

– 2000b. *That the People Might Live: Native American Literatures and Native American Community.* 2nd ed. Oxford: Oxford University Press.

– 2001. *Other Words: American Indian Literature, Law, and Culture.* Norman: University of Oklahoma Press.

Womack, Craig. 1999. *Red on Red: Native American Literary Separatism.* Minneapolis: University of Minnesota Press.

13

Biblical Narrative and the (De)stabilization of the Colonial Subject (Commentary on Part Three)

HARRY O. MAIER

Each of the essays taken up for treatment here offers discussion of the notions of colonial, postcolonial, and decolonized historical agency. All three focus on the colonization of North American First Peoples. Peter Goddard's discussion of the Jesuit Mission to New France challenges a popular misconception that all missionaries to the Americas were guided by biblical narrative, and portrays a different account that qualifies the role of the Bible in missionary activity, one that nevertheless helped to reinforce the privilege of the colonizing historical subject. Laura Donaldson utilizes intertexuality in order to recover Exodus (a text often rejected on account of its uses in the subjugation of First Nations Peoples in North America) and champion an engaged ethic of empathy in rejecting the construction of the subjugated self of Native experience. Jace Weaver calls for a giving up of postcolonial preoccupations when studying Native American cultures, in order to insist on the recognition of the continuing colonization of First Nations in North America and to recognize the ways in which Native agency continues to function amidst efforts at assimilation and cultural annihilation by settler cultures. Donaldson and Weaver take up biblical texts and show how they effected a particular formulation of colonizing/colonized and decolonized subjectivities. Goddard reconstructs a different trajectory, but one I hope to show remains indebted to biblical narrative, though less explicitly so. In what follows, I take up each essay in turn and then, following a summary of the argument, offer my own comments on the ways in which each author exploits colonial and postcolonial notions of the subject. In each instance, I seek to show how the postcolonial notion of the instability of the colonizer/colonized subject opens a space for the renegotiations of biblical texts settled down in colonizing reading strategies. Whether in the theory of moral progress or regress of Jesuit missionaries in New France, or in the return of the Canaanite towards empathy with former slaves who now exercise conquest, or in the recovery of ignored story in those narratives promoting the genocide of pre-existing peoples in the invasion of Canaan, in order to include First Nations peoples as co-inhabitants of the land of promise, in each instance biblical tropes or explicit texts are negotiated and reread for their capacity to shape colonial identities and resist them. This makes biblical narrative a site for both colonial pre/occupation and decolonizing reoccupation, even as historical subjects complexly occupy the intertextual spaces of biblical interpretation and discover themselves both readers of and read by sacred texts.

The Bible and Classical Culture in New France

'The Amerindian in Divine History: The Limits of Biblical Authority in the Jesuit Mission to New France, 1632–1649' urges a revision of the popular conception that European missionary enterprise to the Americas was determined solely by a preoccupation with apocalyptic timetables or the attempt to create a New Jerusalem on earth. Indeed, Goddard argues that in the case of the Jesuit mission to New France the Bible seems to have had a very small role in motivating and guiding missionary activities. In contrast to a literal application of biblical narrative to the evangelization of the Huron and Algonquin people of early Canada, Goddard reconstructs a stadial theory Jesuits deployed in the missionary activities. Not biblical narrative, but metaphors of human development guided their actions. In Goddard's analysis, one is surprised by the lack of biblical narrative inspiring missionary activity. Not the Bible, but a classical view of civilization furnished the theoretical backdrop for Jesuit work among New France's First Nations. Indeed, not only did busy missionary Jesuits have little time for reading and practising exegesis on the Bible, but apart from drawing on it for the purposes of exhortation, they seem to have assigned it a very slight role in helping to win converts. The goal of the Jesuit mission was not to fulfil a prophetic promise but to remediate the loss of civilization and moral righteousness made possible by the long distance separating the original inhabitants of North America from their original ancestors, as represented in the opening chapters of the Bible. To the degree that these missionaries gave theological reflection to their activities, they did not reach in the first instance for the Bible but for Aristotle and the classical heritage as a means to theorize notions of human and cultural progress. Since the Bible was necessarily silent about an entire civilization that had lived for centuries in North America before European contact, these missionaries had to reach for other sources to account for the peoples they met there and for their goals in evangelizing them. 'Aristotle, rather than Abraham, was the authoritative guide to this civilizing process' (p. 267).

Goddard has examined contemporary Jesuit journals, missionary reports, and theological treatises and discovers a dearth of biblical allusion in their narration and theorizing of missionary activities in early Canada. While Protestants placed great weight on the Bible in that narration, post-Tridentine sixteenth- and seventeenth-century Roman Catholics were less inclined to reach for chapter and verse to support and offer rationale for missionary activities. To inspire and sustain missionary activity, Jesuits drew on catechesis, the daily office, hagiography, and texts remembered for their hortatory power. The Bible here was symbolic of rather than a source for divine revelation, the token and promise of God's continuing illuminating presence in a life of missionary service. In fact, because of the Bible's silence concerning North America's original peoples, it was necessary to reach for extra-biblical sources to account for them, including their moral status and lack of civilization. Distance from rather than presence in the biblical narrative accounted for a largely dismal assessment of aboriginal culture. Their 'east of Eden' state was explained as a slow slide towards barbarism in the ever-expanding chronological gap that marked their distance from biblical narrative. Goddard describes this as a post-lapsarian, stadial, and secular history of descent that traces the ever more forceful supremacy of passion over reason as time passed. The antidote to this sorry state was a return to the civilization French missionaries brought with them – a return to origins mediated by European culture and transplanted onto Canadian soil. In rehearsing the depravity chronology had awakened, as an incentive for creating support and enthusiasm for missionary enterprises at home, Jesuit accounts encouraged a view of cultural superiority. Unintentionally, Goddard argues, Jesuit reports of missionary activity abroad helped to reinforce the notion that but for the grace of God, Old France would have been no better off than the new one. A vision of the depraved colonized subject of New France became an incentive for colonizers to embrace their civilization as a token of divine grace. The representation of New France's original inhabitants as savages in need of a Christian civilization would have benefited, Goddard argues, from an application of biblical narrative. Instead, what it came to symbolize was the application of cultural hegemony: 'the cloak of righteousness to be donned [by early Canada's first inhabitants] was often of a French cut, the prescriptions for conversion as cultural as they were religious, designed to promote a model of "civilized" comportment which was likewise the object of pedagogical and disciplinary programs within Europe itself' (267).

The juxtaposition Goddard proposes between Abraham on the one side and Aristotle (and the classical heritage he represents) on the other is informative, not only for Jesuit missions in New France, but for the New Testament itself. For the story of moral transformation is one of the Bible's – especially the New Testament's – favourite tropes. New Testament texts reveal their cultural and imperial location in representing their audiences as people who once lived lives of transgression and impiety and now pursue ethical living in right worship of the one God of Israel. From more theoretical representation of the link of vice and idolatry in Romans 1:18–32 to profiles of salvation that contrast the movement from immoderation towards self-control and virtue (e.g., 1 Thes 1:9; 4:1–8; Col 1:21–2, 3:5–11; 1 Pt 1:14–16), a central theme of the New Testament, especially of the Pauline corpus, is a drama of moral transformation.[1] The choice between Abraham and Aristotle is not a stark one in the biblical tradition; indeed, the cultural situation that shaped biblical portraits of faithfulness, at least in the period associated with the New Testament, is one that draws heavily on Hellenistic ideals of *paideia* in order to redeploy them to help form communities of moral transformation and a particular kind of ethical discourse.[2] It is no accident that Colossians 3:11 ('neither Greek nor Jew, circumcision nor uncircumcision, barbarian, Scythian, slave nor free, but Christ is all, and in all') expresses not only a Pauline ideal of a cosmopolitan unity of all people, but also a Hellenistic one of the unity of peoples under the civilizing power of enlightened culture – more particularly, Roman imperial power.[3] One wonders whether the secular stadial history Goddard discovers in the Jesuit narratives, history, and theology of New France's mission are wholly comprehensible without reference to this overarching biblical drama. The irony of course is that while the New Testament's invocations of moral transformation express evidence of the colonizing influences of Hellenism, especially as they were deployed in the Roman imperial situation, in the later period they have become the expression of a dominant colonizing power. However distant, the Jesuit ideals of a moral recovery echo the themes of moral regeneration that the New Testament voices. To accomplish this does not require an invocation of biblical narratives of occupation, welcome of strangers, Exodus, or exile. Nor does it require even an invocation of Jesus' Great Commission. The imperial situation that offered New Testament authors material to take up, transpose, and re-deploy so as to help promote an alternative social and cultural identity in turn preserved and promoted a legacy to pass on to other generations. Once those other generations were like the original audiences addressed in New Testament texts, no longer strangers and exiles but rather inheritors of Israel's promises, the same narration of transformation was available to apply. In that sense, the story of the use of the Bible in New France invites consideration of the legacy of Hellenistic ideals borrowed not only from a classical cultural heritage, but that cultural heritage preserved in and promoted, under disguise to be sure, in the biblical canon itself.[4]

Strangers to Ourselves

'Joshua in America: On Cowboys, Canaanites, and Indians' invites us by means of Midrash and literary deconstruction to a reconsideration of the *charam* – the command of God to the children of Israel to occupy Canaan by force and annihilate its inhabitants. This is a kaleidoscopic essay that comes aslant to the topics of colonial subjectivity, agency, and potency by way of literary juxtaposition. As such the essay models postcolonial interpretation by refusing to settle down into any single territorial preoccupation, be it that of the liberated conqueror or the oppressed conquered; Donaldson's piece thus urges a reading of biblical narrative from the margins as a means toward a liberating agency. The subtitle of the essay, almost identical to Robert Allen Warrior's 'A Native American Perspective: Canaanites, Cowboys and Indians,' brings her own ideas into conversation with Warrior's oft-reprinted article.[5] Warrior's main point is that Exodus as liberationist narrative is no friend of ab/original peoples, whether in America or anywhere else, however much it is invoked by liberals to celebrate freedom from slavery, exploitation, ignorance, or oppression. This is because what invocations of Exodus too often hide are the ways in which liberation from slavery in the biblical narrative gives way to conquest, assimilation, and annihilation of cultures rendered disposable by divine command. This is a point that Edward Said repeats – now with reference to the history of Palestine – in a lively review of Michael Walzer's *Exodus and*

Revolution.[6] What Walzer calls 'Exodus Politics' signals a progressive history of enlightenment and human promise. But for Said and Warrior, the politics of Exodus is a story of displacement, occupation, and oppression. Israel's liberator Lord becomes conqueror and assimilator. For Said, Exodus erases Palestine. For Warrior, Israel's conquering Lord is especially evident in the long and troubled history of the Christianization of what he names North America's Native Indians. When the Exodus narrative has been applied to Natives, Warrior argues, the result has been no less than the repetition of a self-styled Chosen People bringing its foreign God to already existing peoples and resulting in the extermination/assimilation of Canaanite/Native culture.

Donaldson's essay acknowledges all of this and goes some way towards reinforcing it: her account of the religious justification of the massacre of Native Americans at Lancaster in 1763 shows how biblical narrative, especially that centred around the conquest of Canaan, was at least as determinative as economic/socio-historical factors in the violence of the Paxton Boys against resident Natives, a point already recognized by contemporaries of the event. And, like Warrior, she notices how the conquest of Canaan continues to function as the dark side of invocations of Exodus. Indeed, noticing William Albright's subtle invocation of eugenics as justification for Israel's conquest of Canaan, within scholarship that celebrates its ideals of scientific detachment and patient observation in the reconstruction of a remote Bronze Age past, Donaldson observes how justification of conquest as the underbelly of Exodus is alive and well in the contemporary imagination, and how one may subtly slip from championing the ancient meaning of a biblical text to colonizing the ideal and back again in historical and literary interpretation. It is in the subordinate clauses, where the past is rendered understandable to contemporary readers by invocation of contemporary example, that Albright reveals himself fully at home – however unconsciously so – in a long history of colonial enterprise.

Still, all of this is cannot remain the whole story for Donaldson. Exodus and its aftermath are not forever fated to remain the narrative of an all-conquering Lord urging annihilation or cultural genocide via the politics of assimilation for the peoples of an occupied land. There is too much that such a reading of biblical narrative ignores. The Exodus story is after all the story of the *Israelites* as a colonized people. Genesis 46–7 represents them as guest workers in Egypt, and like immigrants elsewhere, their success provokes envy and hatred among those of the dominant culture. Whatever its aftermath in Canaan as a story of genocide or the politics of assimilation, Exodus nevertheless opens a productive space for consideration of the travail of Native history in America. Here Donaldson urges a reading that – contrary to Warrior and Said – does not pit Israelite against Canaanite, or Exodus against American Indian. Rather, she discovers a commonality between Exodus, the *charam*, and a Native American history that allows for a more deeply empathetic reading of ancient and modern history. In short, her own reading urges a destabilization of the categories of Exodus and Occupation, Israelite and Canaanite, and in so doing she offers an engagement with narrative instability as a means towards retrieving access for the subjugated to a colonizer's favoured narrative (in this case, the settler's version of Exodus, revised by a Native American reader, that foregrounds aspects of a biblical text suppressed by the privileging of one part of a narrative in a colonizing application). In her view, therefore, Warrior and Said are incorrect to dispense with the Exodus narratives so quickly; similarly, Walzer's representation of the Exodus as a story of progress erases too much of the narrative's surpluses of meaning in favour of an excessively simplistic account; Albright's eugenicist musings on the necessary conquest of Canaan in order to preserve Israelite genetic purity similarly turn away too quickly from a more engaged social reading in which the Israelites are colonized subjects, first as guest workers and later as slaves.

Donaldson's aim is not to estrange the reader from the children of Israel, as Warrior and Said effectively do in their readings, but to create an empathetic space for re-engagement with a suppressed moment of history. Midrashic interpretation is the way by which she seeks to open this space. Donaldson follows Daniel Boyarin's understanding of Midrash, which entails the bringing of one's own intertext as a means towards making and finding meaning through the filling in of a text's gaps.[7] Exodus 1:13 and Wendy Rose's poem 'Excavation at Santa Barbara Mission' occasion the reading Donaldson seeks, as well as her own postcolonial resistance to the balkanizing readings of the Exodus offered by Warrior and Said. The 'hard service in mortar and brick' giving way to bitterness in the biblical account finds midrashic interpretation in the empathetic readings of later rabbis, who now bring from the intertext of their own subjugated identities the picture of Jewish babies wedged into Pharaoh's buildings. To be wedged – to be assimilated, to be erased by genocide – this then is brought into conversation with Rose's poem of the Native American archaeologist who, excavating the Christian mission at Santa Barbara, discovers human bones in the uncovered walls. Wendy Rose refuses the cool detachment of the archaeologist, 'the hungry scientist' whose trowel detachedly recovers artefacts, and instead enters into the suffering of Native American genocide by the fourfold lament arising from bones discovered in the mission's walls. This for Donaldson becomes the site of a recovery of Exodus resistant to the too-simplistic hermeneutical moves of Warrior and Said. So it is that Canaanite/Native American is no longer pitted against Exodus Israelite/Israeli/American settler. Rather, Exodus is recovered for making comprehensible Native history – for giving words to the annihilation of Native American cultures, remembering it, writing it down, marking it up as a place to tell one's own stories of brutal servitude and occupation, of bodies wedged, as it were, in the missionary edifices of a colonizing Christianity. It is not, Donaldson argues, through the telling of the biblical story of one people pitted against another (Israelite vs Canaanite) that liberation arises. This is Warrior's move, and in offering it he too easily relinquishes a story – namely, the Exodus – that is productive of political action and transformation. By sharing and mutually recognizing 'those stories that remain wedged into the numerous equivalents of Egyptian walls,' one enters into the supremely human risk of discovering in one's enemy the unlikely neighbour – the discovery that s/he, like me, shares in the suffering and travail of what it means to be human, and wrestles with his/her own colonial pre/occupations.

Donaldson's kaleidoscopic essay models a postcolonial exegesis that insists on the unstable meaning of text. While she recognizes, laments, and resists the colonizing uses of the Exodus story, she rightly insists that the narrative nevertheless retains a surplus of meaning that potentially gives voice to the subjugated Other, and that in turn displaces and decentres straightforward applications which – in the case of the Exodus narratives – transform complex narratives into epic linear narrations of liberation giving way to conquest, colonization, and oppression. This, she implies, is exactly how Warrior and Said read Exodus and its aftermath, and it is their more shrill exegeses, silencing the complexities of story, which she rejects as mirroring the simplistic colonizing applications of story, reduced from its complexity to realize or celebrate a particular political preoccupation. Said and Warrior inadvertently, in giving ground to the colonial way of reading Exodus, grant it the power of their own colonization. It is worth noting that Donaldson's reading exposes a fundamental weakness of Said's approach to narrative more generally, a weakness that is found in his linear reconstructions of the Oriental, which have been rightly criticized as too stable and monolithic.[8]

But does Donaldson's appeal to empathy do enough? From the Canaanite perspectives of Warrior and Said, does discovering in the Conquering Other that the displaced self is languishing under its own bondage do enough to produce that self's own liberating politics of reading? Said, for example, in his review of Walzer's work, is not unsympathetic to the history of Jewish suffering that lies behind a militant Zionist-inspired occupation of the Palestinian Territories. *Palestinian* empathy with the history of Jewish bondage, however, will do little to change an oppressive occupation. Rather, it is Israeli recognition of an Egyptian bondage lived in the borders of its own Promised Land that will unleash the decolonizing power of the biblical narrative. So, similarly, while a Native American reading of Exodus along the lines Donaldson proposes finds meaning in the Exodus story which Warrior's reading ignores or even suppresses, Warrior's main point lies elsewhere: it is to cast into relief how a colonizing reading of Exodus and the *charam* has destroyed Native American culture. Warrior would no doubt be indebted to Donaldson's recovery of the Exodus for naming Native experience, but would he not urge from this a further step: that those arbiters of Manifest Destiny, whose settlers made of the homelands of pre-existing peoples outposts of the Promised Land, learn to recognize themselves as Pharaoh's commanders? Donaldson makes a compelling argument that Native Americans ought not so quickly, as Warrior suggests, throw away the Exodus story as a means for interpreting their own experience. But Warrior's argument does not preclude this, however little his essay fails to recognize this liberating potential of the Exodus narrative. More to the point, again, would be for the colonizer to be retold the biblical narrative in a way that exposes the alleged settler/liberator to the discomfiting reality of being rather more like Pharaoh than Moses. Warrior may be enjoined through empathy to recognize his own oppression in the Exodus story of the conquerors of Canaan's Egyptian captivity. This will do little, however, to name the ways in which the use of Exodus as colonizing text has made defensible what cannot and should not be legitimated – the genocide, by extermination or assimilation, of pre-contact peoples.

I wonder if the good insights of Donaldson's essay and the recovery of a colonizer's text, decolonized for the purposes of liberation, might benefit from the psychoanalytical post-structuralist insights of Julia Kristeva? Herself a Bulgarian émigrée living in France, Kristeva urges in *Strangers to Ourselves* that Western subjects learn from the foreigner, the stranger, the outsider to become acquainted with that foreigner, stranger, outsider in oneself.[9] Too easily is the foreigner escorted to the immigration office, signalling how easily the strangeness of oneself is escorted to those agents of civilization that would resolve the ambiguities of a self and a culture by reference to epic formulations of self and society. As antidote, Kristeva urges a politically situated recognition of Self as Other, which is to say, multiply recognized as both here and there, inside and outside, civilized and untamed. Such a destabilized self, Kristeva insists, makes for good neighbours, for the task of the human life then is not so much to build the good society as to take responsibility for one's own identity. Borrowing from the categories offered for analysis by Donaldson, one would then be Egyptian, Canaanite, liberator, conquered, colonizer, colonized, slave, and free. Such a recognition would create the empathy Kristeva recognizes as foundational for a good society.

That Native Americans, languishing as Canaanites in the post-industrial Promised Lands of the divinely commissioned Colonizer and worthy only of assimilation or worse, can find enough for liberation in these musings from a Parisian psychoanalyst seems unlikely. Kristeva's reflections do, however, seem indispensable for those self-styled Moseses who fail to recognize how their desire to build the Promised Land too often results in commands for underlings to construct its storehouses of prosperity from bricks without straw. And, they may be just enough to wedge open the sealed-up Exodus as epic narrative of liberation and conquest, in order to recognize there the stories of inhabitants of the Promised Land who were themselves, once upon a time, slaves.

Premodern and Postcolonial Subjects

In contrast to the essays of Peter Goddard and Laura Donaldson, which adopt either explicit or implicit postcolonial readings of biblical texts, Jace Weaver resists both the postmodern and postcolonial as 'ahistorical, universalizing, and depoliticizing' (295). This is a bold charge, located (as the sources Weaver cites in favour of rejection) in a critique of deconstructionism as the privilege of the post-industrial Western subject, inheritor of a dominant culture's history, formed by the legacy of Modernity. Such a subject enjoys the luxury of tearing down and ironical detachment with reference to historical agency.[10] Ironical detachment presumes that one has something from which to detach oneself. This points to the deeper reason for his rejection of a postmodern and postcolonial reading of First Nations cultures, alluded to in passing in the course of the footnotes and worthy of fuller explication in order to bring out Weaver's own perspective more forcefully. In 'From I-Hermeneutics to We-Hermeneutics: Native Americans and the Post-Colonial,' Weaver insists that there is no 'post' in the colonial experiences of Native peoples. 'Native Americans remain a colonized people, victims of internal colonialism' (Weaver 1998, 13). Internal colonialism refers to a process of assimilation by a larger settler culture in which the colonized do not exist apart from the colonizer, but are in a state of constant occupation. If postcolonialism takes up the identity formations that arise when the colonizer is absent, or those which survive after the colonized leave, and expresses the hybrid identity as being connected to but no longer directly present to the colonizer, the Native American experience wrestles with the enduring presence of colonization. 'As long ... as those readings and the theologies that spring from them [the dominant literatures and world views of the settler culture] are still taught, as long as denominational factionalism, and Amer-European missionization continue to divide families and force natives to choose between their communities and their religion, the post-colonial moment for Native Americans will not yet have arrived' (Weaver 1998, 15).

The other reason why Weaver rejects the postcolonial as an adequate lens to account for Native American experience arises from his critique and use of Reinhold Niebuhr's concept of irony in history. Again, Weaver's own development is cited rather than explicated in the course of his discussion. In 'Original Simplicities and Present Complexities: Reinhold Niebuhr, Ethnocentrism, and the Myth of American Exceptionalism,' Weaver takes up Niebuhr's account of irony in American history and applies it to Native Americans' experience as colonized peoples.[11] 'American exceptionalism' refers to the idea that on account of an axiomatic assertion of American virtue or divine appointment, standards applied to other nations (for example, the contemporary American prohibition against alleged rogue states possessing weapons of mass destruction) are not applied to the United States. Niebuhr's representation of irony as a hermeneutical stance for reading American history arose from his observation that what America espoused as a democratic nation at the time he was writing, in 1952 at the height of the Cold War, and what America actually was, were so disjunctive as to inspire bemused incredulity. While the United States presumed the mantle of a nation of simple agrarian folk committed to a life of humble virtue, in fact the post–Second World War period had by a series of historical accidents established America as an urban-centred nuclear superpower extending its sphere of military and economic hegemony across the globe. For Weaver, the irony in Niebuhr's representation of the ironic in American history is his acceptance of a period of time when America was constituted by innocent farmers. In fact, Weaver argues, there never was a moment when Americans led lives of humble virtue in the New World. If 1950s America was not living up to the responsibility of global domination because of an outmoded view of itself as a nation of farmers, Weaver argues, Niebuhr himself did not critically assess that account of the settler history of America he took up as historical. On account of his lack of recognition of the Native American experience from contact onward, Niebuhr fails to see that the irony of American history does not begin in the Cold War period or even, further back, after the First World War (where Niebuhr begins to detect it). It rather must be read from the period of first contact, when the myth of a founding nation, as a nation of virtue and innocence, already was hiding the brutal reality of genocide and military occupation. Niebuhr's notion of irony must be extended in order for the full impact of his insight to be driven home and for Americans to come to terms with identities of exploitation and violence. Niebuhr urges Americans to rewrite their present in order not to be blind in future writings – that is, in order to resist the temptation of power to wield pre-emptive war. Weaver, however, urges that this is too little: 'In the end, American Indians remain a colonized people … It is not enough for the colonizer to control the present and future of the colonized, he must rewrite the past as well' (Weaver 2001, 153).

This then sets the tone for the essay's title, 'Premodern Ironies.' Though not fully taken up, Weaver intends by his title the observation hinted at in the piece's subtitle ('First Nations and Chosen Peoples'). The premodern irony to which Weaver refers is the irony of American history that Niebuhr ignores, and it is the reality that Weaver's many stories of Native resistance to Christian evangelization seeks to exploit. These stories that show First Nations peoples offering – by way of ironical quip or amused incredulity – resistance to Christian pleas to conversion both express historical agency by way of resistance *and* reveal the mixed motives of Christian missionaries as agents of colonization. Weaver insists on such premodern irony to demonstrate the abiding power of Native agency, which is able to accept the Christian Gospel without forsaking the importance of being historical subjects, on terms specific to being Native American. Weaver is aware of the contribution of postmodernism to a study to the explication of particular features of Native American cultures. Yet he remains unconvinced that the application of postmodern studies enables a full recognition of Native agency. To conceive of First Nations as chosen peoples is to juxtapose an identity so often stripped from Natives in the colonial history of settlement. This is especially documented in Alfred Cave's patient treatment of settlement debates concerning whether Natives were human, or in the representation of Natives as Canaanites to be conquered and exploited by Europeans who were self-appointed by their reading of the Bible as the Chosen People.[12]

As his subtitle suggests, Weaver offers resistance to the colonizers' history of pre-contact cultures as themselves First Nations *and* chosen peoples. In doing so, he creatively invokes the story of the Gibeonites, who survived Canaan's invasion by Joshua, as well as the lesser-known story of Zelophedad's daughters in Numbers 26–7 and Joshua 17:1–6. Here, Weaver discovers a pre-existing people who are *also*, as the story of conquest unfolds, nevertheless (through their maintenance of cultural and territorial integrity) people 'who by divine sanction enjoyed equally the promise of Yahweh' (301). Quoting from an earlier essay in which this Native American appropriation is similarly developed, Weaver argues: 'American Indians are thus the Hepherites, Zelophedad's daughters, sharing a god with, and living in the midst of, a foreign people, yet preserving their own identity and self-determination.'[13]

The result of these interjections is an essay that, as the title suggests, is deeply ironical. Even as Weaver escorts the postmodern and postcolonial out the front door, he nevertheless seems to bring them in through the back. For what are the postmodern and the postcolonial if not, as Linda Hutcheon has argued with reference to the former, the unmasking of identity by means of ironical juxtaposition?[14] If we can agree that both the postmodern and the postcolonial presume the existence of a historical subject at some remove from a continuing colonization of Native American culture, Weaver's own representations of Native cultures show a form of the postcolonial not as temporal, but as ironic juxtaposition. The 'post' in postcolonial here is not a historical description, but an epistemological one. Further, does his own appropriation of Hebrew Bible texts, championing Natives as coexisting with Canaanites alongside settlers and sharing the title of Promised People, and in the context of an essay that quotes a long history of colonial applications of the conquest narratives, not offer precisely the kind of reorientation of texts and retrieval of historical agency that postcolonial studies seek to identify? In fact, as Donaldson does in her own essay, Weaver seeks the recognition and recovery of Native agency on terms other than those furnished by an occupying culture. But once this is acknowledged, is it not the case that the postcolonial is especially apt for helping to unfold the complexities of subjecthood as both belonging and resistant to dominant culture? Is the postcolonial on these terms about retrieving subjectivity rather than abandoning it in favour of a deconstructivism that always tears down and never builds up? Is Weaver in fact not demonstrating through his own re-rendering of the Israelite occupation of Canaan through the eyes of Zelophedad's daughters a postcolonial reading of the Bible that re-occupies what was once preoccupied with a settler reading? Further, the stories Weaver cites of the evangelized Native turning the missionary enterprise on its head by offering his own kind of appropriation of Christian history point precisely to the instabilities of colonizer identity that the colonized show up. Here is not a choice between abandoning and seizing the historical subject. The historical subject arises, rather, from a complex negotiation of power and story. Weaver's own essay is testimony to that postcolonial negotiation of a Native subject in a situation of colonial occupation.

Responses

Peter Goddard

The 'Call to the Nations' animated the Society of Jesus from its earliest days. Among the first generation of Jesuits, St Francis Xavier demonstrated the missionary vocation when he pushed at the edges of Japan and China. He died in 1552 just off the Hainanese coast, without having introduced the gospel to China, but his example would serve as the model for his fellow Jesuits as they gazed beyond Europe. Xavier, his contemporaries agreed, walked in the footsteps of the apostles. It is worth emphasizing, in response to Harry Maier's observations, that the missionary enterprise as envisioned by these early Jesuits was more Christocentric than bibliocentric. Their source of confidence in their enterprise derived from a mystical sense of unity with Christ; theirs was an *imitatio Christi*. This self-fashioning, from their *Spiritual Exercises* to their humanities-rich curriculum and their classroom vocation, enshrined in a college system that produced nearly every figure in the Canadian mission, allowed Jesuits to see themselves as following Christ, their teacher and ethical example as well as instrument of conversion. To the nations they went, two by two, enflamed by zeal, as the apostles had gone. In Canada, Jesuits did as they had been trained: they relied on meditations upon the personal example of Christ. In this sense, they projected the Christian essentialism Louis Châtellier thought was the chief product of the Catholic reformation that swept much of Europe in the sixteenth and seventeenth centuries.[15]

Yet in another way, Jesuits articulated the values of the first wave of Christian evangelization, as framed in the New Testament and evoked by Harry Maier in his commentary. Specifically, under the leadership of St Paul in the Hellenic Mediterranean, an imperial conception of Christianity coalesced. Tertullian was not wrong to call Paul 'apostle of the heretics' (in *De praescriptione haereticorum*): in his epistles, Paul had developed notions of sin, grace, and their divisive resonances in morality and piety that were far removed from ideas espoused in the Sermon on the Mount. 'Our appeal, therefore, must not be made to the Scriptures; nor must controversy be admitted on points in which victory will either be impossible, or uncertain, or not certain enough,' wrote Tertullian.[16] Jesuits carried this Pauline pitch, sharpened by the Reformation-era battle with the Protestants, and the belated discovery of paganism in the rural enclaves of Europe itself, into the Canadian mission field. The ethnographic lens for viewing aboriginal peoples in their lapsarian state is one that Jesuits derived from Paul, who had a similarly dim view of the failings of Gentile peoples, even as he sought to discern the godly among them and to urge the overthrow of their institutions. But the Bible was not the key to the pagans' conversion; that required a different rhetoric.

The Jesuits were aware of the typology of conversion and castigation laid out in the Pauline epistles, but they absorbed it through the filter of a humanities curriculum that privileged Hellenic ideas of civilization. Given Catholic wariness towards the Bible in the Reformation era, especially in post–civil war France, where fundamentalism had practically wrecked the kingdom, Jesuits had an opportunity to fashion a humanistic program of conversion that was neither literal nor particularly biblical. Instead, in their mission activity as in their sermons and relations, they propounded a notion of conversion that was urgent, total, and uncompromising, even if humanistically tempered.

Profoundly pastoral in their orientation, the Jesuits echoed the rhetoric and the tactics of St Paul rather than his literal message.

Jace Weaver

I want to thank Harry O. Maier for his thoughtful and incisive remarks on my essay 'Premodern Ironies.' He is a generous reader who, in fact, goes beyond the four corners of my article, reading and drawing into the discussion other of my writings, most notably 'From I-Hermeneutics to We-Hermeneutics' and 'Original Simplicities and Present Complexities.' He is quite right in his observation/critique that at certain key points I am impressionistic rather than explicit, and he then seeks to backfill context from my other work.

I wrote 'Premodern Ironies' shortly after the Bush administration invaded Iraq to banish once and for all the post-Vietnam beliefs in the limitations of American power, but before it only served to demonstrate and reinscribe them. Before its adventurism there spun completely out of control. Before Iran and North Korea were able to blithely thumb their noses at the United States by confidently pursuing nuclear weapons – despite President Bush's tough rhetoric that such programs would never be permitted – the United States powerless to intervene because of that adventurism. Late modern ironies, indeed. Were I writing the piece today, it might be very different in some of the ways Maier suggests.

I also wrote that original essay before my book *American Indian Literary Nationalism*, which appeared in 2006.[17] The spark for that book, co-authored with Craig Womack and Robert Warrior, was the backlash by some non-Native scholars against Native scholars who write from a nationalist perspective. In particular, European scholar Elvira Pulitano, in her book, *Toward a Native American Critical Theory*, takes Womack and Warrior (among others) to task for their nationalism and their failure to acknowledge their own hybridity and embrace high theory. Although I do engage and critique Western theoretical discourse in my work, thus undercutting much of her argument, I am dismissed in a footnote as adding 'very little to a discourse on Native American critical theory that is attempting to generate rhetorical strategies of its own.'[18] Pulitano's work spurred us to a sometimes stinging defence of literary and scholarly nationalism. What Pulitano and other critics who contend that Native scholars must employ Western critical methods fail to recognize – or at least admit – is that high theory is not some force of nature that cannot be resisted but rather only a tool (or set of tools) that may be used or not as individual scholars see fit.

Maier makes none of these mistakes in his response to my essay. He understands that postmodern studies is simply an approach, a critical apparatus that may be used or not, in much the same way that the Natives I discuss in 'Premodern Ironies' were able to adopt and adapt Christianity or to reject it outright. Nevertheless, the experience of writing *American Indian Literary Nationalism* with Womack and Warrior has reinforced for me the critical and theoretical position I stake out in the essay upon which Maier reflects. This is not a case, I believe, of Marxian rejectionism – the Marx here being not Karl but Groucho – that is to say, 'Whatever it is, I'm against it.'[19] Rather, for the reasons I originally articulated, I see postcolonial studies as problematic and largely inapt when it comes to the situation of North American indigenes.

Maier writes, however, 'Even as Weaver escorts the postmodern and postcolonial out the front door he nevertheless seems to bring it in through the back.' In my use of irony, he sees me as engaged in the postcolonial enterprise without recognizing it. This strikes me as a little like the 'anonymous Christianity' of Karl Rahner post–Vatican II or, centuries earlier, the doctrine of the *logos*, which permitted Christian theologians to incorporate the wisdom of Greek philosophers into their work and faith. Whatever light there is in pagan religions or philosophies is the light of the Christian god, even though the pagan practitioners cannot see it. That giant sucking sound you hear is not NAFTA pulling American jobs south into Mexico; rather, it is postcolonial studies drawing everything into itself like a sponge. If the postcolonial means only 'ironical juxtaposition,' then it does not seem to mean much.

Maier concludes his response writing, 'Weaver's own essay is testimony to that postcolonial negotiation of a Native subject in a situation of colonial occupation.' Perhaps. In the end, however, I remain unconvinced, despite Maier's erudition and sensitivity. No matter how sumptuous the feast postcolonial theorists set, I and, I suspect, many other Natives as well, will largely bypass the table, though we may occasionally stop by and nibble.

NOTES

1 See Meeks 1997, 18–36 for a thumbnail sketch of the moral ideals of conversion.

2 For an account of the intimate link of Christianity with Hellenism, see Jaeger 1961.
3 Taylor 1981 offers an excellent discussion. See also Mühl 1928.
4 The Hellenistic construction of the 'barbarian' has received enormous attention as a motif of ancient ideologies of colonization. See especially Hartog 1988, 61–111 and Braund 1986, 31–49.
5 Warrior 1995.
6 Said 1986; Walzer 1985.
7 Boyarin 1990, 57–79, 117–29.
8 Moore-Gilbert 1997, 42–53.
9 Kristeva 1994, esp. 169–93, where the strangeness of the other is related to the foreignness within.
10 Weaver develops his arguments against postmodernism and postcolonialism in Weaver 1998, 1–25, citing in particular Shohat 1992, who makes the case for the ahistorical, apolitical, and universal in postcolonialism. See also Dirlik 1997, 52–83; Hall 1998, 242–60; and Frankenberg and Mani 1993.
11 Weaver 2001, 140–53.
12 Cave 1988.
13 See similarly, 'A Biblical Paradigm for Native Liberation' in Weaver 2001, 242–5.
14 Hutcheon 1989, especially her discussion of parody and postmodernism, 93–117.
15 Châtellier 1993.
16 Tertullian, *De praescriptione haereticorum*, xviiii: [Great Evil Ensues to the Weak in Faith, from Any Discussion out of the Scriptures. Conviction Never Comes to the Heretic from Such a Process]. '[1] But with respect to the man for whose sake you enter on the discussion of the Scriptures, with the view of strengthening him when afflicted with doubts, (let me ask) will it be to the truth, or rather to heretical opinions that he will lean? [2] Influenced by the very fact that he sees you have made no progress, whilst the other side is on an equal footing (with yourself) in denying and in defence, or at any rate on a like standing, he will go away confirmed in his uncertainty by the discussion, not knowing which side to adjudge heretical. [3] For, no doubt, they too are able to retort these things on us. It is indeed a necessary consequence that they should go so far as to say that adulterations of the Scriptures, and false expositions thereof, are rather introduced by ourselves, inasmuch as they, no less than we maintain that truth is on their side.' Trans. Peter Holmes, 1870, at www.tertullian.org/works/de_praescriptione_haereticorum.htm; accessed 30 March 2009.

17 Weaver, Womack, and Warrior 2006.
18 Pulitano 2003, 193.
19 Sung by Groucho as Professor Quincy Adams Wagstaff in the movie *Horse Feathers* (1932): 'I don't know what they have to say. / It makes no difference anyway. / Whatever it is, I'm against it.' Video clip available at http://www.youtube.com/watch?v=DtMV44yoXZ0.

REFERENCES

Boyarin, Daniel. 1990. *Intertextuality and the Reading of Midrash*. Bloomington: Indiana University Press.

Braund, David. 1986. 'The Caucasian Frontier: Myth, Exploration and the Dynamics of Imperialism.' In Philip Freeman and David Kennedy, eds, *The Defence of the Roman and Byzantine East*, 2 vols. 1: 31–49. Oxford: BAR.

Cave, Alfred E. 1988. 'Canaanites in a Promised Land: The American Indian and the Providential Theory of Empire.' *American Indian Quarterly* 4: 277–98.

Châtellier, Louis. 1993. *La religion des pauvres: Les missions rurales en Europe et la formation du catholicisme moderne, XVIe–XIXe siècle*. Paris: Aubier.

Dirlik, Arif. 1997. *The Postcolonial Aura: Third World Criticism in the Age of Global Capitalism*. Boulder, CO: Westview.

Frankenberg, Ruth, and Lata Mani. 1993. 'Crosscurrents, Crosstalk: Race, "Postcoloniality" and the Politics of Location.' *Cultural Studies* 7: 292–310.

Hall, Stuart. 1998. 'When Was "The Post-Colonial" Thinking at the Limit?' In Iain Chambers and Lidia Curti, eds, *The Post-Colonial Question: Common Skies, Divided Horizons*, 242–60. London and New York: Routledge.

Hartog, François. 1988. *The Mirror of Herodotus: The Representation of the Other in the Writing of History*. Trans. Janet Lloyd. Berkeley: University of California Press.

Hutcheon, Linda. 1989. *The Politics of Postmodernism*. London and New York: Routledge.

Jaeger, Werner. 1961. *Early Christianity and Greek Paideia*. Harvard: Belnap.

Kristeva, Julia. 1994. *Strangers to Ourselves*. New York: Columbia University Press.

Meeks, Wayne. 1997. *The Origins of Christian Morality: The First Two Centuries*. New Haven: Yale University Press.

Moore-Gilbert, Bart. 1997. *Postcolonial Theory: Contexts, Practices, Politics*. London: Verso.

Mühl, Max. 1928. *Die antike Menschheitsidee in ihrer geschichtlichen Entwicklung*. Leipzig: Dieterich.

Pulitano, Elvira. 2003. *Toward a Native American Critical Theory*. Lincoln: University of Nebraska Press.

Said, Edward. 1986. 'Michael Walzer's *Exodus and Revolution*: A Canaanite Reading.' *Grand Street* 5.2: 86–106.

Shohat, Eila. 1992. 'Notes on the Post-Colonial.' *Social Text* 31/32: 99–113.

Taylor, W.F. 1981. *The Unity of Mankind in Antiquity and Paul*. Michigan: UMI.

Walzer, Michael. 1985. *Exodus and Revolution*. New York: Basic Books.

Warrior, Robert Allen. 1995. 'A Native American Perspective: Canaanites, Cowboys and Indians.' In R.S. Sugirtharajah, ed., *Voices from the Margin: Interpreting the Bible in the Third World*, 277–88. New York: Orbis.

Weaver, Jace. 1998. 'From I-Hermeneutics to We-Hermeneutics: Native Americans and the Post-Colonial.' In Jace Weaver, ed., *Native American Religious Identity: Unforgotten Gods*, 1–25. New York: Orbis.

– 2001. *Other Words: American Indian Literature, Law, and Culture*. Norman: University of Oklahoma Press.

Weaver, Jace, Craig Womack, and Robert Warrior. 2006. *American Indian Literary Nationalism*. Albuquerque: University of New Mexico Press.

14

Epilogue
'Paradise Highway':
Of Global Cities and
Postcolonial Reading Practices

SHARON V. BETCHER

Today global cities are beckoning or 'calling the nations' themselves. If globalization names the most recent form of neo-colonialism, 'globalization as urbanization seems,' as Gayatri Spivak puts it, 'one of the least speculative strands in the thinking of globalization' (2004, 74). Formerly colonized bodies are folded into any of the planet's 'global' or 'world cities,' working out within them new geographies of dwelling. 'In contemporary cities,' writes theorist Jane M. Jacobs, 'people connected by imperial histories are thrust together in assemblages barely predicted, and often guarded against, during the inaugural phases of colonialism. Often enough this is a meeting not simply augmented by imperialism but still regulated by its constructs of difference and privilege' (1996, 4). The sacred texts of various traditions are being read next door to each other – as they are here in Vancouver: along a stretch euphemistically called 'Paradise Highway,' all of the major world religions and others not so catalogued keep sanctuary among a community of persons who share in common merely the recent pattern of migration. These sites, common now in any world city (as is the distance between the cosmopolitan city centre and this outer ring, the migrant labour pool),[1] are among the reasons for reading sacred texts with and through a postcolonial hermeneutic – to affect the dispositions of these bodies, our ways of bearing rights and inscribing responsibility in relation to each other. Given 'the annihilation of the protective capacity of space' (Bauman 2002, 42), how persons religious think about and come to hold sacred text will be articulated in the grammar, the choreography of bodies loosed within these cities.

At the cusp of the twenty-first century, it appears that persons – given the mobilizing desires, if also socio-cultural and psychic dislocations of globalization, either of which can result in the search for identity, belonging, security, purpose – will live in a world significantly shaped by readings of sacred texts. The left-leaning reader's digest *Utne Reader*, in presenting its 2006 Independent Press award to the Jewish magazine of public, progressive theology, *Tikkun*, made this prescient prediction: 'For just as New Age spirituality helped define the cultural landscape over the past 20 years, the battle over mainstream theological doctrine at home and abroad will define the next 20' (Schimke 2007, 6). Because we of various religious convictions, and none, live them within the intimate folds of global cities, how we hold sacred texts and integrate their wisdom into our habituation of civic space (itself never merely 'local,' but with global enthusiasms) has to do from here on not only with peace among nations, but with peace in the 'hood and hopes for the city. Jacobs, who folds postcolonial thought into and through the politics of space, recognizes that within these cities 'imperialism may ... be reactivated in the present through various nostalgias ... [including] the self-conscious elaboration of tradition' – the rhetorical resort to 'tradition' often enough these days sounding something more like the crank of an archeophone than a critically negotiated or ethically discerning engagement of our histories. Equally, however, 'precisely because cities are sites of meetings, they are also places which are saturated with possibilities for the destabilization of imperial arrangements' (1996, 4). The question with which the editors set out in posing this lecture series and then gathering this anthology – specifically, 'What potential does sacred text have as a counter-hegemonic text and how can it be kept from reassimilation to the dominant cultural narrative?' – bears the possible hope of even now, even yet in these conditions, unravelling bodies from the way in which a commitment to honour the ineffable as sacred sovereign/ty has been lived as superiority to others, exclusion of others and/or as en/title/ment to land/s.

Because the editors share that prescient intuition about the debates over theological doctrine shaping the landscape of the next decades, and because we agree with Karla Pollmann's sentiment that we read so as 'to understand the present,' we have hoped that calling upon a postcolonial hermeneutic in relation to sacred texts and religious histories might open out the greater and messier, ambivalent public within texts and on city blocks, might honour the diverse peoples in the worlds of the texts and on-going world/ing of these texts, of the textually informed and striated present within which scriptural interpretations continue to take place. With Pollmann's conviction in mind and thinking into this location of the global city, I offer up in these pages several final engagements with our authors and reflections upon this anthology.

'Can Religions Be Cured?'

Within this volume, Akenson raised most directly the anxious, if now frequently voiced, question regarding religions in the context of globalization, a question aggravated by the histories of multiple religious confrontations over territory and by rationalist worry over the flare of religious passions – namely, 'Can religions be cured?' The structure of the secular, it now becomes clear on the morning of the twenty-first century, does not hold or withhold in quite the way moderns might have presumed. Yet postcolonial scholars themselves – given the historic ways in which texts have been used as 'virtual reality machines' (Akenson), a taxonomy of which has been presented here, and given the temptations before religions in the face of globalization – have often maintained something of the modernist abject relation to religions. Even as there has been broad acknowledgment that religions have not yielded to secularism (as even modern theologians, e.g., Harvey Cox, had predicted); and even as post-structuralists have concluded that 'only an absolute philosophy can feel the necessity of refuting religious experience' (Vattimo 2002, 5), postcolonial theory has been and continues to be 'distinguished by an unmediated secularism, opposed to and consistently excluding the religions that have taken on the political identity of providing alternative value-systems to those of the West' (Young 2001, 338). 'Despite its espousal of subaltern resistance,' postcolonial theory, Robert Young concluded (expressly regarding its interface with religions), 'scarcely values subaltern resistance that does not operate according to its own secular terms' (ibid.).

Analytically speaking, one denotes the presence then not just of intellectual distance, but of an undergirding anxiety, of fear: How do we … how will we carry on, given modernity's great unthinkable – that religions will not stay private, but will be enthusing threads of the dialogue in and about the public square, the city commons? One notices within the venue of postcolonial studies as well as in the scientific and other publics (and do note the recent spate of intellectual denunciations of religions, à la Richard Dawkins, Christopher Hitchens, etc.) worry about whether the religious can be corralled so as not to impede the public. Scarcely the dream that religions might promote our public life – let alone the possibility that religions might deactivate on-going structures of subjective and economic imperialism. I share with those who are wary of religions the hope of disengaging the main lines of a public discourse on the ways in which 'the biblical' has shaped Western assumptions of and about communal identity and nation, and continues to be assumed both into culture wars and as support for American militarization. But I may not share the philosophy of religion that yields to such essentialist questions as 'Can religions be cured?'

Postcolonial theorists are not wrong about the temptations before religious communities, given the razing of relations, dislocation, and loss of purpose, aggravated by globalization as urbanization. Persons may, in the face of these hurts, reach for religions as an alternative power base or may demand from religions solidity of identity and belonging. Educational theorist Andy Hargreaves sums up such insights: 'Economic globalization and homogenization lead many of those who cannot share in its benefits to turn inward to culture, religion, and ethnicity as alternative sources of meaning and identity' (2003, 45). So pressured or tempted, religious communities have not infrequently handed themselves over, promising to their members a sense of security by indulging nostalgia and the reassertion of structures of hierarchical authority, via the claims of 'culture' or 'tradition.' Not only do these psychic demands upon religions tend to increase in the face of immigration and/ or dislocation, but relational truncation changes how all persons access the ancient wisdom traditions: when persons do reach for religious thought, they now pick that up without the critical thickness of generations and communities of reflection and so can receive it in an essentializing mode. That religions arise as resistance to globalization does not imply that religious structures are necessarily healthy. When theologian Linell Cady speaks of 'resisting the postmodern turn,' she writes, as I read her, to warn us of the way in which the release of religion from the grip of enlightenment rationalism's categorical suspicion can all too easily coincide with this nostalgia which uses religion for less than socially constructive purposes, occasioning an all-too-easy assumption of authoritarian impulses hidden within re-appropriated confessionalism. Theological practitioners, too, like postcolonial theorists, can implicitly recognize how easily the status of textual reading as 'an interpretation' can be denied, how the gap between acknowledging a textual interpretation and assuming a metaphysic can be covered over and made into – listen now for the crank of the archeophone! – a history of salvation (Vattimo 2002, 58).

Then again, postcolonial theorists as well as theologians may be tempted to ignore the psychological ramifications of resident cosmopolitanism – with its carnival swirl, cultural and religious pluralism, and disarticulation of the thick of relations. Intriguingly, historian Samuel Laeuchli locates the development of Christianity's tendency towards the patrolling of identity – which one might hope an anthology like this would challenge – within conditions not unlike our own. Roman urbanization, Laeuchli observes, led to the razing of collective identities and the evolution of individuality – a tenuous locus, at least for some, amidst both cultural and religious pluralism. The question of such bodies, 'Where do we belong?' was resolved, writes Laeuchli, with resort to strict rites and discipline – especially that of the sexual body (1972, 109). That sexuality became 'the seismograph of Christian subjectivity' (Peter Brown), a disciplinary path still troubling the Christian communion today, can then in Laeuchli's mind be owed to the *psychological* ramifications of massive, rapid urbanization. The parallel between this stage of globalization as urbanization and Laeuchli's analysis of the development of sexual codes at the fourth-century Council of Elvira suggests how incredibly important will be our attention to the psychology of the postcolonial migrations, especially the psychology involved in urbanization.[2]

Postcolonial theories – assuming the plasticity and pliability of post-structuralist, constructive subjectivities – may not be so alert to or cognizant of the psychological losses and displacements occurring with globalization. As Sanjeev Kumor Uprety has noted in his uptake of the intersection of postcoloniality and disability studies, 'the experience of symbolic castration at the site of cultural hybridity leads to a sense of "lack," and to a subsequent feeling of being … deviant … The in-between space is not only a locale of power and "double vision"; it is also a site of multiple castrations and reiterated pain' (1997, 366, 369). Postcolonial theorists ourselves may be tempted to keep pain at bay and out of mind by intellectually opposing the wielders of rules and identities, by riding the crest of modernity's sense of the mobile and pleasurable pliability of subjectivity, by ignoring the collapse of value into economism. Indeed, among the pains accruing to modernity may be (as religious sociologist Peter Berger analytically surmises) the fact that any number of humans find a 'human existence bereft of

330 Sharon V. Betcher

transcendence ... an impoverished and finally untenable condition'
(1999, 13). For those of us who want to open out more room in cultures
for the pleasures of bodies, for bodies differing, we will need to learn to
navigate these painful social crises otherwise than through denial and/
or intellectual dismissal.

Nevertheless, I wonder what philosophy of religion informs not only
the question 'Can religions be cured?' but also postcolonial theories.
Religion, in Edward Said's view, 'furnishes us with systems of authority and with canons of order ... whose effect is to coerce submission or
aggressive conversion of others' (cited in Sugirtharajah 2003, 111). That
Said gives a functional view of institutional Christendom would be
hard to deny, especially as it reverberates through this collection. But
what if religions, or strands thereof, might be or have been otherwise
motivated – so as, for example, to unhinge us from ideologies? Think of
the Buddhist 'no self,' its practice of the renunciation of ego – a philosophical practice which biblical studies scholar Lawrence M. Wills locates also in certain intertestamental Jewish narratives, for instance,
Greek Esther and Judith as well as the Testament of Job. Of these narratives of 'a stricken, decentered self,' Wills surmises that 'the apparently
individualistic and socially disconnected actions of the ascetic,' when
set as a narrative within a larger ritual experience, 'may express a ritual
language of opposition to social actions, a language of opposition and
deviance that is "ritually" repeated by other[s]' (2006, 911–12). So the
appeal for renunciation of ego may have been socially or ritually, not
simply individually, issued. That these religious tactics only become
reconstructively available amidst decolonizing processes leads one to
wonder, it must be admitted, if such alternative trajectories of traditions have themselves often been colonized by the triumphalisms of the
religious master narrative.

Admittedly, suggesting or reclaiming a locus of the religious conducive to postcolonial concerns remains to be worked out among religious
practitioners – the postcolonial spelling a shift away from the self-
authenticating wholesomeness of modern individualism. As a constructive theologian I hear the challenge in this proposal: How shall religions
– at times like these – work with persons so as to psychically appreciate
living into uncertainty (even if of such is the mortal life), but without
forgoing the empowering of persons for that justice which 'decolonizes
the between-spaces of our interdependence?' (Keller 2004, 14). If 'a destabilized self makes for good neighbours' (Maier), then the challenge

will be for religions to work with persons unmoored and, in such a time, to teach persons to welcome the open-event nature of existence more than metaphysics' structural foreclosures – to find our religious locus as something of a strange attractor, rather than a virtual reality machine. But to be sure, persons living today cannot, as Buddhist David Loy puts it, evade the postmodern turn, given any encounter with religious pluralism: 'Globalization means that today we all participate in the Greek loss of ground and crisis of meaning, whether or not we understand what is happening.' Assuming the on-going 'globalization of educational exchange and intellectual interaction, the postmodern insight' regarding the social construction of our sacred canopies 'can only continue to spread and infiltrate traditional cultures' (2003, 13–15).

And yet what will make the shared public of religions viable, it must be admitted, will be a related insight – our awareness of and responsibility for our interpretive stances. As philosopher Gianni Vattimo puts it, 'It is possible for us today, if not obligatory,' to move from the notion of a 'history of salvation' to a 'history of interpretation'; 'our pre-understanding of this slippage,' our crossing from one sensibility ('salvation') to the other ('interpretation'), Vattimo concludes, 'constitutes our common, historical belonging to the world ... of the religions of the Book' at this time (2002, 57–8). Interpretations, he advises, are forms of 'engaged knowledge,' which do not presume 'an ideal point that would claim to be external to the process' (15). Admitting their interpretative status before the real, religions at their best can hold open the roominess or space of non-correspondence between language and world, and thus between theology and politics, which encourages us to hold all knowledge, all claims, all constructs with humility.

If cautions about the temptations to religions have come to the fore in this text, a final word about the possibility of hybridic religious interactions may be in order. A 'calling of the nations' enfolds differing religious bodies such that, in the global city, religious practices may tickle each other into constructive memory. Some energy like *synekism*, this vitalizing aggregation of energies which draws us to cities themselves (Soja 2000, xv), transpires, I dare say, in the enfolding and overlapping of religions. Religions in proximity don't simply assume oppositional postures; each can catalyse the other, can vibrate through so as to shake open each other's tacit or assumed infrastructure. So Christianity in relationship with indigenous peoples has suddenly remembered that it too is a cosmic, ecologically concerned religion. In relation to Buddhism,

Christianity remembers that at its iconic centre has been the Christic story of ego-death occasioned by a passion for justice that ideologically unhinges us (Loy 2003, 4). And a rereading of 'spirit' – slightly askew from that which mobilized the absence of attention to place of Christian empire (see the subsequent section in this epilogue), because constructively informed or reformed by Vedic notions of *karma* (that our energies, including psychic dispositions, shape not simply our private future) – comes to offer Christians a locus to again think 'soul' (not ego) and to dream 'life' beyond materialism, if not outside the atmosphere of this earth. The mixing, brewing cosmopolitan concrescence of religions need not be so narrowly viewed as ever and again territorially and textually exclusivist.

Religions and the Politics of Place

'Place' constitutes one of the most overt sheaths of consciousness in the Pacific Northwest, especially here in 'Super Natural, British Columbia' (as Tourism BC promotional literature recently regaled us). An Arcadian – or, more particularly, Cascadian – sensibility permeates consciousness along the western edge of North America and has since at least the nineteenth century. The Vancouver Art Gallery has presented this sensibility in several of its recent shows – 'From Baja to Vancouver: The West Coast and Contemporary Art' (2003–4) and '[Emily] Carr, [Georgia] O'Keeffe, [Frida] Kahlo: Places of Their Own' (2002). As a province, British Columbia's lands were never treated from indigenous peoples and so remain in colonial capture – even as we daily indulge in practised ignorance thereof, buying and trading them as some of the most expensive real estate on the continent. This regional sensitivity no doubt also leaves me (a farm kid by birth and an eco-theologian by training) most attentive to 'the land' – the third term among our considerations (bible, postcolonial hermeneutics, and the land) for this anthology.

The essays in this volume have, from diverse angles, offered up a view of one historical, if dominant and long-lived, incarnation of Christianity, which has tried to get its geographical bearings by using sacred text as if this were a map.[3] Sounding much the same alarm as Akenson about a certain Christian-inspired sense of historiography, a sort of hegemonic 'conspiracy theory' projected simultaneously into modern nation-building and knowledge production, biblical scholar Regina Schwartz elsewhere has observed: 'Historiography reveals the inner logic in this randomness of events, and that logic is the course of national development ... Nationalism was the paramount concern in that ... set of founding fictions ... the founding fictions of German historicism' (1992, 184). Text, when engaged by this 'inner obstinacy driving towards a millennial end' (186) generated peoples without ethical attention to the plane of immanence, but with very productive results. For what postcolonial theorists have none too gently noted, especially in relationship to Christianity in the West, has been the relationship between this way of holding sacred text and a religious culture's sense of land en/title/ment. 'While the Hebrew Scriptures speak centrally of the land, its preservation and proper use,' notes theologian Geoffrey Lilburne, 'this concern is entirely lost in the New Testament.' 'By universalizing the scope of God's reign,' he concludes, 'the New Testament appears to trivialize the concern with place and locality and to move its spirituality beyond issues of the land' (1989, 10). Indigenous theologian Vine Deloria wrote his scathing critique of such a Christianity back in 1973: 'By substituting heaven for the tangible restoration of Palestine to the Jews by driving the Romans out, Christians eliminated the dimension of land from religion, and necessarily their theology had to change Hebrew tribal memories of a particular land into a generalized statement about the origin of the world' (1973, 162). Such an abstract sense of truth has all too easily coincided with the imperial imagination – at least in Christian systematic delineation.

In this volume, Karla Pollmann poked at the issue of Christianity's land ethic with more rigorous attention to shifting, historically specific choreographies than these summary judgments allow: 'Christian claims on territory, never well staked in the New Testament,' were easily amenable not only to Eusebius's 'theology and teleology of empire,' but to the comfortable dualism, the productive ambivalence, of the soul/body compromise of Christendom. Modern Christian theology's doctrine of God – of the immaterial Creator who fashioned an object world over which it then held mindful dominion – reflected, though not identically, this earlier spirit/matter distinction and in turn informed the other binary categories of the Christian-enthused West. Transcendence thus took on the muscle tone of imperial, territorial control and empirical force; the choreography of sacred sovereignty, of God's imagined way of relating to the world, was mirrored in assuming responsibility for colonial governance. As true of territorial colonialism in the modern age as of the theology of Prudentius in the fourth century, Christian theology had developed – with and through this dualism – the ability to pull the shades on conscience. On the one hand (and with a view to eternity), 'material and earthly possessions are irrelevant for a Christian'; and yet something in the interpretation of Christian lifestyle advances 'the holdings of fertile land' (Pollmann). Ever and again, under theo-ethical pressure, the land, or materiality, would appear irrelevant to the transcendentalism of Christian identity even as history evinced the moorings of land entitlement.

Even if 'religious wars have always been about land' (as public sentiment seems to insinuate, whether commenting on Israel-Palestine, the Bosnian uprising, or even 9/11), religiously enthused colonialism has – because the text has been assumed as virtual reality machine – often proceeded in feigned theological ignorance of, if not outright material disregard for, the relational web of place – assuming even the vacuity of space and non-cognition of others. Sure that history (a human life-zone hovering above the land relations) promised resolve, Christian theologies invested the category of time, its futurity, its linear stretch, with the promise of sacred activity, whether revelation, epiphanic encounter, or eschatological fulfilment – over against the denigration of nature and place, which but mired humanity in the seasonal, the cyclical, the transient. God, it was said, did 'not manifest himself in the forces and rhythms of nature; he reveals himself in human history, which is determined by his covenant and his promise' (Moltmann 1993, 13). Splitting time-space in this way covered over the fact that much of the coincidence of Christianity and Western political power has resulted in acquiring property rights: 'This distinction between God and world was … seized on by modern theological apologetics as a way of adapting the biblical traditions to the secularizing processes of modern European times. The ruthless conquest and exploitation of nature which fascinated Europe during this period found its … religious legitimation in that ancient distinction between God and world' (ibid., 13–14). So place has been precisely that of which Christianity did not choose to be cognizant, even as it seems now religiously unavoidable. 'History that speaks only of time on the deactivated "stage" of space (space as an "empty interval, a natural given"),' as Jacobs reminds us, 'is imperial history' (1996, 22).

Religions take place in the shared territory of cities and city blocks, whether in Paris and London or in Israel-Palestine or Bosnia or in 'British' 'Columbia' with its unsettled indigenous land claims and its multiply religious, new immigrants. Postmoderns, despite the strident voices of contemporary religious despisers, can no longer assume (as did modernity) that religions will be lived as but a private matter, a posture that hid the way in which Western modern Christian enthusiasms informed secular and subjective infrastructures. So as religions are each in their own way confronted with recognition of their cultural construction of the sacred canopy, the religions of the axial age will now also be challenged to turn towards negotiation of shared place – most notably, the public square, if also the planetary commons. In one turn religions are being challenged – by the encounters incumbent upon globalization – to admit our interpretive, constructive locus; but textual interpretation in turn – foregoing the blinders turned upon spatiality – must also now take account of 'place,' if textual interpretation is to take place without re-enforcing dominative and therefore colonizing power. That is, our interpretations need to assume readings of culture as itself already thick with stories, then to work with the intuitive creativity of jazz musicians, improvising upon a theme so as to open out possible horizons of cultural flourishing.

In other words, theology, like politics by other means, may well need to be done 'by beginning from a site rather than a text' (Magnusson 2002, 2). The ancient historical transcoding (and its supportive metaphysics) must be interrupted by loosing the spatial, through attention to geography (Soja 1989, 10, 24) – along with hospitality, the commitment that makes living together possible. Even as 'there is nothing outside of text,' as Derrida reminded us, nevertheless political sites (like the Arcadian dream city of Vancouver, for example) – textually striated as these are (that is, we inhabit the cultural milieu as a habituated composite of prior interpretations) – will increasingly need to be the practised focus for textual interpretation. 'To activate space, to produce a spatial history, is,' Jacobs advises, 'fundamental to [the] project of taking history beyond imperialism' (1996, 22). Today religious persons' confession of the ineffable must be lived in awareness of religious pluralism and its concomitant, the secular, as an offering of the space of hospitality to all and with the hope of finding ways to be enriched by and in solidarity with the subjective technologies of other confessions.

The postcolonial keeps us from turning towards that which tempted modernity – namely, the ordering power of the binary, as in self/other, culture/nature, civilized/primitive – and that which Frantz Fanon identified as the founding binary, the believer with privileged revelation over and against the supposed non-believer. Treating the complexities of desires by insisting that these be severed and set into a taxonomy of but the two-some – the one as set against the other, the elder twin put in authority over the aberrant other – Western modernity literally engendered empire (though to be sure, Christianity, a reading of which so shaped Western ideation, has not been the only religion tempted to think with and through a Manichean-type dualism). The postcolonial ethically revisits this means of mapping (and so containing by colonizing) desire, especially in our readings of sacred texts and religious histories, if now also the politics of place. If religions can maintain within practice and theology an appreciation for interpretation, for the gap between the ineffable and our understanding, I would suggest here an additional insight for a religious practice appreciative of postcolonial consciousness – that we turn our axial, time-oriented religions on the horizontal, to learn to read with respectful regard for the other, to shape practice with respect to the presence of the religious other, to practise (as per Gianni Vattimo) the secular with religious hospitality. Undoubtedly, the attention given by poststructuralist philosophers such as Julia Kristeva to the issue of hospitality, most fully developed in *Strangers to Ourselves* (1991), has to do with an attentiveness to the politics of place.

The small but still global city of Vancouver, in which the editors of this anthology reside, provides then an interesting study in sensibilities pertinent to the politics, particularly religious, of place. A former British province, British Columbia still attracts the run-off of other former British colonies, from South Africa to Hong Kong. Home away from home for the Dalai Lama, this is a city where New Age spiritualities breed like bunnies, birthed from the overlap of multiple religious traditions, critical thought and immigrants taking leave of their pasts. On a cliff edge, where ocean meets against university campus, sits the Vancouver School of Theology – dressed still in the fascia of Oxford-style architecture, but overgrown now by the affluence of the new international elite, who seem prone to perch on hilltops with ocean views. Here I too am tempted to inhale the spiritual aestheticism of Cascadian transcendentalism.[4]

The school of theology, facing into Christendom's own diminishment and with Christianity having now lost the 'privilege' of whispering visions of social construction into the ear of government, struggles to swerve its 'custodial' relations with indigenous persons towards the practice of religions-in-solidarity. A totem pole ('All My Relations,' 2005), recently erected, holds place on the south plaza of the school of theology. Amidst the simmering politics of indigenous persons being 'colonized' twice over (territorially, religiously), within a province feeling the pull of liberal economics, if also the repercussions from strong theologies yoked with militarism across the 49th parallel, Christianity's trajectory of terrestrially avoidant transcendence has here been hybridically interpolated. If Christian supernaturalism has in Vancouver, following the track of American transcendentalism, sunk itself into 'nature' (hence, 'Super Natural' BC), this idealism easily subtends global cosmopolitan and tourist interests. An indigenous painting titled 'Usufruct' (Lawrence Paul Yuxweluptun, 1995), a sacred textual interpretation in its own way, poses a critical interruption to this economy of value. Challenging this globally sale-able view of the marvellous, the painting assumes – via its brilliant primary colours and classic Northwest coast design – the outline of the Arcadian horizon, only – upon closer consideration – to convey the pained and dying spirits of water, mountain, animal, and earth. Christian understandings of 'transcendence,' critically interrupted and woven into the thick of 'all my relations,' here take on memory, the locus of possible ethical discernment. Textual interpretation could here begin to turn away from the linear, historicist trajectory, which has occasioned numerous historical 'structures of nonrecognition' (Shapiro 1997, 7) so as to stay present to a more decisively territorial economy of value.

Of Spirit, Sovereignty, and the Politics of Cosmopolis

I work as a constructive theologian, something of a different academic voice than the other colleagues on the editorial team. Constructive theologians speak 'resistance' by daring to propose an alternative 'economy' of value.[5] Here in Vancouver, named one of the most livable of the planet's global cities, social Christianity – that 'enabling violence' (Spivak) of the modern era of progress and nationhood, if not itself devoid of commitments to structural justices – has come to an end. Postcolonial studies have challenged the ways in which social mission, both nationally and within Christian community, has inherently carried colonial imbrication, even as the social-justice practices inherent in these liberal traditions have also bequeathed a national infrastructure committed to multiculturalism, social welfare, civil rights, labour rights, and health care. If not directly owing to postcolonial theory, a subconscious decolonizing movement has also occasioned, if not forced, this edge of the western continent, the Pacific Northwest, to dream of a Christianity 'post-Christendom' – if 'Christianity' at all. And yet in this situation – strewn with evangelicalisms, fundamentalisms (New Age and environmental as well as textual), and cosmopolitans (tempted to collapse all sense of value into the discourse of materialism), attention to the complex valences of desires (to which postcolonial theory aspires) has, within lived religious practice, significant political work to do. Given the mobilization of populations via globalization, postmodern public life must assume a religiously plural public square. And yet if the secular can no longer assume to corral and privatize religions, the secular will be served where religions can learn to resist the metaphysical and colonizing assumption – 'the violent appropriation of the real by force' (Vattimo 1999, 9). Theologians work constructively in such a milieu, posing concepts to build solidarity and shared commitment.

I want then to work the Christian textual concept 'Spirit' through post-structuralist analysis in hopes of loosing it for religious practices within the transnational city, a scene of migration and exile, cosmopolitanism and globalization, hybridity and diaspora, if also admittedly as a way of challenging Akenson's structuralist assumptions. Such assumptions, I would suggest, prevent him from reclaiming text for counter-hegemonic practice. Postcolonial theory (as I have explicated in the previous two sections) has not been inclined to credit religions with the potential for colonial subversion and has not been attentive to place, despite the fact that the colonial has precisely to do with the acquisition of land. Given this, and given that I do think religions can encourage entrustment and world wonder, if also ideological unhingement, I want to forward 'Spirit' as a possible, plurally accessible constructive locus: might Spirit be read via postcolonial appreciation as less territorially possessive or presumptive than as elucidated by Akenson? And if so, might it not be a concept well suited for today's religiously plural public?

Akenson asserts that the concept 'New Israel of the Spirit' allowed Christians to replace attention to topography (more precisely, a specific territorial land claim) with the reading of text. So he observes, 'Seemingly Christians ... can live in the land of the spirit, in the Virtual Reality defined by their text, and do not have to acquire real estate to fulfil their divine mission. Text replaces topography.' In Akenson's mind, Christianity's ability to live in the virtuality of Spirit 'breaks apart in practice at the very instant it hits the ground.' Akenson has in fact picked up on the way in which Spirit, in at least a dominant strand of Christianity, has been producing terrestrial avoidance behaviour, has been facilitating affective foreclosures while pursuing the politics of rescue, and with territorially colonizing results. Reading historical effects as a possible site for the ethical discernment of practice (which Christians have regularly and ritually resisted) does seem to prove Akenson's point: the imbrication of Christianity's sense of history with its colonial land grab does seem to write off this concept 'Spirit' as inherently imperially presumptive.

Christian testamental scholar Tod D. Swanson presented a somewhat similar, if more scholastically elaborate argument in an essay that intriguingly assumes an indigenous reading strategy and postcolonial intent (Swanson 1994). Reviewing Mircea Eliade's reprise of Spirit as a foundation for the modern comparative religions project, Swanson comes to connect the concept of Spirit, most expressly developed in the Christian Gospel of John, with Christianity's enervation of attention to place, its presumptive assumption to 'carry [its] message across all boundaries, invading the homelands of other communities' (241). In tracing the history of 'Spirit' as a religiously viable concept, Eliade, in digging into the texts of Hebrew prophets and priests (Genesis, Ezekiel, Isaiah), first found it developed as a sacred metaphor during times of catastrophic dislocation, when religious persons were disarticulated from their sacred lands. If with exile 'space threatened to become permanently emptied of meaning,' Hebrew prophets suggestively constructed 'Spirit' as the placeholder spelling 'the potential sacrality of all spaces,' even 'the decentralized spaces of [peoples'] exile' (242). But if the incarnational insight regarding the immanence of Spirit enervated the clash among various religious centres of meaning (243), this same insight 'into the potential sacrality of all spaces made Christianity exportable' (242) – initially (given the diaspora occasioned by empire), necessarily so.

Spirit – the Gospel of John expressly tying this concept back to the genesis of the cosmos (Genesis 1:1–2) – was broad and spacious enough to gather in those scattered and fragmented by empire, to absolve ethnic and territorial separation (Swanson 1994, 244–5, 251). By performing signs, Jesus had, Swanson concludes, 'already transferred ethnic allegiance from the territorial shrines to his own body … In order to open … the Father's house, the body … of the one who had incarnated the symbols of the patriarchal homelands had to be erased … The dissolution of Jesus' body … clears a space for the coming of the unifying Spirit … The "children of God" who were scattered abroad entangled in their various territories have now been gathered into one spaceless place of the Spirit' (257). Yet, Swanson warns, 'by delegitimizing all territorially based religions it actually staked out a new kind of Christian claim to all of the territories of this world' (257) – thus insinuating Spirit, despite such amazingly hopeful postcolonial insights, as the universal agent, authorizing the 'inva[sion of] the homelands of other communities' (241). 'Coloring a territory Samaritan,' Swanson wryly observes, his work with indigenous land-based religions clearly in mind, 'marks it for a loving, but perhaps still unwanted, invasion' (259).

And yet, even if Spirit did come, given mind/body dualism, to have that texture in the West (a point I would not dispute), need universality necessarily carry forward such a presumptive, because abstract, claim with it? Can we not think of Spirit as an energetic capaciousness relative to – and not merely oppositionally other than – physicality? What if the contours or breadth of Spirit opened not towards an abstract universal, but rather towards 'planetarity' (Spivak)? Might this nominally same concept ('Spirit'), reconstructed – and with particular attention to the choreography of sacred sovereignty – prove to be a locus which evokes religious responsibility towards planetarity today?

Perhaps nothing so much as the confessional conviction of sacral sovereignty has implicitly been coding relations to space among the practitioners of religion. I use the term sacral sovereignty to refer to the way religious persons relate ourselves to the ineffable, such that by this confession (e.g., 'Blessed be God, Sovereign of the Universe') we remind ourselves that we are related to something beyond our own understanding and that we in greater and lesser ways are not wholly in control of our own existence. Sacral sovereignty – a way of talking about the human relationship to the ineffable – has been lived via many different, meaning-making choreographies, even within the 'self-same' religion.

Christian sensibilities towards confessing God as Sovereign of the Universe came during modernity to be 'thought in terms of simple power – the power necessary to assert rule over a people and a territory' (Kuehls 2002, 182), a notion of sacral power which Christians then assumed to represent. Modernity – upon analogy to the way in which God was construed as world sovereign – assumed sovereignty as the structure of the self in terms of the mind's mastery over body and its labour, in relation to the earth in terms of property, in relation to 'the uncivilized' as the responsibility for religious governance. Yet the postcolonial – in striking distinction from scriptural transcoding (a.k.a., 'the biblical understanding'), which today often publicly stands in place of an ethically integral relationship to authoritative text – dynamically multiplies choreographies, complexifies borders, boundaries, relations, personhood, contiguities. If 'any [canonical] text represents a compressed cultural moment in a lost conversation' (Daum), postcolonial hermeneutics rouses other discursants from the compressions of the text and its histories, reading against the grain so as to overhear snippets of that conversation, then calling upon our ethical independence to 'mean' anew.

While this anthology has challenged time and again the dominant arch of Christendom's geography, consideration of the choreography of sovereignty allows us to recognize the fact that there have been 'radical Christianities' which often historically departed from the imperial code. Modern choreography of sacred sovereignty, achieved amidst the contestation we call the Christian Reformation, both swerved from an older technology and was itself not without contestation. Christianity – never but a scene of popular contestation and never then singularly identical to 'the machine of a belief system' (Akenson) – has improvised other choreographies relative to this concept of the ineffable – namely, 'Spirit.' Invoked by the Diggers and the Levellers, among other peasants in the English Reformation, Spirit allowed for substantially different economics, for a different relation to the land. Indeed, Spirit precisely suggested to these textual hermeneuts a communitarian land reformation. The sensibility that 'the Spirit of the Lord fills the Earth,' itself textually informed by 'The Earth is the Lord's and the fullness thereof,' a proclamation of sacral immanence, protested the hierarchical governance model of sovereignty assumed by the aristocracy (all were equally capacious, given Spirit's indwelling) and spelled for these peasant movements a human choreography that refused the presumption of land ownership to any human. Sacred sovereignty implied at the least human-, if not species-, respectful commons and the levelling of human hierarchies – for instance, 'Call no one master.' Spirit here economically served the interests of the peasants being dispersed from common lands by feudal enclosure. Yet such 'radical Christianities' have themselves been colonized by 'the machine of a belief system' (Akenson) and have only become memorially available to us through the interruption of the colonial capture of memory. Nonetheless, Spirit could invite an entirely different choreographic relation to the ineffable, to the sovereign of the universe – one, specifically, that was intensely attentive to land as commons. So postcolonial textual interpretations can loosen our attachment to any singular choreography of sovereignty, among which has been the presumption to dominion of Western modernity, even as we glean insights for possible improvisations of our own.

The hospitality of the commons might very well be the suppressed commitment to the land within this concept Spirit – even as such a commitment has no hard, resistant contours by which to announce or re-enforce itself and therefore can be territorially plundered by presumptions to 'mastery' or empire or tribe or nation. In the face of the multiple civil wars being actively fought in the name of religion and land – Ireland, Palestine, Bosnia, Kashmir, Timor – the texture of Spirit's deterritorializing transcendence cannot wholly be ignored. Intriguingly, it's precisely in this vein that Slavoj Žižek – with the Balkan region in mind – appeals to Christians to remember the land ethic, hospitality, which has been carried in the concept of Spirit. In his text *The Fragile Absolute*, Žižek defines the Christian movement, begun from St Paul: 'Christianity ... introduced into this global balanced cosmic Order a principle ... which, measured by the standards of pagan cosmology, cannot but appear as a monstrous distortion: the principle according to which each individual has immediate access to universality ... of the Holy Spirit, or, today, of human Rights and freedoms' (2000, 120). Then, referring Christians back to the love commandment and its sacrificial ethos ('one has to "die for the law" (Saint Paul) that regulates our tradition, our social "substance"') (127), Žižek concludes that the hard work of love entails 'disengag[ing] ourselves from the inertia that constrains us to identify with the particular order we were born into ... It is this Christian heritage of "uncoupling" that is threatened by today's "fundamentalisms"' (128–9). In the face of superego security demands, id-based hostilities, and narcissistic claims to rights, the energetics and/or dynamic locus of Spirit may capaciously enable thinking towards the planetary commons and shared publics.

If metaphysics has tempted some of us to control and therefore patrol 'the real,' then today, 'infinitely more exigent than the attempt ... to judge or evaluate,' observes theorist Trinh Minh-ha, is the 'state of alert in-betweenness and critical non-knowingness' (234). If Trinh names what I might call a religious 'attention epistemology' for a postcolonial future, she also may – with her sense of 'betweenness' – refer to a way of conceiving the energetic ground or locus of spiritual practice, a locus within which we practise non-duality. As philosopher Philippa Berry notes, the deconstructive style of thinking has itself been drawn to Spirit; such a style of thinking frequently 'presents a new understanding of spirit ... as facilitating a wholly new mode of awareness, which not only invites the thinker to abandon their residual attachment to dualistic thinking, but also offers a potent challenge to their desire for subjective mastery and knowledge' (1992, 4–5). Gianni Vattimo, one practising that philosophical style, challenges Christians likewise to hold open the space of the secular as a hospitality room (2002, 100). Spirit becomes the kenotically open place between, the cleansing breath challenging ideologies of power which vest in secular and scientific as much as religious metaphysical absolutes. Admittedly a reconstructive gesture, the concept Spirit might allow Christians to break through the tacit modernist understanding of the world and our habituation to it, to break away from its virtual reality machine, to try out a new choreography, a relation to place that shifts the ways in which globalizing capitalism serves up resources from South to North. Practising our religious commitments to the ineffable, to the Sovereign of the Universe, requires, if planetarity be our hope, a choreography of confession that does not eclipse the other or his/her taking place, his/her access to 'the commons' (food, air, water, shelter) of life. But that said, Spirit admits that it takes place within the contestation that is Christianity.

Dead Serious?

'Dead Slow' reads the sign over a garage exit as one approaches a pedestrian walkway from the vault of an underground parking lot here in Vancouver. It must be a Britishism, but it worked to shock and shame me, the aggressive American from New Jersey (where 'Terrorism 101' is learned on the Interstate!), to reform my driving habits. Like that sign, modern realism tended to patrol the authoritative religious voice or mood which, when approaching text and ritual, and so as to stay in control, betrayed as little semiotic colour or pulse as possible. Does not this mood – controlled, constrained, authoritative, rational – itself colonize text, including perhaps this one? While postcolonial literature actually sports a rather surprising comedic repertoire, including satire, the trickster, parody, mimesis, and irony, the essays in this anthology seem to treat religious text according to modernist religious sensibilities – in other words, as 'Dead Serious.' Few of our essays actually play with the mood of text (Weaver is one exception), that semiotic registration which cannot exactly be read off the face of a text, but might be intuited from or tried on for theory's sake. Given such a tone, I worry that this collection and its attempted postcolonial engagement has at times a tendency to fall back into the mood of modern realism: Did we lose postcolonial theory's sense of humour – and might that be a sure sign of the onset of that dangerous illness called 'metaphysics'?

'Satire is a prevalent but largely untheorized mode of representation in postcolonial fiction, a way of pointing at and opening out theoretical aporia,' notes literary theorist John Clement Ball, of novels by V.S. Naipaul, Chinua Achebe, and Salman Rushdie (2003, ix). One feels it too in novelist Thomas King's *Green Grass, Running Water*, which implodes the Christian account of Noah's ark with that of the indigenous tradition of Changing Woman. Falling from the sky, Changing Woman lands on an offal-covered deck, among the suddenly animated menagerie of Noah's ark. While Noah insists that, according to Christian rules, animals shall not talk (Quiet, Old Coyote!), the same set of rules leads the sex-starved Noah to see Changing Woman as the gift of a new wife (Noah, despite the fact that his wife had, again according to Christian rules, large breasts, has grown bored with the same wife and children every day and has thrown them overboard). Noah consequently chases Changing Woman across the slippery and fetid deck, demanding procreation, while Changing Woman tries to rid him of his rules. Having failed to catch the wily woman, he deserts her on an island and settles for his rules: 'This is a Christian ship,' Noah shouts back at her as he sets sail with the animals. 'I am a Christian man. This is a Christian journey. And if you can't follow our Christian rules, then you're not wanted on the voyage' (King 1993, 163). As the novel ends, the floods come, a dam – that structure of colonial enclosure (if also of dead seriousness?) – released. Postcolonial theory, I would suggest, might be somewhat more tempted to release religion from the dam of our dead seriousness than this anthology has suggested. Can we not laugh (religiously) at ourselves?

Like King's novel, anticolonial texts – among which we might count at least some biblical pericopes, if not entire books of sacred texts – find occasions for laughter (if sometimes biting) in the contact zone. Religious practices which appreciate the levelling of ego and the unhinging of presumptions and pretensions can be served as much by these moods as by the Zen slap. To work with postcolonial attention invites us to try on the possibility that not all sacred texts have been interested in the project 'history' or linear time or modernity's religious sensibilities. Medieval Christianities, for example, surely did not always play in the mood of dead seriousness, as Bakhtin's notes on carnival make clear. I would suggest then that – insomuch as postcolonial literature actually sports a rather surprising repertoire of satire, comedy, tricksterism, and irony – the (anti-)colonial literature of the Christian testament might itself be – at least at some points – equally humorous.

Postcolonial attention, with its appreciation for mimesis and parody and irony, might allow for a little more religious play – for example, a

Christianity that arrives as cultural trickster. Might we imagine the figure Jesus, for example, as not so much 'a pure, vital and busy healer' set over against the 'miserable wash of humanity' (as the modernist Adolf von Harnack taught us to read him [1908, 101]), but as himself something of a *derisor*? In the ancient monster market, the blind, lame and hobbled, the deaf – monsters all – could be bought and sold, then work the banquet halls as cultural derisors (Barton 1993, 107–8). What of this, I wonder, might have carried over into the crowds of disabled bodies peopling the pages of the Christian ('New') Testament. Might Christianity have at least for some time healed by its satiric wit, rather than its rules? And even if it did not, could we take responsibility for reading it more tongue-in-cheek? Satire, offered as a form of moral engagement (not, then, of mere cynicism), might help us get past the hangover of strong metaphysics within Christianity. Satire challenges or pokes fun at the modern presumption to hold all in, to see all from and through magisterial consciousness.

Contrary to Akenson, who here maintains that 'most successful resistance to imperialism requires using many of the conceptual methods of the conqueror' and that, assuming this mimetic use, there is not 'necessarily much difference between colonial belief systems and those that oppose them,' I contend that comedic energies might make all the difference. In a similar vein as Akenson, Moore observes that 'because Revelation's *anti*colonial discourse, its resistance to Roman omnipotence, is infected with the imitation compulsion, and hence with ambivalence, it contains the seeds of its own eventual absorption by that which it ostensibly opposes' (2006, 114–15).[6] Bhabha appreciated hybridity for its ability to 'reverse the effects of the colonialist disavowal, so that other "denied" knowledges enter upon the dominant discourse and estrange the base of its authority' (1994, 114). Hybridity 'contests the terms and territories of both' the one and the other (28). Of course, the eventual history of Christendom – given its imitation of Caesar's 'gospels,' 'saviour'-status, and 'kingdom' – supports all too well Moore's argument that 'the difficulty of effectively exiting empire by attempting to turn imperial ideology against itself is regularly underestimated by those who acclaim Revelation for decisively breaking the self-perpetuating cycle of empire' (2006, 114). And yet, isn't postcolonial theory's appreciation for the parodic here being over-coded by the virtual reality machine? Even if the canon tried to colonize the comedic, to tame its tongue, parody itself does not assume a never-ending metaphysical circuit.

346 Sharon V. Betcher

To be sure, I don't want to underestimate the fact that 'turn[ing] imperial ideology against itself' may invite something like the mere binary
inversion within cycles of violence. Nor do I want to ignore the fact that
seems to have sealed the deal for Moore – that 'more than any other
early Christian text ... Revelation ... enabled the Roman state effort-
lessly to absorb Christianity into itself' (119). Inversion of the cycles of
violence remains a volatile possibility. But might those with a sense of
humour and an appreciation for postcolonial parody not take text quite
so seriously as replicatory DNA? Readings of the biblical canon do after
all betray an ambivalence about precisely such forms of power. So, for
example, the narratives of 2 Samuel regarding Israel's desire for a king
and kingdom do not rest easily with imperialism: 'Even as the story of
Israel depicts an effort to become "like the nations," it depicts that very
project as pernicious' (Schwartz 1992, 188–9). So the community might
not exactly be 'constructing God or Christ, together with their putatively salvific activities, from the raw material of imperial ideology' (a
reading which I find, given the lens of postcolonial theory, a somewhat
flat sense of creativity, if also a constrained notion of mimicry), but to
have already had in mind 'a conception of the divine sphere' (Moore
2006) quite at odds with this imperial ideology and thus seemingly
laughable, preposterous even, as the community mimed imperial rhetoric. Moore forgets – as much as have Christians enthused with the systematic defence of omnipotence conducive to the great salvation history
– that a variant doctrine of God – recognized as the power of humility
(Philippians) – has often been a theologically appreciated, if culturally
variant, form of power. What made the situation more laughable, a
laughter I 'hear' in Revelation, then, was that some Christians thought
humility the better part of wisdom to put up against that of the holy
Roman emperor. So the resistant community might well have had a different sense of power which, like the Taoist's slow drip of water wearing away stone, allowed them to laugh at cultural presumptions.

If imperialism gives us much to mourn, our mood may well tell on us
– how wary we are, for one thing, of re-entering the religious. Far easier
to assume religions are incurable. Likely we need to have a bit more
tongue-in-cheek when reading some of the anticolonial sacred texts.
The counter-hegemonic may well arrive – as historian of science Donna
Haraway has suggested – on a note of humour: 'Comedy is both object
of attention and method' (1997, 15). The counter-hegemonic may initially claim no more space than a ripple of laughter, a girl's giggle –
humour breaching the 'dead seriousness' of modern realism so as to

open out possibilities under the tacit infrastructure of the great code to which we otherwise are tempted to return. And if religions are to be cured, perhaps they must admit not only their interpretive stance (Vattimo), but also a sense of humour.

In closing, I want simply to reiterate that our intent has not been to turn Christianity or any of the religions of the book into dejects, to give Christianity in the West one more ethical trouncing by way of intellectual denunciation, but to interrupt the temptation to imperialism or dominative sovereignty as it becomes co-incident with the practices of communities within our 'biblical-historical,' even where 'secular,' present. Postcolonial theory, as R.S. Sugirtharajah has shown, opens up a third way in the public debate 'to embrace the book or discard it,' to valorize 'tradition' or to respond with intellectual disgust, eschewing religions as inherently violent. 'A viable way out of this dilemma,' Sugirtharajah insists, 'might be to rely on the postcolonial in-between position. In-betweenness will resist any clear domination of either of these positions and enable us to work through them' (2003, 113). This resembles the position of the constructive, feminist theologian (as I would locate myself) who has had to work out something of a different relation to sacred text than the assumption of the revelation of Divine Providence. A feminist theology has had to recognize that truth is not 'in' the text, but in the facilitation of our capacities to stay 'true' to each other, to keep faith with each other: what's true is that which promotes human and planetary flourishing. Here truth renounces modern and metaphysical propositional assumptions and dares to 'take place' – in and as the event of keeping faith with each other and the earth. Rather than making truth relative to 'revelation,' the postcolonial – here in co-incidence with feminism – suggests that theological truth might itself be more relative to something of a 'situated knowledge.' As William James put it, 'truth happens.'

Yet because Christianity has so shaped and informed the Western symbolic (observes feminist philosophical theologian Grace Jantzen), 'we ignore' the critique of the Western religious imaginary 'at our peril,' especially since 'the heritage of christendom is not being ignored by those who set social and political and economic policies' (1999, 107, 108). Picking up the rhetorical question 'Why should an ancient text matter today?' Sugirtharajah answers in much the same vein as did Jantzen: 'The answer lies with those who are busily using biblical texts to define a narrow vision of biblical faith, especially in the aftermath of September 11' (2003, 2). I might want to claim a creative, cultural wisdom to be forwarded from – and not only a critical, cautionary relationship to – sacred texts. Religious traditions have and can inform bodies towards 'felicity in history' (Luce Irigaray); these do suggest ways of keeping trust with humanity and with the earth amidst transient and passing worlds of meaning – even if I admittedly keep a distance of a different sort (namely, by treating them as wisdom texts and not as the great code of existence). Their wisdoms can address human 'failure to thrive,' can promote entrustment to life, can encourage humans towards planetary sustainability. 'Religious values have functioned to challenge quotidian cultural assumptions and practices that have become naturalized as the only way of seeing or thinking about things,' philosopher Carol Wayne White advises us, adding that 'some sort of active engagement with religious reflection and action is necessary when addressing the ill effects of popularized modernistic values and cultural practices' (2002, 150–1).

'Thinking in radically new ways is,' as Robert Daum has noted, 'enormously difficult.' But this is precisely the possibility that postcolonial consciousness offers religions, already yielding such locations as a 'religionless religion' (Derrida), a God without 'Sovereignty' (Caputo), and a religion without metaphysics (Vattimo). To work with postcolonial theory in relationship to sacred texts might be described from a religious angle as participating in the clearing or emptying of social delusions. But what the postcolonial practice of clearing or emptying delusions opens out upon today is not a vacuum, but a field of dynamic valences, the site-space of today's urban neighbourhoods – places that might yet be enabled to flourish by the practice of hospitality, humility, and solidarity among persons religious. The form of this anthology itself, the give and take among editors and authors, suggests, I trust, something of a model for the ongoing public engagement of religions.

NOTES

1 Within the Canadian scene, the migrants of the last decade – despite often being consigned by immigration laws regarding professional licences or language barriers to working in hothouses, cleaning, driving taxis, etc., and thus finding the housing costs of the cosmopolitan lifestyle out of reach – arrive with higher academic achievements than the settler population.
2 The discipline or practice of sabbath, the sacred day of rest (ritualized in the creation hymn of Genesis 1), also appears to be an answer to ancient urbanization and the desire to root identity. See Brueggemann 1999, 248.

3 Anne McClintock, *Imperial Leather: Race, Gender and Sexuality in the Colonial Contest*, traces how the textually shaped psyche of the Euro-western modern served to map out colonial mission.
4 Consequent to the Reformation, its 'Protestant Ethic,' and modernism, Christians split our relation to the land between the economics of private possession, or real estate, and transcendentalism, or spiritual aestheticism – as, for example, Cascadia.
5 The term 'economy' when deployed within Christian theology addresses how God's love becomes efficaciously present throughout the cosmos. On the imperial inflection of Christianity's notion of divine economy and its doctrine of incarnation, see Elizabeth Schussler-Fiorenza, *Jesus: Miriam's Child, Sophia's Prophet* (Continuum, 1995), 18–24, esp. p. 20. On articulation of religious value as itself a mode of resistance, see White 2002.
6 Stephen Moore was an original participant in the lecture series upon which this anthology is based. His essay from the Green College speakers series, '"The World Empire Has Become the Empire of Our Lord and His Messiah": Representing Empire in Revelation,' was published in *Empire and Apocalypse* (Moore 2006).

REFERENCES

Ball, John Clement. 2003. *Satire and the Postcolonial Novel: V.S. Naipaul, Chinua Achebe, Salman Rushdie*. New York: Routledge.

Barton, Carlin. 1993. *The Sorrows of the Ancient Romans: The Gladiator and the Monster*. Princeton: Princeton University Press.

Bauman, Zygmunt. 2002. 'Living and Dying in the Planetary Frontier-Land.' *Tikkun* 17.2: 33–42.

Berger, Peter, ed. 1999. *The Desecularization of the World: Resurgent Religion and World Politics*. Grand Rapids, MI: William B. Eerdmans Publishing Co.

Berry, Philippa. 1992. 'Introduction.' In Philippa Berry and Andrew Wernick, eds, *Shadow of Spirit: Postmodernism and Religion*. New York: Routledge.

Bhabha, Homi K. 1994. *The Location of Culture*. New York: Routledge.

Brueggemann, Walter. 1999. 'The City in Biblical Perspective: Failed and Possible.' *Word & World* 19.3: 236–50.

Cady, Linell E. 1991. 'Resisting the Postmodern Turn: Theology and Contextualization.' *Theology at the End of Modernity*, ed. Sheila Greeve Davaney, 81–98. Philadelphia: Trinity Press.

Deloria, Jr, Vine. 1973. *God Is Red*. New York: Dell Publishing/Delta Books.

Haraway, Donna. 1997. *Modest_Witness@Second_Millennium: FemaleMan Meets OncoMouse*. New York: Routledge.

Hargreaves, Andy. 2003. *Teaching in the Knowledge Society: Education in the Age of Insecurity*. New York: Columbia University Press.

Harnack, Adolf von. 1908. *The Mission and Expansion of Christianity in the First Three Centuries*. Vol. 1. Trans. James Moffatt. New York: G.P. Putnam's Sons.

Jacobs, Jane M. 1996. *Edge of Empire: Postcolonialism and the City*. New York: Routledge.

Jantzen, Grace. 1999. *Becoming Divine*. Indianapolis: Indiana University Press.

Keller, Catherine. 2004. 'Introduction.' In Catherine Keller, Michael Nausner, and Mayra Rivera, eds, *Postcolonial Theologies: Divinity and Empire*. St Louis: Chalice.

King, Thomas. 1993. *Green Grass, Running Water*. Boston: Houghton Mifflin.

Kuehls, Thom. 2003. 'The Environment of Sovereignty.' In Warren Magnuson and Karena Shaw, eds, *A Political Space: Reading the Global through Clayoquot Sound*. Minneapolis: University of Minnesota Press.

Laeuchli, Samuel. 1972. *Power and Sexuality: The Emergence of Canon Law at the Synod of Elvira*. Philadelphia: Temple University Press.

Lilburne, Geoffrey R. 1989. *A Sense of Place: A Christian Theology of the Land*. Nashville: Abingdon.

Loy, David. 2003. *The Great Awakening: A Buddhist Social Theory*. Boston: Wisdom Publications.

Magnusson, Warren. 2003. 'Introduction: The Puzzle of the Political.' In Warren Magnusson and Karena Shaw, eds, *A Political Space: Reading the Global through Clayoquot Sound*. Minneapolis: University of Minnesota Press.

McClintock, Anne. 1995. *Imperial Leather: Race, Gender and Sexuality in the Colonial Contest*. New York: Routledge.

Minha-ha, Trinh. 1991. *When the Moon Waxes Red*. New York: Routledge.

Moltmann, Jürgen. 1993. *God in Creation: A New Theology of Creation and the Spirit of God*. Minneapolis: Fortress.

Moore, Stephen D. 2006. *Empire and Apocalypse: Postcolonialism and the New Testament*. Sheffield: Sheffield Phoenix.

Schimke, David. 2007. 'Spiritual Stereotypes.' In Editor's Note, *Utne Reader* 139: 6.

Schwartz, Regina. 1992. 'Adultery in the House of David: "Nation" in the Bible and Biblical Scholarship.' In Philippa Berry and Andrew Wernick, eds, *Shadow of Spirit: Postmodernism and Religion*. New York: Routledge.

Shapiro, Michael J. 1997. *Violent Cartographies: Mapping Cultures of War*. Minneapolis: University of Minnesota Press.

Soja, Edward W. 1989. *Postmodern Geographies: The Reassertion of Space in Critical Social Theory*. London: Verso.

– 2000. *Postmetropolis: Critical Studies of Cities and Regions*. Oxford: Blackwell.

Spivak, Gayatri. 2004. 'Globalicities.' *The New Centennial Review* 4.1: 73–94.

Sugirtharajah, R.S. 2003. *Postcolonial Reconfigurations: An Alternative Way of Reading the Bible and Doing Theology.* St Louis: Chalice.

Swanson, Todd. 1994. 'To Prepare a Place: Johannine Christianity and the Collapse of Ethnic Territory.' *Journal of the American Academy of Religion* 62.2: 241–63.

Uprety, Sanjeev Kumor. 1997. 'Disability and Postcoloniality in Salman Rushdie's *Midnight's Children* and Third-World Novels.' In Lennard J. Davis, ed., *The Disability Studies Reader.* New York: Routledge.

Vattimo, Gianni. 1999. *Belief.* Trans. Luca D'Isanto and David Webb. Chicago: Stanford University Press.

– 2002. *After Christianity.* Trans. Luca D'Isanto. New York: Columbia University Press.

White, Carol Wayne. 2002. *Poststructuralism, Feminism, and Religion: Triangulating Positions.* Amherst, NY: Prometheus Books.

Wills, Lawrence. 2006. 'Ascetic Theology before Asceticism? Jewish Narratives and the Decentering of the Self.' *Journal of the American Academy of Religion* 74.4: 902–25.

Young, Robert J.C. 2001. *Postcolonialism: An Historical Introduction.* Oxford: Blackwell Publishing.

Žižek, Slavoj. 2000. *The Fragile Absolute.* London: Verso.

Contributors

Donald Harman Akenson is Douglas Professor of Canadian and Colonial History at Queen's University, Kingston, Ontario. His books include *God's Peoples: Covenant and Land in South Africa, Israel and Ulster* (1992), *Surpassing Wonder: The Invention of the Bible and the Talmuds* (1998), *Saint Saul: A Skeleton Key to the Historical Jesus* (2000), and *An Irish History of Civilization*, 2 vols. (2005–6).

Sharon V. Betcher is Associate Professor of Systematic Theology at the Vancouver School of Theology, British Columbia. She specializes in constructive theology with a pneumatological focus. Her constructive work is informed by critical and cultural theory – especially feminist and disability theologies, ecology, post-structuralism, and postcolonialism. She is the author of *Spirit and the Politics of Disablement* (2007).

Robert A. Daum is Associate Professor of Rabbinic Literature and Jewish Thought and Director of the Iona Pacific Inter-Religious Centre at Vancouver School of Theology, British Columbia, as well as a Faculty Associate of the Centre for Women's and Gender Studies of the University of British Columbia. His research and publications include studies of classical rabbinic rhetoric, poetics, and narratology, as well as of ethics, gender, and authority. He is the author of 'Crossing Crucifictional Boundaries: Transgressive Tropes in Potok's *My Name is Asher Lev*' (in P. Burns, ed., *Jesus in Twentieth-Century Literature, Art, and Movies*, 2007) and 'Verbal Wronging: An Analysis of Speech Banned in *m. B. Metzi'a* 4:10' (*Florilegium* 23.1, 2006).

Laura E. Donaldson is Professor of English and American Indian Studies at Cornell University in Ithaca, New York, where her teaching and research focus on the intersections of literary, religious, feminist, Native, and postcolonial studies. Her books include *Decolonizing Feminisms: Race, Gender, and Empire-Building* (1992) and, as co-editor, *Postcolonialism, Feminism and Religious Discourse* (2001).

Peter A. Goddard is Chair of the Department of History at the University of Guelph, Ontario. His publications include 'Two Kinds of Conversion ("Medieval" and "Modern") among the Hurons of New France' (2004), 'Canada in Early Modern Jesuit Thought: Backwater or Opportunity?' (2002), and 'Augustine and the Amerindians in Seventeenth-Century New France' (1998).

Laura S. Levitt is Professor of Religion, Jewish Studies, and Gender in the Department of Religion at Temple University, Philadelphia, where she directs the Women's Studies Program. She is author of *Jews and Feminism: The Ambivalent Search for Home* (1997) and *American Jewish Loss after the Holocaust* (2007), and co-editor of *Judaism since Gender* (1997) and *Impossible Images: Contemporary Art after the Holocaust* (2003).

Harry O. Maier is Professor of New Testament and Early Christianity at the Vancouver School of Theology, British Columbia, and author of *The Social Setting of the Ministry as Reflected in the Writings of Hermas, Clement and Ignatius* (1991; 2nd ed. 2002) and *Apocalypse Recalled: The Book of Revelation after Christendom* (2002).

Nabil I. Matar is Professor of English at the University of Minnesota. His books include *Islam in England* (1998), *Turks, Moors, and Englishmen in the Age of Discovery* (1999), *In the Lands of the Christians: Arabic Travel Writing in the Seventeenth Century* (2002), *Britain and Barbary, 1589–1689* (2005), *Europe through Arab Eyes, 1578–1727* (2009), and, as co-editor, *Britain and the Islamic World* (2010).

Karla Pollmann is Professor of Classics at the University of St Andrews, Scotland, and Adjunct Professor of Theology at the University of Århus, Denmark. She is the author, most recently, of a commentary, with introduction and text, on Statius, *Thebaid* 12 (2004), and co-editor of *Augustine and the Disciplines: Cassiciacum to 'Confessions'* (2005) and *Poetry and Exegesis in Premodern Latin Christianity* (2007). She is currently working on Augustine's *De Genesi ad litteram* and its reception, and directing an international, interdisciplinary project on the reception of Augustine through the ages (www.st-and.ac.uk/classics/after-augustine).

Mark Vessey is Professor of English and Principal of Green College at the University of British Columbia. He is the author of *Latin Christian Writers in Late Antiquity and Their Texts* (2005) and co-editor of *Holy Scripture Speaks: The Production and Reception of Erasmus' 'Paraphrases on the New Testament'* (2002) and of *Augustine and the Disciplines: Cassiciacum to 'Confessions'* (2005).

Jace Weaver is Director of the Institute of Native American Studies, Franklin Professor of Native American Studies and Religion, and Adjunct Professor of Law at the University of Georgia. He is the author of *That the People Might Live: Native American Literatures and Native American Community* (1997; 2nd ed. 2000), *Other Words: Native American Literature, Law, and Culture* (2001), and *Turtle Goes to War: Of Military Commissions, the Constitution and American Indian Memory* (2002), and co-author of *American Indian Literary Nationalism* (2006).

Ian Wood is Professor of Early Medieval History at the University of Leeds and was director of the European Science Foundation project 'The Transformation of the Roman World,' for which he co-edited a number of volumes. He is the author of *The Missionary Life: Saints and the Evangelisation of Europe, 451–1050* (2001) and is currently writing a book on the use and abuse of the barbarian invasions from 1722 to 2002.

Index

apocalyptic writings: Arab commentary on, 77n21; and missions in
Europe, 203–7, 212; and missions
in New World, 261, 306. *See also*
prophecy
Apple Piety, 301, 303n5
archaeology, 19, 285
Arch of Constantine, 154, *155*,
171n12
archeophone (concept), 9, 12
Archeophone (object), 8–9
assimilation: of American Jews,
95–6; cultural loss, 229–30; of
Nisga'a, 7
Atlas-i-Hümayan, 126
Auerbach, Erich, 13, 21–31, 34n15,
35–6n25, 36nn26, 28–9, 187
Augustine (saint), 25, 161, 187–90,
195–6n67, 196nn68–9, 230, 232–3,
236
Augustus: and *Aeneid*, 177, 179; empire of, 149–50, 152–3
Australia, 280
Avitus of Vienne, 202

Babylonian Talmud, 107, 132n24
Baldridge, William, 299
Ball, John Clement, 344
Baltic regions, 207–10
barbarians: and conversion, 255; and
Roman empire, 151–64; *sauvage*
stereotype, 263–8
Barbeau, Marius, 4–5, 8, 9–11
Bastiaensen, A.A.R., 185
Baumgarten, A.I., 133n17, 185
Bede: and Bible, 212; commentary on
Acts of the Apostles, 203; on mis-
sionary history, 209, 234–5; and
monstrous races, 237–8, 239;
themes of work, 200–1

Bell, Betty Louise, 294
Benjamin, Walter, 21–2, 26–7, 35n23
Berger, Peter, 329
Berry, Philippa, 342
Betcher, Sharon V., 325–51
betweenness, 342
Bhabha, Homi, 86, 95–6, 109, 345
Bible (content of): Acts of the
Apostles, 203; biblical literacy,
128–9, 130, 138n81; *charam*, 273–4;
claims of absolute truth in, 23; as
code, 12, 13, 32–3n4; Deuteronomy,
3; Genesis, 22–3, 186–9; inheritances in, 93, 99n10, 300; interpretations of, 62, 347–8; Psalm 72, 162;
study of early texts, 54. *See also*
sacred texts; theology
Bible (cultural impact of): and
Against Symmachus, 184; and
American culture, 83; and ethnology, 13–20; and mission, 165–6,
204; and missionaries, 210–12,
253–8, 306–9; and moral transformation, 308–9; and nationhood,
12–13, 34n15; technology of, 219–
20; and Western culture, 18. *See
also* Christianity; *Tanakh*
binary, the, 335–6, 342
Binet, Étienne, 256
Blake, William, 12
Bolton, Frank, 4–7
Boniface, 212
Boyarin, Daniel, 104–5, 132n10, 283,
311
Breeding Better Vermonters
(Gallagher), 278
Brightman, Thomas, 71
Bringhurst, Robert, 3–4, 7–8, 11, 31–
2, 37n31
British Columbia, 4, 11–12, 332, 336

Draxe, Thomas, 70
du Peron, François, 256–7, 258

Ecclesiastical History (Eusebius), 157,
  162–3, 180, 193n24
*Ecclesiastical History of the English
  People* (Bede), 200, 234
ego (renunciation of), 330
Elder, John, 274–5, 288n2
Eliade, Mircea, 339
empire: and the binary, 335–6; defined, 10; divinely ordained conquest, 191n4; genocide, 284–7; and
  God, 161; Irish nationalism, 46; resistance to, 345–6; and theology,
  333. *See also* colonialism; exegesis;
  Roman empire
England, Christianization of, 200–5
Epic and Empire (Quint), 178, 229
Estridson, Sven, 207–9
ethnography: defined, 10; of Europe,
  205–10; and Irish nationalism, 46;
  and Jesuits, 319; in medieval
  Europe, 234; of Natives, 260, 298–
  9; of Yahweh faith, 57; of Yeshua-
  faith, 55. *See also* Native power
  (North American)
ethnology: awestruck natives, 5–6;
  as genre, 33n6, 33–4n12; and history, 14; influence of, 17; in modern era, 6; and scripture, 13–20;
  The Indian Speaks, 9–11
Etymologies (Isidore of Seville), 234
eugenics, 277–81, 289n4, 310, 311
Eusebius of Caesarea: and Christian
  nationhood, 224–5, 243n10;
  Christian political theology, 155–6;
  on Constantine's sign of victory,
  223–4, 225; on global unity, 156–
  61; and Great Commission, 165–6;

ideology of empire, 151–4, 180,
  193nn24, 27; and Judaism, 164;
  portrayal of Constantine, 239–41;
  prophetic viewpoint of, 161–4,
  225–6; on public works, 164–70,
  226–8, 243n16. *See also* Constantine
Eusebius of Caesarea (works of):
  Commentary on Psalms, 162,
  172n25; *Demonstration*, 162,
  172n25; *Ecclesiastical History*, 157,
  162–3, 180, 193n24; *In Praise of
  Constantine*, 180; *Life of Constantine*, 160, 164, 182, 223, 225; *Oration*,
  152, 156, 157–8, 162, 163, 164;
  Theophany, 162, 172n25
'Excavation at Santa Barbara
  Mission' (Rose), 281–2, 285–7,
  311–12
exclusionary policy: of Irish nationalism, 46; of rabbinic Judaism, 48;
  of Yeshua-faith, 55
exegesis: defined, 10; and everyday
  life, 259; and Natives, 298–9, 301–
  2, 317. *See also* cartography; empire
exile myth: and Irish nationalism, 46;
  and rabbinic Judaism, 50
Exodus: and Canaanites, *167*, 168,
  277–8, 282, 299–301; Conquest
  Hypothesis, 277–8, 280; Gibeonites, 299, 300, 317; on maps, 60, 62–
  3, 66–9, 68, 76n4; Native American
  reading of, 275–6, 282–5, 309–14;
  in Qur'an, 74–5, 77n21
Exodus and Revolution (Walzer), 275–
  6, 282, 309–10
Explanatio Apocalypsis (Bede), 203

Faces in the Moon (Bell), 294
Fanon, Frantz, 335